SCHILLER AGED TWENTY-EIGHT
Anton Graff

Fr.

SCHILLER

by

H. B. GARLAND M.A. Ph.D.

*Professor of German in the
University College of the South West
Exeter*

GREENWOOD PRESS, PUBLISHERS
WESTPORT, CONNECTICUT

Library of Congress Cataloging in Publication Data

Garland, Henry Burnand.
   Schiller.

   Reprint of the 1949 ed. published by Harrap, London.
   Bibliography: p.
   Includes index.
   1. Schiller, Johann Christoph Friedrich von, 1759-1805. 2. Authors, German--18th century--Biography.
[PT2482.G3 1976]   831'.6 [B]   76-39809
ISBN 0-8371-9084-3

First published in 1949 by George G. Harrap & Co., Ltd., London

Reprinted with the permission of George G. Harrap & Company Ltd.

Reprinted in 1976 by Greenwood Press, Inc.

Library of Congress Catalog Card Number 76-39809

ISBN 0-8371-9084-3

Printed in the United States of America

PREFACE

THE aim of this book is twofold. I have sought in the first place to portray Schiller as a credible person, not the carefully posed, statuesque figure which too often does duty for him. I have attempted to do this by dealing fully with his early struggles, in which he appears particularly clearly as a sensitive, suffering human being. Secondly I have endeavoured to interpret Schiller's work as something which, while transmuting reality, never ignores the truth of human character which is its foundation. In consequence of this double aim the emphasis of the book gradually swings from the events of his life to concentrate, in Schiller's later years, almost exclusively upon his work, as it develops into the object and focus of all his faculties and powers. If I have succeeded in suggesting, in however slight a degree, the integrity of his character and the splendid power of his finest work to some who had not appreciated them before, I shall be well content.

I have quoted from Schiller's works in German; a translation occurs in each case in a footnote. Extracts from letters appear in English, the original wording being available, for reference or verification, in the Appendix. The text of the letters is, except for the one shown in facsimile at p. 150, that adopted by F. Jonas in *Schillers Briefe*. The inconsistency of certain spellings (especially the fluctuations between ' Carlos ' and ' Karlos ') is authentically Schillerian. The map at p. 5 may make some of Schiller's journeyings less abstract.

I wish to express my gratitude for the valuable help I have received from Mr Geoffrey Grant, of the International Book Club, and from my colleagues, Professor I. Levine and Miss Hilda Swinburne.

EXETER,   H. B. G.
June 1949

v

TO

W. G *and* A. M. G.

CONTENTS

vii

ILLUSTRATIONS

PLATES

IN THE TEXT

All these illustrations are reproduced from *Schiller*, by Jacob Wychgram, by kind permission of the publishers, Velhagen & Klasing Verlag, Bielefeld.

MAP

Chapter One

INTRODUCTORY

THE literary sensation of the year 1781 in Germany was the appearance of a powerful extravagant tragedy called *Die Räuber*, by an unnamed author. Rumour in Stuttgart—where it was published—soon identified the anonymous playwright as Friedrich Schiller, the medical officer of one of the local regiments. Among the many who wished to make the acquaintance of the new celebrity was Andreas Streicher, a musical student. Streicher tells us how, expecting to meet a tempestuous fiery fellow resembling the play's hero, he found instead a surprisingly modest, balanced and unassuming young man.

The same contrast between the pre-conceived notion and the real man was experienced later by others. In 1785 Minna Stock, the fiancée of one of Schiller's Leipzig friends, met, not a swashbuckler with top-boots, massive spurs and clattering sabre as she had imagined him from *Die Räuber*, but

a fair-haired, blue-eyed, modest young man, whose eyes were filled with tears and who scarcely dared to address us.

Nineteen years later a sophisticated and intelligent Berlin hostess, Henrietta Herz, was astonished by the same disparity:

I thought he would express himself in a conversation like Posa speaking to King Philip. To my astonishment he appeared as a man of experience and judgment who was particularly cautious in speaking of others.

These all assumed that Schiller created his heroes in his own image. A meeting with the man dispelled the error. As with Shakespeare or Dryden or Fielding or Sir Walter Scott, Schiller's personality as his friends and family knew it is not to be inferred from his work. To discover Schiller the man we must turn to the evidence of his contemporaries.

From a few portraits, a bust, and many descriptions, we can form a fairly accurate physical picture of Schiller. He was tall and upright, though with thin, weedy legs and arms, and a tendency to be knock-kneed. His hair, which he always wore long and brushed back from his forehead, was reddish, his eyes blue, his nose thin and slightly hooked, his lips full and well-shaped. He dressed in

I

plain colours, usually grey or dark blue, and normally wore an open-necked shirt.

To those who expected him to resemble the characters of his plays his manner came as a greater surprise than his appearance. His salient characteristic, remarked by all observers, was his gentleness. He lacked all assertiveness, and curious lion-hunters often found him awkward and unimpressive. Where there was mutual sympathy and sincerity his reserve and shyness disappeared, and a personality emerged which was characterized by unassuming simplicity, unpretentious directness, and warm-hearted kindness. Genast, the *régisseur* of the Weimar Court Theatre, gives a picture of Schiller at the time of his fame in all the unconscious charm of unaffected modesty.

> This year Schiller followed us to the former place [Lauchstädt], and his arrival excited great interest among the visitors, for old and young were much more enthusiastic about him than about Goethe. How different was his behaviour in company from that of Goethe! Crowds worried him, and tributes, which Goethe received as no more than his due, disquieted and embarrassed him; and so he at first chose unfrequented paths in order to avoid the eternal salutations; but as soon as it was reported, " That's the way Schiller has gone," then people chose that way, in order to meet him. He used to walk through the crowd with head bent, replying in a friendly manner to anyone who saluted him. How differently Goethe had strode among these same people (for they scarcely changed from year to year), proud as a king, with head erect, acknowledging a salutation only by a slight gracious inclination.

The same simple friendliness appeared in Schiller's love for children, which grew as his own family increased. He was always ready with a smile and a caress, and would play and romp on the floor happily and without embarrassment.

It is not surprising to find that such a character was free from conceit. He knew his own value and more than once assessed it accurately, but his great successes gave him no arrogance. Madame de Staël, an observer who would not have taken exception to an air of self-importance in so famous a writer, was particularly impressed by the reverse quality in Schiller:

> I found him so modest and so unconcerned about his own successes, so ardent and animated in the defence of what he believed was true, that I vowed him from that moment a friendship full of admiration.

Schiller's modesty was a symptom of his lack of interest in himself. His attention was focused on what he did, not on what he was. Even in his early years, before his personality matured, his ambition was centred, not on personal things, but on the success of his work

He was content with a modest income, and was quietly generous in helping old and new friends.

It was Schiller's unselfish personality that enabled him to overcome the severe handicap of continuous ill-health. For the last fourteen years of his life he was an invalid, and yet the last nine of them were the most productive of his whole career. An introspective character, if he had written at all, would have exploited his own pathological condition. Schiller rose above it. He wrote abundantly, and his writings neither mirror his disease nor betray any influence of it upon his mind. Sickness was an irrelevant nuisance to be ignored as long as possible. Schiller's selfless attitude kept him free from self-pity.

Madame de Staël's keen intelligence had also seen that the single-minded pursuit of truth was as fundamental a feature of the man as his disarming modesty. It was a disinterested quest. Truth was for him its own and only reward. The search for it gave his mature life meaning; and it was the possibility of devoting himself exclusively to its pursuit that made the generosity of his Danish benefactors so important to him. He sought truth first in philosophy and then in art, and always with complete intellectual integrity. His direct truthfulness makes him the most straightforward and open of writers. Nothing is conveyed by innuendo. His conviction of ultimate values would never allow him to be cynical. He could denounce; he could never deride. It was this single-minded devotion to truth, coupled with his modesty and kindness, that won for Schiller the loyal affection of his young students during his professorship. Friedrich von Hardenberg, Fritz von Stein, and others were ready to spend their nights watching by his sick-bed because they sensed his complete integrity and the warm sympathy he brought to their plans and aspirations.

Such a character could hardly consider that an understanding of an author was an essential preliminary for the understanding of his work. Schiller wrote no autobiography, his diary is confined to such factual entries as " Began *Wilhelm Tell* to-day," and he usually burned his manuscripts and notes. His personal life and his work belonged to entirely different worlds, and he saw no connexion between them.

The contrast in this respect between Goethe and Schiller is an obvious one. Goethe's works were all, in greater or less degree, precipitates of personal experience, or, as he himself put it, " fragments of a great confession." Schiller wrote poetry of this intimate kind only on the rarest occasions, and no visible bridge usually links his life and his work. In early youth he wrote a few lyrical poems which were ostensibly concerned with his own personal life;

on closer examination, however, they prove to be the outcome of cool, detached observation; he writes of himself as if he were another person. His early plays, especially *Die Räuber*, *Kabale und Liebe*, and *Don Carlos*, exhibit autobiographical traces, but even here Schiller's creative process has eliminated all identifiable detail. In the mature works hardly anything personal remains. The divergence from Goethe is complete.

Schiller had much difficulty in discovering the style of writing which was congenial to his type of mind. His failure to find himself caused his long silence and apparent infertility after the writing of *Don Carlos*. While rejecting his early manner because of its subjective taint, he could not find the clue to a new style. The first step in the right direction occurred with his marriage in 1790, which gave to his personal life a place distinct from his intellectual activity. His intensive study of history helped to separate the world of his daily life and the world of his imagination. It focused his intellect on things remote from the present. Philosophy took him still further. It showed him truth independent of the senses and accessible only to the intellect; his studies, which foreshadow much later aesthetic thought, confirmed an instinctive conviction that art is the key which reveals truth to the senses. With this recognition Schiller's creative urge reawakened. He did not despise his everyday life, in which he experienced pleasure and comfort, suffering and anxiety; but the most important part of his life was his writing. Unlike that of Goethe, who wrote poetry about his life, Schiller's writing became a part of his life and the more important one. His plays became the focal point of all his highest powers, and the real Schiller is less the sick man bravely struggling against asthma and tuberculosis, against liver and heart disease, than the powerful and versatile imagination which forged his intensely living tragedies.

Schiller's gift was none other than that of the born dramatist; it seems strange that he should not find this out until he was thirty-seven years old. Even then he discovered it only as a consequence of his study of history and philosophy. The cause of this slowness in knowing himself is to be found in the German literature of his day. He had to shake himself free from the hampering tradition of subjective writing in the German drama. The men whose work he had read avidly and secretly at school, Leisewitz, Klinger, Lenz, and above all Goethe, had looked in their hearts in order to write. Schiller followed their example, but the results never satisfied him, and he was aware of failure without being able to determine its source. Hence the slow waning of his early dramatic impulse and the nine years of searching thought before it revived again.

Schiller's career divides itself sharply into successive phases. He

Hamburg

R. ELBE

Bremen

Berlin

Hannover

Magdeburg

Map of
WESTERN
GERMANY
showing places
associated with
SCHILLER

Göttingen

Leipzig

Weimar · Naumburg

Erfurt · Jena

Dresden

Rudolstadt

Meiningen

Bauerbach

Karlsbad

R. RHINE

Frankfurt

Eger

Mainz

Darmstadt

Worms

Männheim

Oggersheim

Nürnberg

Landau

Bretten

Heilbronn

Hohenasperg

Marbach

Ludwigsburg

Neckarems

Nördlingen

Regensburg

Cannstatt

Gmünd

Solitude

Stuttgart

Lorch

R. NECKAR

Esslingen

Tübingen

Augsburg

München

Salzburg

Freiburg

Bodensee

first figures as a dramatist of revolutionary type, criticizing the structure of society; then he becomes a historian, later still a philosopher, and finally a classical dramatist. The impression of shifting aim left by this career is illusory, and caused for the greater part by his early death. If Schiller had lived only as long as Shakespeare—that is, for seven more years—it would have been clear that he had found himself as a tragic writer in 1796 and that his earlier phases were preliminary steps to the main activity of his life. As he died after only nine years of dramatic creation, the last period of his life appears, deceptively, as another phase, instead of the true path of his genius.

Schiller coupled with the gift of the great dramatist that of the great preacher, expressing his lofty and noble ideals in impassioned eloquence. It is no mere chance that the two chief amusements of his early childhood were acting plays and preaching sermons. No man, however, can successfully be preacher and playwright at the same time. Either the dramatist is in control, and then the characters live by their own laws and disregard the moralist's manipulation; or the preacher intrudes himself upon the characters and makes them speak in his own name, sacrificing truth of illusion to nobility of thought. In Schiller's work the two trends held an uneasy truce in the first period of his work. After *Don Carlos* (1787) the historian conquered ground for the playwright, till the philosopher more than redressed the balance. With *Wallenstein* the tragic dramatist came into his own.

Even in these last years Schiller did not entirely conquer the preacher in him. Now and then it happened that a character or a theme roused his enthusiasm to such a pitch that he identified himself with it, and, instead of words dictated by character, there poured forth a stream of Schiller's own rhetorical eloquence. The characters fade, and in their place there stands the figure of an earnest and inspired teacher. Admirable as the sentiments are, they cannot atone for the onlooker's or reader's loss of belief.

Far more often the characters gripped Schiller's imagination without arousing his too enthusiastic participation. When this occurred they live and move apparently of their own accord. Schiller's creative imagination—though not his intellect—is of Shakespearean type. He discards his own identity and enters in spirit into the separate and divergent characters of his work. It is the dramatist's supreme gift, and one which no other German writer and few of other nations have possessed in the same degree. The balanced personality of the playwright has innumerable potentialities which gain no expression in his life, but can be fulfilled at will in his imagination. The state of equilibrium, which according to

KARL EUGEN DUKE OF WÜRTEMBERG

6

TITLE-PAGE TO THE SECOND EDITION OF "DIE RÄUBER"

Schiller is the condition of the mind which has appreciated beauty, is a necessary condition, too, for the objective artist.

The playwright needs to do more than create individual characters. He must knit them together into a convincing, coherent world. His versatile and flexible imagination must intertwine many threads, losing none and giving each its due place. It is a task which many excellent dramatists have accomplished only by simplifying and restricting the world they depict. The greatest (and this is where Schiller takes his place close to Shakespeare) have portrayed a manifold, teeming, and varied world which seems to have its own being, independent of its creator. Schiller's scope in his great plays has the breadth and universality of Shakespeare. He differs—apart from his occasional lapses into moralizing—in the austerity of his conception, which, except in *Wallenstein*, excludes humour.

The weaving of plot, the conception of characters, and the crisis of conflict all depend, however, on language. Living speech is the life-blood of drama, without which all the rest is dead tissue, inert organs, and dry bones. And speech which is alive when written can grow pale and dry, so that the play fades with it. Schiller's *Die Räuber* is an extinct mastodon, exciting wonder, but neither fear nor pity, just because the language which once gave it life has congealed into unnatural forms. Not till Schiller turned in *Don Carlos* to verse did he discover the secret of perennial youth for his plays. Prose being, for him, too close to everyday reality, there crept into his prose dialogue an exaggeration which was an involuntary escape from realism. Verse is by its very nature isolated from ordinary speech, and, once Schiller had adopted it, the need to force his style away from the common tongue disappeared. His verse—as long as it is dramatic verse, governed by character—is much more natural than his prose. Where the moralist penetrates through the mask of the character, and in the poems, where he too consciously strives to remain on the loftiest heights, Schiller fails to achieve this naturalness.

The rhetoric which sometimes escapes control and impairs Schiller's work is at the same time the source of his strength. Where it is properly employed as the servant of character it gives to his verse an eloquent and powerful beauty. It is a style which succeeds only in the hands of the greatest. His many imitators have done him a disservice by associating the label " Schillerian " with their stiff, stilted, tedious productions.

Because Schiller's manifold imagination and his nobly austere intellect were often hard to harmonize his work is inconsistent in quality, but when he was at his best the breadth of his picture, the men and women who people it, and the language they speak are of Shake-spearean calibre. Misunderstood by his countrymen, who have tried in defiance of the facts to make a consciously national poet of him, and neglected by other countries because rhetoric translated so easily turns to bombast, Schiller has still to meet a just valuation. The originality of his aesthetic thought is a minor aspect of his genius. Before all else he is one of the great playwrights of the European tradition.

Chapter Two

CHILDHOOD AND YOUTH
1759–80

FRIEDRICH SCHILLER was born on November 10, 1759, in the little town of Marbach on the river Neckar in the Duchy of Würtemberg, the second child and only son of Lieutenant Johann Kaspar Schiller of the Würtemberg army.

Kaspar Schiller was the son of a baker of the Swabian town of Bittenfeld. He was apprenticed to one of those eighteenth-century surgeons, whose principal practice was the shaving of beards and the pulling of teeth, but he soon abandoned this profession and enlisted in a passing regiment of Bavarian hussars, on its way to the war in the Austrian Netherlands. He served in a number of small actions, skirmishes and marauding forays, was captured by the French, escaped, and rejoined his regiment. In 1748 the Treaty of Aix-la-Chapelle having brought the war and his three years of active service to an end, Kaspar Schiller, now twenty-five years old, made his way back to Würtemberg, sold his horse, while retaining saddle and bridle against an uncertain future, and came to live at the Golden Lion in Marbach with the intention of finding a wife. On July 22, 1749, he married Elisabetha Dorothea Kodweiss, sixteen-year-old daughter of the host of the Golden Lion.

The Kodweiss family was encumbered with debts, and Kaspar Schiller had to draw on his own modest savings in order to placate his father-in-law's creditors. After four years of cramped and anxious existence he gave up his practice and enlisted in the Würtemberg army in 1753 as a quartermaster. In 1757 he was granted a commission as an ensign. The same year he was ordered to Silesia with a contingent of six thousand men provided by Würtemberg under a subsidy treaty with the French. It was an ill-timed departure, for his wife, after eight years of marriage, was expecting her first child. Less than a month after Ensign Schiller had said good-bye she gave birth to a daughter, who received the name Christophine.

Early in the spring of 1758 Ensign Schiller was promoted lieutenant, and in May the Würtemberg force, thinned by disease and wounds to one-third of its original strength, returned home. It was then hat Kaspar Schiller saw his nine-month-old daughter for the first time. In October 1759 he had once again to ride away to war. By an unlucky chance his departure again preceded the birth of a child. Thirteen days after he had left, his son, the future poet and dramatist, was born. He was christened Johann Christoph Friedrich.

Lieutenant Schiller first saw his son in May 1760; he did not, however, return finally to his native land until February 1761. Then, for nearly three years, during which he was promoted captain, his regiment was constantly on the move. During this time his wife and family lived in one room at Marbach. At Christmas 1763, Kaspar Schiller was posted to Schwäbisch-Gmünd as a recruiting officer. He sent for his wife and children, and the family was united for the first time in the New Year of 1764.

Kaspar Schiller was a man of determined character, practical ability, active intelligence, and little education, who, in spite of this handicap, was able in his later years to write a treatise on tree-growing, which was for a time a standard work. Conscious of the shortcomings of his own education, he kept his son steadily at his books, and the children regarded him with an affection which was tempered with awed respect. Frau Dorothea Schiller had married young enough for her husband to be able to guide and mould her character in the first decisive years of their life together. Her lively imagination, gentle motherliness, and sweet temper compensated in the home for the father's rough severity.

Life at Gmünd proved expensive, and before the spring of 1764 the family had moved to cheaper quarters about seven miles away in the village of Lorch, where they remained for three years. Fritz, as he was called at home, spent the happiest time of his childhood in the Rems valley, in which Lorch lay surrounded by dark wooded hills. He listened to his father's stories of campaigning in the Netherlands and Silesia and to his accounts of the greatness and glory of the Hohenstaufens, whose tombs were still to be seen in the monastery of Lorch; and with his sister he played in the woods nearby.

Captain Schiller made a friend in Lorch who exercised a powerful influence on Friedrich. This was Pastor Moser, who began the boy's education, grounding him in Latin and giving him a smattering of Greek. The grave and kind pastor made a deep impression on the six-year-old boy, awakening in him a desire to enter the Church in emulation of his master. He developed for a time a passion for acting the clergyman; dressed in old black clothes, he would climb on to a chair and deliver a sermon. The prestige of Pastor Moser with Schiller was such that, long after the childish mimicry of sermons was forgotten, he used the name of his first teacher for the upright and worthy pastor who appears in the last act of *Die Räuber*.

The happy and care-free life at Lorch came to an end with the transfer of Captain Schiller to Ludwigsburg shortly before Christmas 1776. Ludwigsburg contrasted very sharply with Lorch. It was the residence of the Duke of Würtemberg, and the Court, by its size and influence, dominated the little town. The huge palace overshadowed all other buildings; fashionable dresses, handsome uniforms, luxurious carriages and magnificent horses enlivened the streets. In the opera-house, to which the Schillers, as an officer's family, had free access, the spectators could admire the latest marvels of Italian extravagance and ingenuity in production and decoration. The theatre fascinated Friedrich, and acting displaced preaching as his favourite amusement.

Friedrich Schiller's education was determined by his wish to become a pastor. Candidates for orders attended the " Latin School " (*Lateinschule*) until the age of thirteen or fourteen, when they passed into a higher establishment, the *Klosterschule*. Friedrich Schiller entered the Latin School in 1767, when seven years old. For five years he studied Latin authors, not as poets, historians, and orators, but as compendia of grammar, elucidated by narrow-minded and dreary pedants.

His desire to enter the Church grew stronger. The hope of serving God and simultaneously winning fame as an eloquent and powerful preacher sustained him through the deadly monotony of mechanical learning, and he looked forward eagerly to the next phase of his preparation at the *Klosterschule*. The prospect of seeing him one day in the holy, respected and secure station of a clergyman filled his parents with a pardonable pride.

Late in 1772, however, the Schillers' plans were completely upset by a personal demand from the all-powerful Duke of Würtemberg that Friedrich should be sent to the new school at the 'Solitude' nine miles from Ludwigsburg, where the secular curriculum would make it impossible for him to continue to prepare for the Church. Captain Schiller, torn between his soldierly habit of obedience and his earnest desire to see his son in the ministry, tried hard to evade the demand without causing offence, but it was repeated in a more peremptory tone. Dismay and depression prevailed in the Schillers' house, but there was no escape from the summons. Friedrich Schiller at the age of thirteen found himself for the first time dominated by a power against which the protection of home was helpless.

It was on January 16, 1773, that Friedrich Schiller, accompanied by his father, walked from the house, which had hitherto been his home, to the school which was to replace it for the next eight years. He knew that he had left his home for good and that there would not even be holidays in which he could visit it; he knew too, that he had said good-bye to his dream of becoming a minister. It is small wonder that he was downcast as he walked by his father's side.

Karl Eugen, the Duke of Würtemberg who thus arbitrarily intervened in Friedrich Schiller's life, was a remarkable personality, an absolute despot, who oppressed his subjects for many years and yet enjoyed great personal popularity. Born in Brussels in 1728 and brought up as a Catholic, he had acceded to the ducal throne of Protestant Würtemberg at the age of nine. In 1742 he was sent to learn the duties of a sovereign under Frederick II of Prussia, who found him an apt pupil.

Pronounced to be of age at sixteen, Karl Eugen at first seemed likely to justify the Prussian king's confidence; but as he grew up and grasped the extent of his powers he became impatient of contradiction and ruthless in crushing opposition. Love of ostentation led him to spend vast sums on the Court, with which he hoped to rival and even eclipse the Versailles of Louis XV. Banquets, theatrical performances, balls, hunting-parties, firework displays, all on the most lavish scale, followed one another without pause, and the pace became so furious that his Duchess fled in 1756 to the more sober atmosphere of her native Bayreuth.

Karl Eugen would deny himself nothing. His plans were colossal, and new buildings or extensions of old ones had to be completed in a few weeks by forced labour. His luxurious scale of living far outran the revenues of his state, and the need of money determined his whole policy. He dismissed his tried ministers and replaced them with others more pliable. Three new favourites achieved exceptional notoriety: Philipp Rieger, a coarse and ruthless executor of his master's will; Count Montmartin, a genius at extortion and intrigue; and Lorenz Wittleder, who carried on an unscrupulous and impudent traffic in public offices and appointments. Rieger, a god-father of Fritz Schiller, fell from grace in 1762 in spectacular fashion through the intrigues of Montmartin, and had to endure four years of rigorous imprisonment.

The duty of these new advisers was to extract from Karl Eugen's subjects the vast sums of money the Duke required to gratify his lust for display. The method which achieved the greatest notoriety was the sale of soldiers. It had begun with the Subsidy Treaty which guaranteed troops for the French in case of war, in return for an immediate cash payment. When war came the requisite number of men was rounded up by Rieger in brutal fashion in the years 1757 and 1758. It was with these conscripts that Kaspar Schiller had fought in Silesia. From Subsidy Treaties Karl Eugen graduated easily to the sale of soldiers to France and Holland and then to the sale of untrained young men as recruits for these colonial powers. Few returned from the tropical possessions to which they were sent.

Karl Eugen's acts of violence embraced all the extortions and expropriations, the imprisonment of men and abduction of women traditionally associated with the worst eighteenth-century despots, and any criticism courted an indefinite visit to one of his fortresses. Würtemberg possessed a constitution, but the Duke disregarded its provisions, and when the representative body, the Estates of Würtemberg, ventured at last to protest he retorted by withdrawing his court from Stuttgart to Ludwigsburg. An appeal by the Estates to the Emperor of the Holy Roman Empire, to whom the Duke of Würtemberg was subject, began six years of negotiation, which culminated in 1770 with a compromise, by which Karl Eugen confirmed the rights of the constitution, and the Estates in return undertook to meet most of his debts. Wittleder and Montmartin had already been dismissed.

A remarkable change now occurred in Karl Eugen. His love of ostentation and his ambition persisted, but he satisfied them in less expensive and more useful fields. Almost overnight he became a benevolent despot with a pronounced interest in education. His character did not alter—his intolerance of criticism was still as great, his will as imperious—but his aim and his attitude were new.

It is very likely that Karl Eugen's reformation would have been only temporary, if an important emotional experience had not coincided with it. At the age of forty-one he fell in love with the twenty-one-year-old Baroness Franziska von Leutrum. Karl Eugen carried her off in 1772 to his palace at Ludwigsburg, where she lived as his acknowledged mistress. In 1774 she received the title of Imperial Countess (*Reichsgräfin*) of Hohenheim, and in 1785 Karl Eugen, then a widower, married her. She exercised a beneficial and restraining influence on him, encouraging his interest in useful activities, chief among which was a new school.

In 1770 Karl Eugen had established an orphanage for the children of soldiers, which was to train its pupils for landscape gardening or the ballet. It was a measure of economy by which he hoped in time to replace expensive foreign artists by the cheaper home product. From this beginning there arose in February 1771 the Military College (*Militärische Pflanzschule*), an extension of the original scheme designed to provide officers for the army and civil servants for the administration. The Military College combined school and university (though it had no faculties of medicine and theology) in one institution. It was Karl Eugen's own personal creation and he continued to take a close and lively interest in it for the rest of his life.

The school was at first housed in a building adjoining the rococo palace called the Solitude, and in 1773 was renamed the Ducal Military Academy (*Herzogliche Militär-Akademie*). It was transferred to Stuttgart in 1775, when its scope was extended to include the study of medicine. In 1781 the Emperor Joseph II gratified a long-standing ambition of Karl Eugen when he granted the school a university charter. The Charles University (*Hohe Karlsschule*), as it then became known, did not long survive the death of Karl Eugen in 1793. His successor dissolved it at the suggestion of the older university of Tübingen, which had always been jealous of this new foundation.

When Friedrich Schiller entered this school in 1773 he knew that he would find nothing to compensate for the home that he had been obliged to leave. Life at the school was regulated by military discipline. The administrative staff of officers and N.C.O.'s enforced mechanical uniformity and punctilious attention to turn-out. The boys rose at five, made their beds, and dressed. Then they were marched into the refectory, halted, and, at the order " To prayers," bowed their heads. Morning school lasted from seven till eleven and was followed at twelve by the chief meal of the day, which the Duke and the Countess of Hohenheim often shared. This was a formal parade, and in the hour preceding it the boys had to put on their best uniform—light blue coat with black facings, white waistcoat and breeches, cocked hat and sword. After the meal came a quick change back into working clothes, followed by an hour's organized recreation. Afternoon school lasted from two till seven, when they once again put on full-dress for the supper parade. By nine o'clock they were in bed and lights were put out.

There was no cruelty in this, and there was much less flogging than in English schools of the period. The vice of the Military Academy, however, was its complete organization of every minute of the day. This regimentation was made the more serious by the absence of holidays. A boy could reckon that he would not spend one night outside the school from the day of his entry at twelve or thirteen to the day he left at twenty or twenty-one; not even if his parents were ill or dying would he be granted leave. Deliberate policy dictated this harshness, for Karl Eugen insisted that he was the boys' true father and tried to relegate their real parents to second place.

The educational side of the school was, for its time, exceptionally enlightened. The masters, freed from all administrative duties, lived outside the school, visiting it only when they had teaching periods. Karl Eugen often engaged energetic young men in preference to better-known but less inspiring seniors, and the boys listened to their teachers with a receptiveness which masters forming a part of the repressive disciplinary system of the school could not have commanded. Boys would even wait at the gate for a popular master and escort him back to it when the lesson was over.

Under pressure from the Duke, Friedrich Schiller decided to study law, which meant that he would later enter the Würtemberg civil service. It took him some time to forget his ardent wish to enter the Church, and as late as 1774 he courageously reminded the Duke in an essay that he would much rather be a divine than a lawyer.

Schiller found some outlet for his religious aspirations in literature. Klopstock, the most outstanding of many devotional writers, directly influenced his earliest poetic work, the ode *An die Sonne* (*To the Sun*), written in his first year at the Academy and published nine years later in his *Anthologie*, and it was in emulation of Klopstock's *Messias* that he planned a Biblical epic entitled *Moses*. This remained a mere project.

In spite of a censorship on incoming books, Schiller and his friends read most of the works of the new generation of authors. Schiller the more readily absorbed Rousseau's yearning for simple nature, his admiration for primitive peoples and his abhorrence of laws and conventions because he himself was cut off from a natural life and subjected to paralysing rules. His schooldays coincided with a revolutionary movement in German literature. Goethe, Klinger and Leisewitz opened up new emotional depths to the young men in the Academy, who in their seclusion had no means of checking this poetic world against a real one. Goethe's *Werther* moved them profoundly and led several of them to plan a joint novel in imitation of it. This project made no headway, but Schiller, in whom *Werther* had roused a creative ferment, began to turn into a drama the story of the suicide of a student of Nassau, which he had read in a newspaper. There is little doubt that *Der Student von Nassau*, which he destroyed while still at the Academy, sought to evoke again the raptures and the torments of *Werther*.

This writing encroached upon Schiller's school-work, and he began to lag behind in his legal studies, when in 1775 Karl Eugen kept a promise he had made to the Estates in 1770 and moved his Court back to Stuttgart. The Academy, as his chief hobby, had naturally to follow him. On November 18 the staff and pupils marched the seven miles from the Solitude to Stuttgart, into which they were led by the Duke himself amid the acclamations of the inhabitants.

Here in a former barracks—bleak, monotonous two-storeyed

buildings enclosing three arid courtyards—the Academy underwent expansion. A faculty of medicine was organized. This was a god-send to Schiller, for in medicine all would start level and the ground lost in the study of the law would no longer matter. Schiller was tired, too, of the dry definitions and tedious hair-splitting of the lawyers; he was interested in human beings, and medicine was the study of one aspect of man. Though Kaspar Schiller viewed the change with misgiving—for it seemed to him that much time spent in study and much money spent on books was being wasted—the Duke, on the other hand, eager for recruits for his new faculty, approved, and gave the father a promise of better advancement for his son in the future.

The study of medicine, however, appealed to Schiller less than the lectures given on general subjects to students of all faculties. Professor Jakob Friedrich Abel (1751–1829), who had been appointed in 1772, was the teacher of philosophy. A young man himself, he established friendly contact with his pupils. He drew Schiller's attention to Shakespeare in a lecture on psychology, given early in 1776, by quoting passages from *Othello* in Wieland's translation. So much was Schiller impressed that he begged Abel for the loan of the book.

Shakespeare fascinated and at the same time repelled him; he was at first chilled by the apparent detachment of the author from his characters, and he disapproved of the introduction of comic figures, incidents, and dialogue into tragedy. Influenced by the highly subjective German literature of the day, Schiller felt that the author should take sides for and against his characters. Years after, in *Über naive und sentimentalische Dichtung* (*On Naïve and Sentimental Poetry*), he summed up very clearly his early attitude to Shakespeare:

> Durch die Bekanntschaft mit neueren Poeten verleitet, in dem Werke den Dichter zuerst aufzusuchen, seinem Herzen zu begegnen, mit ihm gemeinschaftlich über seinen Gegenstand zu reflektieren, kurz das Objekt in dem Subjekt anzuschauen, war es mir unerträglich, dass sich der Poet hier nirgends fassen liess und mir nirgends Rede stehen wollte.[1]

It was to be many years before Schiller consciously realized that the objectivity of Shakespeare was exactly what he needed to emulate. In the meantime the powerful attraction that Shakespeare had for him was a sign of congeniality.

---

[1] It seemed to me intolerable that the poet should elude me, should not let me come face to face with him, for an acquaintance with modern poets had induced me to seek the poet in his work, to feel *his* feelings, to reflect together with him, in short to see the object as the subject reflects it.

In 1776 a new German play, Leisewitz's *Julius von Tarent*, roused Schiller's enthusiasm and inspired him to compose a similar tragedy called *Kosmus von Medici*, which he subsequently destroyed.

Four of Schiller's friends at the Academy shared his literary interests; all made their mark in Würtemberg in later years, but not as writers. Friedrich von Hoven, whom Schiller had already known before he entered the Academy, became a distinguished physician; Johann Wilhelm Petersen was Court Librarian at Stuttgart; Johann Zumsteeg achieved some fame as musician and composer; and Georg Friedrich Scharffenstein rose to the rank of major-general in the Würtemberg army.

Schiller soon experienced the joy of seeing one of his works in print. Balthasar Haug, a professor of logic at the Academy, who was also editor of a periodical, *Das schwäbische Magazin für gelehrte Sachen*, published in 1776, without naming the author, a poem by Schiller called *Der Abend (The Evening)*. It is a conventional blend of religion and rural scenes, with no spark of originality, for Schiller had neither the eye for detail nor the ability to see natural objects in a new way, which this kind of poetry required.

A year later Haug published a second, more characteristic poem, *Der Eroberer (The Conqueror)*. Its style is modelled upon that of Klopstock's odes, but its content is Schiller's own. He denounces the conquering tyrant, yet cannot repress an involuntary admiration for him. The attitude of awe and wonder at something wicked but sublime is revealed even more strikingly in Schiller's play *Die Räuber (The Robbers)* with its contrast between the magnificent and diabolical criminal. It is not surprising to find that *Der Eroberer* dates from the time when Schiller conceived the idea of *Die Räuber*.

It was in 1777 that Schiller, who was on the watch for a good dramatic subject, came upon a story which seemed to suit his purpose. It was by Christian Daniel Schubart (1739–91). Schubart, a musician and poet, who had been bitterly satirical at the expense of Karl Eugen and his mistress, was enticed on to Würtemberg soil in 1777, arrested, and thrust without trial into the fortress of Hohenasperg. He spent the first year in solitary confinement, and though the conditions of his imprisonment afterwards improved, it was not till 1787 that Karl Eugen ordered his release. His fate was brought home all the more vividly to Schiller by the presence of Schubart's son at the Academy. The knowledge of this injustice combined with Schiller's growing resentment at the intolerable deprivation of liberty which the school inflicted to provoke an angry hatred of oppression and a passionate yearning for freedom, which found their way into his play, *Die Räuber*.

Writing, however, was consuming time which Schiller ought to have spent on his studies, and so he took at the end of 1777 the drastic resolution of giving up all literary work for two years. He adhered to this decision throughout 1778 and 1779, a time of wearisome preparation for his future profession, during which *Die Räuber* was laid on one side.

This self-imposed renunciation of his one outlet put an additional strain upon his repressed emotional life. Deprived of his writing, he contracted a passionate friendship for his twenty-year-old fellow-student Scharffenstein. An unstable state developed which culminated in a crisis, when it seemed that Scharffenstein had spoken slightingly of Schiller to another youth. Schiller was filled with a sense of shame at misplaced confidence, which found expression in a letter expressing wounded pride and bitter disillusionment glowing at white heat.

> God knows, I forgot everything, forgot all others beside you! I grew in stature at your side because I was proud of your friendship, not that I wanted to appear greater in the eyes of men, but in the eye of a higher world, for which my heart longed and which seemed to cry out to me, " He is the only one you can love "—and yet I was humbled when I looked at you, and I prayed to God that I might be like you! . . . You never really cared for me. How often have I had to hear that from you when you were angry—for otherwise you feigned respect and admiration. . . .

This discovery of the truth about Sangir, as he had called Scharffenstein, constituted a crisis in Schiller's development, probably surpassing the earlier crisis which had wrenched him from home and the Church. When he wrote in this letter, " the Sangir, whom I so loved, existed only in my own heart; and I adored him in you, his image, but how false a one," he had suffered a profound experience of the disparity between the ideal and reality.

In the year 1779 Schiller prepared the dissertation which he hoped would ensure his release from the Academy, whose oppressive atmosphere became the more irksome as he grew to be a man. His subject was *The Philosophy of Physiology*, a theme congenial to him because of its wide scope and general character. The examiners thought his essay showed conceit, false principles, and disrespect for established authorities, and they advised the Duke to reject it. Their advice was accepted, not because Karl Eugen doubted Schiller's capacity, but because he believed that another year at the Academy would have a useful sobering effect.

This was a bitter blow for Schiller, who had endured with patience because he had felt that release was near. The time of his confinement, for so it appeared to the twenty-year-old youth, stretched out apparently interminably in front of him. When the two years of self-imposed renunciation elapsed at the end of 1779 he sought escape in poetic work, which received an additional impulse from the virit, on December 14, 1779, of the author of *Werther*. Goethe was travelling in the suite of Duke Karl August of Saxe-Weimar, who was paying an official visit to the famous Würtemberg College on his way back from Switzerland.

There could be no personal contact with Goethe at this time. The twenty-year-old Schiller, sitting among the senior boys, had published only two poems, and neither had borne his name; on the daïs sat Goethe, ten years older, an author of European repute, and a minister of a sovereign state. Goethe was ignorant of Schiller's existence; Schiller was profoundly moved by the sight of so revered an author, and his enthusiasm for literature redoubled.

Schiller now took up again the manuscript of *Die Räuber*. As the day was governed by a rigid schedule, he frequently reported sick in order to work at *Die Räuber* in the sick-bay, where lights were allowed. In view of the risk of an unexpected visit by the Duke, Schiller kept a medical manuscript handy, which he began to study if he heard steps approaching. In this way *Die Räuber* made good progress, and as he completed the scenes he tried them out on his comrades, often at exciting secret rendezvous in the open air. One such reading, on a Sunday in May 1780, is portrayed in the crude picture by Heideloff, who was one of those present.

Writing *Die Räuber*, however, could not save Schiller entirely from depression. And his gloom deepened rapidly when death for the first time intervened in his life. Early in 1780 he had begun to grow very friendly with Friedrich von Hoven's younger brother, August. On June 13 of that year August died. Schiller's reaction shows him to have been in a nervously introspective state. His poem, *Eine Leichenphantasie* (*A Funeral Phantasy*), written on this occasion, revels in images associated with death, painting in the starkest colours the contrast between the youth's hoped-for future and its grim realization. Writing to von Hoven's father, he spoke chiefly of himself as a young man grown old before his time:

> I am not yet twenty-one, but I can tell you frankly that the world has no attraction for me any more; I no longer look forward to it, and the day of my departure from the Academy, which a few years back would have seemed a special day of rejoicing, will now not even elicit from me a happy smile.

It is clear that Schiller's grief for August von Hoven is inextricably mixed with the frustration caused by the postponement of his release from the Academy.

Schiller's dejection was reinforced by another disturbing experience. A few days before August von Hoven died, Grammont, a school-friend, had asked Schiller to get him some poison. Schiller reported the occurrence, and Grammont was moved to the school sick-bay. Schiller, as his friend and also as a medical student, was given the task of watching at his bedside. It can well be imagined that such close contact with a subject of severe melancholia was likely to deepen Schiller's depression. His fundamental sanity, however, remained unshaken.

During the year 1780 Schiller prepared and wrote his second dissertation, *Versuch über den Zusammenhang der tierischen Natur des Menschen mit seiner geistigen (Essay on the Connexion between the Physical and Spiritual Natures of Man)*. This thesis, which is as general in scope as the first, investigates the influence of the mind upon the body, and of the body upon the mind. Schiller bases his method on Abel's lectures, drawing his examples not from experiment and observation, but from literature. There are many quotations from Shakespeare and a dialogue from *The Life of Moor*, a tragedy by Krake. The encyclopedias will not yield any information about this author, for he is none other than Schiller himself and the play is *Die Räuber*. By converting himself into a bogus Englishman Schiller was able to quote from his own play and also to play a successful trick upon some at least of the examiners; some others probably knew of the deception beforehand.

Schiller's dissertation, which is a bastard product of literature and science of a kind then common, showing more interest in generalized speculation than in exact investigation, satisfied the examiners and thereby achieved its aim; it became his passport to the outside world.

The dissertation was published in the autumn of 1780, but Schiller had to wait until the end of the academic year before he could leave. On December 15, at the age of twenty-one, he emerged as a qualified physician, and, though only his intimates knew this, as a powerful and impassioned writer. The strain of spending his later adolescent years in this peculiar school with its isolation from normal life and lack of privacy had forced his frank and open nature into a partial self-absorption, which obscured his true genius, causing him to spend many years in search of himself.

Chapter Three

STUTTGART AND "DIE RÄUBER"

1781

DUKE KARL EUGEN thought highly of Schiller's ability and had promised that he would be well provided for. Yet Schiller fared worse than his comrades when, at the end of 1780, the list of appointments was made known. He was posted as doctor to the Augé Regiment in Stuttgart. This position did not carry with it commissioned rank, and the regiment contained the dregs of an army which was threadbare and neglected since the Duke had tired of military displays; it was not unknown even for the grenadiers of the Augé Regiment to beg in the streets of Stuttgart. To be the doctor of this assemblage of scarecrows could arouse in Schiller no enthusiasm for his profession. Nor was his uniform—a stiff, ugly, uncomfortable and cheap compromise between that of officer and man—likely to reconcile him with his duties. It would have been a relief to have worn off duty the civilian suits his father had had made for him, but he was expressly forbidden to do so by the Duke himself. Nor was he allowed to supplement by private practice his pay of eighteen talers a month (£1 10s.).

Schiller's duties, in short, were performed in conditions which appeared to him irksome and even degrading. But he was twenty-one years old, for the first time in his life he received pay, however meagre, and he was free from the tyranny of the school. He could live where he liked and, when his duties were over, amuse himself as he pleased.

Schiller shared with another former pupil of the Academy, a Lieutenant Kapf, a ground-floor room in a large house in the street *Am langen Graben*. Their furniture was scanty, consisting of beds, a table, two benches, and a stove. They cooked for themselves, and visitors noticed broken and dirty plates about the room, sacks of potatoes in a corner, and a powerful smell of tobacco in the air. Later, when *Die Räuber* had been published, one corner of the room served as a warehouse for the unsold copies.

Squalid as it was, it was at any rate his own. Here he could entertain his friends to a frugal meal, drink beer with them, or on extravagant days a cheap wine, and pass the evening at cards. More often, however, their meetings took place at the Ox Inn. His frequent visits here, his card-playing and his skittles soon caused the respectable citizens of Stuttgart to look askance at him.

Schiller quickly increased his notoriety by publishing a poem.

I'm beginning to write, and the damned little thing [he wrote] has made me more notorious in this district than twenty years of practice.

The poem which thus blackened Schiller's name was neither frivolous, nor satirical, nor lewd. It was a sincerely written elegy on the death of one of his friends from the Academy, Johann Christian Weckherlin, who died on January 15, 1781.

The *Elegie auf den Tod eines Jünglings* (*Elegy on the Death of a Youth*) recalls Schiller's *Leichenphantasie* of the year before, surpassing it in sincerity and depth, though it is not free from glaring blemishes of taste such as the crass bombast of

Tischt auch den dem grossen Würger auf![1]

There is less effort to make the flesh of the survivors creep and more honest endeavour to react justly to the situation. It was this integrity of purpose which brought Schiller into disrepute, for it led him to bitter and comfortless reflections, far from the conventional paths of funeral oratory.

Schiller's great anxiety in the early months of 1781 was the search for a publisher for *Die Räuber*. The joy and relief at having created the play could not fully unfold until the work had reached the public. As the Stuttgart publishers would not touch it, Schiller turned his eyes ' abroad.' When his friend Petersen travelled to Mannheim in the Rhenish Palatinate he tried, at Schiller's request, to find a publisher for the play there, but without success.

In view of this failure, Schiller took a drastic step. He had the play printed in Stuttgart at his own expense. Not having enough money himself, he borrowed, incurring the first of several debts which later became a serious encumbrance.

On May 6, 1781, the book was published. The title-page is worded, *Die Räuber. Ein Schauspiel. Frankfurt und Leipzig*. 1781. The false place of publication—for the book really appeared at Stuttgart—constituted a deliberate smoke-screen intended to cover Schiller and his printer. The author remained, of course, anonymous. A faint hint of his profession was conveyed by the Latin motto on the title-page:

Quae medicamenta non sanant, ferrum sanat, quae ferrum non sanat, ignis sanat.[2]

---

[1] Serve him up, too, to the great assassin!

[2] Iron cures what drugs cannot, fire cures what iron cannot.

The source of *Die Räuber* (*The Robbers*) was Schubart's story, published in Haug's *Schwäbisches Magazin* in 1777. In this story of hostile brothers—whom Schubart likened to Tom Jones and Master Blifil—Schiller believed that he had found exactly the dramatic subject he needed. He retained the outline of characters and events, amplified them with details and developments of his own, and set his play against the almost contemporary background of the Seven Years War.

When the action begins Karl, the elder son, is at Leipzig University, while Franz, the hypocritical and malevolent younger brother, is living at home with his father Herr von Moor, the ruler of a petty state. Apart from servants, the only other inhabitant of the ancestral castle is the orphan Amalia, betrothed to the absent Karl. A letter from Karl to his father expressing repentance for his excesses is intercepted by Franz, who, substituting a forged letter, magnifies his brother's offences into grave crimes. Herr von Moor, deceived by this rather obvious subterfuge, commissions Franz to write an upbraiding letter to Karl, though he adds, " Bring meinen Sohn nicht zur Verzweiflung."[1]

Karl anxiously awaits the reply to his repentant letter. With several dissolute fellow-students he has fled to the Bohemian frontier in order to elude his creditors. His companions propose to turn brigand if only Karl Moor will agree to be their leader. Karl, on receiving a tersely worded note from Franz informing him that his father will have nothing more to do with him, falls into a paroxysm of rage and agrees to head the newly formed gang of robbers.

In the second act Franz fabricates a false report of Karl's death, throwing old Herr von Moor into a coma so like death that spectators as well as most of the characters are deluded into believing that they have seen the last of him. Franz rules in his father's stead. During these events Karl and his gang have made themselves notorious in the Bohemian Forest. Many of their crimes accord with a kind of rough justice, for they single out the oppressors of the poor as their victims; but many innocent women and children are killed in the desperate rescue of a condemned comrade, which is followed by a resounding victory over the powers of the law.

In the third act Karl Moor, resting near the Danube after the battle, swears a solemn and fateful oath never to abandon his comrades. A new recruit[2] then tells the unhappy story of his love for a woman called Amalia. The mention of the name brings Karl's own love to his mind, and he orders his followers to saddle up for an immediate march to his native region of Franconia.

---

[1] Don't make my son despair.   [2] Kosinsky.

When the fourth act begins the disguised Karl is revisiting his ancestral home, where he finds that his father has apparently died. Amalia, to whom he does not reveal himself, remains constant to his memory. He learns some part of his brother's perfidy and resolves to flee at once, lest he should be driven to fratricide. He rejoins his companions in a wood not far from the castle, where he discovers in an underground vault an old man, locked up with no fire and little food. It is old Herr von Moor, who is thus being starved to death by his wicked son. Filled with the wildest fury at Franz's inhuman villainy, Karl gives orders for the storming of the castle and the apprehension of his brother.

The assault opens the last act. Franz kills himself before the robbers can seize him and hale him before his brother. Karl is reunited with Amalia, and begins to dream of a happy and innocent life with her, when the robbers intervene to remind him of his oath. His last hope gone, he kills Amalia and goes to hand himself over to justice.

As the action is presented in the play, it is divisible into two fairly distinct phases. In the first stage, which extends as far as the end of the third act, the two groups of characters, forming two separate worlds, one around Franz Moor, the other in the train of Karl, remain apart following their own courses. Except for Karl's repentant letter, which is suppressed by Franz, and for Franz's treacherous answer, there is no contact whatever between the parties, who are geographically situated hundreds of miles apart. The second phase is already introduced in the third act in the scene *Gegend an der Donau* (*Scene by the Danube*); there the action, which has come almost to a halt, receives a new impulsion as Kosinsky's story brings Amalia back to Karl's thoughts. With the brigands' journey to Franconia, which falls between the third and fourth acts, the two threads are intertwined into one, and the plot moves swiftly to its catastrophe.

This division of the action emphasizes the contrast between the two brothers, but makes it more difficult to accept them as the closest blood relations. We should have seen Karl and Franz together at a time when the guileless Karl suspected none of the infamy of his brother. By the time they do meet, all bonds are broken. It is inexperience that has led Schiller to take the simple course, instead of adopting a single, more complex action, which would have produced a more concentrated effect. As it is, concentration characterizes the last two acts, which gain by contrast with the dispersion of the first three. It is interesting to note that it was only during the last two acts that the enthusiasm of the audience at the first performance really rose to the pitch of frenzy.

The scene *Gegend an der Donau* links the two actions together and provides the play with a centre of repose, where rural calm, combined with the relaxation following great exertion, reminds the robbers, fresh from the scenes of crime and horror, of another life of hard toil, simple pleasures, and primitive griefs. The initial stage directions themselves strike the right pastoral chord: " Die Räuber gelagert auf einer Anhöhe unter Bäumen, die Pferde weiden am Hügel hinunter."[1]

As the robbers talk of the fertile sunlit countryside before them their crimes, though not forgotten, recede into the background, leaving an atmosphere of idyllic peace, tinged with the melancholy of unspoken vain regret.

> *Moor.* Seht doch, wie schön das Getreide steht! — Die Bäume brechen fast unter ihrem Segen. — Der Weinstock voll Hoffnung!
>
> *Grimm.* Es gibt ein fruchtbares Jahr.
>
> *Moor.* Meinst du?—Und so würde doch ein Schweiss in der Welt bezahlt.[2]

And the mood reaches its height as the setting sun touches the horizon:

> *Schwarz.* Wie herrlich die Sonne dort untergeht!
>
> *Moor [In dem Anblick verschwimmt].* So stirbt ein Held! — Anbetenswürdig![3]

But the spell is fragile and is soon past, the regrets become explicit, the brief contact with another world, where their cares and crimes cease to count, is lost. In the few minutes which this part of the scene lasts Schiller gives the spectator a much-needed rest from horror, and at the same time intensifies by contrast the flaming passions and monstrous crimes of the remainder of the play.

If the events of *Die Räuber* are more extraordinary than the events of real life could be, the style, too, is more inflated than the language of every day. There are in Schiller's speech many reminiscences of Shakespeare and of the Bible, but in spite of allusions and quotations and borrowed phrases, Schiller has created a powerful language of his own. It is a language of white-hot emotion, and it can be

---

[1] The robbers are lying on a hillock beneath the trees. Lower down the slope their horses are grazing.

[2] *Moor.* Look, how strongly the corn is growing. The fruit-trees are almost ready to break with the weight of their crop and the vines full of promise!
Grimm. There will be a good harvest.
Moor. Do you think so? Then at least *some* toil will be repaid in this world.

[3] *Schwarz.* How splendidly the sun sets!
Moor [lost in the sight]. Like the death of a hero! I could kneel before it in adoration!

seen elsewhere at its best and purest in the passionate letter to Scharffenstein.[1]

In *Die Räuber* it is not always pure; here he was writing for an audience, feeling the need to impress, to force his points home. As a result, speech often turns to a scream, and rhetoric to bombast. There is little differentiation of the style at moments of stress between one character and another. And though the heroic is suited to the tirades of Karl Moor, it is out of place on the lips of Amalia, and leads to absurdities such as:

> Ha, Würger! Du kannst nur die Glücklichen töten, die Lebenssatten gehst du vorüber! [*Kriecht zu den Räubern.*] So erbarmet euch meiner, ihr Schüler des Henkers!—Es ist ein so blutdürstiges Mitleid in euren Blicken, das dem Elenden Trost ist — euer Meister ist ein eitler, feigherziger Prahler![2]

And Amalia's resolution to emulate Dido, which follows this speech, rings as false as the allusion to Virginius made by Lessing's Emilia Galotti. Yet beneath the forced emphasis the natural eloquence of Schiller flows unmistakably clear and swift, in spite of wild exaggeration and occasional bathos. In every act examples can be found where the speech of passion carries the stamp of conviction. It cries out, however, for verse.

Die Räuber is a two-man play. Karl and Franz stand out head and shoulders above a host of minor characters. But these lesser figures are not without interest or skill in portrayal. Around Franz are grouped the various members of the Moor family and household. The father, old Herr von Moor, is one of the least satisfactory figures. Weak and credulous, he has apparently not the slightest suspicion of Franz's real nature; Franz, who does not want wit, gives himself no trouble at all in deceiving his father.

If Herr von Moor appears too weak, Amalia, Karl's betrothed, is too heroic. It is evident that Schiller, whose acquaintance with women during the eight years preceding had been confined to reading what was said about them in books and admiring Franziska von Hohenheim from afar, could hardly hope to achieve much success with his first attempt at female portraiture. And in Amalia he did not, in fact, portray a woman at all, but a sensitive and emotional youth. Amalia speaks and feels as he himself had spoken and felt in the days of his friendship with Scharffenstein. And with such inexperience it could scarcely be otherwise; his daily conversation, his sharing of hopes and fears, his confiding of

---

[1] See above, p. 18.

[2] Ha! Assassin! You can only slay the happy, the unhappy you pass by! [*She creeps to the robbers.*] Take pity on me, you disciples of the hangman! There is a bloodthirsty mercy in your looks, which brings consolation to the wretched— your master is a vain, cowardly boaster!

ambitions, of attractions and loathings, were all confined to a circle of youths. It is this which explains Amalia's rhetorical speech and her heroic conduct, whether she is repelling Franz's advances with his own sword, or demanding death from the robbers. Schiller had not yet learned, nor had he had the slightest chance to learn, that a woman's character cannot be created merely by slightly softening that of a man.

Two other figures occur in the Moor household, Hermann and Daniel. Hermann, resentful of past injury and filled with remorse at his own evil actions, is but lightly sketched. The portrayal of Daniel, also conventional, is fuller and more successful because the character of the faithful and honest retainer, striving to maintain his integrity in the service of a wicked master, excited greater sympathy in Schiller than a mere second-rate evil-doer such as Hermann could arouse. On the fringe of this group stands Pastor Moser (whose name and irreproachable character recall Schiller's first teacher in Lorch), a figure of simple integrity, the living symbol of the truth of religion and the moral law which Franz would like, but does not dare, to deny.

The people around Franz are not his adherents; by his very nature he could have none. Those who surround Karl Moor are in the strictest sense his followers, all bound together by their wicked trade of robbery and murder. The level of portrayal is higher here, and each figure is deftly and appropriately differentiated. Most prominent among the robbers, because he talks the most, is the boastful Spiegelberg, the original author of the proposal that the fugitives should band themselves together and take to robbery. Spiegelberg has a fertile and active, but mean, mind and lacks any quality of leadership, though he is bitterly resentful when his companions ignore his pretensions and unanimously acclaim Karl Moor as their chief. Spiegelberg is the natural criminal with no inhibitions and no shame: "Wart', und wie man Handschriften nachmacht, Würfel verdreht, Schlösser aufbricht und den Koffern das Eingeweid' ausschüttet—das sollst du noch von Spiegelberg lernen!"[1]

He boasts of the grandeur of the criminal's life and end, but his metal proves to be base. Certainly he is ready for any wickedness, provided that it involves him in no personal danger. He recruits for the gang by morally perverting his victims and leads a brutal raid on a defenceless nunnery, but he recoils from any serious conflict with a worthy opponent. In the battle in the Bohemian Forest it is he who raises the cry "Können wir nicht mehr entwischen?"[2]

---

[1] Wait, you'll have to learn from Spiegelberg how to forge documents, load dice, force locks, and extract the inside from strong-boxes.

[2] Isn't there any possibility of escape?

Contrasting with the vicious and despicable Spiegelberg is Schweizer. He is Karl Moor's right hand, a devoted follower with entire and unquestioning confidence in his leader. Schweizer has no judgment of his own and accepts at once Karl Moor's orders. He is capable of violent crime, but not of deliberate cruelty. No man in the gang, not even Karl Moor, has higher courage, and none is more trustworthy. Schweizer's word, once given, is binding; and nowhere is this more striking than in the manner of his death. Having promised to deliver Franz alive or not to show himself again, Schweizer finds him dead by his own hand; with the words " Mich sieht er nicht wieder "[1] he straightway blows his own brains out. His affection for Karl has a touching, dog-like quality about it, a desire to render little services unasked, such as the helmetful of water that he brings to Karl by the Danube's bank. And when Karl swears the oath which is later to tear him from a happiness apparently within his grasp it is Schweizer who warns him, " Schwöre nicht! du weisst nicht, ob du nicht noch glücklich werden und bereuen wirst."[2]

The other members of the gang are less fully, but still adequately delineated. Roller resembles Schweizer, but is more intelligent. Schwarz and Grimm, faithful adherents also, are more cultivated and less crude than Schweizer and Roller; it is to them that Karl turns when so moved by rural peace and beauty in the scene by the Danube. Razmann is intelligent and brave, but without firm convictions and easily persuaded to disloyalty by Spiegelberg's insinuating tongue. Schufterle, cynical and unscrupulous, is dismissed from the gang by Karl Moor for an act of atrocious cruelty during the rescue of Roller.

By the time of the catastrophe Schweizer, Roller and Spiegelberg are dead; Schufterle and Razmann have been dismissed. And it is noteworthy that none of the original group of faithful followers has any hand in holding Karl Moor to his oath. The active hostility to Karl and the insistence on the oath come from more recently joined and anonymous brigands. Of the recruits only one is named, the upright Kosinsky, whose presence is a tribute to the character of Karl and his power of attracting noble minds.

The focal-point of the play is the antithesis of the two brothers. Generosity and goodness in the guise of evil confront wickedness and vice in the cloak of respectability. Two figures face each other who know no half-measures; both are extremes of their types.

Franz Moor, the ' respectable ' brother, is the personification of

---

[1] He won't see me again.

[2] Don't swear! You cannot tell whether you will not some day become happy again and repent.

cold and calculating iniquity, of unimpassioned, relentless pursuit of an evil aim. Wickedness and cruelty afford him pleasure, and the accession to power in his feudal territories elicits from him a ghoulish joy at the torments he will be able to inflict upon his defenceless subjects:

> Mein Vater überzuckerte seine Foderungen, schuf sein Gebiet zu einem Familienzirkel um, sass liebreich lächelnd am Tor und grüsste sie Brüder und Kinder. — Meine Augbraunen sollen über euch herhangen wie Gewitterwolken, mein herrischer Name schweben wie ein drohender Komet über diesen Gebirgen. . . . Ich will euch die zackigte Sporen ins Fleisch hauen und die scharfe Geissel versuchen. — In meinem Gebiet soll's so weit kommen, dass Kartoffeln und Dünnbier ein Traktament für Festtage werden, und wehe dem, der mir mit vollen feurigen Backen unter die Augen tritt! Blässe der Armut und sklavischen Furcht sind meine Leibfarbe: in diese Liverei will ich euch kleiden![1]

Franz's wickedness is subtle, deceptive, and treacherous. He disregards the spirit of the law, but observes its letter. It is partly for this reason that he exerts all his ingenuity to avoid direct participation in the crimes he conceives. It is by the shock of grief that he seeks to kill his father and by the hand of a servant that he attempts to murder Karl. But his flinching from direct action is also the result of cowardice. Franz fears the consequences of his own acts and tries to argue his misgivings out of existence. When his conscience at last asserts its claims too insistently to be denied he is paralysed with terror.

The one infallible guide in which Franz puts his trust is his reason. And in Schiller's view reason and intellect alone, without any intuitive perception of good, without any assistance from the heart, must lead to evil. The consequences of this overweighting of the intellectual faculties of man emerge in the three powerful soliloquies in which Franz develops his attitude and belief. In the first of them[2] he expresses his resentment at the ugliness which nature has given him, but then, like Richard III, consoles himself with the thought that she has granted him a bountiful compensation—" Gab sie uns doch Erfindungsgeist mit."[3]

---

[1] My father coated his demands with sugar, made his territory into a family circle, sat smiling kindly at the gate and greeted them as his brothers and children. My eyebrows shall lower above you like thunder-clouds, my lordly name hover above these mountains like a threatening comet. . . . I will drive the keen-rowelled spurs into your flesh and let you feel the sharp scourge. In my land things shall reach the point when potatoes and small beer are fare for a holiday, and woe to him who comes before my eyes with round and ruddy cheeks! The pallor of poverty and slavish fear shall be my colours! That's the livery I'll clothe you in!

[2] Act I, scene i.

[3] Yet she gave us the inventive mind.

He derisively rejects the dictates of laws and of conscience, and
goes on to analyse the ties of blood. Cold dissection leads him to
the conclusion that no affection is due to a brother, the mere chance
product of the same womb, no love or respect to a father, who consulted only his own pleasure in the begetting of his son. Spurning
all regard for others, Franz proclaims his motto as, " Schwimme, wer
schwimmen kann, und wer zu plump ist, geh' unter! "[1]
And his final resolve, pronounced at the end of this speech, formu-
lates the same idea with greater preciseness:

> Ich will alles um mich her ausrotten, was mich einschränkt, dass
> ich nicht Herr bin. Herr muss ich sein, dass ich das mit Gewalt
> ertrotze, wozu mir die Liebenswürdigkeit gebricht.[2]

Franz's second soliloquy[3] touches on a theme which fascinated
Schiller at this time. The interdependence of mind and matter
and the subordination of the mind to the body had formed the subject of his passing-out dissertation. It is no surprise to find Franz
preoccupied, too, with this theme, and it is without doubt an allusion
to Schiller's own work when Franz says, " Philosophen und Medizi-
ner lehren mich, wie treffend die Stimmungen des Geistes mit den
Bewegungen der Maschine zusammenlauten."[4] This principle Franz
exploits when he plans to kill his father by despair, destroying
the body by attacking the mind (den Körper vom Geist aus zu
verderben).[5]
Franz's purposeful denial of all human values reaches its climax
in his third soliloquy (Act IV, scene ii). Here he justifies murder,
even the murder of a brother, as an act having no more significance
than the thoughtless begetting of a human being:

> Den Vater, der vielleicht eine Bouteille Wein weiter getrunken hat,
> kommt der Kitzel an — und draus wird ein Mensch, und der Mensch
> war gewiss das letzte, woran bei der ganzen Herkulesarbeit gedacht
> wird. Nun kommt mich oben der Kitzel an — und dran krepiert ein

[1] Let him swim who can, and he who is too clumsy can sink.

[2] Everything which hinders my absolute power I will destroy. I must be
master, so that I can obtain by force what I cannot by charm.

[3] Act II, scene i.

[4] Philosophers and physicians teach me how closely the moods of the mind
coincide with the movements of the body.

[5] To attack the body through the mind. Spiegelberg, the black sheep among
the brigands, holds a similar view: " denn incidenter muss ich dir sagen, du richtest
nichts aus, wenn du nicht Leib und Seel verderbst." (*For I must tell you, by the
way, that you won't achieve anything unless you corrupt both body and soul.*)

Mensch, und gewiss ist hier mehr Verstand und Absicht, als dort bei seinem Entstehen war.[1]

And yet the moral prejudices, as Franz considers them to be, possess for him a disquieting power and tenacity. To be sure, he attributes them merely to early education and association, but the very terms in which he speaks of them pay unwilling tribute to the hold they have upon his imagination:

> Verflucht sei die Torheit unserer Ammen und Wärterinnen, die unsere Phantasie mit schröcklichen Märchen verderben und grässliche Bilder von Strafgerichten in unser weiches Hirnmark drücken.[2]

Franz, in spite of all his parade of rationalism, has an imagination in which extravagant ideas and visions run riot. He is no genuine rationalist, but a romantic, whose rationalism has succeeded only in turning his romanticism inside out. He bestows sentimental attachment and emotional admiration on evil rather than on good, on things ugly and repellent rather than on things beautiful and attractive. He wallows in muck, delights in degrading man to the level of the animals, and sees only filth in man's physical life.

The climax of his inverted romanticism is reached in a passage which might, on internal evidence, be the joint work of Hamlet, Leopardi,[3] and Bishop Odo of Cluny:

> Der Mensch entstehet aus Morast, und watet eine Weile im Morast, und macht Morast, und gärt wieder zusammen im Morast, bis er zuletzt an den Schuhsohlen seines Urenkels unflätig anklebt.[4]

With such a character, the cringing fear of imminent death is no concession by Schiller to a conventional punishment of sin, it is a part and parcel of the contradictory nature of the man himself, with his superficial rationalism and the fundamental faith which he would so willingly deny. Franz's reasoning seeks by a continuous, but always precarious, effort to triumph over or explain away his intense irrational fear and his unacknowledged belief in God and immortality.

So great is the contrast between Franz and Karl, that it is difficult

---

[1] And the urge comes upon the father, who has perhaps drunk a bottle of wine more than usual—and the result is a human being who was certainly the very last thing thought of during the whole Herculean labour. And now the urge comes on me—and a man dies; and certainly there is more sense and purpose here than in his begetting.

[2] A curse on the folly of old women and nurse-maids who pervert our imagination with horrible tales and imprint upon our tender brains terrifying pictures of the punishment of sin.

[3] è fango il mondo.

[4] For man comes from muck, and wades for a while in muck, and returns to muck and rots in muck, till he one day filthily sticks to the sole of his great-grandson's shoe.

to credit that the two are brothers.   If Franz exalts his reason, Karl places his reliance on emotion and intuition.   He is capable of wrong actions, not of evil intentions; he can be misguided, he cannot be malicious.   Impetuous and quick-tempered, the offences which he commits before the fateful decision to become a robber are merely the expression of youthful high spirits.

Circumstance transforms him into a mighty and sublime criminal, but though it may pervert his good impulses it cannot replace them with evil ones.   Karl can be hard, ruthless, pitiless, but never mean or grasping or avaricious.   In Schiller's own words: " Er hätte sich bälder zehen Mordtaten als einen einzigen Diebstahl vergeben."[1]

His temperament is quick and impressionable; the very first scene in which he appears reveals him as a man incapable of accurate reaction, one from whom stimuli evoke exaggerated responses. After a wild youth, during which he has not troubled himself at all about his father, he writes a candid and repentant letter home, confidently expecting that all will be immediately forgiven and that he will be welcomed and feasted like the Prodigal Son of the Bible. He should have had some uncertainty, even though he knew Herr von Moor to be a most indulgent father.   And when, in this state of complete unpreparedness, he receives Franz's treacherous letter he is angry, not with Franz alone, nor with his family, but with mankind; indeed he declares war upon the whole of humanity:

> Menschen haben Menschheit vor mir verborgen, da ich an Menschheit appellierte: weg dann von mir, Sympathie und menschliche Schonung! — Ich habe keinen Vater mehr, ich habe keine Liebe mehr, und Blut und Tod soll mich vergessen lehren, dass mir jemals etwas teuer war! . . . Und Glück zu dem Meister unter euch, der am wildesten sengt, am grässlichsten mordet, denn ich sage euch, er soll königlich belohnet werden.[2]

This unpredictable violence is responsible for Karl's misfortunes. If he could have responded accurately and justly to the situations which confronted him there would have been much less bloodshed and possibly no tragedy.   This is a vital aspect of the character of Karl Moor, but it was one of which Schiller was not fully conscious, for he himself, in consequence of the stresses to which he was subjected in his adolescent years, was suffering from the same emotional malady as Karl Moor.

[1] He would have forgiven himself ten murders more easily than a single theft. [*Selbstrecension im Wirtembergischen Repertorium.*]

[2] Human beings concealed humanity from me when I appealed to humanity; begone then sympathy and humane regard! I have now no father, no love; bloodshed and death shall teach me to forget that anything was ever dear to me!—and good luck to him who proves a master among you, who starts the most furious fires and carries out the most atrocious murders, for he shall receive a royal reward. [Act I, scene ii.]

This is not to say that Karl Moor is to be identified with Schiller. But something of the violence and quickness and vehemence of Schiller's own character at this time has gone into the character, just as it has permeated many scenes of the play. It is, for instance, Schiller's own experience—a typical school experience—which is embodied in the famous words, the first spoken by Karl Moor in the play, " Mir ekelt vor diesem tintenklecksenden Säkulum, wenn ich in meinem Plutarch lese von grossen Menschen."[1]

This denunciation of the dry scholar's conventional approach to the classics, a denunciation which continues in a language surpassing in coarseness and frankness that of Goethe's *Götz*, is the reaction of a youth for whom the stories of former greatness are vivid, present reality: " Schöner Preis für euren Schweiss in der Feldschlacht, dass ihr jetzt in Gymnasien lebet und eure Unsterblichkeit in einem Bücherriemen mühsam fortgeschleppt wird."[2] Plutarch, so much admired by Schiller, is also his hero's favourite reading; and Karl Moor is himself one of the great characters with immense capacities for good or evil of whom Plutarch wrote.

Karl Moor leads a life not of goodness, but of wickedness, and another and more modern author influenced Schiller in depicting this development. Rousseau's portrayal of the corrupting effect of society determines the fate of Karl Moor. A fundamentally good and great man is driven to frightful crime by the narrow, soulless, and wicked world around him. In a more natural, simple, and upright environment he would have applied his strength and his talents to worthy ends. The fearful crimes he commits (though he himself must bear the direct responsibility for them) are also an indirect condemnation of civilization as Schiller, aided by Rousseau, then saw it.

His fundamentally good character endeavours to combat the passions which the evil-doing of others arouses in him. As long as he knows of Franz's perfidious conduct towards him alone, mildness and magnanimity prevail, despite distant flickerings of anger and resentment.

Ich fliehe aus diesen Mauren. Der geringste Verzug könnte mich wütig machen, und er ist meines Vaters Sohn. — Bruder, Bruder! du hast mich zum Elendesten auf Erden gemacht, ich habe dich niemals beleidigt, es war nicht brüderlich gehandelt — Ernte die Früchte deiner Untat in Ruhe, meine Gegenwart soll dir den Genuss

[1] When I read about great men in my Plutarch, then this ink-smudging age nauseates me. [Act I, scene ii.]

[2] A fine reward for your sweat in the battle, that you should now live in the public schools and have your immortality carried about fastened up in a bookstrap. [Act I, scene ii.]

nicht länger vergällen — aber gewiss, es war nicht brüderlich gehandelt.[1]

In such a speech the dualism of Karl Moor is laid bare. Hard and
ruthless on the surface, he is sensitive and vulnerable beneath it.
His rough exterior protects him against the injuries inflicted by the
world and prevents his conscience from determining his conduct.
But conscience, which first stirs when he realizes that his brave
and reckless rescue of Roller has cost the lives of eighty-three
innocent people, gives him thereafter no rest. The warning he
gives to Kosinsky, his newest recruit, is proof of the questioning
and self-condemnation which is going on in his inmost heart, seldom
though he expresses it. And the torments he suffers on seeing Amalia
testify to his awareness of the degradation into which he has sunk.
His conviction of ever-increasing guilt is the cause of further crimes,
as it impels him to surround himself with callous unconcern as with
an impenetrable wall: " Glaube mir, man kann das für Stärke des
Geistes halten, was doch am Ende Verzweiflung ist—Glaube mir!
mir! und mach' dich eilig hinweg."[2] So he speaks to Kosinsky in
one of those rare moments when the significance and errors of his
career appear pitilessly clear to his unclouded judgment.

Karl Moor's fate is the consequence of a decision, the portrayal
of which reveals Schiller as no slavish follower of Rousseau, but as
a sturdy and independent mind with his own standard of judgment.
Karl Moor does not confine himself to condemning modern parasites
on the magnificent body of antiquity; he extends his attack from
the emasculating effects of culture and education to the sins of the
law; and not of bad or badly applied laws, but of any laws what-
soever. He begins in fact as an anarchist:

> Ich soll meinen Leib pressen in eine Schnürbrust und meinen
> Willen schnüren in Gesetze. Das Gesetz hat zum Schneckengang
> verdorben, was Adlerflug geworden wäre. Das Gesetz hat noch
> keinen grossen Mann gebildet, aber die Freiheit brütet Kolosse und
> Extremitäten aus.[3]

---

[1] I must flee from these walls. The slightest delay could throw me into a rage,
and he is my father's son.—Brother, brother! you have made me the most wretched
man on earth, and yet I never offended you, it was not a brotherly act.—Reap the
fruits of your crime in peace, my presence shall no longer poison your enjoyment—
but it was no brotherly act.

[2] Believe me, one can take for strength of mind what is in reality despair—
believe *me*, *me*! and go swiftly away.

[3] I am to confine my body in a corset and lace my will into laws. The law has
turned into a snail's crawl what could have been the flight of an eagle. Laws
have never made a great man, but freedom breeds colossi and monstrosities.

It is clear that Schiller does not fully endorse Karl Moor's words. If it is deplorable that laws do not produce great men, freedom from law, which breeds " colossi and monstrosities," is not wholly admirable either. Karl Moor's words express his momentary anger and impatience at the humiliating treatment he has recently suffered at the hands of the law. In such a mood and with such an attitude he becomes a chief of brigands and finds himself obliged to put his precept into practice, to become his own standard and to disregard all laws but that of his own personality; to be, in the most literal sense, a law unto himself. The consequences are appalling. He longs for justice and inflicts injustice; he wishes to aid the poor and infirm, and he massacres them by the score; and for every crime of which he himself knows, a dozen are committed by his followers. The recognition of the wickedness of his chosen course comes to him early: " Und ich so hässlich auf dieser schönen Welt—und ich ein Ungeheuer auf dieser herrlichen Erde."[1]

Though these words, like all his thoughts, are emotionally conditioned, the acknowledgment of guilt, once made, cannot be ignored and insists on repetition, till it brings him to the terrible denial of the value of his whole life.

O über mich Narren, der ich wähnete, die Welt durch Greuel zu verschönern und die Gesetze durch Gesetzlosigkeit aufrecht zu halten. Ich nannte es Rache und Recht — ich masste mich an, o Vorsicht, die Scharten deines Schwerts auszuwetzen und deine Parteilichkeiten gut zu machen — aber — o eitle Kinderei — da steh' ich am Rand eines entsetzlichen Lebens und erfahre nun mit Zähnklappern und Heulen, dass zwei Menschen wie ich den ganzen Bau der sittlichen Welt zu Grund richten würden.[2]

It is the emotional expression of a deeply felt truth, the agonizing admission that his course has been wrong from the outset. And as his whole life has been based on exaggeration and extremes, so Karl Moor exaggerates here his potential influence on world history. But that does not detract from the genuineness of his remorse or the truth which underlies it.

Exaggeration is the keynote of *Die Räuber*, and with its aid Schiller has created a work of enormous dramatic power. It was at this time his natural means of expression. His artistic vision was a powerful magnifying apparatus. Action, characters, style, all are on the grand

---

[1] And I so ugly in this beautiful world—a monster on this splendid earth.

[2] Oh, what a fool I was to dream that I could improve the world by atrocities and maintain laws by lawlessness! I called it vengeance and justice. I presumed, O Providence, to straighten the edge of your sword and to counteract your little partialities, but—what childishness it was—now I stand at the end of a dreadful life and learn with weeping and gnashing of teeth that *two men like myself would destroy the whole moral structure of the world.*

scale. The world of this play is not our everyday world, but a distinct, independent world—larger, more violent, more heroic, and more wicked. What happens in it is credible and convincing, if its scale is accepted. But it is not only larger than the world of every day, it is purer and more concentrated. All the little irrelevancies of normal life, all that is inessential, is omitted. This concentration and intensification run parallel with the urge to exaggerate, and are an aspect of it.

Schiller strove for emphasis and has not escaped the danger of over-emphasis. It is a frequent defect of his early work, and arises partly from the literary style and outlook of his day and partly from his own peculiar circumstances. Exaggeration was in the air. The avoidance of violent passions, characteristic of the seventeen-forties and fifties, had yielded in the late sixties to a phase in which, it was felt, passion ought to be portrayed and could not be too violently expressed. What Gerstenberg had begun with *Ugolino*, Goethe continued with *Götz von Berlichingen* and *Die Leiden des jungen Werther*. Even the sensitive and retiring Leisewitz followed the prevailing fashion in the speeches of Guido in *Julius von Tarent*. All were outdone by Klinger, whose plays greatly impressed young Schiller. Literary influences, however, were supplemented by personal ones.

Though Schiller was certainly not downtrodden or broken by the Academy, he suffered its repression, and as he grew older became more and more aware of the contrast between the liberty prevailing in the outside world and the restraint in which he was at that time held. The narrowness and confinement of school-life engendered in him a state of repressed longing and smouldering resentment which made itself felt with exceptional force in the outlet which dramatic writing afforded him. And his condition was considerably aggravated by the insistence of the authorities on his remaining at school for the year 1781.[1] It was during this hated year, his twenty-first, that he finished *Die Räuber*. The very writing of it was part of his fight against the negative discipline and interference with personal liberty which characterized the Academy. For he wrote it secretly by candlelight, and every page of his manuscript was a victory over the system he loathed. The need of constant vigilance contributed to an atmosphere of tense excitement, which the darkness and the shadows thrown by the candle did nothing to diminish. Small wonder then that the starkest and sharpest contrasts and a violently exaggerated tone prevail. The miracle is rather that the play is not spoiled by the combined effect of literary fashion and military repression.

[1] See above, p. 18.

Schiller's urge to exaggerate in *Die Räuber* was not, however, only a matter of passing fashion. It corresponded to something in his mental structure. He was not concerned primarily with himself; the desire to communicate was conscious and important in him, and had manifested itself in his early preaching and play-acting games, just as it appeared at school in the poem on the death of August von Hoven. Schiller was driven by irresistible impulse to pass his ideas and attitudes on to others. It was a form of conflict; other ideas must be vanquished if his own were to gain the day. The consciousness of this necessity leads in the young and immature to overstatement, over-emphasis, exaggeration. This bent of mind underlies the cat-tearing bombast of *Die Räuber* and the powerful rhetoric of Schiller's later work. The former is an immature, the latter a mature, instrument for the convincing and persuasive presentation of his message.

The consequence of Schiller's approach in this play is the creation of a world which is not the real world. It lives its own life, cut off not only from the spectator, but from past and future. Its only reality is its intense and burning present. Within its limitations it vibrates and glows and pulsates with a fierce life of its own. Once this is realized and accepted, the absurdities fade and cease to matter. For Schiller has created a group of characters, who live in spite of exaggerations and defects, has set them in a world, not our own, but receiving our belief, and has engaged them in a conflict which lays bare the innermost recesses of their souls. Obscenity smudges the picture here and there, bombast obscures but cannot wholly conceal the convincing truth with which Robber Moor and his scheming, hypocritical brother are portrayed. Nor does it detract from the power of the conception in which two men, each in his own way, seek to stifle their conscience and fail, set their will against the moral law and perish. The implementation of such a huge design exceeded the powers of an inexperienced youth, but the dynamic force and energy of the play cannot be denied.

Die Räuber was preceded by a preface—it was Schiller's second, his first having been scrapped as inadequate and uncomplimentary to the public. Having disclaimed any idea of stage production for his play, Schiller analyses the characters of Franz and Karl Moor, defending the play against hypothetical accusations of immorality.

Ich darf meiner Schrift zufolge ihrer merkwürdigen Katastrophe mit Recht einen Platz unter den moralischen Büchern versprechen; das Laster nimmt den Ausgang, der seiner würdig ist. Der Verirrte tritt wieder in das Geleise der Gesetze. Die Tugend geht siegend davon.[1]

Anxiety about the play's reception explains the defensive tone of this preface.

Outside Würtemberg the identity of the author was not at first known. In Stuttgart it was no secret that this electrifying play had been written by the doctor of the Augé Regiment. Gradually the name of the author became known in other parts of Germany, and Schiller, as a new celebrity, began to receive calls from visitors to Stuttgart.

If he could regard with satisfaction the stir his work had caused, the financial aspect was less gratifying. The original edition was exhausted within a few months, but it had comprised only eight hundred copies and failed to balance the cost. Schiller then ordered a second edition, which only increased his liabilities. This new edition is mainly important for the fact that the authorship of " Friderich Schiller " is for the first time acknowledged on the title-page. It bears also the famous vignette depicting a raging lion with lashing tail and one paw angrily raised, beneath which are read in small, shy italics the words *in Tirannos*.

---

[1] In consequence of its remarkable catastrophe I can justifiably promise my work a place among moral books. Vice meets the end it deserves. The erring hero returns to the path of law. Virtue carries the day.

Chapter Four

"*DIE RAUBER*" *PERFORMED*
1781–82

BEFORE publishing *Die Räuber* Schiller had sent proofs of the play to the Mannheim bookseller and publisher Schwan in the hope that he would buy up the entire edition. Schwan declined, but he asked for a copy of the book when it should appear. This Schiller sent him in May 1781. Schwan, who had seen theatrical possibilities in the play, mentioned it to Baron von Dalberg, Director of the Mannheim National Theatre, who wrote to Schiller in the summer of 1781, asking for a stage adaptation of *Die Räuber* and intimating that he would welcome future plays from Schiller.

This offer was as flattering as it was unexpected. Mannheim, the capital of the Electoral Palatinate, which lay to the north-west of Würtemberg, possessed at this time one of the best theatres in Germany. The Mannheim National Theatre, founded in 1778, had at one time hoped to secure Lessing as its first director. It had had to content itself with Baron von Dalberg, who, though deficient in taste, was enterprising and energetic. In Schiller's eyes Mannheim seemed a vital centre of culture, far superior to Stuttgart. A letter went off to Dalberg in which the open-hearted and inexperienced young man made no secret of his intense delight. The antipathy to stage performance expressed in his preface vanished at once, and he set to work on the adaptation, which he promised to have ready by the end of August. It took longer than he expected, and it was October 6, 1781, before he sent it off to Dalberg.

The preparation of the play for the stage caused Schiller much heart-burning. He had to make alterations which were no improvements, but were dictated by the requirements of the theatre. He had to listen and defer to the opinions and demands of his patron Baron von Dalberg, and some of these seemed to him ill-conceived and even perverse. There was one request that he tried particularly hard to resist. The burning actuality of the play in its almost contemporary setting probably disquieted the aristocratic director and led him to press for its transference to the year 1495 in the reign of Emperor Maximilian I. Dalberg was in a position to dictate and carried his point.

Another dispute arose about the death of Amalia. Dalberg wished her to take her own life instead of perishing at the hands of Karl. Again he had his way, but Schiller felt so strongly about this alteration that he retained his version of the catastrophe when the stage adaptation was printed.

There were other changes. Schiller allotted a more important role to Hermann at the expense of the simpler figure of Daniel. An important modification also took place in the interview between Karl and Amalia. In the stage version the latter is attracted to the Count, but fails to recognize him as Karl. She is instinctively true to her lover, while believing herself to be inconstant, a subtlety most unsuited to stage representation, where it involves her kissing the disguised Karl and failing to recognize him in consequence of a large hat and a pair of false moustaches. A considerable alteration is also made in the last act. Franz no longer dies by his own hand, but is judged by the robbers and condemned to perish in the dungeon in which he had confined his father. The desire of the virtuous public to witness the punishment of the malefactor was satisfied, but the catastrophe loses in nobility. Bad taste has also crept in with the episode in which Karl exposes Amalia's bosom to his comrades in order to prove how much he loses by her death.

Apart from these changes Schiller made liberal cuts, especially in Franz's soliloquies, in the robbers' scenes in the first and second acts, and in the scene by the Danube. Even then the play still took four hours in performance. The stage version was published by Schwan in 1782, but for Schiller the original form remained the authoritative text, and was the basis of subsequent editions.

A criticism of *Die Räuber* in its stage form written by K——r in *Das Wirtembergische Repertorium*[1] was really the work of Schiller. An interesting combination of humour and critical detachment, it shows his gift for coining the memorable phrase when he speaks of Karl Moor: " Er ging auf wie ein Meteor und schwindet wie eine sinkende Sonne."[2] And his words on the style of the play reveal a just judgment, ironical humour, and cool impartiality:

> Die Sprache und der Dialog dörften sich gleicher bleiben und im ganzen weniger poetisch sein. Hier ist der Ausdruck lyrisch und episch, dort gar metaphysisch, an einem dritten Ort biblisch, an einem vierten platt. Franz sollte durchaus anders sprechen. Die blumigte Sprache verzeihen wir nur der erhitzten Phantasie, und Franz sollte schlechterdings kalt sein. Das Mädchen hat mir zu viel im Klopstock gelesen. Wenn man es dem Verfasser nicht an den Schönheiten anmerkt, dass er sich in seinen Shakespeare vergafft hat, so merkt man

[1] See below, p. 44.
[2] He rose like a meteor and departs like a setting sun.

es desto gewisser an den Ausschweifungen. . . . Wo der Dichter am wahrsten fühlte und am durchdringendsten bewegte, sprach er wie unsereiner.[1]

For Schiller at this time one crowning thought overtopped all else—*Die Räuber* was to be produced by one of the best theatres of Germany. As the day of the first performance drew near Schiller was consumed by a desire to be present. This would mean a journey across the frontier into another state, something for which he could not possibly hope to obtain permission, since the Duke would regard his play-writing as a waste of time. Since he could not get leave, he resolved to go without it. The performance, originally fixed for January 10, 1782, was postponed until the thirteenth at Schiller's request, since duty would detain him in Stuttgart on the earlier day. He made the journey to Mannheim with Petersen, saw the placards with the synopsis he had written for Dalberg, and watched the stream of early arrivals for the performance which, because of the play's length, was due to begin at five.

To see the curtain rise on the first performance of his first play on one of his country's leading stages is a great and inspiring moment for any man. For the twenty-two-year-old Schiller, raised in the intellectual desert of Würtemberg, tied apparently for life to an ill-paid and tedious calling, it was an hour of immense joy and triumph, which brought with it a sense of freedom and release from all the pettifogging restrictions of his everyday life.

At first the pleasurable sensations were neutralized by a strong dose of anxiety. Wonderful though it was to have the play performed at all, there was still a wide gulf to be crossed. The play might fail, the ' mob,' whom he had so scornfully condemned in his original preface, might misjudge it as he had asserted they would. The play began, and a rapt and attentive audience listened spellbound to the tirades of Karl and followed fascinated the diabolical cunning of Franz. From the third act onward, the point at which the threads of the two actions join, silence gave way to loud and repeated bursts of applause, and the final curtain fell amidst a scene of wild enthusiasm.

Enraptured with success, Schiller returned to Stuttgart, where he learned to his relief that his absence had not been detected. But

---

[1] The language and the dialogue might well be more consistent and could on the whole be less poetic. The style is now lyrical and epic, now metaphysical, in a third place it is Biblical, in a fourth dull. Franz ought to speak in a completely different manner. Only when it comes from an ardent imagination can we excuse flowery speech, and Franz should be perfectly cold. The girl has read too much Klopstock for my liking. If the author's beauties don't reveal that he is crazy on Shakespeare, then his extravagances certainly do. . . . When the author's feelings were most genuine and their effect most moving, he spoke as you and I do.

D

though it cheered him to find that no interview with his commanding officer threatened, he was oppressed by a sense of desolation and dreariness in the intellectually somnolent atmosphere of Würtemberg. The champagne of Mannheim had spoiled his palate for Stuttgart small beer. Würtemberg could offer him no better task than holding sick parades and making reports at guard-mounting. The first performance of *Die Räuber* was a turning-point. It gave him an outside standard by which he could measure conditions in Würtemberg; and he found them wanting.

His dissatisfaction was not new; it was more articulate, more certain, more decisive. But there had been a sign of it before. Schiller had planned an *Anthologie auf das Jahr* 1782 (*Anthology for the Year* 1782) in the autumn of 1781. This collection of lyrical poems was in reality a polemical work, intended as a retort to the *Schwäbischer Musenalmanach auf das Jahr* 1782 (*Swabian Muses' Almanach for the year* 1782), published by a young man named Stäudlin in September 1781. Irritated by Stäudlin's pretensions to be the leader of Swabian literature, Schiller decided to publish a rival collection. The *Anthologie* contains some poems by his friends, but by far the greater number are by Schiller himself. These form a survey of his poetry from the *Ode to the Sun*, written when he was sixteen, to love poems of the year 1781. It also contains *Semele*, a neo-classical operetta.

The most notable poems of the *Anthologie* are the odes addressed to Laura. " Laura " seems to have been Frau Vischer, from whom Schiller rented his room. There are six poems in all, five of which Schiller incorporated in his collected works. They reflect no joy, only acute sensuality and deep gloom at the thought of transience. The minutely observed sensuality is seen most clearly in *Phantasie an Laura* (*Imagination*):

> Und was ist's, das, wenn mich Laura küsset
> Purpurflammen auf die Wangen geusst?
> Meinem Herzen raschern Schwung gebietet,
> Fiebrisch wild mein Blut von hinnen reisst?
>
> Aus den Schranken schwellen alle Sinnen,
> Seine Ufer überwallt das Blut,
> Körper will in Körper überstürzen,
> Lodern Seelen in vereinter Glut.[1]

This is the expression in strained and involved verse of burning

---

[1] What is it that pours deep red flames on to my cheeks when Laura kisses me? What makes my pulse beat faster, my blood course feverishly? . . . The senses transcend their bounds, the blood overflows its banks, body seeks to fuse with body, souls to blaze in a combined glow.

physical desire. The combination of sensual passion with intellectual analysis recalls the English metaphysical poets, but Schiller is still attached to the artificial diction of his age; thus a dissonance arises between the vivid realism of his vision and the gilded elegance of the style in which he seeks to convey it. Not that his style lacks personal qualities; in his hands it becomes more tense, more elliptical, more closely packed with meaning. But it is still not an instrument adapted to what he has to say.

The concentration on physical desire, of which these poems are the expression, leads him in *Melancholie* to lament the ravages of time in a tone more reminiscent of the depths of Webster than of the sentimentality of Klopstock:

> Weh! entblättert seh' ich deine Rosen liegen,
> Bleich erstorben deinen süssen Mund,
> Deiner Wangen wallendes Rund
> Werden rauhe Winterstürme pflügen,
> Düstrer Jahre Nebelschein
> Wird der Jugend Silberquellen trüben;
> Dann wird Laura — Laura nicht mehr lieben,
> Laura nicht mehr liebenswürdig sein.[1]

Whether he shudders at the thought of old age or closely observes the symptoms of his passion, it is sensual love poetry, in which the author is more interested in his own reactions than in the object of his love.

The polemical aim of the *Anthologie* emerges in the dedication and preface. Schiller's purpose was to seize from Stäudlin's grasp the leadership of the literary movement in Würtemberg and to expose the unoriginality and dullness of Swabian culture as Stäudlin exhibited it.

The chief interest in the collection lies in the light which it throws on a phase of Schiller's development. It suggests that his talent was not a lyrical one. Most of the poems tend in some degree towards philosophical, narrative or dramatic poetry.

The *Anthologie* was complete and in the printer's hands before the decisive visit to Mannheim took place. Once he had seen his play produced, he abandoned the writing of poetry and began to concentrate his energies upon a new play, which was to be even better than *Die Räuber*. Its subject was the conspiracy headed by Count Fiesco in fifteenth-century Genoa. Through the next eight months in Stuttgart this play absorbed Schiller's chief interest.

---

[1] Alas! I see the petals of your roses strewn, deathly pale your sweet lips, the swelling round of your cheeks will be furrowed by rude winter storms, the dim light of sombre years will cloud the silver springs of your youth; then Laura will not love any more, nor be capable of inspiring love.

More and more Schiller disliked the prosaic and Philistine atmosphere of Stuttgart. But he was tied there by his military appointment and could see no prospect of escape, so he tried to make the best of it. Early in 1782, in collaboration with Professor Abel and Petersen, he planned a quarterly periodical, *Das Wirtembergische Repertorium der Litteratur* (*The Würtemberg Repertoire of Literature*), the first number of which appeared at Easter 1782. Only Nos. 1 and 2 appeared under Schiller's editorship; the third, which was also the last, was edited by Petersen, for Schiller was by then in another land. Schiller's contributions included two dialogues, *Der Spaziergang unter den Linden* (*The Walk beneath the Lime-Trees*), and *Der Jüngling und der Greis* (*The Youth and the Old Man*), an essay on the German theatre, and various reviews, chief among which was the full-length criticism of *Die Räuber* already referred to.[1] Of these the most important are the first dialogue and the essay on the theatre.

Der Spaziergang unter den Linden is a conversation between a pessimist and an optimist, the former of whom has rather the better of the argument. The pessimist is also a materialist, and, like so many materialists, an inverted romantic, and his observations on mortality and transience accord closely with the reflections of Franz Moor and the attitude embodied in the odes to Laura:

> Dachtest du je, dass dieses unendliche Rund das Grabmal deiner Ahnen ist? dass dir die Winde, die dir die Wohlgerüche der Linden herunterbringen, vielleicht die zerstobene Kraft des Arminius in die Nase blasen?[2]

" Why may not imagination trace the noble dust of Alexander till he find it stopping a bung-hole? " Hamlet's question had taken root firmly in Schiller's mind. His joyless boyhood, his recent acquaintance with death, and his medical training all combined to provoke these sombre speculations, to which Hamlet has given the supreme expression. But there is an interesting development at the close of Schiller's dialogue. The young student of psychology, who had written on the interdependence of body and soul, points out that the philosophical opinions of his characters are subjective, being determined by their different experiences.

In the essay *Über das gegenwärtige teutsche Theater* German authors, public, and actors are weighed and found wanting. But the most interesting thoughts in it concern the conception, so widespread in the eighteenth century, that the moral effect of literature

---

[1] See above, p. 40.

[2] Did you ever consider that this infinite sphere is the grave of your ancestors? that the wind, which brings you the sweet scent of the limes, perhaps blows into your nostrils the dust of strong Arminius?

or the drama is directly to encourage virtue and to discourage vice. Schiller refuses to endorse this view, and states his attitude in words that convince by their sound common-sense and impartiality:

> Wenn der teufelische Macbeth die kalten Schweisstropfen auf der Stirne, bebenden Fusses, mit hinschauerndem Auge aus der Schlafkammer wanket, wo er die Tat getan hat — welchem Zuschauer laufen nicht eiskalte Schauer durch die Gebeine? Und doch, welcher Macbeth unter dem Volke lässt seinen Dolch aus dem Kleide fallen, eh' er die Tat tut? oder seine Larve, wenn sie getan ist? — Es ist ja eben König Duncan nicht, den er zu verderben eilet. Werden darum weniger Mädchen verführt, weil Sara Samson ihren Fehltritt mit Gifte büsset? Eifert ein einziger Ehemann weniger, weil der Mohr von Venedig sich so tragisch übereilte?[1]

Schiller's visit to Mannheim for the first performance of *Die Räuber* lost nothing in retrospect. He felt that if he could only live in such a congenial artistic climate his genius, so cribbed and confined in Würtemberg, could unfold freely. Living there seemed impossible, but at least he might pay a second visit and so repeat the stimulus which his first had provided. The temptation was very strong; he could once more undergo the same exciting experience and renew and extend important personal contacts. And the thought of a new visit was given a heightened charm by the prospect of accompanying two ladies, eager to see his play. He would not only enjoy the thrill of seeing his own work on the stage, but would be able to sun himself in the warmth of their sympathetic enthusiasm.

One of the ladies so anxious to accompany Schiller to Mannheim was his landlady, Frau Vischer. The other was Frau Henriette von Wolzogen. The widow of a petty noble, Frau von Wolzogen was at this time thirty-eight years old. She was a woman of generous and unselfish temper. Her estate lay away to the north near Meiningen, but she had friends at Stuttgart, and all four of her sons were being educated at the Karlsschule. Her attention was drawn to Schiller by her eldest son, Wilhelm, who was filled with enthusiasm for *Die Räuber*. Frau von Wolzogen admired Schiller's ability, his integrity, and his courage, and could also see how many difficulties his sanguine and incautious temperament must encounter in the future.

Schiller wrote to Mannheim asking for a performance of *Die*

[1] When the diabolical Macbeth, cold drops of sweat upon his brow, staggers with uncertain tread and glazed eye from the chamber where he has done the deed, what spectator is there whose very marrow does not feel the icy shudder? And yet, what real Macbeth drops his dagger from his cloak before he does the deed—or his mask of innocence, if he has already done it? It is after all not King Duncan, whom he is about to slay. Are fewer girls seduced because Sara Samson paid for her slip with poison? Is one single husband less jealous because the Moor of Venice acted with such tragic haste?

Räuber to be arranged for May 28. This proved impossible, but he nevertheless profited by the absence of the Duke to undertake the journey with his two companions. Once more Mannheim wove its spell about the young man. On the return journey, however, the shades of Würtemberg began to close upon him. That he could only pay rare visits to the cultural paradise of Mannheim was bad enough. But the journey had been undertaken without permission; his colonel had turned a blind eye, and if word of the visit were to leak out Schiller would have to accept full responsibility. As the carriage jolted along the rough road doubts, fears, and regrets succeeded one another, and across them all lay the shadow of the prisoner of the Hohenasperg. Till now the sympathy and the indignation Schiller had felt about Schubart's fate had been disinterested. And suddenly it seemed possible that there might be a closer connexion. What had happened to Schubart might also happen to him; it was a novel, arresting, and disturbing thought. To make matters worse, he felt feverish and ill; his condition deteriorated with every mile of the journey, and he arrived in Stuttgart with every symptom of fever.

However, it was a safe arrival. No picket stopped the carriage at the city gate, no guard was waiting at Schiller's lodging to arrest him on his return. Yet uneasiness persisted. It helped to reinforce the idea of escape from Würtemberg which the palpable superiority of Mannheim had already implanted in him.

A few days after his return Schiller took the first step. On June 4, 1782, he wrote to Dalberg:

> And yet I almost regret the happiest journey of my life, which, by the most repulsive contrast between my fatherland and Mannheim, has brought me to the state when Stuttgart and all Swabian scenes are intolerable and nauseating to me. Soon none can be so unhappy as I. I am conscious enough of my sad situation, and perhaps conscious enough, too, of deserving a better fate, and in both cases there is only *one* prospect.
> Excellent sir, may I throw myself into your arms?

And his feeling of frustration leads him to paint the contrast in the most striking colours:

> I am still little or nothing. I shall never prosper in this arctic region of taste, whereas more propitious stars and a *Grecian climate* would make of me a true poet.

It is a moving but naïve document; the cool and well-bred Dalberg was more embarrassed than touched by such impulsive confidence. Schiller, moreover, did not stop at proposing that he should come to Mannheim, but suggested that Dalberg should write to Karl

Eugen to ask for Schiller's release. As to Dalberg's readiness to employ him he had no doubt at all. Dalberg, who had been profuse in assurances, drew back alarmed when he found that this vehement young man was expecting action to follow talk. He wrote no letter to the Duke of Würtemberg.

Meanwhile news of Schiller's visit to Mannheim leaked out, and towards the end of June the Duke learned of it. Schiller, whose sense of security was growing with the passage of the weeks, was summoned to Ludwigsburg and a horse placed at his disposal for the journey. On arrival at the palace he was shown in to a very angry Duke, who regarded his trip to Mannheim as equivalent to desertion and an act of personal ingratitude. Not only did Karl Eugen upbraid him, he forbade him to continue literary work and finally awarded him fourteen days' detention. No horse being forthcoming for the return journey, Schiller, with rage, indignation, and misgiving in his heart, made his way back on foot over seven long miles of road. He reported to the guard-room, handed in his sword, and began to serve his sentence.

This interview with the Duke and the award of detention were decisive. Schiller was animated by a lively sense of injustice and a feeling of deep humiliation. Behind his resentment lay an uneasy fear. At any hour of any day the Duke's police might enter the guard-room to carry him off to Hohenasperg, where Schubart had already languished for five years without any sign of reprieve. The blacker his present situation seemed, the more alluring was the thought of enlightened Mannheim.

To leave Würtemberg seemed to Schiller the only solution. How could he, with his irresistible creative urge, abstain from writing as Karl Eugen demanded? And to write another word in Stuttgart invited the worst. Schiller yet hoped that he might be able to avoid a complete breach; his parents must remain in Würtemberg and were dependent on the Duke. To ask for permission to go, he knew, was hopeless. But if he fled and successfully reached Mannheim, then perhaps Dalberg could be persuaded to placate the angry Duke. He therefore wrote again on July 15 to Dalberg, who in the meantime had replied politely but evasively to Schiller's ardent letter of June 4. Schiller waited in vain for a further answer.

In Stuttgart the situation deteriorated. In August Schiller received a second summons to Ludwigsburg. Karl Eugen, in a furious temper, accused Schiller of involving him in a diplomatic incident. The facts were these. Spiegelberg, the most scoundrelly of the robbers in Schiller's play, refers to the canton of Grisons (Graubünden) in Switzerland as "the crooks' Athens." This allusion, isolated from its context and exaggerated by malicious persons (including a personal enemy of Captain Schiller), had at length provoked a semi-official *démarche* by the government of the canton. Here was the cause of Karl Eugen's anger. The interview culminated in a formal ban on the publication by Schiller of any but medical works, infringement of which would be followed by imprisonment. Schiller knew what this meant. He knew also that he could not comply with the Duke's orders. Far from being a shock to him, the interview made his path clear. He returned to Stuttgart pale and quiet, but determined.

Schiller knew that there was nothing for it but flight, with its possible consequences for his family if he succeeded and its much graver consequences for him if he failed. He needed—and found—a friend whom he could trust entirely. This friend was Andreas Streicher, the young musician who had sat in the gallery of the Academy at the passing-out dinner of 1780 and had been so much impressed by the frank open look of one of the seniors, whose name he did not then know. Some six months later Streicher was presented to the author of *Die Räuber*, and found to his pleased surprise that Friedrich Schiller was the young Academician whose bearing he had so much admired.

Streicher became one of Schiller's intimates and his most loyal and reliable supporter. Without his aid it is doubtful if the flight would ever have taken place, or, if it had, extremely probable that it would have failed. It was Streicher who made the practical preparations.

Meanwhile Schiller made a last attempt by letter to ease the conditions imposed by Karl Eugen. The Duke returned no direct answer to Schiller's letter, but through his commanding officer the young man learned that he would be placed in detention if he again wrote to his sovereign.

Towards the end of September the visit of a Russian grand-duke and his consort was to be greeted with festivities of exceptional brilliance. It seemed a moment when movement would not be obvious and vigilance might be relaxed. Streicher, displaying the most generous friendship, changed the plans for his own musical education and drew from his mother the money reserved for it, in order to accompany Schiller on his flight. Little by little Schiller's luggage was unobtrusively transferred to the house where Streicher lived with his mother, in order to avoid the suspicious sight of a carriage being loaded outside Schiller's lodging.

A final ordeal faced Schiller; he must pay his last visit to his parents and sisters who now lived at the Solitude. Captain Schiller was left in ignorance of his son's plans, so that he could conscientiously say that he was not a party to the flight. But Frau Schiller and Christophine had been let into the secret. It was a depressed and heartsick, but still resolute, young man who journeyed with Streicher back to Stuttgart after his farewell visit to the Solitude.

The flight was fixed for the evening of September 22, 1782. That night " one of Schiller's most tried friends " (clearly Scharffenstein) would command the guard at the Esslingen Gate. The morning of the twenty-second broke. Streicher completed his own preparations and hastened to see how Schiller was faring with his. To his dismay he found scarcely anything done. Schiller, in packing, had picked up Klopstock's *Odes*, had read, become absorbed, and from that gone on to compose a poem himself. Streicher had to sit and cool his heels until this was finished and read out.

At last the packing was done. At nine in the evening Schiller was at Streicher's house; the loading of their two trunks and Streicher's piano began. At ten they moved off. Tense anticipation held the two occupants of the carriage. Slowly they lumbered towards the Esslingen Gate. The challenge " Halt! Who goes there ? " followed by a shout for the sergeant of the guard raised their anxiety to the utmost. Streicher, leaning forward so as to obscure his friend, reported Dr Ritter and Dr Wolff bound for Esslingen. The sergeant was satisfied, the coachman flicked his horses, and as the carriage moved on the two occupants leaned forward to gaze up at the unlighted window of the officer's room, where Scharffenstein, indistinguishable in the darkness, relaxed with a feeling of intense relief.

But the travellers could not yet relax. They had left by the eastern Esslingen Gate in order to avoid arousing suspicion and, if the worst happened, to mislead their pursuers; and before they could gain the Mannheim road they must make a circuit of the town to the north-west. In silent awareness of the danger, which still threatened, they leaned back in the cushions while the carriage made the circuit at a foot-pace. The road passed close to the Solitude. When, near midnight, they saw a bright glow from the ducal fireworks and illuminations, Schiller, in an anguish of home-sickness, involuntarily exclaimed " My mother! "

On the Mannheim road progress was faster and soon after one o'clock they halted at Enzweihingen, where by candlelight and over a cup of coffee Schiller declaimed to his friend unpublished poems of Schubart, including appropriately that powerful indictment of tyranny, *Die Fürstengruft*. Once horses had been changed they set out again, and when the sun rose were only two hours' journey from the frontier. About eight o'clock the blue-and-white frontier posts of the Palatinate came in sight beside the black-and-red of

Würtemberg, and a few minutes later Schiller was safely on foreign territory.

He had successfully accomplished a decisive and far-reaching step. The medical career in Würtemberg, for which his education had prepared him, was closed to him from now on. Exiled by his own act in a foreign land, he could no longer depend upon his parents or visit them. He stood fairly upon his feet, and must fight for his own existence and for his justification as a poet. Just how much he would have to fight, he himself could not at that time realize.

Chapter Five

WITH "FIESCO" IN MANNHEIM

1782

WITH the passage of the frontier the dangerous phase of Schiller's journey was over. At ten o'clock he and Streicher halted for breakfast at the village of Bretten in the Palatinate; at nine in the evening they were at Schwetzingen, close to Mannheim. There they decided to spend the night, as the gates of the city would be closed before their arrival.

Schiller's mood was one of great optimism. He had escaped from the forces that hampered his development and from the fears which menaced his future. He had left behind the petty Philistinism of Würtemberg, the dreary routine of professional duties, the ill-fitting uniform and the tassel-less N.C.O.'s sword, which had seemed a badge of servitude; behind him, too, lay the fear of sudden arrest and consignment to gaol. And the advantages of the place to which he now came were as great as the drawbacks of that from which he fled. He was coming to a capital as intellectually light as Stuttgart was dark, to a theatre whose director had been lavish with praise and liberal with promises. Nor did he come empty-handed. The author of *Die Räuber*, one of the greatest successes of the Mannheim Theatre, brought with him the manuscript of *Die Verschwörung des Fiesco zu Genua* (*Fiesco's Conspiracy at Genoa*), complete except for its catastrophe. And *Fiesco*, he felt, was a much better play than *Die Räuber*.

On the morning of September 24 Schiller and Streicher made the short journey from Schwetzingen to Mannheim and went straight to the house of Meyer, the producer, who had been very helpful to Schiller during his previous visits. Director Dalberg was still in Stuttgart, attending the festivities. Schiller's arrival was a surprise, but the news that he came as a fugitive from Würtemberg was a shock for Meyer, who advised him at once to write a conciliatory letter to the Duke. Schiller felt obliged to comply with this suggestion, and composed without much conviction a letter to Karl Eugen expressing his willingness to return on terms which included permission to write and publish literary works, to wear civilian clothes and to visit neighbouring states, by which he meant the Palatinate, whose capital was Mannheim. The letter was dispatched, and some days must pass before he could expect an answer. In the meantime he would seek to establish himself in Mannheim.

Die Verschwörung des Fiesco zu Genua was Schiller's trump-card, and he and Streicher eagerly sought an opportunity to witness the astonishment and admiration it would evoke from the connoisseurs. Meyer invited a number of actors and actresses to a party at which Schiller read his play. The first act was heard in silence, and the guests were obviously relieved when the second act came to an end and refreshments were handed round. Instead of remaining to hear the rest of the play, they dispersed, leaving only Schiller, Streicher, and Iffland with the hosts. *Fiesco* had failed as far as the company was concerned. Schiller was depressed and irritable; the dumb-founded and crestfallen Streicher had to reassure Meyer in private that Schiller really was sole author of *Die Räuber*, which the producer, esteeming *Fiesco* the worst play ever written, was inclined to doubt; and the party broke up early. Back at their lodging, Schiller, after denouncing the obtuseness and spite of the actors, declared his intention of himself going on the stage, since none, he maintained, could declaim as well as he.

Meyer had asked to be allowed to retain the manuscript over-night. When Streicher called in the morning he was astonished, relieved, and delighted to find Meyer enthusiastic about the merits of the play. He attributed the disaster of the previous day to Schiller's pronounced Swabian accent and exaggeratedly rhetorical delivery. Streicher, feeling that this was not the moment for critic-ism, concealed from Schiller this verdict on his reading, and in-formed him only of Meyer's revised estimate of *Fiesco*. Their hopes were raised still further by Meyer's assurance that the play would be accepted for performance.

Already before the reading of *Fiesco* an unexpectedly prompt reply to his letter to Karl Eugen had been received by Schiller. It was from General Augé; it ignored Schiller's conditions and merely advised him to return as the Duke was then in a very gracious mood. Schiller therefore wrote a second letter, repeating his conditions, which received an identical reply. With the recollection in his mind of the way in which Schubart had been enticed on to Würtemberg territory, Schiller dared not deliver himself defenceless into the hands of Schubart's tormentor. It was clear that his flight was final.

The first reports from Stuttgart of the reactions to Schiller's clandestine departure showed that it had caused a great sensation. Some even feared that Karl Eugen might ask for Schiller's extradi-tion. All opinions in Mannheim concurred that he would be well advised to remain in some sort of concealment for the present. The two friends decided to go for a short time to Frankfort, where they could await developments in safety. As they were already running short of money, they went on foot. Three days of walking overtaxed Schiller's delicate constitution and he had difficulty in accomplishing the march from Darmstadt to Frankfort on the third day.

They selected a cheap-looking inn in the suburb of Sachsenhausen and agreed a price with the host beforehand. As the situation looked desperate, Schiller wrote the following morning to Dalberg requesting an advance of money. The letter is a candid and moving document. Schiller admits his difficult and precarious situation: " As soon as I tell you, *I am a fugitive*, I have told you my whole situation." Considering the success of *Die Räuber*, the profits it had brought to the Mannheim Theatre, and the encouragement Dalberg had given Schiller's request for an advance on *Fiesco*, the request was not an unreasonable one.

Three days passed without any mail from Mannheim, and the expectations of the two friends became daily more anxious. On the fourth day they were relieved to find a bundle of letters. Their contents were not reassuring, for most of the writers considered the danger of extradition still to be a real one. There was a letter from Meyer, which Schiller left till last. He opened it with trembling hands and read. When he had finished he said nothing, but gazed through the window across the river Main. Streicher waited anxiously till Schiller could bring himself to reveal the contents of the letter. Dalberg had refused everything; he would not advance money, nor accept *Fiesco* in its present form, nor undertake to accept it when revised. It was only ten days since Schiller had left Stuttgart and already all his confident hopes had proved illusory. Schiller and Streicher had not even enough money to pay their score in Frankfort and must for the present remain there. Schiller's hope of reducing his debts in Stuttgart was gone and he was living at Streicher's expense. It was bad enough to be in a foreign country without means. But now Schiller was without prospects also.

But he had certain assets, though they would not have been accepted by a creditor. The selfless devotion of Streicher was assured. Schiller's youth, reinforced by a fierce determination, would not yield to despair. And his creative powers were already at work forging a new play, which brought fresh hope and at the same time diverted his thoughts from an uncertain and ominous future.

The next day brought material relief. Streicher received a remittance from his mother. They were now able to pay their bill and leave Frankfort. They travelled by barge to Mainz, and next day walked southward to Worms. There they found a letter from Meyer proposing a rendezvous at Oggersheim next day. Schiller and Streicher arrived punctually at the Viehhof Inn in Oggersheim, where they met Meyer and his wife and two others. Meyer was confident about the eventual chances of *Fiesco*, once Schiller had revised it; but in the meantime it was thought wise for him to live away from Mannheim, as long as the danger of persecution by Karl Eugen persisted. The two friends therefore remained at Oggersheim.

From the first week in October until the end of November they lived in this Rhineland village. The autumn was cold and damp, with frequent mists; but they were comfortable in their room. When darkness closed in, Streicher would play the piano while Schiller walked up and down working out his scenes. But the play with which he was preoccupied was not *Fiesco*, which he ought to have been preparing for Dalberg, but the new drama, which had taken shape in his mind during the journey to Frankfort. All his energy and interest were devoted to the future *Kabale und Liebe*.

But if his immediate financial situation were to improve at all, he must complete and revise *Fiesco*. Reluctantly he went to work, and early in November it was ready. He sent it to Dalberg with hopes which were not entirely free from misgiving. Day after day he waited and no reply came. By November 16 the tension and uncertainty had become such that he felt he must write a reminder to Dalberg; and so unsettled did he feel that the very same day he and Streicher set out for Mannheim to get news by hook or by crook.

Arrived at Mannheim, they went straight to Meyer's house, where they found themselves beset with a new anxiety. It was a matter of personal safety. The Meyers, in a state of great agitation, told Schiller that an officer of the Würtemberg forces had called and inquired for him an hour ago. Hardly had they heard this news than a friend arrived breathless to say that the officer was pursuing his inquiries about the town. Thoughts of arrest, extradition, imprisonment—thoughts which had recently been half-buried though not forgotten—were in a moment once more pressing and dangerous realities. Meyer's house was not safe and Oggersheim, where they were equally well known, out of the question. None could think of a secure refuge, till at last a Frau Curioni solved the problem by offering Schiller and Streicher sanctuary in the palace of Baron von Baaden, whose housekeeper she was. The young men accepted her offer with alacrity and gratitude, and spent the night in luxurious comfort as well as in safety. In the morning it was learnéd, to the relief of all, that the Würtemberger had already left.

Though the immediate danger was over (indeed there had never been any, for the officer was a friendly acquaintance trying to pay a social call), both Schiller and his friends had become acutely conscious of his dangerous and precarious situation. Encouraged by those around him, he began to consider leaving the Mannheim area, at any rate for a time.

The departure, which now seemed advisable, became a necessity a few days later. Dalberg would have none of *Fiesco* and declined to make Schiller even a token payment. The last hope which Schiller had brought with him from Stuttgart had now been frustrated. He was down and out; he had no money and no home; he had appreciable debts; in delicate health, he had to face an unsympathetic world with no assets other than the devotion of his friends and his confidence in his own talents.

Some time earlier Frau von Wolzogen had generously offered Schiller a refuge in her own house at Bauerbach near Meiningen, if he should at any time have need of one. Schiller decided that the time had come to accept this offer. He and Streicher knew that they must part. Streicher decided to earn his living by giving music lessons in Mannheim. A few days before Schiller's departure he moved from Oggersheim to the city. Meanwhile Schiller, who believed that he would never see his home again, met his mother and eldest sister secretly at Bretten, near the Würtemberg border.

On the raw, cold morning of November 30 his actor friends and Streicher called for him at Oggersheim and the whole party walked to Worms by a road thick with snow. Between Schiller and Streicher no words were spoken; they exchanged a long, firm handshake. Streicher and the rest returned to Mannheim. Schiller spent the night at Worms and set out by coach the next morning, thinly clad, in bitter December weather, on the sixty-five-hour journey to Meiningen.

Schiller owed much to his friends. The generosity of Frau von Wolzogen came to his aid when that of Streicher could no longer help him. But he did not sponge, and all his friends felt that their confidence and esteem were justified. His qualities excited admiration, his circumstances sympathy. And the friendships, which aided him so materially, reflect as much credit on his warm-hearted character and unwavering integrity as on the discernment, generosity, and loyalty of Streicher, Frau von Wolzogen and, later, Körner.

Streicher remained for a few years in Mannheim and then migrated to Vienna, where he prospered as a dealer in pianos. The period which he spent with Schiller remained the event of his life. His simply written book, *Schillers Flucht aus Stuttgart* (*Schiller's Flight from Stuttgart*), published in 1836, is a reliable and detailed source of information about Schiller at this time. It is also a glowing tribute to Schiller's qualities and an unassuming, but none the less impressive, monument to Streicher's own selfless devotion.

Before leaving Mannheim Schiller disposed of the manuscript of *Fiesco*. He sold it to the bookseller Schwan, who paid him eleven and a half *louis d'ors* (£10) for it, making a handsome profit on the transaction. This sum enabled Schiller to pay his score at the Viehhof in Oggersheim, but it was a miserable fulfilment of the hopes he had associated with the play, which, in his view, was so immeasurably superior to *Die Räuber*.

It was a passage from Schiller's favourite author Rousseau which, in Academy days, had drawn his attention to the character and story of Fiesco; and Schiller had mentioned Fiesco with approval in the dissertation of 1780. No sooner were the piles of newly bound copies of *Die Räuber* beginning to litter the room Schiller shared with Kapf, than he set to work to plan a tragedy based on the story of Fiesco.

Rousseau's brief remarks were inadequate as a source, and Schiller applied himself diligently to the study of historical works, of which the most important, according to his own statement in the preface, were Robertson's *History of Charles V* and Cardinal de Retz's *Conjuration du comte Jean Louis de Fiesque*.

Born in 1524, Fiesco, a typical Renaissance figure, headed a conspiracy in 1547 against Andrea Doria, Duke of Genoa, with the object of re-establishing the republic. The revolt succeeded, but Fiesco in the moment of his triumph slipped from a plank while boarding a galley and was drowned. The struggle of republican against despot was especially dear to Schiller, and he was also attracted by the consummate skill of Fiesco in pretending to be absorbed only in his own pleasure, while in reality ruthlessly preparing a plot. There seemed to be great dramatic possibilities in the story. Schiller adhered in the main to the pattern of historical events, but it was obviously necessary for him to devise a new ending. An accidental slip of the foot may happen in real life, but it has no business to occur in tragedy. It was not till Schiller was working on the play at Oggersheim in October 1782 that he was able to devise a catastrophe that satisfied him. Once it had occurred to him to make Fiesco die by the hand of an intransigent republican, the character of his hero acquired a new interest; for the simple struggle between republican and despot became complicated by the powerful motive of personal ambition.

In Schiller's play Genoa is well ruled by the self-appointed duke, Andrea Doria, a despot, though an enlightened one. But Doria's nephew Gianettino, a selfish, coarse, brutal fellow, reveals himself as a true tyrant. Fiesco, the most admired nobleman in Genoa, resolves to overthrow the Dorias, but he conceals his design so successfully behind a mask of flippancy and dissipation that none suspects his real aims. In order to deceive his enemies he makes love to Gianettino's sister, whereby his own wife suffers much unhappiness. He presently discloses his plans to certain other malcontents, chief of whom is Verrina, an inflexible republican, whose inveterate hatred of tyranny has been doubled since Gianettino violated his daughter. Fiesco, Verrina, and three others become the nucleus of the conspiracy of which Fiesco is determined to be sole head. Reluctantly the others agree, but Verrina's suspicious eye has already detected the ambition of Fiesco, and, believing that the latter's aim is merely to overthrow Doria and to take his place as duke, decides that Fiesco must be assassinated in the hour of victory. The revolt takes place, and the party of Fiesco, who by an unhappy chance kills his own wife in the fighting, is successful. Urged by the majority of his supporters, he readily accepts the crown which is thrust upon him. Verrina implores him to decline the proffered greatness; when Fiesco rejects all his pleas Verrina pushes him into the harbour.

Die Verschwörung des Fiesco zu Genua has a more compact and better constructed action than *Die Räuber*. Schiller has an eye for contrast between scenes which recalls Shakespeare. The shallow brilliance of the festivities in Fiesco's palace yields to the deep gloom of the scene in which Verrina learns of the rape of his daughter. Verrina's sinister avowal of his intention to kill Fiesco, made at deepest night amid bare rocks and crags, is succeeded by Fiesco's monologue of ambition, as from his balcony he watches the sun rise upon the fair city of Genoa. Schiller's skill in dramatic construction has improved with practice, though he has not yet entirely solved the problem of presenting an action upon the stage; the fifth act in particular contains an imperfectly understood imitation of Shakespeare's battle scenes.

Apart from unnamed noblemen, servants, and so on, *Fiesco* contains no fewer than nineteen characters, of whom twelve are prominent persons of the play. All of these are differentiated and several made to live. Andrea Doria and his nephew Gianettino are a complementary pair, the enlightened and the tyrannical despot. Yet each lives, each is comprehensible without the other. Gianettino is the more fully portrayed. Though he occasionally rants, Schiller is most successful with his tyrant in remarks which unguardedly reveal his boorish arrogance and presumption: " Lavagna, wir danken für deine Bewirtung. Ich war zufrieden."[1]

---

[1] Lavagna, we thank you for your hospitality. It was satisfactory.

E

The republican party consists of Fiesco, Verrina, Bourgognino, Sacco, and Calcagno. Of these Sacco and Calcagno are men of courage but lacking in principle. They take part in the conspiracy because they hope for personal advantage from it. Bourgognino is a fresh and active youth, and Schiller has in a phrase characterized his nervous impatience—" Ich sitze ungern, wenn ich ans Um-reissen denke "[1]—while the others sit in solemn council. Verrina presented a more difficult problem. A man of stern determination and uncompromising principle, a lean and hungry Cassius, he should have been sparing in word and gesture. Instead, he expresses himself all too often in fervid eloquence. It is odd, too, that a man of this apparently selfless political temper should have to be galvanized into action by purely personal misfortune.

All these figures are political partisans, who are also credible characters. They serve politics. Fiesco on the other hand makes politics serve him. Superbly skilled in intrigue and dissimulation, he deceives all around him into a complete misjudgment of his character and aims. His wife and his fellow-conspirators, with the exception of Verrina, are as much taken in as his enemies. The main-spring of Fiesco's actions is ambition, and his complete egoism allows it to unfold without any check from conscience or self-criticism. Fiesco's other guiding passion, the desire to shine in the eyes of the world, is closely linked with his ambition. When, having revealed his patri-otic plans to Verrina and his companions, he walks up and down, pausing to consider his future course, and finally resolves to be a true republican, it is the dazzling greatness of the renunciation, not the rightness of the act, which prompts his decision: " Ein Diadem erkämpfen ist gross, es wegwerfen, ist göttlich."[2] But a renunci-ation, however divine, cannot command the continued admiration which is paid to the exercise of power. And Fiesco's ambition and desire to shine must be constantly fed. His virtuous resolution lasts but a short time, and when he next reflects alone it is to see the autocratic ruler in his most favourable light: " Zu stehen in jener schrecklichen Höhe — niederzuschmollen in der Menschlichkeit reissenden Strudel. . . ."[3]

At such a moment Fiesco uses almost the very words of Schiller's poem *Der Eroberer*[4]; he has the same intoxication for precarious heights, the same insatiable desire to out-top all his fellow-men. He is a sublime egoist. He must be head of the conspiracy or

[1] I cannot sit down when I am thinking of this revolution.

[2] To win a diadem is *great*, to discard it is *divine*.

[3] To stand on that terrifying height—to frown from above upon the swirling stream of humanity. . . .

[4] See above, p. 17.

nothing: " Wenn ich nicht der Souverän der Verschwörung bin, so hat sie ein Mitglied verloren."[1] He regards his fellow-conspirators with contempt: " Schlugen sie nicht um gegen das Wort Subordination wie die Raupe gegen die Nadel? "[2] He admits, not without pride, to a fox's cunning: " Ein Fuchs riecht den andern."[3] His egoism is as complete in private life as in public. Not only is his wife subordinated to his political schemes, and suffers grievous insult, but Fiesco, in avenging these slights, makes it clear that he is satisfying, not his wife's wrongs, but his own sense of honour: " Sie waren Zeugen — retten Sie meine Ehre in Genua."[4]

When Leonore attempts to persuade Fiesco to abandon his ambitious plans and to seek happiness with her in private life she meets with blank incomprehension—

> *Leonore.* ... Mein Gemahl ist hin, wenn ich den Herzog umarme.
> *Fiesco.* Das verstehe ich nicht.[5]

Though she shakes his determination, it is for a moment only, and he leaves her without a word of farewell. For three short minutes her death by his own sword produces in Fiesco all the symptoms of frenzied grief, but the love of display immediately reasserts itself and he consoles himself with the idea that her funeral rites shall dazzle all beholders with their pomp: " Kommt! dieser unglücklichen Fürstin will ich eine Totenfeier halten, dass das Leben seine Anbeter verlieren und die Verwesung wie eine Braut glänzen soll."[6] When he meets Verrina shortly afterwards he is so full of his new greatness that it does not even occur to him to mention Leonore's death. Fiesco is, in short, a figure of dazzling brilliance, completely immersed in himself and lacking any of the profounder qualities of heart which stir the sympathy and pity of the spectator for the hero of tragedy.

The character of Muley Hassan, the Moor, is an addition to the plot, for which there was no historical model. He performs all kinds of tasks which the proud Fiesco will not undertake himself. An unprincipled rogue who enters Fiesco's service after an abortive attempt to murder him, Muley Hassan is a figure of comedy, whose

---

[1] If I am not the leader of the conspiracy, then it has one member fewer.

[2] Did they not writhe at the word *subordination* like a caterpillar at the needle transfixing it?

[3] One fox smells out another.

[4] You witnessed this—redeem my honour in Genoa.

[5] *Leonore.* ... When I embrace you as a duke I have lost you as a husband.
Fiesco. I cannot see that.

[6] Come! I will give this unfortunate princess such a funeral, that life shall lose its admirers, and decay shall shine like a bride.

alert wit, ready invention, and droll humour, win for him more sympathy and indulgence than he loses by his blatant wickedness. He combines the wit and ability of Spiegelberg with the courage and staunchness of Schweizer. And in the end he accepts his fate and goes uncomplaining to his death. He is really no greater criminal than his master, and the association is a tacit condemnation of Fiesco.

There are two women in the play. In the sweet-tempered and domestic Leonore, Schiller has achieved a success which is the less surprising since this play was written after he had emerged from the cloistered seclusion of the Academy. The attempt to portray the high-level harlotry of Julia, however, is conventional and 'literary,' and achieves only a caricature.

The style of *Fiesco* is extremely uneven. In the speech of Muley Hassan, of Gianettino, and occasionally of other figures Schiller has coined the characteristic phrase and cadence. Elsewhere the distortions by bombast and hyperbole are crass. It was perhaps inevitable that a political tragedy should express itself by exaggerated and superficial rhetoric, since the political passions themselves lie near the surface of the personality. Schiller, as he confessed in his preface, felt a certain coldness in his theme, and this drove him to try to force warmth into it. The effort resulted in bombast and such absurd stage-directions as "indem er heroisch aufspringt,"[1] and " heroisch auf und nieder "[2] and all the deliberate attitudinizing which passes so easily into bathos—such, for instance, as the speech of Bourgognino which brings down the curtain of the first act: " Ich habe schon längst ein Etwas in meiner Brust gefühlt, das sich von nichts wollte ersättigen lassen. — Was es war, weiss ich jetzt plötzlich — Ich hab' einen Tyrannen!"[3]—an unfortunate use of the worm metaphor.

The same deliberate effort to impress infects whole scenes. The most conspicuous example is the confession of Verrina to Bourgognino that he plans to murder Fiesco. The old gentleman could have whispered it quite conveniently at home; but no, he drags his prospective son-in-law out into the wilderness in order to have a suitably flesh-creeping background, and then, having uttered his fearful message, unsociably makes his way home alone, leaving Bourgognino to follow.

This scene is perhaps the clue to the most serious defects of *Fiesco*. Verrina, Fiesco, and various other characters do not behave like ordinary human beings. Yet the play, notwithstanding its

---

[1] Leaping up heroically.

[2] Heroically striding up and down.

[3] I have long felt something in my breast which nothing could satisfy. Now, all at once, I know what it was. I am suffering from a tyrant.

historical remoteness, deals with normal life; the exaggerations and distortions are therefore more obvious than in *Die Räuber*, where the whole conception, in spite of the contemporary setting, was grandiose and superhuman. In *Fiesco* a realistic conception is treated in heroic and inflated style. The resulting incongruity between style and content becomes very easily absurd and unintentionally comic.

In *Fiesco* Schiller attempts for the third time to portray the sublime criminal. Robber Moor and his brother Franz had represented two widely differing, convincing, yet extraordinary versions of the type, which exercised such a powerful fascination on Schiller from the days of the poem *Der Eroberer*; Fiesco is convincing but ordinary; he is striking but not sublime. Schiller comes very near to seeing through the meretricious disguise that covers the mean and shabby reality. But he has just failed; he still asks us to accept Fiesco at his own valuation, though it is patent that it is a gross overestimate. Rousseau's praise had prevented Schiller from drawing the right conclusions from the self-revelation of Fiesco. This fault in valuation is as great a cause of failure as the extravagant style.

Regarded by itself, *Fiesco* must be classed as a failure embodying some notable achievements. Compared with *Die Räuber*, it is an imperfect transition from a world of fantasy to a world of reality, and an essay in improved dramatic construction. It is also Schiller's first incursion into history. Its rhetorical language suggests as strongly as *Die Räuber* that Schiller would be more at home in poetry than in prose.

Chapter Six

BAUERBACH: " KABALE UND LIEBE "
1782–83

IT was on November 30, a Saturday, that Schiller left Worms on his long and slow journey to Meiningen. The roads, bad at any time, were now covered with snow, the weather raw and frosty, and it was not till the morning of the next Saturday, December 7, that the coach halted at the Hart Inn in Meiningen. Even now Schiller's wearisome journey was not quite at an end, for his destination was Bauerbach, which lay two hours southward by deep and miry roads.

It was dark before Schiller reached Bauerbach. Though the snow reflected a faint light, he could distinguish little. Trees loomed in black contrast, and here and there a wan light gleamed in a cottage window. When at last he halted at the house he found that he was expected by the servants, whom Frau von Wolzogen, then living at Stuttgart, had charged to make him welcome. He was shown upstairs to a large room with a comfortable bed and a stove burning in expectation of his arrival. Comfort and warmth meant much to this young man, fresh from seven days of slow and jolting travel in bitterly cold weather. Even more welcome and more precious to him was the consciousness that here was a home, offering shelter in a hostile world.

Sunday morning revealed to him more of the house in which he was to live and of the landscape in which it was set. The village of Bauerbach, of which Frau von Wolzogen was the feudal mistress, was a collection of poor, ill-built cottages, situated in a sombre and bleak valley whose dominant colour was the dead black of the pine-trees. The manor-house itself was nothing but a good-sized cottage, enlarged by the addition of an upper storey. It was a primitive, poor, and lonely environment.

But Schiller viewed it with favourable eyes. Eighteen months of lodging uncomfortably in Stuttgart had been followed by two months in which insecurity and fear for the future had aggravated material discomfort. Bauerbach was a haven of rest and security, a quiet refuge in which he could work at his newest play, *Luise Miller in* (later to be known as *Kabale und Liebe*). Most important of all, it was a place of solitude; and solitude was what he wanted most.

Schiller was no recluse. He needed the stimulus of contact with his fellow-men. But in December 1782 he was sick at heart. He had gone out into the world, full of confidence, of hope, and of trust in human nature. The persecution of Karl Eugen and the cold unconcern and disregard of all but personal gain displayed by Dalberg (for in this light his conduct appeared to Schiller) had bruised a heart naïvely expecting to find help and understanding, and quite unprepared for hostility or indifference. The twenty-three-year-old Schiller had left Mannheim with a cynical contempt and a suspicious mistrust of mankind. As he sat in his room on that Sunday morning and wrote to Streicher he crystallized the bitter experience of the last two months in the words:

Whatever you do, dear friend, keep this practical truth, which has cost your inexperienced friend so dear, always before your eyes. When one needs men, one must either become a scoundrel or make oneself indispensable to them. One or the other, or else one goes under.

The solitude of Bauerbach was an essential remedy for Schiller's wounded spirit. Signs of an improvement are to be found in a letter written to Frau von Wolzogen four weeks after his arrival in Bauerbach:

It is a misfortune, my dearest friend, that kind-hearted people are so easily driven into the opposite extreme of misanthropy when a few unworthy characters deceive their open-hearted judgment. So it was with me. I had embraced half the world with the warmest affection, and in the end I found I had nothing but a cold lump of ice in my arms. [January 4, 1783.]

These words indicate a certain detachment from his earlier mood; he is able to define and judge it. In the same letter, too, are two sentences which reveal a true appreciation of his own character and show why the seclusion of Bauerbach was no permanent solution for his problems: " You have no idea how essential it is for me to find people of noble mind. I need them to reconcile me with the whole human race with whom I had almost fallen out." A similar note is struck more than two months later in a letter to Reinwald: " A friend shall reconcile me with the whole human race, which has shown me certain ugly features. He can catch up and bring back my Muse, which is already half-way to Cocytus." (March 27, 1783.) The last few months of want, humiliation, and disillusionment had left their mark on Schiller, but his heart was sound and his mental health fundamentally unimpaired.

Wilhelm Friedrich Hermann Reinwald, to whom this letter was addressed, was twenty-two years older than Schiller. A man of considerable literary talent and enormous industry, Reinwald had spent the prime of his life ill paid and unappreciated in the service of the dukes of Meiningen. He was conscious of the waste of his abilities, but felt powerless to avert it. He laboured painstakingly on in the library, very much aware that he had passed his best.

From contact with Schiller's glowing youthful personality the middle-aged librarian derived a new and fresher outlook and an interest in a character now unfolding and needing his help. Reinwald's diary reveals the impression made on him by Schiller:

> There dwells in him an exceptional spirit, and I believe that Germany will one day speak his name with pride. I have seen the fire that springs from these eyes, saddened by fate, and recognized the rich spirit they bespeak.

A friendship sprang up between the two, for each had something to give the other. Reinwald was for Schiller the only cultivated contact within reach of Bauerbach; he had the experience and intelligence to understand Schiller's aims and to give him sensible advice. For the older man Schiller was a means of rejuvenation, a contact with his own lost youth. The friendship was to have a permanent effect on Reinwald's life. A letter of Christophine Schiller's, which Reinwald chanced to read, led to an acquaintance, conducted at first by letter, which culminated later in their marriage. It was a union to which Schiller was opposed because of the disparity of age and temperament.

In the earliest days of Schiller's stay in Bauerbach Reinwald's acquaintance had a practical value for him. He was determined to make his solitude profitable by industrious reading. Reinwald, as librarian, could supply his wants; and with his assistance Schiller read very widely. Rural seclusion offered an opportunity for writing, and Schiller made rapid progress with *Luise Millerin*. By the middle of December he was able to write to Reinwald that he hoped to have it finished within a fortnight. The estimate was over-optimistic, and it was not completed till mid-February.

At the end of December, after Schiller had spent three weeks in his solitude, Frau von Wolzogen came to spend a few days at her house, bringing with her her sixteen-year-old daughter Charlotte, whom Schiller had met once in Stuttgart.

In the solitude of Bauerbach and at the moment at which he was beginning to recover his regard for human beings after an attack of misanthropy, her attraction for him was multiplied many times, and the sweetness and artlessness of the girl led him to believe that there was some return of love on her side. When in April 1783 the visit of the ladies was again imminent, and it seemed that they would be escorted by a young man of the name of von Winckelmann, Schiller's passion blazed up, fanned by jealousy. He hastily scrawled a letter, expressing his detestation of Winckelmann and the impossibility of remaining if he were to come, in language of a vehemence which must finally have opened the eyes of Frau von Wolzogen, if indeed they were not opened already.

Frau von Wolzogen was disturbed. Such a match would be a social misalliance for her daughter; and Schiller was showing altogether too great a readiness to renounce his literary career and bury himself in Bauerbach. She revealed to Schiller that her daughter loved von Winckelmann and sent her away from Bauerbach. Schiller's attraction to her, though it remained powerful as long as he was in an environment abounding in associations with Charlotte, gradually subsided after he had left the district.

The gap which Lotte von Wolzogen's departure in June left for Schiller was to a large extent filled by his work. Two tasks shared his chief attention ; the adaptation of *Luise Millerin* for the stage, and the conception of a new play based on the story of the son of Philip II of Spain, Don Carlos. Schiller had toyed for some time with the idea of two other new themes, one of which was a play on the story of Mary, Queen of Scots. They were abandoned when his imagination was kindled by the theme of Don Carlos. Work on the new play was interrupted by his love-affair and further delayed by the revision of *Luise Millerin*. Dalberg had approached Schiller in March and asked for the new tragedy of which he had heard. Schiller's reply was dignified and cool, but he was too sensible to reject this offer, and began to prepare the play for production in Mannheim. He worked slowly and reluctantly, for his heart was now in his new tragedy.

As the winter passed away and spring approached, new energy and new hopes stirred in Schiller. " Soon, my dear friend, that splendid time begins when the swallows return to our skies and emotions to our hearts. With what longing I await them." So Schiller had written to Reinwald on March 27, and had gone on to speak of his previous disillusionment in terms which show that it was a temporary phase, now largely overcome:

> Loneliness, discontent with my lot, hopes which miscarried, and perhaps also the change in my mode of life, have, if I may so express myself, falsified the notes of my spirit and untuned the instrument of my feelings, which was once so pure. Friendship and the month of May will, I hope, set it right again.

Spring when it came, however, brought new unrest. It became increasingly clear to all, including Schiller himself, that rural seclusion was not the right permanent environment for him. His mind needed intellectual intercourse and the regular interchange of ideas if it was to remain sharp, clear, and productive. The danger of running to seed was a very real one for him in Bauerbach. The first to observe it was Reinwald, who intended to make a journey to Gotha and Weimar, taking Schiller with him and introducing him to various men of letters of note there. Schiller, at first enthusiastic, eventually declined to accompany Reinwald in order to be near Lotte. The librarian was sure that Schiller was losing sight of his proper course and expressed this view in a letter to Christophine Schiller:

> Your brother must know many characters, because he must portray them on the stage, he must be stimulated by talk about nature, and art and sincere and friendly conversation. A second winter in the district where he is now will make Dr S. completely hypochondriacal.

The presence of Schiller, with his youth, his enthusiasm, and his genius, meant much to Frau von Wolzogen, and his departure would leave a gap in her life; reluctantly she came to the same conclusion as Reinwald. Schiller, too, realized the need of at least a temporary change. With Frau von Wolzogen's encouragement he planned a visit of some six weeks to Mannheim. On July 24, 1783, he travelled from Bauerbach, leaving his belongings behind, for he counted with confidence on returning in September.

Schiller had spent nearly eight months there. They had given him safety and security, restored much of his trust in human nature, and afforded him leisure in which to complete one masterpiece and to conceive another.

Luise Millerin, first performed in Mannheim on April 15, 1784, did not acquire the title *Kabale und Liebe* (*Intrigue and Love*) till late in 1783, and the name was given, not by Schiller, but by the actor Iffland. But as *Kabale und Liebe* it was published and performed, and by that title it has been known ever since.

Tradition attributes the first conception of the play to the fourteen days spent in detention in Stuttgart in July 1782. The idea of the work certainly preoccupied him during the September days when he and Streicher walked to Frankfort. From then on *Luise Millerin* was his primary interest, and it was only with great reluctance that he had torn himself away from it in order to revise and adapt *Fiesco*. Amid the autumn mists of Oggersheim and the December snows of Bauerbach he had worked enthusiastically at the play, and by February 1783 it was practically completed. When, shortly afterwards, a new project, later to become the tragedy *Don Carlos*, superseded *Luise Millerin* in his interest and affection, his revision of the play became as unwilling as had been that of *Fiesco* the year before.

Kabale und Liebe is a domestic tragedy (*bürgerliches Trauerspiel*). Its most obvious predecessors are Lessing's *Emilia Galotti* and

H. L. Wagner's *Die Kindermörderin,* both of which Schiller knew well. In *Die Räuber* Schiller had created his own form, in *Die Verschwörung des Fiesco* he had made a free adaptation of Shakespearean construction as he understood it; in *Kabale und Liebe,* however, he used an established and fashionable type of play without any attempt at technical innovation.

The domestic tragedy of the eighteenth century in Germany was a very narrow form. Of English origin, it had been introduced into Germany by Lessing with *Miss Sara Sampson* in 1755 and had decisively gained the favour of the public in the seventeen-seventies. Its characters are drawn from the world of its own day, and its manner of presentation and language purport to be realistic, though the element of literary fashion in the style has become more obvious with the passage of time. Imagination and fantasy were absent, the language was prose, the setting prosaic. With domestic tragedy there was always a risk of the commonplace; but it gave on the other hand an opportunity for social and political criticism.

Indignation and anger, recurring and accumulating over a period of years, gave the original impulse to *Kabale und Liebe.* They dated back to the first shock Schiller sustained, when despotic power snatched him from his family and his chosen calling. Occasional flickerings and outbursts showed that in spirit he had not submitted. The writing of *Die Räuber* was itself an expression of his refusal to be subdued by the tyrannical atmosphere of the Academy. And *Die Räuber* contained one episode which displayed open social criticism. It is the history of Kosinsky. Undoubtedly this story owes much to Lessing's *Emilia Galotti,* but it was not a mere echo. Schiller knew of episodes in the recent history of his own land as outrageous as the fate of Kosinsky's Amalia and of favourites as unscrupulous as Kosinsky's minister. In the part played by the latter, in the relegation of the sovereign to the background and the projected marriage between the young nobleman and the middle-class girl, there is more than one point of contact with *Kabale und Liebe.* Kosinsky's story is its seed.

Schiller had personal experience of tyranny. A deed, entered into in his childhood by his parents, bound him permanently to the Duke of Würtemberg's service. Schubart at Hohenasperg showed him another and grimmer side of despotic oppression. The detention which followed his second visit to Mannheim did no more than put a match to these inflammable experiences. The figure of the Duke, endowed with absolute power and inspired by caprice and resentment, overshadowed Schiller's life in the few months he remained in Stuttgart and the fear of extradition and of the long arm of the tyrant continued to dominate his life throughout the weeks and months at Mannheim, Oggersheim, and Bauerbach. Both the walking-tour to Frankfort and the journey to Bauerbach were conceived as a flight from apprehension; even during his stay at Bauerbach Schiller felt obliged from time to time to write misleading letters as to his location and plans, with the aim of putting the Duke of Würtemberg off the scent. Tyrannical oppression was a real and urgent theme for Schiller.

The plot is Schiller's own, but it obviously owes something to *Emilia Galotti*, to Wagner's *Kindermörderin*, and even to Lessing's *Miss Sara Sampson*. But the borrowed elements have been combined with incidents and characters which Schiller derived by hearsay from the most recent history of his native country. It is a story of star-crossed lovers, whose tragedy is determined not by the fatal enmity of families, but by the artificial, rigid, and insurmountable barrier separating class from class. Ferdinand von Walter, the son of the President (the Prime Minister and favourite of the Prince), loves Luise Miller, the daughter of a humble musician. Both of them realize the obstacles to the match, and Ferdinand has till now concealed his attachment from his father. But the folly of Luise's mother estranges the President's creature Wurm, who himself had wished to marry the girl. Wurm denounces the affair to Ferdinand's father, who at first makes light of the matter, as he does not believe it possible that his son can seriously intend to marry a girl who is not of noble birth. Such a match would derange his plans to marry Ferdinand, for reasons of political influence, to Lady Milford, the Prince's English mistress. When the President reveals this scheme to Ferdinand he discovers that Wurm's estimate of the gravity of the situation is right and his own judgment wrong.

The President wastes no time, but seeks by a show of violence and a threat of public disgrace for Luise (he orders her exposure in the pillory) to weaken her hold upon his son's affections. He achieves the exact opposite and is checkmated by Ferdinand's threat publicly to denounce the foul crime by which his father has risen to his present station.

It is Wurm who whispers to the baffled President a scheme by which the separation of the lovers can yet be achieved. Miller and his wife are to be arrested and Luise told that the only means of securing their release is to write a letter to Wurm's dictation. This note, addressed to the vain and foppish Court Chamberlain von Kalb, is designed to fall into the hands of Ferdinand and to arouse his jealousy. Luise is to swear an oath not to reveal how the letter really came to be written. The plan succeeds. Ferdinand, beside himself with rage, torments the wretched Luise and poisons her and himself as well. Before she dies Luise reveals to Ferdinand the real authorship of the fateful letter. The President, summoned by a note from Ferdinand, arrives in time to witness his son's last moments. Wurm, appalled at the results of his cunning, betrays himself and his employer, and the President surrenders to justice after receiving his dying son's forgiveness.

Schiller has constructed his play with a skill resulting from natural ability perfected by experience and careful thought. He was considerably helped by writing in a well-established form. The first scene gives all the necessary information and a foreboding of the tragedy. Before the first act has ended, the shape of the threat to the lovers is visible. In the second act the storm gathers and breaks, but the lightning, which had flickered so ominously, fails to strike home, and the clouds recede; the President, to the spectator's relief, is outwitted at the last moment and forced to retire. The third act witnesses a renewal of the threat to the lovers; this time the plans are laid with greater care and are therefore all the more dangerous. In the fourth act the plot succeeds, but as its final issue is to occur in the fifth act, there is a pause which is filled by the interview between Lady Milford and Luise. The last act sees the miscarriage, fatal for the lovers as for the plotters, of the subtle and intricate plot, on whose " diabolically fine mesh " the President had complimented Wurm.

The action of the play, based on the unbridgeable gulf between the noble caste and the rest of humanity, is designed as a vehicle for social criticism. The tragedy is a passionate indictment of conditions prevalent in that age in many of the courts of Germany.

Each of the principal characters has a social significance. The President himself, descended from an ancient noble family (Ferdinand refers to his pedigree of five centuries), is the embodiment of ruthless determination to grasp power and hold it, at whatever cost to others. He has risen to his present station by a crime, whose cold-blooded and treacherous character is indicated by the words of Wurm:

> Ich besinne mich mit welcher Offenheit Sie Ihren Vorgänger damals zu einer Partie Picquet beredeten und bei ihm die halbe Nacht mit freundschaftlichem Burgunder hinwegschwemmten, und das war doch die nämliche Nacht, wo die grosse Mine losgehen und den guten Mann in die Luft blasen sollte.[1]

Intelligent, cool, and calculating, the President can simulate whatever mood or manner is needed for his plan. Far too clever for his impetuous and upright son, he plays with him as a cat with a mouse,

[1] I recollect with what candour you persuaded your predecessor to play picquet with you, and how you drank half the night away together as friends over the burgundy bottles, and yet that was the very night when the great mine was to go off and blow the good fellow sky-high.

now feigning paternal concern, now outraged authority, now genial benevolence. He handles von Kalb with equal adroitness.

The President's standards of conduct rigidly exclude moral scruples. Twice he outlines his views: power and rank are his values, success in attaining them the only criterion of conduct. In conversation with Wurm he speaks thus of his son's love-affair:

> Dass mein Sohn Gefühl für das Frauenzimmer hat, macht mir die Hoffnung, dass ihn die Damen nicht hassen werden. Er kann bei Hof etwas durchsetzen. Das Mädchen ist schön, sagt Er; dass gefällt mir an meinem Sohn, dass er Geschmack hat. Spiegelt er der Närrin solide Absichten vor — noch besser — so seh' ich, dass er noch Witz genug hat, in seinen Beutel zu lügen. Er kann Präsident werden. Setzt er es noch dazu durch — herrlich! das zeigt mir an, dass er Glück hat. — Schliesst sich die Farce mit einem gesunden Enkel — unvergleichlich! so trink' ich auf die guten Aspekten meines Stammbaums eine Bouteille Malaga mehr und bezahle die Skortationsstrafe seiner Dirne.[1]

In his view the whole affair can be no more than a diversion, in which Ferdinand pretends and lies with a watchful eye on a successful future career, determined to do nothing which could compromise it.

A further illustration of the President's doctrine of influence and success is provided by his words to Ferdinand:

> Du bist im zwölften Jahre Fähndrich! Im zwanzigsten Major! Ich hab' es durchgesetzt beim Fürsten. Du wirst die Uniform ausziehen und in das Ministerium eintreten! Der Fürst sprach von Geheimenrat — Gesandtschaften — ausserordentlichen Gnaden! Eine herrliche Aussicht dehnt sich vor dir — die ebene Strasse zunächst nach dem Throne — zum Throne selbst, wenn anders die Gewalt so viel wert ist als ihre Zeichen. — Das begeistert dich nicht?[2]

A fundamental difference in standards of value divides the two men, as Ferdinand points out in his reply: " Weil meine Begriffe von Grösse und Glück nicht ganz die Ihrigen sind."[3]

---

[1] That my son is attracted by this woman makes me hope that the ladies will not hate him. He can be a success at court. You say the girl is good-looking; it pleases me to find that my son has good taste. If he holds forth to the little fool about his honourable intentions, so much the better—that shows that he has wit enough to tell lies. He can become President. If he brings it off, splendid!— that proves that he has luck—and if the foolery ends with a healthy grandchild, still better!—I'll drink an extra bottle of Malaga in honour of the good prospects of my house and pay the maintenance of his mistress.

[2] You were an ensign at the age of twelve, major before you were twenty. That was my doing with the Prince. Now you shall take off your uniform and enter the Cabinet. The Prince spoke of Privy Councillor—of missions to foreign courts—of exceptional favours! A splendid prospect opens up before you, a clear path to the place nearest to the throne, to the throne itself, if power is worth its promises. And doesn't that thrill you?

[3] Because my ideas of greatness and happiness are not exactly yours.

The great gulf which separates even more widely the standards of the aristocracy and of the middle classes is clearly recognizable in the dialogue between the President and Wurm concerning the oath which Luise is to swear:

> *Präsident.* Einen Eid? Was wird ein Eid fruchten, Dummkopf?
> *Wurm.* Nichts bei uns, gnädiger Herr! Bei dieser Menschenart alles.[1]

President Baron von Walter is the key to the social significance of the play. He is, as he claims to be, the representative of the princely power. The standards and methods he chooses to adopt are also inevitably the standards and methods of the state. Two other figures of the corrupt court are placed beside him to complete the picture.

Court Chamberlain von Kalb has as much consciousness of rank as the President. When Baron von Walter proposes that Kalb should allow his name to be used as a bait in the intrigue which is to prise Ferdinand away from Luise the following dialogue ensues:

> *Hofmarschall.* Dieser andre?
> *Präsident.* Müssten Sie sein, Baron.
> *Hofmarschall.* Ich sein? Ich? — Ist sie von Adel?
> *Präsident.* Wozu das? Welcher Einfall! — Eines Musikanten Tochter.
> *Hofmarschall.* Bürgerlich also? Das wird nicht angehen. Was?[2]

But von Kalb, though he is as proud as the President, has neither the latter's intelligence nor his ruthlessness. He is a narrow and restricted being, whose whole sphere of interest is comprised in dress, court functions, and questions of precedence and fashion. Ferdinand's contemptuous summing-up of his life is a fair one:

> In einem Augenblick siebenmal kurz und siebenmal lang zu werden wie der Schmetterling an der Nadel? Ein Register zu führen über die Stuhlgänge deines Herrn und der Mietgaul seines Witzes zu sein?[3]

Kalb's moral sense is as much atrophied as that of the President, and it is with astonishment that he learns that Ferdinand, because he loves another, refuses to marry Lady Milford:

> *Präsident.* . . . Er liebt eine andere.

---

[1] *President.* An oath? What's the use of an oath, you fool?
Wurm. None at all with *us*, your Excellency. But, with such people as *these*, of the very greatest use in the world.

[2] *Chamberlain.* And this other?
President. Must be you, Baron.
Chamberlain. I? I?—Is she noble-born?
President. Why should she be? What an idea!—No, a musician's daughter.
Chamberlain. A bourgeoise then? Can't be done. What?

[3] To bow down to the ground and straighten up again seven times in a moment like a butterfly on a pin? To keep a record of your master's visits to stool and to be the hack of his wit?

Hofmarschall. Sie scherzen. Ist das auch wohl ein Hindernis?
Präsident. Bei dem Trotzkopf das unüberwindlichste.
Hofmarschall. Er sollte so wahnsinnig sein und sein Fortune von sich stossen? Was?[1]

In contrast to the President, who can be detested but not despised, von Kalb is a figure of derision and contempt even to many in his own restricted aristocratic circle.

To the unscrupulous minister and the vain and foppish courtier Schiller adds a third figure, the mistress of the Prince. Lady Milford has excellent qualities, but they are personal ones, and she possesses them not because of her privileged position, but in spite of it. She is even more powerful than the President, for she has access to the Prince's ear when he is most inclined to listen:

> Wer sich herausnimmt, Beleidigungen dieser Art einer Dame zu sagen, die nicht mehr als eine Nacht braucht, ihn ganz zu verderben, muss dieser Dame eine g r o s s e Seele zutrauen oder — von Sinnen sein.[2]

Without ever knowing that they exist she can bring ruin upon the Prince's subjects; for he sells seven thousand of them as soldiers to a foreign power in order to buy her the most superb diamonds. The wealth and welfare of the land is at the mercy of her caprice:

> Wahr ist's, er kann mit dem Talisman seiner Grösse jeden Gelust meines Herzens wie ein Feenschloss aus der Erde rufen — er setzt den Saft von zwei Indien auf die Tafel — ruft Paradiese aus Wildnissen — lässt die Quellen seines Landes in stolzen Bögen gen Himmel springen oder das Mark seiner Untertanen in einem Feuerwerke hin-puffen.[3]

Whilst her position at court and the favours shown her by the Prince reveal the vicious corruption of the nobility and the reckless tyranny of the ruler, her warm and generous qualities of heart enable her to expose and castigate the crimes committed merely to give her a fleeting moment's pleasure.

These three, minister, chamberlain, and mistress, represent the visible power and ostentatious display of the ruler of the despotic state.

---

[1] *President.* . . . He loves someone else.
Chamberlain. You are not serious. Can that be an obstacle?
President. With this obstinate fellow an insuperable one.
Chamberlain. He is so foolish as to turn his back on such wonderful good fortune? What?

[2] Whoever dares to utter insults like this to a lady who needs only one single night to ruin him utterly, must either believe she has a truly noble soul or—be out of his senses.

[3] It is true that with the spell of his greatness he can conjure up out of the earth every whim of my heart like a fairy palace. He can set the fruits of the two Indies on my table—turn wildernesses into paradises—can let the springs of his land arch in fountains to heaven or squander the strength of his subjects in a firework display.

But the despot himself does not appear, and Schiller acted wisely in withholding him. Each of the three figures is a symbol, yet each is also an individual fully alive with personal qualities, now attractive, now repellent, which distract from his or her value as a representative. The personality of the Prince is concealed. He stands invisible in the background, but the shadow of his power falls across the play, unblurred by any personal feature; we see the crimes his rule provokes, the oppression, the callous indifference; the vice and the luxury; the insuperable barrier between Prince and subject: " Sie sind verschanzt, eure Grossen — verschanzt vor der Wahrheit hinter ihre eigne Laster wie hinter Schwerter der Cherubim,"[1] cries Luise in her distress, and audience and reader feel alike the same sense of impotence to reach the source of evil, the same awareness of the remote intangibility of the Prince. His absence from the stage emphasizes his inaccessibility and suggests that he neither knows nor cares about the flagrant wrongs done in his name.

The fourth and last person in the play drawn from the nobility is the President's son, Ferdinand von Walter. As he is the hero of a play about living people, his personal qualities must outweigh any capacity to represent a class. But he stands for the young generation, for the new age, opposed to class barriers, which, however severely it may suffer for the moment, will in time replace the old corrupt order and bring into the world a new social spirit.

In the middle-class world (and *Kabale und Liebe* shows the lower middle class, and not the well-to-do ladies and gentlemen of *Miss Sara Sampson* and *Emilia Galotti*), there is, too, a representative of the new generation. Luise Miller proves that with education and a suitable environment the musician's daughter can stand on the same plane as the nobleman's son. When she is treated as a lady, she becomes a lady. The gulf that remains is the artificial one of rank and station, maintained by tradition, prejudice, and the self-interest of a small minority.

Luise's parents complete the middle-class picture. Miller is the embodiment of integrity and simple goodness, with a touch of obsequious humility forced upon him by the arrogance and power of the ruling class. His wife exemplifies the effects of ignorance and a petty environment on a character without natural distinction. Frau Miller is opinionated and ambitious, and it is her presumption in imagining that she can bridge the social gulf that occasions the tragic events of the play.

Wurm, a commoner by birth, is a despicable jackal of the great, without principle or compassion, ready to help in the work of

---

[1] They are entrenched, the great, entrenched behind their own vices as securely as if these were the swords of Cherubim.

oppression for a small share in the profits. The aristocratic system has perverted him.

Class faces class in inescapable antagonism. A small proportion of society, notorious for its corruption, oppresses the mass of simple, right-thinking people. Only in the young is there hope. But it is a strong and bright glow of hope that is not put out by the disaster which overtakes Ferdinand and Luise. The moral victory, which they gain over the forces of evil by their purity and goodness, is translated at the close into a material victory, for their tragic end compels the fall of the President and Wurm. Virtue and honour perish, but in their fall they shake the foundations of the palace of corruption, though its final ruin is not yet.

If there is any play of Schiller to which the motto of *Die Räuber*, *in Tirannos*, should have been attached, it is this one. The play attacks the very foundations of eighteenth-century despotism and of the existing organization of society. It gains in power by its fairness. Not that Schiller could help taking sides. He had seen and heard of the consequences of despotism; he knew of Schubart's misery and of the sale of soldiers, and he had suffered the frustration of his own planned career and the attempt to suppress his writing. He had heard of the mismanagement and corruption of favourites, of Montmartin and Wittleder, undoubted models for the President and Wurm; and he knew personally one of the famous despots of the eighteenth century. He knew likewise that beyond the borders of Würtemberg there were scores of other princes of the same type. He had seen all this and made up his mind to denounce. Yet he denounced with moderation and reason. And he does it in the best possible way, allowing the events and characters to speak for themselves.

The play is more, however, than a propagandist work. Schiller has written a play about real people. Though the President and Miller, von Kalb and Wurm, Ferdinand and Luise, are representative, they are also characters of flesh and blood with virtues and vices existing side by side. The President is not a stage villain, but a man with genuine feelings, which he has deliberately repressed; and the change in him, which the death of his son evokes, though too rapid, is not an impossible one. Even so, in the court characters the representative element is predominant. In the other figures the personal, individual aspect is more important.

The Millers are superbly portrayed. Frau Miller's combination of vanity, cupidity, and conceit, and the impossibility of silencing her are real, convincing features. Her selfishness is disguised in the vicarious satisfaction she derives from the prospect of her daughter's elevation, in which her own vanity and social ambition and not

Luise's interests are consulted. Miller's touching affection for Luise, his sincerity and his quaint, engaging and irrepressible humour reveal him as a complete, credible, and lovable character.

Ferdinand and Luise presented a more difficult problem. Because they are the principal figures, Schiller could not apply to them the technique of economy which he used so effectively with the Millers, von Kalb, and Wurm. Nor could rank and station give the keynote to their characters, as they do with the President. There were subtle difficulties too. Luise must be devoted to her father and yet be led by her heart to cross his wishes. She must be all love for Ferdinand and yet alienate him by her seeming coldness. Schiller has successfully solved this problem; he never forgets Luise's humble origin, which is not merely an arbitrary obstacle to her union with the baron's son, but also divides, through different upbringing, her mode of thought from that of her lover. Her sense of family and of filial duty offend the more individualistic and selfish passion of Ferdinand. Only in her scene with Lady Milford is Luise not quite credible. She says here what the spectator wants her to say, yet knows that she could not. In the scene in which Wurm goads her into writing the letter the true presentation of mental torment almost reaches the limit of the bearable.

Ferdinand von Walter is a rapturous, but jealous and quarrelsome lover. He is a romantic, who forms his own conception of the world and is then, like Karl Moor, angry with reality because it does not coincide with the ideal he has created. This romanticism underlies his differences with Luise and causes him to fall into the trap which his father and Wurm have baited for him; the distortion of values to which it gives rise is also the reason for his murder of Luise. Ferdinand reacts in the same exaggerated fashion. Whether he cries ecstatically: " Du, Luise, und ich und die Liebe !"[1] or mutters with murder in his heart, " Und ich verdiene noch Dank, dass ich die Natter zertrete, ehe sie auch noch den Vater verwundet,"[2] in either case he overshoots the mark. Wrapped up in his own thoughts, he cannot perceive accurately what goes on around him. His blind refusal to see and hear anything but what he has made up his mind to see and hear is very clearly indicated when von Kalb, in fear for his life, reveals the truth about the dictated letter. Far from recognizing the deceit which has been practised upon him, Ferdinand is unable to grasp the clear and unmistakable meaning of von Kalb's words, because they do not fit in with his conviction of Luise's guilt.

---

[1] *You*, Louise, and *I* and *love!*

[2] And I deserve thanks for crushing the viper before it bites the father too.

Ferdinand's sudden jealousy confronted Schiller with a difficult problem of motivation. He has grappled with his dilemma in two distinct ways. Even in the first scene he has made a slight rift between Ferdinand and Luise, a rift which is a consequence partly of different upbringing and environment, partly of the intransigent and exacting character of Ferdinand. But he has also introduced a quarrel between the two just before Ferdinand finds the dictated love-letter, and this unresolved dispute is interpreted by Ferdinand's jaundiced mind as confirmation of his suspicions.

A most important feature of *Kabale und Liebe* is the humour which pervades the whole play. There had been sardonic humour in *Die Räuber*. *Fiesco* had contained in Muley Hassan a consciously comic figure, but in *Kabale und Liebe* both humour and wit impregnate the play and find their expression consciously or unconsciously in almost every character. The President's ironical turn of mind makes his otherwise vicious character tolerable and more real, when, for instance, he replies to von Kalb's invitation to a firework display:

> *Hofmarschall.* . . . das süperbeste Feuerwerk — eine ganze Stadt brennt zusammen — Sie sehen sie doch auch brennen? Was?
> *Präsident.* Ich habe Feuerwerks genug in meinem eignen Hause, das meine ganze Herrlichkeit in die Luft nimmt.[1]

and so proves that he can turn his humour against himself. In the scene in which he threatens Luise with the pillory his caustic humour is an effective antidote to the attitudinizing of Ferdinand:

> *Präsident.* . . . Wie lang kennt Sie den Sohn des Präsidenten?
> *Luise.* Diesem habe ich nie nachgefragt. Ferdinand von Walter besucht mich seit dem November.
> *Ferdinand.* Betet sie an.
> *Präsident.* Erhielt Sie Versicherungen?
> *Ferdinand.* Vor wenig Augenblicken die feierlichste im Angesicht Gottes.
> *Präsident (Zornig zu seinem Sohn).* Zur Beichte deiner Torheit wird man dir schon das Zeichen geben. (*Zu Luisen*) Ich warte auf Antwort.
> *Luise.* Er schwur mir Liebe.
> *Ferdinand.* Und wird sie halten.
> *Präsident.* Muss ich befehlen, dass du schweigst? — Nahm Sie den Schwur an?
> *Luise.* Ich erwiderte ihn.
> *Ferdinand (Mit fester Stimme).* Der Bund ist geschlossen.

[1] *Chamberlain.* The most superb fireworks—a whole city on fire. You will come and see it burn, too,—what?
President. Thanks, I have fireworks enough in my own house that look like setting my whole position on fire.

Präsident. Ich werde das Echo hinauswerfen lassen.[1]

A breath of sanity and proportion springs from such passages as
this. The President also helps most effectively to characterize von
Kalb, when he likens him to " Ein Bonmot von gestern, die Mode
vom vorigen Jahr."[2]

The ridiculously self-important figure of von Kalb can stimulate
even Ferdinand and Lady Milford to humour. In this character and
that of Miller, Schiller has tried his hand with great success at
comedy of character. The achievement with Luise's father is
greater than with the Chamberlain, for, unlike von Kalb, Miller
has to retain our sympathy. Miller is comic because of his odd
incongruous mixture of qualities—defiance and obsequiousness,
independence and love of money. He is, besides, a character who
cannot help expressing himself humorously, however grave the topic
and however serious his own views. The contrast between serious-
ness of aim and comedy of expression heightens the effect of the
humour:

> *Frau.* . . . da sieht man's ja sonnenklar, wie es ihm pur um ihre
> schöne Seele zu tun ist.
> *Miller.* Das ist die rechte Höhe! Auf den Sack schlägt man, den
> Esel meint man. Wer einen Gruss an das liebe Fleisch zu bestellen
> hat, darf nur das gute Herz Boten gehen lassen.[3]

Schiller himself, to judge from his letter to Dalberg, had scruples
about the propriety of this mixture of the comic and the tragic.
Though it was something he did not repeat, it was in its place in this
play. *Kabale und Liebe* is Schiller's one attempt at realism, the

---

[1] *President.* How long have you known the President's son?
Louise. I know nothing of the President's son. But Ferdinand von Walter
has paid me visits since November.
Ferdinand. And he adores her.
President. Did he make you promises?
Ferdinand. The most solemn assurance in the face of God just a few minutes
ago.
President (angrily to his son). You will be told when to confess your follies. *(To
Louise)* I'm waiting for an answer.
Louise. He promised me love.
Ferdinand. And will keep his promise.
President. Must I order you to be quiet? *(To Louise)* Did you accept it?
Louise. I reciprocated it.
Ferdinand (in a firm voice). The bond is forged.
President. I'll have the echo thrown out.

[2] Yesterday's quip, last year's fashion.

[3] *Wife.* You can see as clear as daylight that he's only concerned with her
beautiful soul.
Miller. That's the right tune! That's the tree they all bark up. When they
want to go to bed with a girl they all start by getting the heart to act as a go-
between.

only play in which the little irrelevancies, the accidental accompaniments of everyday life, are deliberately retained. By aiming at complete presentation he deprived his tragedy of universality and intensity. This realistic style was not truly congenial to him. The rhetoric of the scenes which matter most to Schiller—those between Ferdinand and Luise, or between either and Lady Milford—contrasts with the detailed realism of the remainder. Schiller's desire to portray the essence rather than the surface led, in *Kabale und Liebe*, to dissonances of style and passages of false tone. He could only achieve his end when he turned to verse.

Chapter Seven

FALSE DAWN: MANNHEIM
1783–85

ON July 24, 1783, in sweltering summer weather, Schiller left Bauerbach. For ten months his only revenue had been the sum Schwan had paid him for *Fiesco*, and that had gone immediately to settle his most pressing debts. The generous hospitality of Frau von Wolzogen had fed and housed him free for eight of those months, but there were out-of-pocket expenses which he had to meet himself, and his only recourse was to borrow. Frau von Wolzogen herself had lent him money and had stood surety with certain other creditors. But this was only a part of his financial embarrassment. He still had debts in Stuttgart, contracted mainly for the publication of *Die Räuber* and *Das wirtembergische Repertorium*. The thought of these encumbrances had dulled the enjoyment of his Bauerbach retreat. And it was for this reason most important that he should now make some pecuniary gain from his new play *Luise Millerin* and, perhaps also, from *Die Verschwörung des Fiesco*.

His stay in Mannheim was to be short. He would make arrangements about his plays and return to Bauerbach, which he quitted even for this short period with great reluctance. He was a good deal in love with Lotte von Wolzogen; he was sincerely and gratefully attached to her mother; and he dreamed of settling for life in the only place which had been a home for him since he had been uprooted and transplanted to the Academy ten years before. Now, as he jolted to and fro in the coach on the road to Frankfort, all his thoughts were directed backward to the friends and the house he had left.

He travelled as fast as he could, with the object of transacting his business quickly and returning to Bauerbach. From Wernarz and from Frankfort he sent hurried letters to Frau von Wolzogen, expressing his longing to rejoin her. On July 27 he arrived in Mannheim, where the heat was intense and the air oppressive. Streicher, still in Mannheim, was surprised by Schiller's arrival, and the two friends had much to tell each other. But the real object of Schiller's visit had to wait for its attainment, for Dalberg was out of town and did not return until August 10.

Dalberg's attitude to Schiller had changed much since their last meeting nine months before. His fears that Schiller's presence might cause political trouble with Würtemberg had been allayed, and his hopes roused by all he had heard of the new play Schiller had written in Bauerbach. He was cordial in greeting and lavish with praise. Schiller, however, could not forget his earlier experience and was very little disposed to accept Dalberg's assurances at their face value. He could now write to Frau von Wolzogen : " The man is full of fire, but unfortunately it is no more than a flash that blazes up and then is gone as quickly as it came."

Dalberg promised a performance of *Die Räuber* for August 31, in order to display again the excellence of Mannheim acting. Meanwhile he proposed to Schiller an engagement as house-dramatist, and pressed him to accept it. It was a very tempting offer, for it seemed to show a way of escape from the financial *impasse* in which Schiller found himself. But the pull of Bauerbach was still strong, and Schiller might have declined the proposal if Dalberg's efforts had not received unintentional support from Bauerbach. Frau von Wolzogen announced that Herr von Winckelmann was coming to spend two months there. Schiller felt that an immediate return was out of the question and promptly closed with Dalberg's offer.

Schiller's engagement as house-dramatist was to last from September 1, 1783, to August 31, 1784. His salary for the year was three hundred florins, of which two hundred were paid at once and the balance in December. He undertook to provide the theatre with three new plays, two of which, *Die Verschwörung des Fiesco* and *Kabale und Liebe*, were already written. He was also to draw the receipts from one performance of each of these plays, to retain the publication rights, and to have a seat on the managing committee.

Schiller was naturally prone to sanguine expectations, and the caution and reserve, which he had tried at first to maintain, were foreign to his temper and soon vanished. He began to calculate what he considered to be his certain income and arrived at the generous figure of 1,200 to 1,400 florins. He might, he felt, devote four to five hundred to the reduction of his debts, a thought which lifted an enormous load from his mind; he could now, as he wrote to Frau von Wolzogen, look forward to a peace " which I have not enjoyed for a long time, because the uncertainty of my prospects and the gnawing thought of my debts pursued me relentlessly."

The uncertainty of his calculations was quickly demonstrated. He went down with fever on his first day of office. The unusually hot summer weather had caused an epidemic in the ill-drained, dirty town, and at one time as many as one-third of the inhabitants were affected. Schiller's most reliable friend in the theatre, the producer Meyer, died of the disease on September 2, the day after Schiller had taken to his bed. Schiller himself was delirious for a time and had to remain in his room for most of the month of September. He spent the whole winter in very indifferent health. By temperament he was impatient of the frailty of his constitution, and the fulfilment of his contract, too, weighed heavily upon his mind; though *Fiesco* and *Luise Millerin* were written, they needed considerable rehandling before they could be put into rehearsal. Schiller felt that he must work in spite of ill-health, as he wrote to Frau von Wolzogen at New Year, 1784:

> In order to satisfy both the impatience of the theatre and the expectations of the public, I have had during my sickness to work with my head and to maintain my feeble strength with such strong doses of quinine that this winter may have witnessed permanent damage to my health.

Schiller began in Mannheim to pay attentions to Margarete Schwan, the daughter of the bookseller. He wrote home about her with sufficient warmth to lead Captain Schiller to believe that a marriage was imminent. It was a match which he would have welcomed, for Schwan was a man of substance and of the same rank in society. The old gentleman at Ludwigsburg had always viewed with misgiving his son's attraction to the noble-born Lotte. But Margarete Schwan was a self-possessed young lady who was in no hurry to marry, preferring for the present to play one suitor off against another.

Schiller's appointment at Mannheim had led at first to an improvement in his relations with his father. Captain Schiller had been shocked at his son's flight and very little edified by his achievements since. This new post seemed to give a promise of better things. The project of a visit to Mannheim by Frau Schiller and Christophine was discussed, but was abandoned because of expense. Schiller's appointment had the drawback that it raised the hopes of his creditors, who understandably felt that the time had come when their loans should be repaid. On this matter Schiller could not see eye to eye with his father, nor could he accept the suggestion that he should petition the Duke of Würtemberg for pardon. A strained situation arose which lasted throughout the winter.

Meanwhile Schiller, who had taken his seat on the theatre committee on October 15 during a lull in his illness, had by mid-December completed the stage version of *Die Verschwörung des Fiesco*. The difficulties he experienced with this adaptation were not solely caused by his illness, nor even by his reluctance to alter a published work; they arose from the need to make at Dalberg's request changes which

Schiller himself could not approve. He had faced a similar problem with *Die Räuber*, but the changes Dalberg proposed for *Fiesco* were even more far-reaching. Two undoubted faults in the play disquieted the director. He felt that the tragic ending was not satisfactory and wished to see it replaced by a happy solution. And he feared that the happy marriage of Bertha in the fifth act, following upon the rape she suffers in the first, might prove unacceptable to the audience. Schiller reluctantly made the changes demanded.

Schiller's original version had used the violation of Bertha to rouse the republican fury of Verrina, but had ignored it as far as her match with Scipio Bourgognino was concerned. In the stage version Bourgognino declares that he cannot marry the violated Bertha, who protests against his rash assumption in words of an unctuous morality which ring strikingly untrue: " Der allmächtige Blick der beleidigten Tugend entwaffnete den feigen Verführer. Er floh mit Beschämung fort, und die Vorsicht rettete Bertha, eh' er eine zwote Bestürmung wagte." [1] These hollow and pretentious words are not only false in the mouth of the person who utters them, they also describe conduct which is manifestly inconsistent with the character of the seducer, Gianettino; and the preservation of Bertha from rape has made of Verrina's curse a pointless and unjustifiable exaggeration.

In order to give the play a happy ending considerable alterations had to be made. Leonore's death was cut out, leaving her story incomplete. Fiesco makes up his mind to renounce the crown, conceals this decision, is almost (but not quite) murdered by Verrina, and then announces, to the admiring astonishment of all beholders, his refusal of the ducal dignity. His motives are as selfish in this version as in the original. This conclusion, in which incense is burned to the egoist, and the spectator asked to applaud his thinly veiled selfishness, is as offensive in spirit as it is inconsistent with the characters and the development of the play.

Other alterations diminished the importance of Julia and of Calcagno and Sacco; the number of characters was reduced by making Bourgognino the object of Gianettino's affront in the Senate; and Muley Hassan escapes in this version with his life. Bertha too is released from her dungeon by Bourgognino, and Verrina makes his distrust of Fiesco known to his prospective son-in-law in a room instead of dragging him off to the wildest and most desolate spot he can find. Both these alterations are improvements. A large number of the changes made for brevity and concentration or eliminated awkward changes of scene. But the total effect is a negation of the

---

[1] The all-powerful gaze of injured virtue disarmed the cowardly seducer. He fled ashamed and Providence rescued Bertha before he could dare a second assault.

tragedy, a falsification of its characters, and a cheapening of its values.

Die Verschwörung des Fiesco zu Genua was performed in this version on January 11, 1784, without achieving any great success, which is hardly surprising in view of the deformations it had undergone.

No sooner was *Fiesco* disposed of than Schiller set to work to prepare *Luise Millerin* for the stage. Here the work was less arduous and the alterations slighter, for his third tragedy had been written after he had acquired some experience of the stage and with the very actors in mind by whom it was eventually performed.

Schiller's circumstances, too, seemed to be taking a turn for the better. On January 10, 1784, he was unofficially informed that he had been elected a member of the German Society of the Palatinate (*Kurpfälzische deutsche Gesellschaft*), founded in 1775 "to further good taste, and the use of the German language." On February 21 he received the official diploma with the Elector's assent, the effect of which was to grant him Palatine nationality, a useful and encouraging development for the fugitive Würtemberger. This official recognition did something to appease Captain Schiller, who still viewed his son's chosen career and way of life with steady displeasure.

In the course of February the actor Iffland, who was beginning industriously to write plays, submitted one to Schiller with the request that he should name it. Schiller gave it the title *Das Verbrechen aus Ehrsucht*, and as such it was performed in March. Schiller returned the compliment by asking Iffland to do the same for *Luise Millerin;* the result was the title *Kabale und Liebe.*

Kabale und Liebe was first performed on April 15, 1784, when it achieved an outstanding success, though it did not maintain its place in the repertoire so well as *Die Räuber.* Schiller, who was warmly applauded, felt a sense of personal triumph, which was renewed when the play was produced at Frankfort in his presence at the beginning of May. He returned to Mannheim busy with new ideas and more than half resolved to stay on permanently as house-dramatist and make the city his home.

In the course of May he made several new acquaintances. Early in the month a Herr and Frau von Kalb spent a day or two in Mannheim on their way to the garrison town of Landau, to which von Kalb, an officer in the French service, had been posted. Frau von Kalb, who came from the neighbourhood of Meiningen, bore a letter for Schiller from Reinwald, and the three spent some hours together in Mannheim. She impressed Schiller as a woman of intelligence. About three weeks later a Frau von Lengefeld, passing through Mannheim with her son-in-law and two daughters, left cards on Schiller, but the meeting left scarcely any impression on the poet. The ladies, who knew of him only as the author of *Die Räuber*, were surprised at his meek appearance and gentle manner. They were to meet again four years later.

The month of June opened with a very pleasant surprise for Schiller in the shape of a parcel from Leipzig containing presents from unknown admirers. Two men and two ladies united in this tribute. One of the ladies sent him a handsomely embroidered brief-case, the other had done the portraits of all four admirers in pastel, and one of the men sent him a musical setting of Amalia's song, *Schön wie Engel*,[1] from the third act of *Die Räuber*. Schiller was beside himself with delight, which he expressed to Frau von Wolzogen in words glowing with emotion:

> You see, my dear one, quite unexpected joys sometimes befall your friend, joys which are the more valuable because free will and pure disinterested emotion have given rise to them. Such a gift from unknown persons, occasioned only by pure esteem, having no other cause but the wish to express recognition for a few pleasant hours I have given them—such a present is a greater reward than the loud applause of the world, the only sweet compensation for a thousand gloomy minutes.

Such recognition based on sympathy and understanding seems to him the true fame for which he has striven:

> And if I pursue the thought further and consider that there are perhaps more such circles in the world, who love me unknown to me and would like to make my acquaintance, that perhaps in a hundred years or more, when my ashes have long been dispersed, my memory will be blessed and people will pay me a tribute of tears and admiration when I am in my grave, then, my dearest friend, I rejoice in my calling and am reconciled with God and my hard fate.

The brief-case lay on his desk and the four pictures were hung on the wall above it; but although he learned the names of his four admirers, he did not answer their letters.

He was busy at this time preparing his inaugural address to the German Society of the Palatinate. Conscious now more than ever of the nobility and dignity of his mission as a dramatic poet, aware, too, of the doubts as to his ability and importance which were beginning to circulate in Mannheim, Schiller determined to make his speech a justification of himself and of the art he served. The title he chose for the speech, which he delivered on June 26, 1784, was *Was kann eine gute stehende Schaubühne eigentlich wirken?* (*What Actual Effect can a Good Permanent Theatre have?*)[2].

---

[1] *Lovely as Angels.*

[2] In 1802 Schiller altered the title to *Die Schaubühne als moralische Anstalt betrachtet* (*The Theatre considered as a Moral Institution*).

In noble and eloquent prose Schiller enumerates the moral functions of the theatre. It can be the handmaid of religion and law, supporting their tenets by illustration. The theatre helps us to support the blows of fate, and is the only voice which can point out to the rich and powerful their follies and crimes. It is an important instrument of education and enlightenment, and a means of bringing about national consciousness: " wenn wir es erlebten, eine Nationalbühne zu haben, so würden wir auch eine Nation."[1] It is the best and most wholesome recreation:

> Die Schaubühne ist die Stiftung, wo sich Vergnügen mit Unterricht, Ruhe mit Anstrengung, Kurzweil mit Bildung gattet, wo keine Kraft der Seele zum Nachteil der andern gespannt, kein Vergnügen auf Unkosten des ganzen genossen wird.[2]

Schiller's address is a powerful defence of the drama. He allots it a place in the state beside religion and law. In many respects it stands, he considers, higher than they. He interprets its moral value in subtler and more realistic terms than his predecessors had devised. The illustration of morality, the exposure of folly, the castigation of vice, and the lauding of virtue—all these he sees as functions of the drama; but he considers the direct moral effect, the cure of vice or the prevention of crime, to be a relatively unimportant one.

The vital aspect of his theory is the contention that the theatre is the best form of recreation, for he treats this recreation as necessary for mental health and as *a moral value in itself.*

> Wenn Gram am Herzen nagt, wenn trübe Laune unsre einsamen Stunden vergiftet, wenn uns Welt und Geschäfte anekeln, wenn tausend Lasten unsre Seele drücken und unsre Reizbarkeit unter Arbeiten des Berufs zu ersticken droht, so empfängt uns die Bühne: in dieser künstlichen Welt träumen wir die wirkliche hinweg, wir werden uns selbst wiedergegeben, unsre Empfindung erwacht, heilsame Leiden-schaften erschüttern unsre schlummernde Natur und treiben das Blut in frischeren Wallungen.[3]

The effect of the drama is to achieve a balance of mind: " Der Unglückliche weint hier mit fremdem Kummer seinen eignen aus,

---

[1] If we could have a national stage, we should be a nation.

[2] The stage is the institution which combines pleasure with instruction, amusement with education, which develops no spiritual faculty to the detriment of another, no single pleasure at the expense of the whole.

[3] When grief gnaws at the heart, when depression poisons our lonely hours, when the world and our affairs nauseate us, when a thousand burdens press upon our souls and the cares of our callings threaten to stifle our sensitivity, then, in such moods, the stage receives us: in this artificial world we dream the real one away, we return to ourselves, our feelings revive, healthy passions shake our sleeping constitution and send our blood pulsing more freely through our veins.

der Glückliche wird nüchtern, der Sichere besorgt."[1] And the art
of the theatre is a social art; men gather to laugh together and to
mourn together, and this community of joy and suffering and the
bond between man and man which it forges are the supreme moral
values of the drama.

It is a noble conception of the part which the theatre can play
in the life of the individual and of society. For Schiller it was a
justification of his own chosen path. One passage, omitted from the
final version of 1802, was a passionate protest against the shortsighted and narrow views of those who saw in the theatre only a
trivial amusement or a means of making money, and regarded the
dramatic writer as a lower creature than the civil servant or the
scholar because his life was more precarious. It is Schiller's own
experience in Mannheim which throbs beneath his anger and
contempt:

> Man verurteilt den jungen Mann, der, gedrungen von innerer
> Kraft, aus dem engen Kerker einer Brotwissenschaft heraustritt und
> dem Rufe des Gottes folgt, der in ihm ist? — Ist das die Rache der
> kleinen Geister an dem Genie, dem sie nachzuklimmen verzagen. . . ?
> Nichts ist bekannter und nichts gereicht zugleich der gesunden Vernunft
> mehr zur Schande als der unversöhnliche Hass, die stolze Verachtung,
> womit Fakultäten auf freie Künste heruntersehen.[2]

Schiller's mind was now occupying itself with many theoretical
problems relating to his art. He conceived the idea of a periodical
dealing with the drama and forming a Mannheim counterpart to
Lessing's famous *Hamburgische Dramaturgie*. Schiller first mentioned it to Reinwald in a letter of May 5, 1784, and formulated
the detailed plan in a memorandum to Dalberg of July 2, 1784.
Very likely Dalberg, impressed by Schiller's speech to the Society,
had in conversation expressed some interest in the scheme. Schiller's
programme embraced a history of the Mannheim Theatre, an
account of its constitution, biographies and criticisms of the actors,
an annotated record of the repertoire, and essays on dramatic art.
It was this item that interested Schiller most. Yet though he undertook to carry out all clerical tasks and business arrangements, as well
as to edit the journal—and all for an honorarium of fifty florins a
year—Dalberg was not to be tempted. He was beginning to weary
of Schiller, who still showed no sign of delivering his third play.

---

[1] The unhappy man weeps away his own sorrow with that of others, the happy
man becomes thoughtful, he who fancies himself secure becomes anxious.

[2] People condemn the young man, who, driven by a power within him, quits
the narrow prison of a professional career and follows the call of the god within
him. . . ? Is this the revenge of little spirits, who dare not follow the genius as he
scales the heights? Nothing is more familiar and nothing more disgraceful to
reason than the irreconcilable hatred, the proud contempt with which the faculties
regard the liberal arts.

On May 5, 1784, Schiller had written to Reinwald that his continuation as house-dramatist for another year was regarded as settled. Late in June Dr. May, the theatre's doctor and a friend of Dalberg, called on Schiller and passed on a message from the director, advising a return to the study of medicine. It was a plain hint that the contract would not be renewed. So far was Schiller, however, from realizing this, that he interpreted the message as a sign of a sympathetic interest in his career and fortunes, and imagined Dalberg perhaps ready to extend a helping hand. The next day he wrote thanking Dalberg for his interest and asking him to advance the money for one year's study of medicine, after which he would again be at the service of the theatre. According to his usual practice with letters which he found embarrassing, Dalberg wrote no answer.

No doubt he regretted ever having engaged Schiller. He could more cheaply have bought the two plays already written, for that is all he had gained from the contract. There was still no word of the third play, and he thought it extremely unlikely that he would ever see it. Other authors could deliver plays promptly—plays which suited the public taste better than Schiller's. Dalberg's discovery in this year had been Iffland. For some time one of the leading actors in Mannheim, Iffland had suddenly emerged with *Das Verbrechen aus Ehrsucht* as a dramatist of talent. To the modern eye, enjoying the advantage of viewing them from a distance, Iffland's plays are clearly hack-work, designed for popular taste. But for the contemporary it is more difficult to divide the wheat from the chaff, and for Dalberg a play was a good one if it filled the house. With such an excellent and dependable dramatist in his company Dalberg felt that he could dispense with the house-dramatist.

It had really been a mistake of Dalberg's to create this post, and of Schiller's to accept it. A dramatist of power and originality could not bind himself to deliver plays at stated intervals; and Schiller's reputation was not yet sufficiently firmly established for his mere name to be a valuable asset to the theatre.

To Dalberg's impatience was soon added Iffland's jealousy. A master of intrigue, Iffland undermined Schiller's position, while maintaining a show of disinterested friendship. The climax came when the comedy *Der schwarze Mann*, by F. W. Gotter, was performed in Mannheim on August 3, 1784. One of the characters, named Flickwort (word-patcher), is a house-dramatist and is the principal butt of Gotter's wit. Iffland played the part dressed and made up to look like Schiller. This stroke of malice delighted the audience, and Schiller, who was then in the neighbouring village of Schwetzingen all ignorant of what was going on, became overnight an object of derision.

This episode, which shook Schiller's reputation in Mannheim, made, however, little impression on him, for he already had troubles enough on his hands. In mid-July, while his sister and Reinwald were visiting him, Schiller suffered the severest blow he had yet sustained. The guarantor for one of his debts in Stuttgart, pressed by the creditors, fled to Mannheim, was there arrested for debt, and thrown into prison. It was Schiller's evident duty to rescue his surety. But where was he to find the money? He had none himself, and neither Reinwald, Christophine, nor Streicher had the means to pay off this debt. The situation seemed utterly desperate, when help came from a most unexpected quarter. The mason, Anton Hölzel, and his wife, with whom Schiller lodged, were simple, kindly folk who had taken a liking to the young man. Hearing of his straits, they advanced the two hundred florins necessary to dispose of the debt and release the surety. It was an act of touching kindness, for the sum represented a large part of their savings. Years afterwards Schiller was glad to have an opportunity to render them some service when they in turn were in need.

These more pressing worries drew Schiller's attention away from the attempt to lampoon him in the performance of *Der schwarze Mann*. But August was a black month, for the days drifted on and still Dalberg spoke no word either about a renewal of the contract or about the loan Schiller had requested for his medical studies. A few days before the contract ran out Schiller wrote again to Dalberg in terms implying that he would continue in his post, but this effort to elicit a reply from Dalberg failed, and Schiller automatically ceased to be employed by the theatre on September 1, 1784. He was now again without income; he had no salary outstanding, for he had drawn the last of it as early as December 1783. Relations with his father, too, had deteriorated again; Captain Schiller wrote sombre, reproachful letters, to which his irritated and worried son returned unjust answers. Even the relationship with Frau von Wolzogen was disturbed, for, powerless to pay her what he owed her, he had been ashamed to write.

It would have been an intensely gloomy autumn but for his ever more intimate acquaintance with Frau von Kalb. Debarred by French custom from living with her husband in a garrison town, she had taken up residence in Mannheim in August. The acquaintance with Schiller, begun in May, was renewed. Charlotte von Kalb was a woman of great sensitiveness and emotional instability, which had been augmented by an unhappy childhood. She was two years younger than Schiller. As Fräulein von Marschalk-Ostheim, she had been married for reasons of fortune and family interest to Heinrich von Kalb in the previous year. She did not love her husband and, when Schiller met her, seemed to have renounced all claim to happiness.

Schiller became a regular visitor to her house soon after she had established herself at Mannheim. The friendship was then an intellectual one, for Charlotte von Kalb was intelligent and starved of cultural interests. Meanwhile the relations between Schiller and von Kalb continued cordial. Schiller's enthusiasm and poetic fire brought a new interest and a warmth of sympathy into her life; and he, for the first time, met a woman who had some understanding for his work. Throughout the autumn her friendship consoled Schiller for the shocks and the neglect which he encountered elsewhere.

During the late summer and the autumn he worked at his tragedy about Don Carlos. In striking contrast to all his previous plays, it was in iambic verse. Eventually he read a portion of the work to Frau von Kalb, who, to his disgust and dismay, told him it was the worst thing he had yet written. Schiller went away in dudgeon, leaving his manuscript behind him. Left alone, Frau von Kalb read the scenes herself and was entranced. Schiller's exaggerated ranting, as once before with *Fiesco*, had distorted his work and prevented his hearer from appreciating it.

Towards the end of the year Charlotte von Kalb rendered Schiller a very practical service. Duke Karl August of Weimar, Goethe's patron, paid a visit to Darmstadt in December. Frau von Kalb furnished Schiller with a letter of introduction to a lady of the Hessian court at Darmstadt. Armed with this, and carrying the manuscript of the first act of *Don Carlos* in the brief-case given him by his Leipzig admirers, Schiller arrived at Darmstadt on December 23, 1784. He was well received, and on Boxing Day was invited to read his fragment of *Don Carlos* to the assembled court, which included the important guest from Weimar. Schiller had profited by Charlotte von Kalb's tuition both in recitation and in social behaviour, and his performance made an excellent impression. In conversation with Duke Karl August he expressed his hope of some form of public recognition, which was fulfilled the following morning by a cordial note from the Duke granting him the title of Saxon-Weimar Counsellor (*Sachsen-Weimarischer Rat*). The official patent reached him on January 14, 1785. It was more to him than a mere title; it meant that in the eyes of the world he enjoyed the recognition, patronage, and protection of a prince famous in Germany for his encouragement of literature; it meant that he could parade a visible dignity which would appease the anxiety and allay the scepticism of his father; and it gave him an air of respectability which might ease the pressure of his creditors.

G

But he could not live on an honorary title, however welcome it might be. His life seemed to be one involved financial tangle and he had to devise some scheme by which he could attempt to unravel it. He decided to venture again into journalism. He conceived the idea of publishing a bi-monthly periodical concerned mainly with the theatre. It was a development and broadening of the *Mannheimer Dramaturgie* which he had suggested to Dalberg in July. The title of the journal was to be *Die rheinische Thalia*. In November Schiller wrote a prospectus which he had printed and distributed to many notable men of letters and to every friend he could recollect. It contained not only his programme together with the price and terms of subscription, but also a brief autobiographical sketch in which he summarized his career at the Academy and spoke with cool detachment of *Die Räuber*. However dynamic the work, its glaring faults must inevitably cause Schiller to reject it, once he reached some degree of maturity. His epigrammatic dismissal of his first play in this essay as the issue of " der naturwidrige Beischlaf der Subordination und des Genius,"[1] though only a half-truth, proves that he had turned his back on the extravagances of his adolescence.

Schiller's sanguine temperament did not desert him when he began to calculate the probable success of *Die rheinische Thalia*. Basing his estimate on a probable subscribers' list of five hundred, he reckoned that his annual net income from the enterprise would be a thousand florins. In fact, the number of subscribers was so small that he had to abandon his plan of printing a list of their names in the first number for fear of making his journal an object of ridicule. He had worked very hard and devoted great energy to the commercial side as well as to the literary contents of the periodical, but it was all to no purpose. His hopes of financial gain proved once more to be illusory.

The first number of *Die rheinische Thalia* appeared in the middle of March 1785. It was to be the only issue to bear this title. It contained Schiller's inaugural address to the German Society of the Palatinate, the translation of an episode from Diderot's *Jacques le Fataliste*, various small items concerning the Mannheim theatre, and a fictitious letter about the Hall of Classical Sculpture (*Der Antikensaal zu Mannheim*). This is the first hint of the opening up of a new world for Schiller, a panegyric on the nobility of Greek art, which is " Eine unwidersprechliche ewige Urkunde des göttlichen Griechenlands."[2] But the most important by far of Schiller's contributions to *Die rheinische Thalia* was the first act of *Don Carlos*, dedicated to his new patron, Duke Karl August of Weimar.

[1] The unnatural cohabitation of subordination and genius.
[2] An incontrovertible eternal document of divine Greece.

Die rheinische Thalia appeared when spring was almost at hand. Its preparation had occupied four long winter months, filled with bitterness, agitation, and worry. Schiller's relations with the direction and company of the Mannheim Theatre became strained; his debts were undiminished, though the pressure of his creditors had relaxed; his father still viewed his present life and future prospects with misgiving. Only his visits to Frau von Kalb brought some light into his life as the year drew to a close.

Fits of depression became frequent, in which the outlook seemed hopeless and all his efforts bound to fail. On December 7, 1784, he was a prey to just such a mood, when he suddenly remembered the tributes he had received six months before from Leipzig. They had given him such joy at the time, it seemed incredible that he had made no acknowledgment then nor sought to make contact with his friends there since. In the bleakness of his situation as he saw it that evening, the disinterested regard of his Leipzig admirers was the only bright gleam. He sat down at his desk with the four portraits on the wall before him and began to write " to the circle of Leipzig admirers." His letter was apologetic, grateful, and open-hearted, and it included a wish to correspond further and the hope that he might be able to visit them in Leipzig, perhaps on his way to Berlin.

A delay ensued before this letter was answered. Meanwhile Schiller was honoured by the Duke of Weimar, worked at *Die rheinische Thalia*, and paid more and more attention to Frau von Kalb. At last, in the second half of January, letters from the Leipzig friends arrived. In words full of understanding and warm regard Gottfried Körner honoured Schiller's talent and invited him to visit them all in Leipzig.

Without either party being aware of it, Schiller's friendship with Charlotte von Kalb had meanwhile developed into something more intimate and more passionate; and soon it was clear that they were in love. But they were separated by rank and even more decisively by Charlotte's marriage. Passionate revolt flamed up. Into his poem *Freigeisterei der Leidenschaft* (*The Passionate Protest*)[1] Schiller, normally so unwilling to write purely personal poetry, poured his fierce anger against the barriers of society and convention:

> O, zittre nicht — du hast als Sünderin geschworen,
>   Ein Meineid ist der Reue fromme Pflicht.
> Das Herz war mein, das du vor dem Altar verloren,
>   Mit Menschenfreuden spielt der Himmel nicht.

---

[1] Published in a severely shortened form which disguises its personal significance and with the non-committal title *Der Kampf* (*The Conflict*).

Zum Kampf auf die Vernichtung sei er vorgeladen,
   Auf den der feierliche Spruch dich band.
Die Vorsicht kann den überflüss'gen Geist entraten,
   Für den sie keine Seligkeit erfand.

Getrennt von dir — warum bin ich geworden?
   Weil du bist, schuf mich Gott!
Er widerrufe, oder lerne Geister morden,
   Und flüchte mich vor seines Wurmes Spott.[1]

The quivering personal note, the cry of torment in these lines, omitted by Schiller on publishing the poem, are unmistakable. It is the only occasion when the fire of his tragedies glows in his poetry. And for one so averse from public display of his emotions, to have written such a passionate and subjective poem proves how acute and grave was the crisis in his life.

He was not the man to carry on a clandestine love-affair. Either he must possess Frau von Kalb, a married woman, in the eyes of all the world, with all the social and economic consequences such an act would entail; or he must renounce her and sever the relationship. Whichever choice he made was torment, and his present indecision torment, too. At last in February he put an end to his doubts and hesitations by breaking matters off.

Schiller's experience in these days after his renunciation of Frau von Kalb is vividly conveyed by the letter to Körner and his friends in Leipzig which he began on February 10, and left unfinished on being interrupted by a visitor. When he took up his pen again twelve days later the thing had happened:

> (Here I was interrupted by an unexpected visitor, and in these last twelve days a revolution has taken place in my affairs and my heart that gives this letter more importance than I had dreamed—which marks an epoch in my life.) I cannot stay in Mannheim any longer. . . . There is no soul here, no single soul that can fill the void in my heart, neither man nor woman; and the one who could *perhaps* be dear to me is parted from me by convention and rank.

It is a cry of pain, and it is followed by an urgent cry for help. Schiller proposes to come to Leipzig. The more intolerable his situation in Mannheim appears to him, the more golden is the prospect of Leipzig.

---

[1] Oh, do not tremble, your solemn oath was a sin and to obey the pious duty of repentance would make you forsworn. Your heart was mine before you gave it at the altar, heaven does not sport with human joys.

I challenge him to whom that solemn word bound you to a combat of annihilation. Providence can determine which is the superfluous spirit, for whom it designed no happiness.

Parted from you—why was I born? God created me because he made you. He must recant or learn to destroy souls and so save me from his creature's scorn.

Something great, something inexpressibly pleasant must await me there, for the thought of my departure turns Mannheim into a prison, and the horizon weighs upon me like the thought of a murder upon the murderer—Leipzig seems to my dreams and premonitions like the rosy dawn beyond the hills.

All his interest, all his energy is concentrated on leaving Mannheim as soon as possible. It will only take three or four weeks, he thinks, to wind up his affairs there. He talks of going on from Leipzig to Weimar, there to present himself to his patron Karl August; but it is the new friends, the prospect of a life with sympathetic spirits who understand him and his work, that fill Schiller's mind at this time.

One serious practical difficulty still lay in the way of his departure. He must be able to settle his debts in Mannheim and above all to repay the Hölzels' generous loan. He therefore wrote to Leipzig on February 28, asking Huber, one of the group of friends, to arrange for a bookseller to take over the *Thalia* and to make Schiller an advance of three hundred florins on it. Göschen in Leipzig accepted the journal, and Körner's generosity provided Schiller with the sum he needed to put his affairs in some sort of order before leaving Mannheim.

He remained all impatience to leave, and though his original estimate of three to four weeks proved too short, he was ready early in April. The night of April 8 he spent with Streicher. The two friends stayed up the whole night discussing the time they had spent together and their hopes and plans for the future. In the early morning of April 9 Schiller said good-bye to Streicher—as it proved, for life—and left on his journey to Leipzig.

Schiller's departure from Mannheim for Leipzig closed more than a chapter in his life. This journey was the first obvious boundary stone marking the turning-point in his mental and artistic development. The restraint of school had driven him into the furious reaction of *Die Räuber*—" Seine ganze Verantwortung sei das Klima, unter dem es geboren ward,"[1] he wrote in the prospectus for *Die rheinische Thalia*. Fear, uncertainty, and want had prolonged that state, but a new and positive attitude, no longer a mere reaction to outward stress, demanded free room and scope in which to unfold. Through the four years which had elapsed since he had left the Academy he had slowly and imperceptibly changed. He had grown out of the realistic tradition of domestic tragedy. He had developed an increasing antipathy to the obviously personal in literary work, even going so far as to suppress two-thirds of his one

---

[1] Let the responsibility for it be attributed to the climate in which it was born.

genuinely personal poem, *Freigeisterei der Leidenschaft.* His gaze was more clearly turned outwards, his interest was in the actions and thoughts of others. Hitherto literary tradition and an unsettled and disturbing life had prevented him from developing the impersonal and universal art to which he tended. The beginnings had been made; his speech *Die Schaubühne als moralische Anstalt betrachtet* was his first flight into the sphere of aesthetic theory, his essay *Der Antikensaal zu Mannheim* revealed his gathering admiration for the impersonal art of the Greeks, and above all the magnificent first act of *Don Carlos* proved that he had found and forged a style which purged intense personal experience of all that was local and particular till it glowed with another and, as it seemed to him, a purer fire.

These were beginnings, but a hopeless love-affair, debts, personal enmities, and daily cares dogged his step and diverted him from his goal. " So far adverse fate has hindered my schemes. My heart and my poetry had simultaneously to succumb to necessity," he wrote to Körner. He needed a new climate, new friends, new contacts, emotional calm, and freedom from care—in a word, a complete change of environment, which would allow him to develop his new style, free from the associations of the old. It was this that he hoped to gain from Leipzig.

Chapter Eight

LEIPZIG AND DRESDEN
1785-87

SCHILLER had left Mannheim on April 9, 1785. Winter still maintained its grip on the countryside, and mud, snow, and flood delayed his progress. During the nine days that he was on the road (two more than the journey normally demanded) Schiller had ample leisure to speculate about the friends he was going to meet and about his future course.

It was no part of his plan to live at Körner's expense. He still had great hopes for *Die rheinische Thalia*, in spite of the disappointing public response to the first number. And while he earned his living by journalism, he might, he thought, study the law, a plan which he had discussed with Streicher the night before his departure, for he already felt the need of some assured financial basis. He also nourished a vague hope that a visit to his new patron, the Duke of Weimar, would somehow benefit his career.

On April 17 he at last arrived at the Blue Angel Inn in Leipzig, wearied and bruised from the jolting and swaying of his long journey. His first step was to send a note to Huber, the younger of his two men admirers; the other, Körner, was not in Leipzig, but at his home in Dresden.

Schiller now met three of his four new friends, Huber and the two Stock sisters. Ferdinand Huber was an intelligent youth of twenty-one, whose will-power had been inhibited by the strict control of a domineering mother. He was engaged to Dora Stock, the elder daughter of Goethe's Leipzig drawing-master. She was twenty-five, slightly deformed, and possessed appreciable artistic gifts— she had executed the four portraits sent to Schiller. Her attractive younger sister, Minna, the embroiderer of Schiller's brief-case, was engaged to Körner.

Christian Gottfried Körner, whom Schiller met some weeks later, was the most notable personality of the four. Born in 1756, Körner had studied law and had then at the age of twenty-three travelled as the companion of a Saxon count, visiting the Low Countries, France, Switzerland, and England. In 1783 he received an administrative appointment in Dresden. In the previous year he had become engaged to Minna Stock against the wishes of his parents, and a long period of betrothal seemed inevitable. But early in 1785 the death of his father left him comfortably off and opened up the prospect of an early marriage. Körner was a just judge of others' ability and scope. His own creative capacity was slight, though contact with Schiller aroused in him a desire to write which he could rarely fulfil. Generous, true and unselfish, he constantly sought in a practical yet discreet way to help others.

The company of two girls, both engaged to be married, made Schiller very much aware of his own solitary state. Exactly a week after he had arrived in Leipzig he wrote a letter to Schwan in Mannheim formally asking for Margarete's hand. Schwan rejected the proposal without informing his daughter, and Schiller, who had acted on a sudden impulse, let the matter drop.

At the beginning of May Schiller moved to the village of Gohlis, a popular summer resort. Huber and the Stock sisters were there, too, and a friend of Körner's, the young publisher Göschen (who had taken over *Die rheinische Thalia*), came to share Schiller's lodgings at the end of May. On July 1, 1785, Schiller and Körner met at last at the village of Kahnsdorf, close to Leipzig. They took to each other at once, and Schiller's extravagant enthusiasm was expressed in a long letter written to Körner two days later. "How beautiful and how divine is the contact of two souls, who meet on their way to the Godhead," he wrote, and went on to compare the drinking of Körner's health by Göschen, Huber, and himself to the Last Supper.

On August 7 Körner and Minna Stock were married in Leipzig, and Dora Stock went to live with them in their new home in Dresden. Schiller remained alone at Gohlis, for Huber and Göschen, though they often came out to visit him, had returned to their Leipzig quarters. As the weather deteriorated and autumn set in early, depression and gloom descended upon Schiller in his solitude.

He was to move to Dresden as soon as Huber obtained an appointment there, but this uncertain prospect was too slow for him, and early in September he wrote to Körner, asking if he might come at once. In reply there came a cordial invitation, which reached him at dusk on the evening of September 10. He packed at once and left the next morning before first light.

In the afternoon of September 12 the four friends moved out to Körner's country house and vineyard at Loschwitz, about three miles outside the city. "These are going to be divine days," Schiller wrote to Huber on September 13. Happiness, good humour, and harmony prevailed, and Schiller hoped to press on with his *Don Carlos*; but progress was slow. Perhaps there was too much harmony; the hours when he was not writing were too agreeable.

He also grew more and more conscious of the gaps in his historical knowledge, and his writing came almost to a halt because of the necessity for more and more thorough preparation. His studies for *Don Carlos* resulted in his first modest historical work, a translation of a French essay on Philip II by Louis-Sébastien Mercier, which he published in *Die Thalia* in February 1786.

Though the harmony and concord of Schiller's days in Dresden were no help to his work on *Don Carlos*, they inspired him to write a poem praising the joys of friendship. The famous ode *An die Freude* (*To Joy*) was the first of his poems to become popular, and Beethoven's use of it nearly forty years later as the text in the last movement of the Ninth Symphony has achieved for it an even wider fame. The poem, which is first mentioned in a letter to Göschen dated November 29, 1785, was written some time during that autumn. It is a dynamic hymn praising joy as a social, cosmic, and moral force. Schiller sees it as the power which breaks down the barriers separating man from man:

> Deine Zauber binden wieder,
> Was die Mode streng geteilt,
> Alle Menschen werden Brüder
> Wo dein sanfter Flügel weilt.[1]

Joy is the great driving force in nature, whether animate or inanimate:

> Freude heisst die starke Feder
> In der ewigen Natur,
> Freude, Freude treibt die Räder
> In der grossen Weltenuhr.[2]

It brings humanity to man—

> Unser Schuldbuch sei vernichtet!
> Ausgesöhnt die ganze Welt![3]

Under its magic influence the poet together with his friends swears an oath to lead a noble and upright, charitable and courageous life:

> Festen Mut in schwerem Leiden,
> Hilfe, wo die Unschuld weint,
> Ewigkeit geschwornen Eiden,
> Wahrheit gegen Freund und Feind,
> Männerstolz vor Königsthronen—

[1] Your magic unites again what fashion has rigidly parted, wherever your gentle wing pauses all men become brothers.

[2] Joy is the strong spring in eternal nature. It is joy that drives the vast machine of the universe.

[3] Let all resentment be wiped out, the whole world reconciled.

Brüder, gält' es Gut und Blut:
Dem Verdienste seine Kronen,
Untergang der Lügenbrut ![1]

The poet and his friends are to swear this *together*, for the ode is
social in form, consisting of stanzas separated by choruses to be
sung by the full choir of friends; and friendship is celebrated as the
supreme source of joy—

Wem der grosse Wurf gelungen
Eines Freundes Freund zu sein.[2]

Schiller's love and his desire for joy cannot be confined to the
narrow circle of his own immediate friends, but must enfold the
entire human race—

Seid umschlungen, Millionen!
Diesen Kuss der ganzen Welt! [3]

The Schiller who wrote this reveals his identity with the author of
Die Räuber ; Karl Moor's anger had condemned all men, Schiller's
joy embraces all. Whatever the youthful Schiller does, he must do
with all his heart and with all his soul. His optimism is as excessive
as his depression. Hating all that is lukewarm, he must feel every
mood with the utmost possible intensity. Not only must he scale
the supreme heights and plumb the profoundest depths, but an
innate impulse drives him constantly from narrow detail to the broad
sweep, from isolated experience to universal validity. This desire
to generalize produces a style full of fire and eloquence, but without
tenderness or individual subtlety. The exalted emotion is carried
along on a surging torrent of impetuous and cosmic rhetoric.

The tense and concentrated quality of this poem creates a fragile
mood, easily damaged by ridicule. Schiller was capable of humour
when it was not inhibited by intensity of feeling or thought, and
various minor works in addition to *Kabale und Liebe* reveal that he
could not only laugh at others, but also at himself. But it was only in
trifles, such as his *Bittschrift* (*Petition*), and *Körners Vormittag*
(*Körner's Morning*), private jokes written in Dresden for the benefit
of his own circle of friends, that he was ready to satirize himself.

Schiller's progress with *Don Carlos* remained slow. He found it
easier in that pleasant environment to compass short works than to
devote the continuous time and effort necessary for so large an
enterprise. The need to earn his living by something yielding quicker

---

[1] Firm courage in deep suffering, help where innocence weeps, eternity for
sworn oaths, truth against friend and foe, manly pride before kingly thrones.
Even if it cost us life and wealth: merit shall be rewarded, the lying brood shall
perish!
[2] To all who have laid the great wager and won a friend.
[3] O ye millions, I embrace you, I give this kiss to the whole world!

profits also made itself felt. Though Körner had declared, " For a year at any rate let me have the pleasure of saving you from the necessity of earning your bread," Schiller was determined to be independent if he could. Under the title *Die Thalia* (for *Rheinisch* was inapplicable once he had left Mannheim), the second number of his journal appeared, nearly a year overdue, in February 1786. It contained the second act of *Don Carlos*, the translation of Mercier's *Philippe II*, the ode *An die Freude*, the two poems inspired by the crisis of Schiller's love for Charlotte von Kalb,[1] and a short story called *Der Verbrecher aus Infamie.*

Der Verbrecher aus verlorener Ehre (*Crime and Dishonour*), to use the new title given to it by Schiller in the revised edition of 1802, is a terse, compact work. In some twenty pages it covers the life history of a criminal, from childhood to execution. The central figure of Schiller's story is Christian Wolf, an innkeeper's son, who takes to poaching. Convicted three times, his third sentence of three years' penal servitude turns him into a real criminal, who, when the chance comes, murders the man who years before had informed against him. After this Wolf takes to the woods and becomes head of a robber gang; but his nature is not wholly corrupted and he seeks a chance to live usefully; all his petitions for pardon, however, are rejected, and he eventually surrenders and is executed. The original of Schiller's hero was Johann Friedrich Schwan, born in 1729 and executed for robbery in 1760 at Vaihingen in Würtemberg. Schiller no doubt heard in very early life of his exploits, for in his childhood the execution was still a recent occurrence, and Vaihingen was within easy walking distance of Stuttgart and the Solitude. But if he had heard of Schwan's career then he had forgotten it again; and it was while he was a pupil of the Academy that his attention was directed to it by Professor Abel, whose interest in the story led him to write an account of it.[2] Abel had a personal connexion with Schwan's story, as his father was the magistrate to whom Schwan surrendered.

Schiller's direct and simple story employs two methods of narration: he himself tells the beginning and the end, and allows the criminal himself to tell the middle part. He deals perfunctorily with Wolf's crimes, because he is not interested in them; what does interest him is how Wolf could commit them. For this reason he touches but lightly on the execution, mentioning Wolf's end at the beginning before the reader's sympathies are enlisted, and stopping the story as soon as Wolf admits his identity to the magistrate.

[1] *Der Kampf* and *Resignation.*
[2] *Lebensgeschichte Friedrich Schwans* (*Life History of Friedrich Schwan*), published in 1787, one year after Schiller's version, but written earlier. Schiller was clearly acquainted with it.

As Schiller's interest was psychological, he does his story-telling
tersely and economically.   Two pages of introduction reveal
Schiller's thesis.   Many persons of abnormal capacity for evil, he
considers, never discover or exercise their criminal tendencies, because modern life gives them no scope:

> Wie sehr würde man erstaunen, wenn man so manchen, dessen
> Laster in einer engen bürgerlichen Sphäre und in der schmalen Umzäu-
> nung der Gesetze jetzt ersticken muss, mit dem Ungeheuer Borgia in
> einer Ordnung zusammenfände.[1]

Schiller claims sympathy for the criminal, who has more in common
with the rest of mankind than is usually supposed: " Wir sehen
den Unglücklichen, der doch eben in der Stunde, wo er die Tat
beging, so wie er in der, wo er dafür büsset, Mensch war wie wir,
für ein Geschöpf fremder Gattung an."[2]   The truth-seeking psycho-
logist finds the cause of crime and abnormality " in der unveränder-
lichen Struktur der menschlichen Seele und in den veränderlichen
Bedingungen, welche sie von aussen bestimmen."[3]

Schiller closes this introduction with a noble defence of his
humane and understanding approach to the problem of crime:

> Wenn ich auch keinen der Vorteile hier in Anschlag bringe, welche
> die Seelenkunde aus einer solchen Behandlungsart der Geschichte
> zieht, so behält sie schon allein darum den Vorzug, weil sie den grausamen
> Hohn und die stolze Sicherheit ausrottet, womit gemeiniglich die
> ungeprüfte aufrechtstehende Tugend auf die gefallne herunterblickt,
> weil sie den sanften Geist der Duldung verbreitet, ohne welchen kein
> Flüchtling zurückkehrt, keine Aussöhnung des Gesetzes mit seinem
> Beleidiger stattfindet, kein angestecktes Glied der Gesellschaft von
> dem gänzlichen Brande gerettet wird.[4]

It is an intellectual and sober sympathy for the criminal, not a
sentimental one.   He frankly admits the bad elements in Wolf;
but he considers that society, having once condemned Wolf as a

---

[1] One would stand amazed to discover so many men, whose vices are now
stifled in a confined social sphere and the narrow limits of laws, placed in the same
category as the monster Borgia.

[2] We see the unhappy man as a creature of another order, and yet at the moment
when he committed the crime, as in the moment when he suffers for it, he was a
human being like ourselves.

[3] In the fixed structure of the human soul and the variable external circumstances which determine it.

[4] Even if I do not put forward any of the advantages which psychology derives
from such a treatment of history, this method still deserves preference because it
puts an end to the cruel scorn and the proud and secure aloofness with which
untried and unsullied virtue regard virtue which has fallen; and because it
propagates the gentle spirit of tolerance without which no fugitive will return,
no reconciliation will take place between the law and him who offends against it,
no infected member of society be preserved from utter ruin.

criminal, drives him to further crime: " In allen Entwürfen getäuscht, an allen Orten zurückgewiesen, wird er zum drittenmal Wilddieb."[1] Schiller touches one of the weak spots of all prison systems, the difficulty experienced by the released prisoner in finding employment. When he speaks of Wolf's third sentence he attacks the other vice of prisons, their tendency, by herding prisoners together, to deprave rather than to reform: " Ich betrat die Festung als ein Verirrter und verliess sie als ein Lotterbube."[2]

The message of *Der Verbrecher aus verlorener Ehre* is made the more impressive by the convincing and consistent portrayal of the character, actions, and motives of Christian Wolf. Though it is a frankly moral work, its noble message of sympathy with the outcast is not obtrusive, because the author has eliminated comment from the narrative, confining it to his introduction. Dignified restraint intensifies its effect.

No sooner was the number of *Die Thalia* published in which this story appeared than Schiller began to prepare for the third issue, which was published in May. Its most important feature was again an instalment of *Don Carlos*; it also contained a pseudo-philosophical essay entitled *Philosophische Briefe* (*Philosophical Letters*). The four letters purport to be written by two friends, three by Julius and one by Raphael; and the last letter of Julius contains Schiller's views stated in an essay entitled *Die Theosophie des Julius* (*The Theosophy of Julius*). It had been Schiller's intention that the work should consist of an interchange of letters between himself (Julius) and Körner (Raphael), but Körner was much occupied with business, and was besides fastidious and dilatory in writing, so that in the end Schiller himself wrote all four of the letters.

The *Philosophische Briefe* link the enthusiasms of Schiller's first year in Leipzig and Dresden with his earlier ideals of friendship. *Die Theosophie des Julius* assumes perfection as the aim of man and happiness as its result. As the perception of happiness renders us even happier, so we seek to spread happiness to others; and this endeavour is love in its most spiritual sense. Such a love is the enthusiastic friendship that he felt for Körner. The link with his youth is revealed by his quoting his own poem *Die Freundschaft*, first published in the *Anthologie* in 1781. The ideas embodied in this essay have no philosophical originality or intrinsic importance, but they help to throw a light on Schiller's mind at this time, revealing the continuity between this first year in Dresden and the period that preceded it.

[1] Disappointed in all his projects, repulsed at every point, he becomes for the third time a poacher.

[2] When I entered the prison I was one who had erred, I left it as a criminal.

Schiller's conception of friendship has an important connexion with his early work. Three years before he had written to Reinwald: "The poet must be less the *painter*, than the *beloved*, the *bosom friend* of his hero." In the *Philosophische Briefe* he goes further and maintains that the poet identifies himself so closely and so enthusiastically with his hero, that he becomes identical with him: "Ich bin überzeugt, dass in dem Momente des Ideals der Künstler, der Philosoph und der Dichter die grossen und guten Menschen wirklich sind, deren Bild sie entwerfen."[1] It is an important revelation of his early, subjective method of creation, which involved the temporary subordination and transformation of himself into his hero.

Schiller soon found his journalistic work for *Die Thalia* a strain. It brought him no pleasure, and prevented him from living as he would have wished. In April the Körners and Huber spent a fortnight in Leipzig, and Schiller, who remained behind to work at *Don Carlos* and *Die Thalia*, experienced a sensation of barrenness and frustration. With his friends away he could not settle down, and his letters are restless and dissatisfied, punctuated with sudden outbursts of emotion, such as—"Oh, my dear friends, how I long for you. And how much out of humour this friendless solitude makes me." When, however, the Körners came back Schiller found that he could not regain his former happiness. The fortnight's separation had provoked a crisis. He was disturbed by his semi-dependence upon Körner, and alarmed at the persistence of his irritability and unproductiveness after his friends' return.

In his earlier years he had created out of conflict, and the atmosphere of conflict had permeated his whole life. Discord had stimulated him, opposition had struck fire from his soul. Now he was happy and lived in harmony, but happiness, he found, was a mental narcotic, and under its influence his creative powers seemed to be waning; and the consciousness of this decline became a source of new unhappiness. But the root of the trouble lay deeper. Schiller had outgrown his youth and found nothing to replace it. Even if he had never gone to Dresden he could not have continued writing as he had done hitherto. He must find a new approach and a new style, and to do that he must wrestle with himself. His present happiness distracted him from this task. To leave the Körners seemed to be the only solution to his dilemma, but it was one which he was not yet prepared to face.

Meanwhile he was dissatisfied with himself for another reason,

---

[1] I am convinced that in the matter of the ideal the artist, the philosopher, and the poet really are the great and good men whose image they are portraying.

as yet only dimly connected with the future of his creative genius. The further he progressed with *Don Carlos*, the more acutely he became conscious of his ignorance of history. He felt more and more that he was building his new tragedy upon sand. The work on *Don Carlos* became even slower as the urge to study history grew in force. On April 15, 1786, he had written to Körner: "History becomes dearer to me every day." In May he advised Huber to turn to historical writing. In August he undertook to edit for the publisher Crusius a collection of monographs on great conspiracies and rebellions. But though he stimulated others to write, he confined himself at this time to reading more and more widely in history.

Schiller's affection for the Körners enabled him to weather the crisis of May. He stayed on in Dresden and settled down again to work at *Don Carlos* and *Die Thalia*. No. 4 of this periodical was to contain not only the usual instalment of his new tragedy, but the beginning of an entirely new work, *Der Geisterseher (The Man who saw Ghosts)*. For Schiller it was a fresh venture, for *Der Geisterseher* was a novel, which he proposed to publish in instalments. The background of the book was the growing interest in supernatural phenomena, stimulated by the discovery of electrical forces and of hypnotic and mesmeric powers, to which many, whose minds were wearied by the narrow rationalistic outlook of the age, turned with eagerness and hope. The new discoveries became the pretext for an extravagant reaction, for beliefs in spirits and apparitions and for the practice of alchemy. This new occultism was exploited and put to great commercial profit by skilful impostors, of whom the most famous is Cagliostro.

The first part of *Der Geisterseher* deals with the summoning of a dead man's spirit and its exposure as a very clever fraud. But the theme of the whole book is a complex and successful Catholic intrigue, which aims at the conversion of the Protestant heir to the throne of a German state. Five instalments appeared in Nos. 4 to 8 of the *Thalia* (1787–89); the last of these, called *Der Abschied (The Parting)* is termed a "fragment from the second volume." But the rest of the second volume never appeared. Schiller grew to detest this novel. Nothing in its theme was of vital importance to him, and the necessity of delivering fresh instalments of what he felt to be a trivial work exasperated him.

In spite of his irritation with it, the story achieved considerable success. The theme was a popular one, the narrative style was fluent and clear, the construction designed to create a maximum of suspense. Financial reasons impelled Schiller to continue the instalments even after his interest in the work had almost entirely

lapsed. But his ever-increasing reluctance led him to make an
early end. In 1789 he quickly put the instalments together, inserted
Der Abschied in the middle of the fourth, added a perfunctory
conclusion, and published the book as *Der Geisterseher, Erster Teil.*
Readers from all over Germany clamoured for the second part, but
nothing could prevail upon Schiller to devote himself seriously
to it again—though he occasionally toyed with the idea of finishing
it. It remained a fragment, not only lacking an adequate conclusion,
but containing many discrepancies and gaps which had arisen through
the intermittent manner of Schiller's work on it and had remained
uncorrected through his loss of interest. The air of mystery of the
first book and the absorbing and intricate story of its unravelling
show that Schiller had the ability to write a good detective novel.
But the book has other qualities besides suspense and an intricate
plot; it gives a vivid account of life in Venice, its analysis of character
is shrewd, its movement rapid, and its presentation economical and
direct.

In the autumn of 1786 a chance to leave Dresden presented
itself to Schiller. An actor acquaintance in Mannheim wrote to him
suggesting that Schröder, the director of the Hamburg Theatre,
would be glad to produce *Don Carlos.* Schröder was well known
throughout Germany as one of the greatest actors and most intelligent
producers of the day, and Schiller immediately perceived all the advantages of this proposal. On October 12, 1786, he wrote to Schröder
offering him *Don Carlos* and all his future, yet unwritten, plays.

Schröder was prompt in his reply. He accepted *Don Carlos* and
proposed that Schiller should come to Hamburg as house-dramatist
on his own terms. This was a startling and tempting opportunity,
for no greater opportunity for dramatic fame existed at that time
than a close association with Schröder's stage. If would provide the
solution, too, to his worrying financial problem, for it meant an
assured income and freedom from the hack-journalism which took
so much time from his creative work and brought but a meagre
reward. On the other hand there were two reasons which weighed
against an acceptance of the Hamburg proposal. It was only two
years since Schiller had relinquished his appointment at Mannheim,
and the bitter contrast between his great expectations and their
fulfilment had remained fresh and vivid in his memory. He was so
happy, too, with the Körners that, in spite of the persistent feeling
that he ought for the sake of his creative powers to go, he was
reluctant to take a step which would place hundreds of miles between
them. For two months he hesitated, then on December 18, 1786, he
declined the invitation to Hamburg, though he agreed to Schröder's
request for *Don Carlos.*

Schiller's offer of his future plays was to prove valueless. *Don Carlos* was his last dramatic work for many years to come. The play with which he intended to follow it, *Der Menschenfeind* (*The Misanthropist*), remains a fragment, consisting of eight scenes in prose which give no clear idea of plot and development. The central figure, Herr von Hutten, bitterly disappointed by the conduct of his fellow-men, brings up his daughter to break their hearts. At the point where he makes this announcement the fragment breaks off. The source of the play had been Schiller's own bitterness and disillusionment; the mellowing effect of his stay in Dresden made it impossible for him any longer to write a tragedy on such a theme. But he could not make a comedy of it either. After it had lain for several years Schiller published it in 1790 in No. 9 of the *Thalia* under the title *Der versöhnte Menschenfeind*.

Schiller had undertaken to send the stage version of *Don Carlos* to Schröder in January; but when the time came it was not ready. It was not unusual for him to be behindhand with revision, but in the New Year of 1787 he was delayed by an unexpected distraction. He fell suddenly and desperately in love with an attractive nineteen-year-old girl, Henriette von Arnim, whom he met at a carnival ball. Her mother encouraged Schiller, not because she favoured the match, but because the presence of a well-known playwright lent distinction to her drawing-room and attracted other wealthier admirers of Henriette. Two months passed by during which he neglected his work entirely.

During a temporary absence of the Arnims from Dresden Schiller was at length persuaded by his friends, who viewed his passion and its object with misgiving, to spend some time in April at Tharandt, a village some nine miles from Dresden. The holiday, which the Körners hoped would diminish Henriette von Arnim's power over him, began badly amidst snow and hail. But in spite of initial discontent and restlessness he gradually found his thoughts turning from Henriette to his work. On his return to Dresden in May his eyes were opened to her flirtations with other admirers, and the episode came gradually and quietly to a close. Schiller returned to his work and at last had *Don Carlos* ready for Schröder in June.

The end of his brief passion for Henriette von Arnim was the signal for his departure from Dresden. It needed only some such disturbance of his pleasant associations to bring him to a decision; for it had been more and more borne in upon him that he must leave before long. The crisis of May 1786 had been followed by another in December, when the Körners had spent Christmas away from Dresden. In their absence Schiller was as restless and miserable as he had been at Easter. Much as he liked them, the sense of dependence upon them could not but be humiliating, for they as a happily married couple were independent of him.—" Will *my* image not fade more quickly with you than *yours* with me? . . . You meant so much to me, and I so little to you," he wrote on December 29, 1786. It is this sense of inequality in their relationship which led him later to write: " If I had not felt the degradation of my spirit so profoundly before I went away, I should never have left you."

He did not, however, contemplate leaving the Körners for good. He needed, it seemed to him, a temporary change, a period in which he could learn to live alone again and to feel independent. He decided to go to Weimar, the residence of his only patron, Duke Karl August. In a letter written on May 24, 1787, he had already made contact with Wieland, one of the best known of the small group of celebrated men of letters living in Weimar. Meanwhile the atmosphere in Dresden was as cordial as ever. On the evening of July 19 the five friends sat together and drank to their next meeting. On the following day Schiller set out for Weimar.

Schiller's two years spent with the Körners constitute the beginning of a much longer period of transition in his life. He emerged from years of solitude, ill-health, and financial embarrassment to find himself sheltered, cared for, and befriended. It is small wonder that his response to the new friendship and concord in the early months was an exaggerated one. Even after the first enthusiasm had subsided, he could not adapt himself properly to the new life. He was right in the high value he set upon Körner's combination of warm regard, tact, intellectual integrity, and rock-like solidity. But he was wrong about the way in which it could be of value to him. By a natural reaction he had leaned too heavily upon Körner. It was long before he realized this error and still longer before he could bring himself to act upon its recognition. But in the end he had to act.

The Körner household did not turn out to be the final haven he had so confidently believed it to be in the autumn of 1785. It was a port in which he was able to refit for a fresh voyage with a better compass and chart, and a secure base with which he could remain in contact. In the two years spent with the Körners he learned first the value of friendship and then the importance of standing on his own feet. The complete change which his life there underwent facilitated and quickened in his intellect and creative imagination a deeper development, which was imminent but unrealized before he came. With Körner's assistance Schiller set out to find himself. He alone could make the final discovery.

Chapter Nine

" *DON CARLOS* "

1787

SCHILLER'S departure from Dresden for Weimar coincided with the publication of the complete *Don Carlos*. Its beginnings reached back to the days in Stuttgart before he fled to Mannheim. His attention had first been drawn to the subject by Dalberg in May 1782, and in July of that year he had written of it as one of the subjects which he would treat in the near future. In Bauerbach the story had begun to engross his interest, and his first request for books after his arrival at Frau von Wolzogen's house included *Dom Carlos: nouvelle historique* by the Abbé de Saint-Réal, a seventeenth-century version of the fate of the only son of Philip II of Spain.

Saint-Réal's story is history romanticized. On the death of his first wife, Philip II married the young French princess Elizabeth, who was already betrothed to Philip's son Don Carlos, whom she had not yet seen. When they met, Don Carlos and Elizabeth fell in love. The jealousy of a lady of the court, Princess Eboli, obliged them to extreme caution, and they employed Carlos's friend, Marquis Posa, as a go-between. The King became suspicious of Posa and had him assassinated. Carlos meanwhile asked Philip for the governorship of the Spanish Netherlands, but his request was refused. He then planned to flee to the Netherlands and to lead a revolt against his father. The plot was discovered, he was arrested, and condemned to death. Shortly afterwards Elizabeth too died, apparently from poison.

Saint-Réal's sensational story pays little attention to historical truth. There is no evidence of a love-affair, and Carlos was not executed, but imprisoned in his own room. Neither was Marquis Posa a historical figure. Not that Saint-Réal had any obligation to adhere to facts; he quite frankly called his little work a " historical novel."

The inaccuracy of this story was immaterial. It gave scope for dramatic situations and the portrayal of character. On March 27, 1783, Schiller wrote as follows to Reinwald:

> I find that there is more underlying unity and interest in this story

than I had thought formerly, and that it gives me an opportunity for vivid portraits and powerful or moving scenes. The character of a youth, who is at once great, ardent, and sensitive, and is at the same time heir to several thrones; of a *queen* who, in spite of all the advantages of her situation, meets disaster through the attempt to compel her love; of a jealous father and husband; of a cruel and hypocritical inquisitor and barbarous Duke of Alba, etc.—all these could hardly fail.

This passage makes it clear that Schiller's interest at this time was not in history, but in a story; his attention was concentrated not on the political significance, but on the private characters of his persons. His reference to Philip II speaks of him only as husband and father; Marquis Posa, later to be so important a mouthpiece of the political purport of the play, is not so much as mentioned. More than a year later Schiller explicitly stated his intention of making the work a personal, and not a political, tragedy: " Carlos would decidedly be no political play, but rather a family drama in a princely house " (August 24, 1784).

About this time, too, a letter to Dalberg mentioning the important persons of the play: " Four great characters of almost similar scope; *Carlos, Philip*, the *Queen* and *Alba*," again made no allusion to any important part played by Posa. Indeed, Schiller's original plan, drawn up at Bauerbach and still extant, concentrates on the love of Carlos and Elizabeth, and in such a play Posa can only play a minor part.

From its first inception till the middle of the year 1786 (for in No. 3 of the *Thalia* Schiller repeats that the play is a family drama set in a royal house) Schiller's aim was to present a deeply moving picture of human passions; the rank and station of the persons would heighten the colour and dignify the tone of the tragedy. It was a play conceived on the lines of *Hamlet*, a comparison which Schiller himself had in mind, to judge from a letter written to Reinwald on April 14, 1783: " If I may use the comparison, Carlos's soul comes from Shakespeare's Hamlet, his blood and nerves from Leisewitz's Julius, and his *heart-beat* from me."

Superficial points of resemblance between the situations of Carlos and Hamlet are obvious. Each is crown prince, each hates his father and loves his mother. Philip's suspicious distrust of his son recalls Claudius's attitude to Hamlet. But Shakespeare was, on Schiller's own avowal, not the only writer to influence his conception. The violence of Carlos's passion for Elizabeth, who is separated from him by the laws of the state and of religion, owes something to the similar love of the hero of *Julius von Tarent;* and, like Julius, Carlos is determined to gain his end, cost what it may. If Carlos owes something to Hamlet and to Julius, he owes most of all to his creator. Not that Carlos is ever to be identified with Schiller, who, even in his most subjective early years, did not dramatize himself. He did, however, at this time of immaturity take sides, and so he writes of Carlos: " I must confess that he is almost like a sweetheart for me. I carry him in my heart—I go about the countryside round Bauerbach in raptures over him " (April 14, 1783).

This enthusiasm for the character of Carlos was the guiding force while Schiller was conceiving the play. If he could have written the work at once without interruption it would no doubt have been a love-tragedy in which Carlos himself was the outstanding figure. But circumstances delayed its progress. The adaptation of *Fiesco* and of *Kabale und Liebe*, sickness and financial worry, diverted Schiller's attention, so that he was more than a year without working at the play at all. In June 1784 he took it up again, intending that it should be the third play which he had contracted with Dalberg to write. For this purpose it was already too late. The attachment to Frau von Kalb, which developed in the autumn and winter of 1784, renewed his interest in it; for the relationship of Carlos and Elizabeth, drawn together by love, yet definitively parted by a rigid convention, offered a poignant situation closely resembling that in which he and Charlotte von Kalb found themselves. It was a love-tragedy that Schiller brought with him " in his head," as he put it, when he left Mannheim for Leipzig in April 1785.

The final version, which was published in 1787, is a very different one from that which Schiller had planned in 1783. Posa's politics prevail over Carlos's personal passion. Carlos loves Elizabeth, as in the earlier conception. His secret, which he must conceal from all the priests and courtiers, who watch to profit by his first false step, becomes an oppressive burden to him, until his former friend Marquis Posa returns from abroad. To him Carlos can reveal the fearful truth that he loves his stepmother. Posa is the advocate of a new, enlightened political order and plans to achieve his ideals with Carlos's assistance. He daringly arranges a meeting between Carlos and the Queen, who persuades her stepson to renounce his love and go as governor to the Netherlands.

But Carlos's new political resolutions encounter immediate difficulties, for Philip, fearful and jealous of his son, refuses him the governorship. Frustrated of his hope of escape and misled by a letter, which he wrongly believes to come from Elizabeth, Carlos relapses into his former criminal love. He recklessly betrays himself to Princess Eboli, who had believed herself loved by him, and the princess, in a fury of jealousy and spite, informs the king's advisers of Carlos's love for the Queen.

Though Philip's jealousy is stimulated to the utmost and disaster seems imminent, the situation takes a turn for the better, when, angered at the obvious delight with which his confessor and the Duke of Alba impart Carlos's secret, Philip suspects their motives and declines to accept their conclusions. Alone at the centre of his vast and populous empire, Philip feels desperately the need of the disinterested opinion of an honest man. He scans a list of deserving nobles, and his choice lights on Marquis Posa, whose forthright manner and contempt of flattery win the King's entire confidence.

Dazzled by his suddenly acquired power over Philip, Posa hesitates for a moment in his resolve to send Carlos to the Netherlands, for Philip might offer a more direct way of achieving his political ends—but it is only for a moment; affection for his friend and a preference for youth lead him back to his original plan. By devious paths and subtle intrigue he prepares the way for Carlos's flight. But his plans miscarry. Faced with sudden emergency he arrests Carlos, who is about to betray himself for the second time to Princess Eboli, and then writes letters deliberately diverting the King's suspicion from his son to himself, the new favourite.

Philip's reaction on discovering Posa's duplicity is swift. Without warning, the Marquis is shot. Carlos, instead of profiting by Posa's assumption of blame and fleeing to the Netherlands, delays out of mistaken fidelity to his friend until it is too late. He is discovered and handed over by Philip to the Inquisition.

In this later form of *Don Carlos* two momentous changes have taken place. Firstly, the love of Carlos and Elizabeth is replaced as the centre of interest by the political ideas which Posa represents; and secondly, Marquis Posa, a minor figure of the original plan, now overshadows Carlos and has become the real hero of the play. Schiller's whole conception had altered, as he himself freely admitted in the *Briefe über " Don Carlos "* (*Letters on " Don Carlos "*) of 1788 —" Neue Ideen, die indes bei mir aufkamen, verdrängten die frühern."[1]

Yet Schiller was already committed to the earlier conception, for half the play was already in the hands of the public. The first act had appeared in *Die rheinische Thalia* as early as March 1785, the second act in *Die Thalia* in February and May 1786, and a portion of the third in December 1786.[2] He had now the task of completing the work so as to incorporate in it a quite different set of ideas and values. Careful additions and minor alterations in the opening acts do something to prepare the mind for the developments which are

[1] The earlier ideas were displaced by new ones which had in the meantime arisen within me.

[2] The second act in *Die Thalia* comprises scenes i–xiii of the present text, the third act scenes xiii–xv of the present Act II and Act III, scene i to the middle of scene vii.

to follow, but the emotional key of the first act could not be altered without destroying it and starting anew. No piecemeal modification could displace Carlos from his central position, and the expectations aroused in the first act are therefore not fulfilled in those that follow. Schiller himself realized that the broadening of his conception had confronted him in *Don Carlos* with insoluble difficulties:

> Ich hatte mich zu lange mit dem Stücke getragen; ein dramatisches Werk aber kann und soll nur die Blüte eines einzigen Sommers sein. Auch der Plan war für die Grenzen und Regeln eines dramatischen Werks zu weitläufig angelegt.[1]

The first two acts of *Don Carlos* were conceived by a dramatist whose main interest was the passions of the human heart; the last three acts are the work of a more mature and calmer Schiller, whose mind was filled with the lessons of history and the humanitarian ideals of his age. The change was due partly to Körner's influence and the improved circumstances of Schiller's life, and partly to the historical reading to which *Don Carlos* itself had led him. Most of all, it was due to the maturing of Schiller's own character. It was a gradual development, but its critical phase took place in the spring of 1786. The first Schiller had loved Carlos, the second admired more moderately Marquis Posa, not for his character, but for the views he held and the cause he served. *Don Carlos* ceased to be a personal and became a political tragedy.

It was not necessary for Schiller to make any alterations to the character of Carlos; only his valuation has changed. Eager, ardent, and impetuous, Carlos has the misfortune to find himself obliged to retain in his breast a secret which he would give anything to impart. No man is less suited for repression and constraint, and Schiller has shown, by the suddenness of Carlos's relief on seeing Posa, how deep was the torment before:

> O, jetzt ist alles wieder gut. In dieser
> Umarmung heilt mein krankes Herz.[2]

When, some minutes later, he confesses his love for Elizabeth the long-confined passion jets forth like a stream of molten metal:

> Ich liebe ohne Hoffnung — lasterhaft —
> Mit Todesangst und mit Gefahr des Lebens —
> Das seh' ich ja, und dennoch lieb' ich.[3]

The one consistent feature in Carlos's character is his love for

---

[1] I had been working at the play too long; a dramatic work can and must be the fruit of one summer and no more. The plan, too, was too broad for the limits and rules of a dramatic work. (*Briefe über " Don Carlos "*.)

[2] Now everything is well again. In this embrace my heart which was so sick regains its health.

[3] I love without hope—sinfully—in fear of death and in danger of my life—I know it all, and yet I love.

Elizabeth, which in the end is sublimated into political ardour, into the resolve to free the Netherlands because she wishes it.

Apart from this one dominant passion, sudden and incalculable change marks Carlos's personality. His good resolution fails at the first encounter with Philip's suspicion; his incautious impetuosity misleads Princess Eboli into the belief that he loves her; and in spite of experience and Posa's warnings, he impulsively entrusts his fate to her power for the second time. Carlos can act generously and nobly, but always from personal not public motives. He inevitably misinterprets Posa's attachment, for, capable only of personal and emotional relationships, he cannot appreciate that with his public-spirited friend the state comes before the individual. A consequence of the change in Schiller's plan is the diminishing scale on which Carlos is portrayed. As Schiller himself lowers his valuation of personal motives, the figure of Carlos decreases in stature.

Saint-Réal had made Queen Elizabeth a passionate lover, like Carlos himself. In Schiller's play she has become the embodiment of dignity, honour, and just, sensitive thinking. Her innate moral sense will always prevent her from doing any mean or unjust act, or from thinking any thought of which she could afterwards feel ashamed. She loves Carlos, but she exerts every effort to turn his passion to more productive and hopeful ends, and seconds Posa's endeavour to win him for his political plans. Her best portrait is in the words of Posa:

> In angeborner stiller Glorie,
> Mit sorgenlosem Leichtsinn, mit des Anstands
> Schulmässiger Berechnung unbekannt,
> Gleich ferne von Verwegenheit und Furcht,
> Mit festem Heldenschritte wandelt sie
> Die schmale Mittelbahn des Schicklichen,
> Unwissend, dass sie Anbetung erzwungen,
> Wo sie von eignem Beifall nie geträumt.[1]

Simple, natural, and unselfish, she is ill at ease in the rigid artificiality of the Spanish court, yet no more articulate complaint escapes from her than the words in which she ostensibly refers to Princess Eboli:

> Es ist
> Ein hartes Schicksal, aufgeopfert werden.[2]

Schiller's change of plan has, however, complicated his portrayal of Elizabeth. In the later stages of the play she descends on occasion to political intrigue.

[1] In quiet, natural radiance, devoid of thoughtless gaiety, ignoring all pedantic calculation, remote alike from rashness and from fear, with firm heroic pace, she treads the narrow path of right, unaware, because she never dreams of applauding her own conduct, that she compels adoration.

[2] To be sacrificed is a hard fate.

To King Philip II Schiller's change of plan has brought a much
fuller treatment. Originally one of the main figures in a family
drama, Philip has developed into the representative of the old
political order which Posa seeks to overthrow. But he is still involved in a personal tragedy, and the need to illuminate all aspects
of his character has led Schiller to treat him at exceptional length.
Philip is the despot, whose negative rule, enforced by death and
destruction, is based on a contemptuous valuation of mankind.
In the great tenth scene of the third act Posa holds up to him a
pitiless mirror:

> Sie wollen pflanzen für die Ewigkeit
> Und säen Tod? Ein so erzwung'nes Werk
> Wird seines Schöpfers Geist nicht überdauern.
> Dem Undank haben Sie gebaut — umsonst
> Den harten Kampf mit der Natur gerungen,
> Umsonst ein grosses, königliches Leben
> Zerstörenden Entwürfen hingeopfert.
> Der Mensch ist mehr, als Sie von ihm gehalten.[1]

Philip rejects Posa's persuasion, believing his own conviction to
arise from a superior knowledge of human nature:

> Ich weiss,
> Ihr werdet anders denken, kennt Ihr
> Den Menschen erst wie ich.[2]

This is the root of the problem. Philip's low opinion of mankind
is based on his limited experience, on the men of his court, flatterers
and exploiters of the despotic system, of whom the brutal and
arrogant Alba and the tortuously intriguing and hypocritical confessor, Domingo, are typical. It is a disaster for the despot that
these are the men he knows.

It is also a misfortune of the system of absolute government that
the personal and the political are inextricably mixed. What the
tyrant wills is law, regardless of the motive prompting his will.
And so Philip, though he appreciates Posa's aims more justly than
does any other character except his queen, reacts with mean personal
resentment to Posa's desertion of him:

> Er sei gestorben als ein Tor. Sein Sturz
> Erdrücke seinen Freund und sein Jahrhundert!
> Lass sehen, wie man mich entbehrt. Die Welt
> Ist noch auf einen Abend mein. Ich will
> Ihn nützen, diesen Abend, dass nach mir

[1] Planting for eternity you would sow death? Such artificial work will not
outlast the mind of its creator. You have built for ingratitude—in vain have you
fought a hard fight with nature, in vain have you sacrificed to destructive plans a
great and kingly life. Man is more than you have taken him to be.
[2] I know that you will think otherwise, once you know man as I do.

> Kein Pflanzer mehr in zehen Menschenaltern
> Auf dieser Brandstatt ernten soll. Er brachte
> Der Menschheit, seinem Götzen, mich zum Opfer;
> Die Menschheit büsse mir für ihn! [1]

A private grudge determines the most far-reaching political decisions. Philip is neither a despicable nor a bad character, but he exercises power which no single man should wield. Absolute power has corrupted him.

Schiller reinforces the condemnation of despotism by his portrayal of the creatures who surround the ruler and use him for their own ends. Domingo and Alba are their typical representatives. The subtle, insinuating, and unscrupulous priest is the more dangerous. One of Schiller's earliest aims, announced in a letter to Reinwald (April 14, 1783), was to avenge mankind for some of the wrongs it had suffered at the hands of a worldly and corrupt Church, and much of his bitter contempt has been embodied in the figure of Domingo, whose disregard of moral principle, evident throughout the play, is crystallized in this dialogue with Princess Eboli:

> *Prinzessin*
> . . . obschon Sie mir bewiesen,
> Dass Fälle möglich wären, wo die Kirche
> Sogar die Körper ihrer jungen Töchter
> Für höh're Zwecke zu gebrauchen wüsste.
> Auch diese nicht — Dergleichen fromme Gründe,
> Ehrwürd'ger Herr, sind mir zu hoch —
>
> *Domingo*
>   Sehr gerne,
> Prinzessin, nehm' ich sie zurück, sobald
> Sie überflüssig waren. [2]

The policy which Domingo pursues by such unscrupulous methods is a reactionary one, summed up in his judgment of Carlos, spoken to Alba:

> Sein Herz entglüht für eine neue Tugend,
> Die, stolz und sicher und sich selbst genug,
> Von keinem Glauben betteln will. — Er denkt!

[1] Let his death reveal his folly. Let his fall crush his friend and his age! They shall see whether they can do without me. For one more evening the world is still mine; and I will use this evening so that no seed shall prosper for ten generations where my fire has burned. He sacrificed me to mankind, his idol. Mankind shall atone in his stead.

[2] *Princess.* . . . although you proved to me that cases were possible in which the Church could use even the *bodies* of its young daughters to further higher ends. These, too, have not convinced me. Such pious reasons, reverend father, are above my head.
Domingo. Very willingly do I withdraw them, princess, the moment they become superfluous.

Sein Kopf entbrennt von einer seltsamen
Chimäre — er verehrt den Menschen — Herzog,
Ob er zu unserm König taugt? [1]

Domingo is treacherous, Alba is brutal. Arrogant and ambitious, he is as ruthless as Domingo, but his coarse fibre expresses itself, not in intrigue, but in violence.

The interplay of these courtiers with the King exposes still other shortcomings of absolute government and dictatorship. The monarch alone bears the responsibility, but the decisions he takes are based on biased and even false information provided by those around him, who while evading all responsibility, thus become the real rulers. It is true that Philip for a moment detects the snare that Domingo and Alba have set for him:

Ich bin der Bogen, bildet ihr euch ein,
Den man nur spannen dürfe nach Gefallen?
Noch hab' ich meinen Willen auch — und wenn
Ich zweifeln soll, so lasst mich wenigstens
Bei euch den Anfang machen. [2]

But Philip's tardy discovery only underlines the condemnation of the system, and his desperate prayer for the help of an honest man proves how dependent on those around him is the apparently independent absolute monarch:

Jetzt gib mir einen Menschen, gute Vorsicht —
Du hast mir viel gegeben. Schenke mir
Jetzt einen Menschen! [3]

In Marquis Posa Philip believes that he has found the answer to his prayer. But Posa is more than an honest man, he is the representative of the new order, of the coming age. Opposite the ageing despot and tyrant stands the young democrat with his ideas of equality:

Werden Sie
Von Millionen Königen ein König! [4]

and his ardent advocacy of freedom of thought and religion—

Ein Federzug von dieser Hand, und neu
Erschaffen wird die Erde. Geben Sie
Gedankenfreiheit! [5]

[1] His heart is afire for a new virtue, which in its pride and confidence and self-sufficiency refuses to beg from any faith. He *thinks*! A strange chimera has caught his imagination—he honours mankind—Duke, is he really fitted to become our king?
[2] You take me for the bow which you can bend at will? As yet my will's my own, and if I am to doubt, let me at least begin with you.
[3] Give me a man, O kindly Providence, you have given me much, grant me now a man.
[4] Become a king amid millions of kings!
[5] A stroke of your pen, and the earth is recreated. Give us freedom of thought!

Posa's ideals are the noble, humanitarian ones of tolerance and freedom of thought and speech, and harmonious collaboration between all the members of the state:

> Sanftere
> Jahrhunderte verdrängen Philipps Zeiten;
> Die bringen mildere Weisheit; Bürgerglück
> Wird dann versöhnt mit Fürstengrösse wandeln,
> Der karge Staat mit seinen Kindern geizen,
> Und die Notwendigkeit wird menschlich sein.[1]

For a moment his unexpected conquest of Philip's regard causes him to hesitate and consider whether he might with the king's new-found support achieve his aims. But his plans are far-reaching, his thoughts are with the future, and a very short period of reflection turns his hopes from Philip's setting star to the rising sun of Carlos:

> Was kann ich auch
> Dem König sein? — In diesem starren Boden
> Blüht keine meiner Rosen mehr. — Europas
> Verhängnis reift in meinem grossen Freunde![2]

He does not shrink from the thought of revolution; the new order must be achieved by whatever means:

> Er mache
> Den span'schen Thron durch seine Waffen zittern.
> Was in Madrid der Vater ihm verweigert,
> Wird er in Brüssel ihm bewilligen.[3]

Posa's political passion provides the clue to his friendship for Carlos. It is not the enthusiastic emotional adoration of the eighteen-year-old Schiller for Scharffenstein, nor of the Bauerbach Schiller for his Carlos. It is a balanced and mature regard which is subordinated to his ruling idea. Its basis is Carlos's capability by rank and outlook to make Posa's ideals reality. The Marquis's love is given to the whole of mankind. At his very first appearance he describes himself to Carlos as:

> Ein Abgeordneter der ganzen Menschheit,[4]

---

[1] Gentler ages will succeed the time of Philip; they will bring a milder wisdom; the happiness of the subject and the greatness of the prince will then be reconciled and go hand in hand; the kindlier state will spare its children and harsh necessity become humane.

[2] What can I be to the King?—No roses of mine can bloom in that barren soil. Europe's fate ripens in my great friend.

[3] Let him shake the Spanish throne with armed force. What his father refused him in Madrid, he will grant him in Brussels.

[4] A representative of the whole of humanity.

and Carlos becomes for him the individual symbol for humanity:

> Mein Herz,
> Nur einem einzigen geweiht, umschloss
> Die ganze Welt! — In meines Carlos Seele
> Schuf ich ein Paradies für Millionen.[1]

His actions are not always those of a friend. A higher principle than friendship leads him to take risks himself and to cause Carlos to take risks that a purely personal regard must have avoided. Philip's judgment on Posa (endorsed by Schiller himself in the *Briefe über " Don Carlos "*) is this:

> Und wem bracht' er dies Opfer?
> Dem Knaben, meinem Sohne? Nimmermehr.
> Ich glaub' es nicht. Für einen Knaben stirbt
> Ein Posa nicht. Der Freundschaft arme Flamme
> Füllt eines Posa Herz nicht aus. Das schlug
> Der ganzen Menschheit. Seine Neigung war
> Die Welt mit allen kommenden Geschlechtern.[2]

Yet Posa is a man as well as a political idealist. There is inevitably a personal element in his affection for Carlos; and he has serious faults in his intense pride and his leaning towards intrigue. This is his chosen weapon; it fails him and dooms his friend; and pride impels him to the vain and needless sacrifice of his own life. There is some truth in Elizabeth's remark:

> Sie haben
> Nur um Verwunderung gebuhlt.[3]

Posa's pride is intimately related to a romantic heroism which Schiller himself clearly recognized in his hero:

> Wer entdeckt nicht in dem ganzen Zusammenhang seines Lebens, wie er es hier in dem Stücke vor unsern Augen lebt, dass seine ganze Phantasie von Bildern romantischer Grösse angefüllt und durchdrungen ist, dass die Helden des Plutarch in seiner Seele leben, und dass sich also unter zwei Auswegen immer der heroische zuerst und zunächst uns darbieten muss?[4]

Schiller's admiration for the heroic, which had pervaded *Die Räuber*

[1] My heart, dedicated to one alone, embraced the whole world! In my Carlos's soul I created a paradise for millions.

[2] And for whom did he make this sacrifice? For that mere boy, my son? Never. I cannot believe it; Posa dies for no mere boy. The poor flame of friendship cannot fill a Posa's heart, which beat for the whole of humanity. His love was for the world and all coming generations.

[3] You craved only astonished admiration.

[4] Who can fail to detect in the whole texture of his life, as it is lived before us on the stage, that his whole imagination is filled and pervaded with images of romantic greatness, that Plutarch's heroes live in his soul, and that of two courses his eye will turn more readily to the more heroic? [*Briefe über " Don Carlos."*]

and *Fiesco*, emerges again in Posa. It is an outlook which Schiller cannot help but impart to those characters he admires, and Posa was certainly an object of admiration for him:

> Auch gestehe ich, dieser Charakter ging mir nahe.[1]

But the mature Schiller of *Don Carlos* will not allow his emotions to bias his judgment, and adds:

> Aber was ich für Wahrheit hielt, ging mir näher.[2]

That truth is, that the political idealist, for all his pure motives, in practice often treats human beings in as arbitrary and capricious a manner as the most absolute despot, because he tries to force reality to take on the form he has conceived in his own mind. By recognizing this in the *Briefe über " Don Carlos,"* Schiller admits the cardinal error of the romantic personality and passes judgment on his own attitude of four or five years before. In turning from the subjective hero Carlos, whom he had uncritically worshipped, and substituting for him the figure of Posa, whom he appreciates with cool detachment, Schiller has taken the first important step towards the objectivity of his best work. It is an attitude which he achieved with difficulty and maintained with effort. The plays created under its influence reveal his kinship with Shakespeare and are his finest products.

Schiller has successfully portrayed the sensual passion of Princess Eboli, the simple integrity of Count Lerma, and the bleak and rigid conventionality of the Duchess Olivares. The most important of the secondary figures is the blind Grand Inquisitor, whom Philip summons, once he has decided to sacrifice his son. The Inquisitor administers to the King a severe and crushing rebuke for daring to think humane thoughts during his brief contact with Posa. Aged as well as blind, the Inquisitor is the scarcely living symbol of the negative, destructive forces of bigotry, which Posa (and Schiller) opposed and detested. The Inquisitor is devoted to death and eager for prey:

> *König*
> Kannst du mir einen neuen Glauben gründen,
> Der eines Kindes blut'gen Mord verteidigt?
>
> *Grossinquisitor*
> Die ewige Gerechtigkeit zu sühnen,
> Starb an dem Holze Gottes Sohn.
>
> *König*
> Du willst
> Durch ganz Europa diese Meinung pflanzen?

[1] I admit, too, that this character meant much to me.

[2] But what I took to be truth meant even more.

Grossinquisitor
So weit, als man das Kreuz verehrt.

König
                                    Ich frevle
An der Natur — auch diese mächt'ge Stimme
Willst du zum Schweigen bringen?

Grossinquisitor
                                    Vor dem Glauben
Gilt keine Stimme der Natur.

König
                              Ich lege
Mein Richteramt in deine Hände — Kann
Ich ganz zurücke treten?

Grossinquisitor
                            Geben Sie
Ihn mir.

König
            Es ist mein einz'ger Sohn — Wem hab' ich
Gesammelt?

Grossinquisitor
            Der Verwesung lieber als
Der Freiheit.[1]

The dark forces represented by the Inquisitor gain the day. Yet though catastrophe overtakes the human protagonists of the new age, we know that their efforts are not vain. The ideas are not destroyed with the individuals who have proclaimed them. It is a background of hope, faint and far off, yet certain; without it this tragedy of vain endeavour and futile sacrifice would have been unbearable.

The change in Schiller's attitude to the play brought with it difficulties of construction as well as of characterization. With conscientious craftsmanship he tried to weld the tragedy into a unity, while retaining the published acts in something like their original

---

[1] *King.* Can you found for me a new faith which will defend the bloody murder of a child?
Grand Inquisitor. To expiate eternal justice God's Son died upon the cross.
King. Will you spread this opinion through the whole of Europe?
Grand Inquisitor. Everywhere that the cross is honoured.
King. I perpetrate a crime against nature—can you silence this powerful voice within me, too?
Grand Inquisitor. The voice of nature counts for nothing in the eyes of faith.
King. I lay my office as judge in your hands. Can I withdraw entirely?
Grand Inquisitor. You need only give it me.
King. It is my only son—for whom have I gathered territory and wealth?
Grand Inquisitor. Better for death and decay than for freedom.

form. He could only do it by expansion, and the play is in consequence overloaded and excessively long. But there was one feature of *Don Carlos* which dated from his first beginnings upon the theme and went far towards unifying the play. This is its style. *Don Carlos* is Schiller's first play in verse. Four years before Schiller conceived his tragedy at Bauerbach, Lessing had published *Nathan der Weise*, the first play in blank verse to secure attention and applause throughout the whole of Germany. It is this metric pattern which Schiller chose because, as he wrote to Dalberg in August 1784, it would give his tragedy dignity and brilliance.

The rhetoric of *Die Räuber* and *Fiesco* had seemed to cry out for verse. A reaction against *Kabale und Liebe* and a sense of his vocation as a writer of high tragedy had led Schiller to adopt verse. Poetry is one of the chief agencies by which a play can be decisively removed from the trivialities of everyday life. Verse sets a play in a known and instantly recognizable category and frees it from any obligation to reproduce the details of the world we know; it is a sign that the poet will present to us an essential reality shorn of the incidental and irrelevant. Schiller was convinced that this, and not the realism of domestic prose tragedy, was his appropriate style. Writing to Dalberg he had said of *Kabale und Liebe* and *Don Carlos*:

> I cannot now forgive myself for being so obstinate, or perhaps so vain, as to wish to shine in a contrary sphere, so wish to restrict my imagination within the limits of domestic tragedy, when high tragedy offers such a fertile field and exists, if I might say so, for me; for in this form I can achieve greatness and brilliance and earn more thanks and astonishment than in any other; in this field I can perhaps not be equalled, in the other I could be *surpassed*. [August 24, 1784.]

Verse was the outward sign of the discovery of the tragic form in which, he felt, he could achieve his best.

Schiller's blank verse in this play shows no trace of being the work of a beginner. Its language is rich, its rhythms subtle; its expression leaves a feeling of perfect rightness. Its faults are occasional luxuriance (though successive prunings by Schiller himself have lopped off most of what was superfluous) and some limitation of range. The same noble rhetoric characterizes the utterances of Posa and the Inquisitor, of Carlos and Domingo. This uniformity certainly impedes characterization; on the other hand it provides this rather diffuse and sprawling play with a much-needed unifying element.

The rhetorical verse of *Don Carlos* has power and verve; it can achieve its effect by accumulation:

Ich habe niemand — niemand —
Auf dieser grossen, weiten Erde niemand.

So weit das Zepter meines Vaters reicht,
So weit die Schiffahrt unsre Flaggen sendet,
Ist keine Stelle — keine — keine, wo
Ich meiner Tränen mich entlasten darf,
Als diese.—[1]

or by short sentences of the greatest simplicity:

Ja, es ist aus. Jetzt ist
Es aus. — Ich fühle klar und helle, was
Mir ewig, ewig dunkel bleiben sollte.
Sie sind für mich dahin — dahin — dahin —
Auf immerdar! — Jetzt ist der Wurf gefallen.
Sie sind für mich verloren. — O, in diesem
Gefühl liegt Hölle — Hölle liegt im andern,
Sie zu besitzen.[2]

The words group themselves with complete naturalness, the rhythm quickens and drags with the tempo of the emotion. Clearly marked in both passages is the use of pause and repetition, as characteristic of Schiller as the light amid darkness in Rembrandt. Repetition is not only a feature of single speeches, but is used with telling effect in dialogue:

Marquis

.   .   .   .   .

Auf Kaiser Karls glorwürd'gem Enkel ruht
Die letzte Hoffnung dieser edeln Lande.
Sie stürzt dahin, wenn sein erhab'nes Herz
Vergessen hat, für Menschlichkeit zu schlagen.

Carlos

Sie stürzt dahin.[3]

There is perhaps no better instance of the way in which Schiller's verse in *Don Carlos* rises and falls with the emotion of the speaker than a passage in Philip's speech about the dead Posa, with its slow, depressed beginning, its mounting strength, and final dying away in discouragement:

Im Grabe
Wohnt einer, der mir Achtung vorenthalten.
Was gehn die Lebenden mich an? Ein Geist,

---

[1] I have no one—no one—in all this wide earth no one. As far as my father's sceptre rules, as far as Spanish ships carry our flag, is no place—no place—none, where I can pour forth my tears, but this. [*Don Carlos*, Act I.]

[2] Yes, it is finished, now it is finished.—Now it is clear and open to me, which should for ever and for ever remain hidden. You are lost to me—lost—lost—for ever! Now the die is cast. I have lost you.—Oh, hell is in this feeling, hell, too, in the thought of possessing you. [*Don Carlos*, Act I.]

[3] *Marquis*. The last hope of these noble lands rests on the glorious descendant of the Emperor Charles. It will perish if his heart no longer beats for humanity.
Carlos. It will perish.

I

Ein freier Mann stand auf in diesem ganzen
Jahrhundert — einer — er verachtet mich
Und stirbt.[1]

Don Carlos was first performed in Hamburg on August 30, 1787. For the Leipzig production in the same year Schiller prepared a prose version (for the actors could not speak verse), in which Carlos kills himself instead of being handed over to the Inquisition. The verse text appeared in four different forms. The fragments in *Die Thalia* were followed by the edition of 1787, which had the phenomenal length of 6,282 lines, more than 2,000 in excess of *Hamlet*. In new editions published in 1801, 1802, and 1805 Schiller made appreciable cuts, so that the work in its present form is reduced to the still considerable length of some five thousand lines. The causes of this excessive bulk were Schiller's change of plan and the breadth of his second conception. He had not yet acquired the discipline which would impel him to sacrifice a successful detail for the sake of the whole.

Don Carlos is the climax of Schiller's youth; and it also reaches out beyond it to embody something of the reflection and maturity of his Leipzig and Dresden years. All his works up to this point had been impressive experiments, which led him no farther. He had not fully solved his dramatic problem with *Don Carlos*. From the intensely personal conception of the opening act he had swung over to the excessive abstraction of a political problem. But though he had not yet found the combination which suited him, with the impersonal treatment of the personal situation he had, as the quality of his dramatic verse proves, at least hit upon the form of tragedy appropriate to his genius.

---

[1] In the grave lies one who refused me respect. What can the living mean for me? *One* mind, *one* free man rose up in this whole century, just one—he despises me and dies.

Chapter Ten

AT WEIMAR
1787–89

THE little town of Weimar, the capital of a minute state, had attained in the seventeen-eighties a repute out of all proportion to its size, wealth, or political importance. Enlightened policy, personal sympathy, and chance had attracted to it some of the greatest writers of the age. The literary invasion had begun in 1772, when the Dowager Duchess Anna Amalia had appointed Wieland, most versatile of poets, as tutor to the young Duke Karl August and his brother. In 1775 Goethe, at the urgent invitation of Karl August, came on a visit and stayed for life; and in the following year the philosopher and critic Herder was at Goethe's instance appointed Court Chaplain and General Superintendent of the Church. The presence of these three was sufficient to make Weimar one of the most important cultural centres in Germany.

Schiller's first and most obvious motive in visiting Weimar was to bring himself again to the notice of Duke Karl August, who had heard nothing of him since he had granted him the title of Weimar *Rath* at the end of 1784. The moment seemed to favour a new approach. The first act of *Don Carlos* had earned the Duke's approval two and a half years before; now Schiller brought with him the newly published tragedy. His hopes were not, however, confined to the Duke, for the great men of Weimar might also exercise a powerful influence upon his future. He felt that *Don Carlos*, so new and different in style from his earlier work, was by far the best play he had yet written and would serve him as a letter of recommendation. He certainly hoped for much-needed financial advantage from his visit, but he was eager, too, to secure from these established men of letters the recognition that he also was a writer of the first rank.

His journey to Weimar began unfavourably. Scarcely an hour before Schiller arrived at the post-inn in Naumburg Duke Karl August had passed through on his way to Berlin, and the date of his return was quite uncertain. It was a discouraging start. On his arrival the sight of Weimar provoked a second disillusionment, for it proved to be a large sleepy village, full of low-built, insignificant houses, many of them roofed with mossy and rotting thatch.

Schiller had also been attracted to Weimar by Charlotte von Kalb's presence, but when they met their love was no longer what it had been before. In the last two and a half years Schiller had given himself little time to think of her. He lacked any tendency to make a pleasure of former pain, and his life had brought him change and new interests. But Frau von Kalb had lived and fed her mind upon those agonizing hours in February 1785; in her recollection she had given them a magic and a sweetness, greater perhaps than they had ever possessed. For her the meeting with Schiller was a more momentous event than it could possibly be for him. A gap had opened between them. There was affection, kindness, consideration on both sides; the thought of divorce and remarriage was to occur to Charlotte and to be entertained for a moment by Schiller. But the seeds of separation were there.

Charlotte had discouraging news for him. The greatest of the Weimar celebrities was absent. Goethe had left for Italy the year before and, contrary to all expectations, had not returned, nor was there any word of his coming. The young Duchess, who was known to be an admirer of Schiller's work, was away, too, and of the important figures only the dowager Duchess Anna Amalia, Wieland, and Herder were in residence.

The hopes he had placed in Weimar were already fading, but he determined at least to make the most of those opportunities still available. On July 23, two days after his arrival, he paid his visit to Wieland and on the following day to Herder. Wieland, whom Schiller respected for his translation of Shakespeare and envied for his light touch and supple style, received the visitor with cordiality, and the two men spent two hours in stimulating discussion. As to Herder, he knew nothing at all of Schiller's work, but Schiller felt a liking for him, which seemed to be mutual.

Schiller pressed copies of *Don Carlos* on Wieland and Herder. He was presented to the Duchess Anna Amalia and passed an agreeable hour in the informal atmosphere of her court. She did not, however, appreciate *Don Carlos*, which was read to her early in August by Gotter, author of the comedy in which Iffland had lampooned Schiller three years before. Influenced by a coolness towards Schiller in the best circles of Weimar, Wieland dropped the contact which had begun so promisingly, and managed for some weeks to evade the necessity of committing himself to a criticism of *Don Carlos*. Only from Herder did Schiller hear approval of his play.

He was not sorry in the second half of August to spend a week in an entirely different environment. With Charlotte von Kalb he made the journey to Jena, to pay a visit to Professor Reinhold,

Wieland's son-in-law. Schiller's impression of Jena gained by his irritation with Weimar, but it had manifest advantages of its own. It was a town of some dignity, and its atmosphere of liberal scholarship and the absence of a court with its snobbery and petty despotism exercised a strong attraction for Schiller.

Reinhold gave Schiller a hint that he would have no difficulty in being elected to a chair at Jena, a thought which fell on fertile ground. It seemed a possible solution to his ever-present problem of financial insecurity. Reinhold was also a fanatical disciple of Kant, whom he viewed as the new Messiah; such was his enthusiasm and persuasiveness that when Schiller left he determined to read the new philosophy for himself.

By September Schiller was more at ease in Weimar. He spent many hours a day preparing a history of the revolt of the Netherlands against Spanish domination in the sixteenth century. The genesis of this task was the interest in the period of history which *Don Carlos* had engendered

The history of the rebellion of the Netherlands was to be Schiller's own contribution to a serial work giving short accounts of great conspiracies, of which he was general editor. When the first volume of *Die Verschwörungen* (*The Conspiracies*) appeared in 1788, a year later than originally planned, it contained, however, nothing by Schiller. His constantly increasing interest in the revolt of the Netherlands had led him to expand his plan to such a degree that his book was out of proportion to the other monographs and required separate publication.

The hint that an academic chair might be within his reach gave Schiller an added stimulus in his task, and through the autumn, winter, and spring he worked steadily at the book. Körner, with whom he corresponded regularly, viewed with disapproval and alarm the sacrifice of poetry to history. Schiller's answer reveals his irritated contempt of the public which neglected *Don Carlos*, and also the hopes he placed in his new work:

> With half the value I am capable of giving to a historical work I can achieve more recognition in the so-called learned and polite world than the full expenditure of my mental energy on such frivolity as a tragedy can achieve.
>
> From my Carlos, the result of three years of endeavour, I have had nothing but annoyance. My History of the Netherlands, the work of five or at most six months, will perhaps earn me respect and reputation.

The most important reason behind his new devotion to history, however, was the need for an intellectual activity which he could pursue steadily without having to wait for moments of inspiration. The slow development of *Don Carlos* and the increasing rarity of the creative mood had roused in him the fear that he might be nearing the end of his poetic vein. On January 18, 1788, he wrote to Körner: " Is it true or false that I must think how I am going to *live*, once my poetic springtime is over? "

There was justification for his fear. In the years 1780 to 1783 he had written three tragedies, and at the beginning of that period a quantity of poems. In the next four years he had produced only one tragedy, a mere handful of poems, and one or two prose works to which he attached little value. The new tragedy he had projected, *Der Menschenfeind*, made no progress and he had to abandon it. Poets who write themselves out in youth are not rare, and Schiller feared that he might be one of them—" I am in danger in this way of writing myself out," (letter to Körner, January 18, 1788). It was time, he felt, since he lived by writing, that he should employ his pen on some literary task which was worth doing and which he could still do well. In history he believed that he had found it.

Die Geschichte des Abfalls der vereinigten Niederlande von der spanischen Regierung (*The History of the Secession of the United Netherlands from Spanish Rule*) appeared in October 1788. It did not cover the whole revolt, but only the period from 1560 to 1567. The history proper was preceded by an introduction, which had already been published separately in the January issue of Wieland's *Der teutsche Merkur*, in order to whet the appetite of the public. Schiller wrote it with enthusiasm; the consequence is a flowing rhetorical style.

> Gross und beruhigend ist der Gedanke, dass gegen die trotzigen Anmassungen der Fürstengewalt endlich noch eine Hülfe vorhanden ist, dass ihre berechnetsten Plane an der menschlichen Freiheit zuschanden werden, dass ein herzhafter Widerstand auch den gestreckten Arm eines Despoten beugen, heldenmütige Beharrung seine schrecklichen Hülfsquellen endlich erschöpfen kann.[1]

This essay, of which the basic idea is the victory of freedom of thought over religious intolerance, is not a truly historical work. The poet in Schiller has arranged, selected, and adapted, in order to present as vividly as possible events and characters and their meaning. It breathes Schiller's own enthusiasm and, with its persuasive rhetoric and striking images, constitutes a brilliant overture, rousing our interest by a rapid and sparkling treatment of themes from the work itself.

The history itself is of a different character. Schiller has collected and marshalled his facts with painstaking thoroughness and then

---

[1] Great and consoling is the thought that there is at the last a bulwark against the defiant presumption of princely violence, that its most calculated plans are confounded by human freedom, that a vigorous resistance can strike down the upraised arm of the despot, heroic endurance exhaust his terrible resources.

unfolded the history of the revolt in fluent, clear, and noble prose. His interest is concentrated mainly on the political events, the great figures, and the moving incidents, though he does not neglect the background of intellectual, religious, and economic life. The result is a vigorous, convincing, and readable presentation of historical events, well suited to the general reader. Schiller's own claim, made in his letter to Körner of February 12, 1788—"In my hands history will become here and there something which it has not been before"—is amply fulfilled. He opened up history in Germany to the general reader and was the first German writer to raise historical writing to a high literary level.

For the specialist Schiller's work is less satisfying. His background, for all his hours of mole-like industry, was not quite adequate, his judgment on the value of his authorities not always reliable. There are errors of fact and false estimates. The book is not an original contribution, but an able, vivid, and brilliant presentation of existing knowledge. If his newness in the historical field caused some shortcomings in his book, it also gave it a freshness and sparkle which the routine historian often lacks.

This historical work was one of Schiller's greatest commercial successes. It was eagerly bought, and the public waited with interest for the promised continuation. This, however, was never to be written, though it was several years before Schiller abandoned the idea. At first thrust into the background by other urgent tasks, it was finally dropped when Schiller's interest in history was replaced by an enthusiasm for philosophy.

While he had been writing *The History of the Secession of the Netherlands* Schiller had continued to live in Weimar. He saw a great deal of Wieland, with whom he had become reconciled in October 1787. Wieland proposed that Schiller should become his co-editor on *Der teutsche Merkur*, with which *Die Thalia* should be amalgamated. The scheme did not mature, but Schiller became a frequent contributor to the *Merkur*.

Late in November Schiller set out for Meiningen to revisit Frau von Wolzogen and his sister Christophine, now Frau Reinwald. The landscape which had aroused in him such enthusiasm five years before failed to rekindle his imagination. Those early emotions refused to be revived. But it was pleasant to renew contacts with his friends, and particularly Frau von Wolzogen, whom, as she died in the following August, he was seeing for the last time.

Schiller and Wilhelm von Wolzogen decided to return to Weimar together on horseback. They broke their journey at the village of Rudolstadt, where the Lengefeld family, distant relatives of the Wolzogens, lived. Schiller had already met Frau von Lengefeld and her two daughters for a few moments in June 1784, as they passed through Mannheim on their way back from a visit to Switzerland. The elder daughter, Caroline von Beulwitz, was married, not very happily; the twenty-one-year-old Lotte was not yet engaged. They were enthusiastic readers of the literature of the day, including the early work of Schiller, whose visit was a great event in the monotonous round of their winter occupations. Schiller immediately took to both sisters, and they showed a sympathy and regard for himself and his work, such as he had experienced only in the Körners' circle. The landscape pleased him even in its December bareness, and it was soon agreed that he should revisit Rudolstadt in the summer.

Back in Weimar he was soon immersed in his historical task, working twelve hours a day and only going out to make a short evening call on Herr and Frau von Kalb or on Wieland. At the same time he produced for *Der teutsche Merkur* of March 1788 the first poem of importance that he had written for three years.

This, *Die Götter Griechenlands (The Gods of Greece)*, is a pointer to the direction in which Schiller's mind was moving. His interest in the great days of Greece and Rome had at first been limited to their heroism alone, as it appears in Plutarch. In *Die Götter Griechenlands* his vision has widened. The poem is a lament for all that the modern world has lost in replacing the Greek supernatural world by a lifeless scientific materialism.

The contrast between the serene abundance of antiquity and the gloomy austerity of the present, repeated in ever sadder variations, culminates in praise for the rich polytheism of the Greeks, which he contrasts with the bleak monotheism of Christianity. This thought earned Schiller much adverse comment and a particularly bitter attack from Friedrich von Stolberg in August 1788 in the periodical *Das deutsche Museum*. Schiller later recognized the justice of some of the criticisms and revised the poem drastically in 1793, cutting out eleven of its twenty-five stanzas and adding two new ones including the famous final lines—

> Was unsterblich im Gesang soll leben,
> Muss im Leben untergehn.[1]

Published in 1800, this is the authorized form of the poem.

Die Götter Griechenlands is a milestone on the road of Schiller's development. Guided by Wieland, he had come upon a new and hitherto unsuspected world; but it was a world which, for all its attractions, was gone past recall. The poet can only express vain regret for beauty irretrievably lost. It is a document of Schiller's growing admiration for antiquity, not an attempt to imitate it.

---

[1] That which shall live for ever in song must perish in life.

Towards the end of January 1788 Schiller again met Lotte von Lengefeld, who had been sent by her mother to Weimar to acquire experience of court society. He was attracted by her youthful freshness and unassuming modesty and touched by her sincere admiration of his talent. They did not meet often at Weimar, but they planned a summer together in Rudolstadt. When she left Weimar in April it seemed a natural thing for them to maintain a correspondence.

Schiller made the short journey to Rudolstadt in the middle of May. Lodgings were ready for him in the house of the choirmaster of Volkstädt, a mile and a half from Rudolstadt. He brought with him his partly written history of the Netherlands, *Der Geisterseher* and *Der Menschenfeind*. The landscape in May more than fulfilled the expectations it had aroused in December. A walk with Lotte von Lengefeld and her sister Caroline and a quiet evening over their coffee-cups was the reward for the day's work. Eventually Schiller took his papers to Rudolstadt with him and worked in Lotte's study. It was a time of serene happiness, and the affection which he and Lotte felt for each other quickened imperceptibly into a love of which they were as yet only half-conscious.

This development was not lost upon Lotte's conventional mother, who was perturbed at the idea of a union between her daughter and a commoner. Lotte was sent away on short visits to Frau von Stein, Goethe's former friend in Weimar, and to friends at Jena. These separations did not diminish their unavowed love. Schiller stayed on into November in order to spend his birthday with Lotte and her family, and then returned to Weimar, saddened by the parting, but full of hope for the future, as his last note to Lotte before his departure shows: " The thought of our reunion is a bright and cheering one. Everything shall and will bring me back to it. Everything will recall you and be the dearer for that recollection."

Those pleasant summer and autumn months at Rudolstadt had not been so productive of work as Schiller had hoped. He had prepared his history for the press, and had written some instalments of *Der Geisterseher*. But he had made no progress at all with *Der Menschenfeind;* the moments of inspiration seemed to have gone and the former fire to burn low.

> " The times are past when I could concentrate all my powers on a single object,"

he wrote to Körner on August 20, 1788. But, though he could not create anything new, he wrote during this period one of his best critical works. *Die Briefe über " Don Carlos "* (*Letters on " Don Carlos "*), published in *Der teutsche Merkur* in 1788, were a reply to some of the criticisms and also to some of the praise which his newest tragedy had evoked. Some reviewers had considered Posa's actions to be inadequately explained, others had interpreted the play as an apotheosis of ardent personal friendship. Schiller set out to refute both of these views. Though his justification of Posa's actions is here and there too ingenious, his comments are shrewd and well argued, his tone moderate yet firm, and his readiness to admit faults quite disarming.

Schiller's interest in classical antiquity, which earlier in the year had inspired *Die Götter Griechenlands*, grew in strength during these summer months. With the Lengefeld sisters he read the *Odyssey* in Voss's hexameters, the *Iliad* in Stolberg's prose.[1]

Schiller turned next to the Greek tragic dramatists and began in the autumn of 1788 to translate Euripides' *Iphigeneia in Aulis* into German blank verse. A version of scenes from the *Phoenician Women* followed, and he conceived, but failed to carry out, a plan to translate the *Agamemnon* of Æschylus. He published his translations in *Die Thalia*. He was consciously seeking to steep himself in the style, methods, and spirit of the Greek authors, as he wrote to Körner:

> I intend in the next two years to read no more modern writers. Many of *your* points have convinced me. None of them does me any good. They all lead me away from my true self. The Ancients give me real enjoyment. At the same time I need them in the highest degree in order to purify my taste, which, through its subtlety, artificiality, and cleverness, was getting very far from true simplicity. You will find that familiar intercourse with the Ancients will do me a great deal of good—will perhaps give me a classical quality. [Letter to Körner, August 20, 1788.]

The interest and enthusiasm with which Schiller now approached the study of classical literature seemed to bring him into Goethe's orbit. Through the whole of Schiller's first year in Weimar the absent Goethe had been constantly in his mind. Weimar was full of wholehearted admirers of Goethe, and the prevailing outlook was influenced by his realistic and experimental approach, so very different from the intellectual and idealistic outlook of Schiller. The prestige of Goethe's name, the regard in which he was held in Weimar, and the quality of his writings all contributed to establish his ascendency in Schiller's mind.

After an absence of nearly two years Goethe returned to Weimar in June 1788, while Schiller was at Rudolstadt. In September the Lengefelds contrived, through their friend, Frau von Stein, to arrange a meeting between the two men. It took place on September

---

[1] Voss's verse translation of the *Iliad* was not published till 1793.

7, when Goethe came out to Rudolstadt, accompanied by three ladies. Schiller found Goethe's manner stiff and formal, though he was much impressed by the liveliness and warmth with which Goethe spoke of his experiences in Italy. The meeting left him with a sense of dissatisfaction and with the feeling that the difference in age (he was then twenty-eight, Goethe thirty-nine) involved a divergence of outlook which might well preclude any close intellectual contact. A copy of *Der teutsche Merkur* for March had been artfully left open at *Die Götter Griechenlands*, and Goethe, after reading a few stanzas, asked leave to borrow it, and slipped it into his pocket, but this was the only episode in the whole afternoon which would bear any favourable interpretation.

Schiller could not then know the state of dissatisfaction and unrest in which Goethe had found himself since his return. Nor did he suspect the dislike with which Goethe, the classicist, regarded him as the representative of Nordic violence, exaggeration, and distortion. For Schiller, one classicist was speaking to another; Goethe was meeting the author of *Die Räuber*, which he hated as the symbol of something which he had himself outlived and which threatened all that he now stood for.

A few days after this meeting Goethe read in the *Allgemeine Litteratur-Zeitung* Schiller's review of his *Egmont*. Though he had much to praise, Schiller also had faults to point out, and underlined them without diffidence. This newcomer to Weimar ventured, despite the difference in rank and years, to criticize Goethe as an equal. The frank tone of this review seemed to the older man an impertinence; it placed one more obstacle in the way of any fruitful contact between them.

Now that he loved Lotte Lengefeld, Schiller lived a very different life in Weimar from that which he had led on his first arrival more than a year before. He no longer needed social engagements to keep him happy, but contentedly shut himself up in his rooms to work at *Der Geisterseher* and at his translations from Euripides. He also wrote at this time a short story called *Das Spiel des Schicksals* (*The Shifts of Fate*), recounting the career of Colonel Rieger, whose catastrophic fall from grace had been a Würtemberg sensation twelve years before. It is little more than a pot-boiler written for *Der teutsche Merkur*, which published it in 1789, but its psychology is as truly observed and as consistently logical as that of *Der Verbrecher aus verlorener Ehre*.

Schiller's hopes of marriage were clouded by the insecurity of his life; he felt his profession of letters to be a precarious and ungrateful one. Suddenly in mid-December there came a new development. A professor in Jena retired, and Schiller, whose

reputation as a historian had been established by his history of the
Netherlands, was offered the appointment on Goethe's recommendation and with Duke Karl August's approval. Though he had toyed
with the idea of such a professorship for more than a year, he did not
yet feel qualified for it; but, faced with the necessity of making a
quick decision, he consented to take the post. Over Christmas he
had leisure to ponder the advantages and disadvantages of his new
appointment. The gains seemed few, the drawbacks many. It
would give him a higher standing and might be a stepping-stone to
a more remunerative post at another university. Money, or the
lack of it, was the chief drawback to the chair at Jena, for it carried
no stipend, and the professor, if not a man of means, had either to
live by writing, or else starve on the meagre fees paid by the students
attending his lectures.

The financial inadequacy of the post was the more disappointing
because he reckoned on his first permanent appointment to enable
him to marry Lotte Lengefeld and to free him from the perpetual
strain of journalistic work. A great source of irritation, too, was the
thought that he would lose his summer at Rudolstadt, the prospect
of which had helped to speed the winter.

Schiller was to take up his appointment in May 1789. Through
the five months that remained he could do little to prepare himself
for the summer's lecturing. His profitable but tiresome novel,
Der Geisterseher, had first to be finished, and took much of his time.
Another project of these months seemed likely to combine
financial with academic gain. This was the publication under his
editorship of a serial work comprising various historical memoirs.
It was modelled on a French enterprise which had been extremely
successful. With the assistance of Körner and his brother-in-law
Reinwald, Schiller hoped to issue four volumes a year, to provide
himself with a steady income, and to extend his historical knowledge.

He was also at work upon a poem. *Die Künstler* (*The Artists*)
had been conceived and written during the autumn of 1788 at
Rudolstadt. Two thorough discussions of the poem with Wieland
in the first months of 1789 resulted in such drastic revision that the
final form in which it appeared in *Der teutsche Merkur* in March
1789 was not only three times the length of the original, but appre-
ciably different in character and thought.

The basic attitudes underlying *Die Künstler* are the grandeur of
man and the importance of art in his life. Schiller's noble and lofty
humanism optimistically proclaims the moral progress man has made:

> Wie schön, o Mensch, mit deinem Palmenzweige
> Stehst du an des Jahrhunderts Neige
> In edler stolzer Männlichkeit,

> Mit aufgeschlossenem Sinn, mit Geistesfülle,
> Voll milden Ernsts, in tatenreicher Stille,
> Der reifste Sohn der Zeit. . . .[1]

Man, as Schiller sees him, has risen to his present height through the helping hand of art:

> Nur durch das Morgentor des Schönen
> Drangst du in der Erkenntnis Land.[2]

Art reveals swiftly and easily truths which the speculative and scientific intellect discover late and with difficulty; and it surpasses science, for only in the artist's hands can truth have its full effect upon man:

> Der Schätze, die der Denker aufgehäufet,
> Wird er in euren Armen erst sich freun,
> Wenn seine Wissenschaft, der Schönheit zugereifet,
> Zum Kunstwerk wird geadelt sein.[3]

It is the high responsibility of the artist to care for the spiritual dignity and welfare of mankind:

> Der Menschheit Würde ist in eure Hand gegeben,
> Bewahret sie!
> Sie sinkt mit euch! Mit euch wird sie sich heben!
> Der Dichtung heilige Magie
> Dient einem weisen Weltenplane,
> Still lenke sie zum Ozeane
> Der grossen Harmonie.[4]

In *Die Künstler* Schiller confronts for the first time the dilemma of philosophical poetry. Philosophy requires clear exposition, unclouded by the emotions; poetry pays little attention to clarity and much to feeling. But a compromise is possible, if the poet endeavours, not to put forward a logical argument, but to combine and align ideas and attitudes. This is what Schiller has attempted in *Die Künstler*, though without entire success. The sudden transitions often cause obscurity; a wealth of imagery overtaxes the mental agility of the reader; and Schiller tends, as in many of his early poems, to concentrate too much meaning into too little space.

---

[1] How beautifully, O man, do you stand in the century's closing years, the palm of victory in your hand, proud, noble, manly; your senses alert, your mind enriched with many thoughts, full of mild gravity, quietly encompassing so much, the maturest son of the age.

[2] Only through the morning-gateway of the Beautiful did you enter the land of knowledge.

[3] Only in the artist's arms can the thinker enjoy the treasures he has piled up, when his knowledge, ripening towards beauty, is ennobled into a work of art.

[4] The dignity of mankind is placed in your hands, preserve it! Whether it sinks or rises depends upon you. The holy spell of poetry serves a wise world order, may it guide man to that great sea where harmony prevails.

The result is a poem difficult to read and not wholly satisfying, even when the difficulties have been surmounted. Schiller's luxuriant style has overloaded it and obscured its meaning.

If *Die Künstler* is only a partial success as a poem, it is an important document in Schiller's development. It represents his growing conviction that art is the noblest activity of man. It seems strange that this proud apologia for his own poetic calling should be published at the moment when he was to turn his back on creative work for several years. His stay in Weimar of nearly two years had had unexpected consequences. Intellectual commerce with the great men of the age had not stimulated new poetic activity. Three poems,[1] one of them the merest trifle, make up his total poetic production for this time. Ceasing to be a poet, he had become a professional historian. The paralysing hand of Weimar, which had laid itself upon Goethe and reduced him almost to poetic silence for many years, seemed to have lamed the pen of Schiller. He too became absorbed in the study of the classics. More and more conscious of the high importance of the poet's calling, Schiller decided that he must prepare himself by hard study and serious thought for his great task.

He was in a state of ferment and change; he did not like his former style of writing and had not yet hit upon a new one. *Don Carlos* already pointed the way to his later style, but he was too conscious of its stormy beginnings and its structural weakness, and so he failed to realize the importance it could still have for him. He was twenty-nine, his youth was behind him, and he feared that with his youth he had lost his creative power.

Schiller's doubts about himself were reinforced by his acquaintance with Goethe. During the early months of 1789 he met Goethe several times, but no closer contact ensued. The older man, less inclined than ever, since his return from Italy, to make close friendships, kept Schiller at a distance; Schiller on his side experienced for Goethe a combination of repulsion and attraction, of love and hate.

> To be often with Goethe would make me unhappy; he is never effusive, even with his closest friends; one can never get at him. I believe he is an exceptional egoist. He can win men, and can make himself agreeable by attentions great or small, but he never gives himself. He makes his presence felt by the good he does, but remains as remote as a god. This seems to me to come from a logical, deliberate plan, aiming at the highest egoistic enjoyment. Such creatures ought not to be allowed. I detest him for it, although I thoroughly admire his mind and think him great. (Letter to Körner, February 2, 1789.)

[1] *Die Götter Griechenlands, Die Künstler, Die berühmte Frau.*

The source of Schiller's divided mind about Goethe is a conflict in himself. He felt the power of Goethe's genius and recognized it as greater than his own; but his proud ambition would not let him be content with second place. A disharmony resulted, which was expressed in contradictory emotions and wavering judgments: " I won't measure myself with Goethe if he puts out his full powers. He has far more genius than I, wider knowledge, more accurate observation, and an artistic sense refined and purified by experience " (letter to Körner, February 25, 1789).

A fortnight later he repudiated this humility and allowed his resentment of Goethe's easy course and tacit assumption of superiority to well up in angry and bitter words: " This fellow, this Goethe, bars my way and reminds me so often that fate has treated me ill. How easy has been his lot, and how must I struggle to this very moment " (letter to Körner, March 9, 1789).

Deep down, however, Schiller had not lost confidence in his own genius. In the midst of this hesitancy and doubt he had written to Körner in that very letter of February 25, 1789, affirming his faith in his own powers as a tragic dramatist:

> I have made a drama suited to my own talent, which gives me a certain excellence in it just because it is mine. If I go in for realistic drama I am very much aware of the superiority of Goethe and of many other writers of the recent past.

He knew that his genius was for a drama that dealt in essentials and disregarded details; but he also knew now that luxuriance, exaggeration, and complexity had hitherto been the principal defects of his plays and that he must strive for the simplicity which *Don Carlos* had entirely lacked.

Schiller's almost complete abandonment of creative work was partly the consequence of weariness. Obliged to live by his pen, he found the moments of inspiration ever rarer. Yet it was also in part deliberate. He set himself the highest standard, and felt that he could only attain it after a complete change of mental occupation and prolonged study. His love for Lotte Lengefeld helped him by resolving and harmonizing personal conflicts which had hitherto hampered his development.

Chapter Eleven

MARRIAGE AND LIFE AT JENA
1789–91

HAVING moved to Jena on May 11, 1789, Schiller found that he disliked his new life less than he had expected. The atmosphere of a university town proved at first congenial, and he had for the first time in his life the feeling that he belonged to a community. He gave himself a fortnight to settle down before delivering his inaugural lecture in two instalments on May 26 and 27. To avoid any appearance of presumption he had chosen to hold it in Professor Reinhold's moderate-sized lecture-room. It was due to start at 6 P.M., and so great was the interest in the new professor, who was still best known for his sensational play *Die Räuber*, that by half-past five there was not a seat left, though numbers of would-be hearers were still arriving. Stairs and landings were packed full, and some began to drift away again. Schiller consulted his colleague Reinhold, and it was decided to hold the lecture in the largest hall the university possessed, which lay at the other end of the town. The crowd of students streamed through the streets, and soon the

SCHILLER'S SIGNATURE

This reads: " J. C. Fridrich Schiller Herzogl. Meining Hofrath und Professor zu Jena in Sachsen "

new lecture-room, too, was packed so full that Schiller had difficulty in reaching the dais. He had dreaded this moment, but as soon as

CHRISTIAN GOTTFRIED KÖRNER IN 1790
Wagener

SCHILLER IN 1794
Dannecker

he began to read, all his misgivings fell from him and he felt confident in his power to hold his audience. It was clear that his first lecture was a triumphant success, and that evening the students sang a serenade beneath his windows.

Schiller published his inaugural lecture in November 1789 under the title *Was heisst und zu welchem Ende studiert man Universal-geschichte?* (*What is Universal History, and why do we study it?*). It falls into two distinct parts. The first distinguishes the true scholar (*der philosophische Kopf*) from the false one (*der Brotgelehrte*), for whom the academic life means, not the pursuit of truth, but a living. The second part deals with the study of universal history. Since there are always gaps in our knowledge and much that has reached us is untrustworthy, the historian must supplement the assemblage of facts by deduction, infusing into the chaos of contradictory and fragmentary testimony a spirit of order which is in himself:

> Er nimmt also diese Harmonie aus sich selbst heraus und verpflanzt sie ausser sich in die Ordnung der Dinge, d.i. er bringt einen vernünfti-gen Zweck in den Gang der Welt und ein teleologisches Prinzip in die Weltgeschichte.[1]

This was Schiller's view of the task of the historian, and in his peroration he affirms the power of history, so written, to broaden the mind, to lead man beyond the narrow limits of his own life and imperceptibly to merge the individual in the species. By making us acquainted with the efforts of those who have gone before us, history leads us, too, to exert ourselves to improve the lot of future generations.

The lectures reveal how far Schiller has travelled since the days when he idolized Rousseau. Civilization is no longer, as it had been in *Die Räuber*, the corrupter of man; primitive peoples no longer the only possessors of virtue: " Wie beschämend und traurig aber ist das Bild, das uns diese Völker von unserer Kindheit geben! "[2] The European situation seemed to Schiller one of moral progress. The pursuit of arts and sciences had become international, laws had succeeded tyranny and become humane, wars had given way to peace: " Die europäische Staatengesellschaft scheint in eine grosse Familie verwandelt."[3]

Schiller's noble belief in the grandeur of man and in his steady upward progress was consistent with the world he saw round him.

[1] He takes this harmony from himself and transplants it into the order of things —*i.e.* he imputes a reasonable purpose to the course of the world and a teleological principle to history.

[2] How sad and humiliating is the picture which these peoples reveal to us of our own childhood!

[3] The European society of states seems changed into a great family.

K

It was a hundred and forty years since Germany had known total war, and nearly thirty years since the much less savage Seven Years War; religious hatred was sinking, and intellectual intercourse disregarded the frontiers of the many separate states; a spirit of rational freedom, impatient with obsolete restraint, pervaded France; and far off in America the British colonies had vindicated the cause of freedom and enlightenment and established their independence. Humanity seemed to be moving towards a better, more harmonious, and happier world. In May 1789 Schiller did not foresee the bloody revolutions, catastrophic wars, and inhuman industrial development which were about to overtake Europe.

The University of Jena was recovering from a period of stagnation in the middle of the century and developing into a centre of the new Kantian philosophy. With nearly a thousand students, it dominated the little town of about four thousand inhabitants. Its atmosphere, which at first had charmed Schiller, proved on closer acquaintance to be parochial and petty. An episode typical of its internal jealousies occurred when Schiller's inaugural lecture was published in November. In all good faith Schiller had styled himself on the title page Professor of History. Though he did not know it, he was Professor of Philosophy and not of History, and the holder of the latter chair, Professor Heinrich, tried to have the lecture confiscated. Schiller could regard several of his colleagues only with contempt and soon tired of this society of professors and their wives. His absent friends contrasted favourably with the dullness of his acquaintance in Jena. He regretted his stimulating discussions with Körner in Dresden, and he thought how excellent it would be to make a real contact with Goethe in Weimar. Above all he deplored his absence from the Lengefeld sisters at Rudolstadt.

In June he paid the Lengefelds a very short visit, and early in July the sisters called on him on their way to friends at Lauchstädt. By now Schiller's love for Lotte had reached the point where it must soon disclose itself. But he was diffident about her feelings and feared a rebuff. On August 2 he left Jena for Leipzig and called at Lauchstädt on the way. Too sensitive even now to risk a setback, he sounded Caroline about his chances with Lotte and received the answer for which he hoped. But his time was short and no opportunity came of speaking with Lotte alone, so he had to defer his proposal till he had reached Leipzig. As soon as he arrived there he wrote to her declaring his love and asking her to be his wife. In simple and sincere words, which mirror her quiet happiness, she wrote back her acceptance. A few days later they met in Leipzig and decided, in consultation with Caroline, to keep the engagement secret for the present, in order not to worry Frau von

Lengefeld ; for Schiller's insecure financial position would perturb her even more than the prospect of her daughter marrying a commoner. They planned to tell her as soon as his situation improved.

Schiller had reached the first stage towards the fulfilment of his happiness, and yet the obstacles seemed just as great as before. He regretted his Jena appointment, which brought him status, but no money, making him poorer by diminishing the time available for his journalistic work. He repeatedly thought of going to Berlin, but he had no influential connexions there.

There was a more hopeful prospect of employment in Mainz, where Huber, now in the Saxon diplomatic Service, had drawn the attention of Baron Karl Theodor von Dalberg to Schiller towards the end of 1788. Dalberg, the elder brother of the director of the Mannheim Theatre, was a Catholic priest and chosen heir to the Electorate of Mainz. The Coadjutor, as he was styled, had been made governor of Erfurt, an enclave belonging to the Elector of Mainz and situated some fifteen miles to the west of Weimar. He was anxious to assist Schiller, but powerless to offer any appreciable help until he succeeded to the Electorate. But the reigning Elector, though old and feeble, survived for many years, and Schiller soon realized that he must regard his chances in Mainz as uncertain and remote. He thought next of a solution which seemed simpler, since it depended less upon factors he could not control. He planned to give up his academic career, ask Karl August for a small pension, and live at Rudolstadt, earning his living by his pen. But this scheme must wait until the secret of the engagement was revealed to Frau von Lengefeld.

Meanwhile the lovers wrote letters and arranged visits. But the secrecy caused an irksome feeling of restraint, and apart from this Lotte soon began to feel very unhappy. The cause lay with her sister Caroline. Schiller sent most of his letters to both sisters, and in conversation addressed himself more often to the more mature and articulate Caroline than to his shy and retiring fiancée. Lotte concluded that he had not understood his feelings when he proposed to her. She thought of breaking the engagement, but was dissuaded by a friend, Caroline von Dacheröden, who, as the wife of Wilhelm von Humboldt, later became one of the close friends of the Schillers in Jena. In November a letter from Schiller reassured her and restored her self-confidence.

In the same month the first volume of *Memoirs* appeared. Schiller's only contribution was an introductory essay, *Über Völkerwanderung, Kreuzzüge und Mittelalter* (*On the Migration of Peoples, the Crusades and the Middle Ages*). This unsatisfactory work consists of a swift survey of the Crusades against the background of preceding centuries, followed by a sketch of the feudal system of the Middle Ages. It contains serious errors of fact and judgment, revealing the pitfalls which beset Schiller in turning historian without the foundation of a long and close study of history. It had been written in haste, for Schiller was at this time lecturing daily, and he found the enormous amount of preparatory reading an almost intolerable burden. His literary work was practically at a standstill.

As the weeks and months passed by he became more and more eager to advance the date of the marriage. He grew restless, impatient, and irritable, and at last in December the more enterprising Caroline revealed the engagement to her mother. To their relief Frau von Lengefeld accepted the situation with a good grace. Schiller was able to bring her a small social consolation when the Duke of Meiningen granted him the title *Hofrat* (Court Counsellor), which he had requested in order to narrow the gap in rank.

Frau von Lengefeld, however, would not hear of Schiller resigning his chair and coming to live at Rudolstadt. Schiller then hoped that his financial problem might be solved by a small pension from the Duke of Weimar. After Frau von Stein had prepared the way, Schiller made a formal request, and early in January Karl August told him that he would grant a small pension of 200 talers a year (£30). It removed the last obstacle in the way of his marriage. Lotte had already been promised an allowance of 200 talers by her mother, lecture fees would probably bring in 200, and Schiller reckoned that he could earn the remaining 200 (for he put the annual cost of living at Jena at 800 talers) by his literary work.

Early in the New Year Frau von Lengefeld agreed to fix an early date for the marriage. It was to be at Jena, since Schiller could not get away for long enough to acquire the residential qualification for Rudolstadt, and it was fixed for February 22, 1790. As Schiller was particularly anxious that the wedding should be held quietly and in private, it took place in the little church of Wenigenjena just outside the town of Jena. Apart from the bridal pair and the clergyman, only Frau von Lengefeld and Caroline were there. Having escaped the notice of students and professors, the wedding party drove to Schiller's apartment. This, with two additional rooms, was to be the home of the newly married couple. They did not propose to keep house themselves, and they had meals sent in by their landladies. In spite of their modest income, they lived quite comfortably, maintaining a servant apiece.

The marriage drew Schiller and his parents more closely together. Ever since he had obtained the chair at Jena his father's opinion of him had risen, and this unimpeachable marriage was further evidence that Fritz really had settled down to a steady and ordered existence. Schiller, too, was much moved and worried by the news that his mother was seriously ill. In the many months of her convalescence he thought more of home and wrote to his parents more often than for many years past.

Relations with Körner, somewhat strained during his engagement, also became more cordial now. Schiller had concealed his growing love for Lotte from his friends in Dresden, and when he at last announced his impending marriage, a coolness developed between the two men. But the good-humour and serenity which came upon Schiller with his marriage, together with Körner's good sense, soon cemented the bond between them as firmly as before.

The young couple were very happy. Lotte was adaptable and full of sympathetic understanding, and Schiller repeatedly wrote of his joy in such words as these to Christophine: " We lead the happiest life together, and I cannot imagine how I lived before." The disturbing influence of Caroline had been neutralized by Lotte in a spirited discussion with her sister, and the couple remained contented with each other's company, seeing very little of the academic society of Jena.

Schiller still hoped later on to find a congenial post in Mainz; he had been much encouraged by the gracious and friendly attitude of the Coadjutor when he and Lotte had visited Erfurt shortly before their marriage. But a slight shadow now lay across these future prospects. In July 1789, some three weeks before Schiller's engagement, the Bastille had been stormed in Paris, though the echo of its fall was then heard but faintly in Germany and not at all by Schiller. But through the winter of 1789–90 the ferment grew till it could no longer be ignored. To Schiller it spoke of war, and he foresaw its enormous scope: " I tremble at the thought of war, for we shall feel it throughout the length and breadth of Germany " (Letter of April 15, 1790).

The first year of his marriage was a period of intensive work. He was lecturing daily on universal history, and also giving a course on tragedy, based on his own past practical experience. The severest tax upon his time and energy was, however, a history of the Thirty Years War which he had begun to write. Towards the end of 1789 Göschen had offered him 400 talers for a readable account of this great struggle, to be published in the *Historischer Calender für Damen* (*Historical Calendar for Ladies*) for 1791 and following years. The payment was so good that Schiller, with Lotte to care for as well as himself, could hardly have declined it. But he was attracted, too, by the period, which had gripped his imagination as early as 1786, when his interest in history was new.[1]

[1] See Schiller's letter to Körner, April 15, 1786.

Though it must be readable, Schiller was determined that his history of the Thirty Years War should also be sound and reliable. The available sources were immense, and Schiller found his task a colossal one. The writing was the easiest part of it; the greater part of his time had to be given up to reading, annotating, and collating. He worked very long hours, often fourteen a day, and made appreciable progress. By September 1790 he had finished the manuscript of the first part (Books I and II), which takes the narrative as far as the battle of Breitenfeld (1631), and he could take a well-earned and much overdue rest at Rudolstadt. When it was published late in the autumn this first instalment achieved immediate success, and the edition of seven thousand copies—a very large one for those days—was exhausted before the end of the year. A second impression had to be printed.

Die Geschichte des dreissigjährigen Krieges is avowedly popular and Schiller omitted the learned apparatus of footnotes, which he had employed in his *Geschichte des Abfalls der Niederlande*. There are gaps caused by his own incomplete knowledge. There are also faults of conception; for instance, Schiller wrongly attributes to Gustavus Adolphus the ambition to seize the imperial crown of Germany; and he assumes through most of the book that Wallenstein was a calculating and deliberate plotter of treason, but in the end shifts his ground and invalidates his whole previous conception with the terse formulation: " So fiel Wallenstein, nicht weil er Rebell war, sondern er rebellierte, weil er fiel." The reason for such errors is Schiller's inability, through inexperience, to assess the trustworthiness of his sources.

The book also lacks proportion. Well over three-quarters is devoted to the war up to the assassination of Wallenstein (1634) and the fourteen years remaining are dealt with cursorily in the last sixty pages. The Peace of Westphalia is omitted altogether. The sketchiness of the last book arises from the nature of Schiller's interest in the period. His attention was focused on two great men, Gustavus Adolphus and Wallenstein. When these had left the scene his enthusiasm vanished. He approached the period with the eye of a dramatist. This is the source of the weakness of his book, but also of its strength. Despite many faults of detail and some of conception, *The History of the Thirty Years War* is a vivid and clear account of a complex and obscure period. Schiller has marshalled the unwieldy mass of facts with skill, has bound them together with a sound general conception, and presented his work in a dignified

¹ Thus Wallenstein fell, but not because he was a rebel; he rebelled because of his fall.

and flexible style. The German public could for the first time read a history which was popular in the best sense of the word.

This book did not exhaust Schiller's historical activity in the year 1790. He also edited the second and third volumes of *Memoirs*, prefixing to Volume III a sound essay on the reign of the Emperor Frederick I. For succeeding volumes, which were to contain the memoirs of Sully, he planned and began to write an account of the wars of religion in France. *Die Geschichte der französischen Unruhen, welche der Regierung Heinrichs IV. vorangingen* (*The History of the French Troubles which preceded the Reign of Henry IV*) remains incomplete. Published in five parts with the first five volumes of Sully's memoirs, it covers the reigns of Francis II, Charles IX, and Henry III up to the eve of the Massacre of St Bartholomew (1572); sixteen years between that event and the accession of Henry IV remain untouched. Though only a fragment, this version of fourteen tormented years of French history is a solid and yet lively piece of work, giving a competent and clear account of events with brief vivid portraits of the principal figures.

Three other historical essays—dealing with the origins of society, the mission of Moses, and the legislation of Lycurgus and Solon—had their source in university lectures. They helped fill numbers of *Die Thalia* in the autumn of 1790.

The year 1790 saw the climax of Schiller's historical work. Though *The History of the Thirty Years War* and *The History of the French Troubles* were to occupy him as late as 1792 and one or two minor essays came from him even later, he did not again concern himself so closely with history as during this year. His interest was at its height, his ambition and energy roused. He wrote to Körner in November 1790: " I cannot see why I should not, if I really try, become the first historian in Germany." (Letter of November 26, 1790).

History had at first been an ancillary to tragedy, but as he felt his creative powers flag he realized that he must divert his energies to some activity less dependent than is poetry on uncertain inspiration; and his interest in history lay ready to hand. It was not a new enthusiasm. Plutarch's lives of great men had fascinated him long before he had begun to study history for *Fiesco* and *Don Carlos*.

When he turned in 1788 to the intensive study of history it was with all his customary ardour. This enthusiasm was both a virtue and a fault. It ensured vivid presentation, but it led to extravagance. The vices of his historical approach appear most clearly in his introduction to *The History of the Secession of the Netherlands*, with its bold, sweeping statements which neglect fact and detail. Contact with Herder and the reading of Kant on history made matters no better, and the same fault characterizes his lectures and the essay on the Crusades and the Middle Ages. Schiller later became conscious of this defect and devoted more and more time to the acquisition of facts, for which *The History of the Thirty Years War* shows a proper respect. As his enthusiasm waned, his style acquired a sobriety better suited to his task.

Schiller's perpetual difficulty was the scantiness of his background. He had come to the study too late in life, lacking the normal student's preparation. Only too well aware of the inadequacy of his knowledge, he lived, as a historian, from hand to mouth. He did not know enough facts and he did not know the relative value of his sources. Körner had diagnosed the root trouble in his letter of March 31, 1789: " Your ideal of universal history is excellent, but in order to achieve it to your satisfaction you would have to give up all other activity. It needs a man's whole powers for his whole life."

Schiller's industry was enormous, and by 1790 he had made great strides forward and considerably reduced the handicaps under which he was working. Yet in spite of this expenditure of energy the end of 1790 saw his interest decline, and as soon after as it was financially practicable he abandoned the study and writing of history.

The reason lay in Schiller's mental make-up. The convincing presentation of history requires an artistic skill which Schiller possessed and delighted to employ. Its basis, however, is an attention to detail and minute fact, which he was most reluctant to give. In arranging the amorphous mass of facts which confronts him, the historian may not reject things because they displease him; and his conclusions should emerge from the facts. Schiller's mind worked in quite another way. The idea was formulated complete in his mind and he then selected the facts and details which were essential and relevant to his idea. His ideas are generally true— or he would not be a great writer—but he does not arrive at them as an historian should. By temperament and mental constitution he was unsuited to the historian's task. As an artist he could be free, as an historian he was tied to facts; and freedom was his highest good.

For one whose very nature was at variance with the principles of historical study, Schiller had reached a remarkably high level in his chief historical works: *The History of the Secession of the Netherlands, The History of the Thirty Years War, The History of the French Troubles,* and *The Siege of Antwerp*[1]. He made himself the first historian in Germany for the general public, and embodied in his

[1] *Die Belagerung von Antwerpen,* written for *Die Horen* in 1794.

work those noble, eighteenth-century, humanitarian ideals—
tolerance and the moral progress of man.

The services which history rendered to him were greater however
than the services he gave to history. It provided him with themes
for his later dramatic works; it gave him a sure political sense in the
treatment of historical subjects; and, most important of all, it
brought his mind, however reluctantly, into contact with the discipline of facts. The effect of the three years 1788-90 on his mind
was a permanent one. He had sensed the importance of his study
of history when he had written to Körner on April 15, 1786:
" I wish I had studied history for ten years together. I believe
I should be quite a different fellow. Do you think it is too late
now? "

The study of history proved a valuable corrective to the one-
sided addiction to idealistic speculation and to generalization which
had characterized his mind. He had profited by a visit to the world
of facts, even if he found its climate uncongenial.

Schiller's intense activity in the autumn of 1790 was almost
exclusively historical. Only in one short work did he maintain
contact with the world of poetry, and even that was concerned, not
with creation, but with principles; it was a critical review of the
poetry of Gottfried August Bürger (1747-94). *Über Bürger's
Gedichte* (*On Bürger's Poems*) appeared in the Jena *Allgemeine
Litteratur-Zeitung* for January 15, 1791. Like all reviews in this
journal it was unsigned. Schiller's essay was a dignified but severe
attack on Bürger's popular poetry. He conceded to Bürger many
excellent qualities, but denounced his failure to eliminate vulgar
traits. Every poem is marred by some such flaw. In this demand
for a purified poetry Schiller champions the claims of the type of
poetry which suited his own genius. He seeks a consistent and
essential nobility, and emphasizes the close connexion between
nobility of mind and nobility of work. For the first time he explicitly
puts forward the demand for idealization and the presentation of a
purified and concentrated truth, which affords, in his view, a truer
picture than the complex chaos of irrelevance which the unpurged
reality presents:

> Eine notwendige Operation des Dichters ist Idealisierung seines
> Gegenstandes, ohne welche er aufhört seinen Namen zu verdienen.
> Ihm kommt es zu, das Vortreffliche seines Gegenstandes (mag dieser
> nun Gestalt, Empfindung oder Handlung sein, in ihm oder ausser ihm
> wohnen) von gröbern, wenigstens fremdartigen Beimischungen zu
> befreien, die in mehrern Gegenständen zerstreuten Strahlen von
> Vollkommenheit in einem einzigen zu sammeln, einzelne, das Ebenmass

störende Züge der Harmonie des Ganzen zu unterwerfen, das In-
dividuelle und Lokale zum Allgemeinen zu erheben.[1]

These words accurately describe Schiller's own method of creation.
In his criticism Schiller was clarifying his own views on literature,
and his attack on Bürger is therefore unfair, though his criticism
is measured and just in tone.

Schiller's exertions in the year 1790 had been immense. He had
achieved much and could be well pleased with his status as an
historian and with the financial reward of his long and arduous
hours of research and writing. He worked over Christmas 1790,
but for the New Year he planned a brief rest, when he and Lotte
would visit Coadjutor Dalberg at Erfurt.

They left Jena on December 30, and began their holiday filled
with agreeable thoughts of future prosperity under the Coadjutor's
patronage. On January 3, 1791, Schiller was suddenly taken ill at a
banquet. He was taken to his lodging suffering from fever and a
severe pain in the chest. He spent one day in bed and was confined
indoors for several more, during which the Coadjutor visited him
and made plain his high regard and future intentions. At the end
of the first week in January 1791 Schiller and his wife began their
return journey, reassured after the first shock which his sudden and
alarming illness had caused. Schiller stayed a day or two at Weimar
and left Lotte there with Frau von Stein, returning himself to Jena
on the eleventh in order to press on with his work.

On the following day his symptoms returned in an acuter form.
The illness at Erfurt had been no more than a warning of this
grave attack. His temperature rose rapidly and the pain became
more severe. On the fourteenth he began to cough up blood. It
was time Lotte was sent for, and on the fifteenth Schiller wrote
her a short note which is a touching attempt to combine anxiety
for her return with the wish to allay her fears. When Lotte came
she found his consumptive symptoms complicated by gastric
disturbances. For six days he could eat nothing, and was so en-
feebled that he fainted when lifted from the bed. He became
delirious, and the doctor feared for his life, but after three days
he began slowly to mend. By the end of January the improvement
was decided, though it was mid-February before he could write a
normal letter.

[1] A necessary operation for the poet is the idealization of his subject, without
which he ceases to deserve his title of poet. It is his business to free from cruder,
or, at any rate, from foreign elements the excellent features of his subject (whether
this is form, emotion, or action, existing in himself or outside him); he must
gather up the strands of perfection, dispersed through several objects, into one,
must subdue to the harmony of the whole those elements which disturb its sym-
metry, and elevate the individual and local into the general.

The only light in these dark days was the loving care of his wife and the devoted attention of some of his students, chief among them Frau von Stein's son Fritz and the eighteen-year-old Friedrich von Hardenberg, better known as the poet Novalis.

The long period of overwork in 1790 and the years of late hours and irregular meal-times which had gone before it had taken a bitter revenge. The shock for Schiller had been profound, and he realized the need to spare his strength and his lungs and to follow exactly the directions of his doctor. But he had to live, and could not hope for a long time to earn anything by lecturing. He could count only on a total of four hundred talers from the Duke of Weimar and Frau von Lengefeld, and must at least double that sum by writing. At the end of his first year of married life he was faced with the terrible dilemma: rest and starve, or work and fall ill. He chose the latter, as he must, for he had his devoted Lotte to think of as well as himself. And so, slowly and cautiously, he began work on the second instalment of *The History of the Thirty Years War*, encouraged by a generous review by Wieland and by the news that the first edition was exhausted.

In the hope that recovery would be aided by rural calm, a change of air, and the recollection of happy hours two years before, they moved in April to Rudolstadt. There, on May 7, a new illness overtook him in the form of asthmatic hindrances to breathing, which were so distressing that it seemed doubtful if he could survive. After a few hours the spasms subsided, only to return the next evening and to reach a crisis on the tenth. His hands and feet grew cold, his pulse low and fitful, he could no longer speak. He and those who stood by believed that he was near his death. Lotte and her sister redoubled their efforts to maintain life and warmth, and presently he fell into a gentle sleep. When he awoke the asthmatic spasms returned, but they were less violent; his voice came back, and he whispered to Lotte and Caroline as they stood beside his bed: "It *would* be nice if we could stay longer together."

Schiller had been thrust to the brink and then withdrawn, and in the days when the issue seemed undecided the thought of a mission unfulfilled had been very painful to him. Even before this attack he had written to Wieland in March: "I would so much like to reach the goal towards which an obscure awareness of my powers sometimes impels me" (Letter of March 4, 1791).

Had Schiller died in May 1791, at the age of thirty-one, as he seemed likely to do, he would have appeared as one whose early promise remained unfulfilled. Three impressive but faulty plays in prose, written in early youth, a noble but overgrown verse tragedy standing alone without posterity, an unfinished novel, and two incomplete historical works would have made up the catalogue of his important works. It would have seemed that he had written himself out with *Don Carlos* and turned from inspired creation to the routine writing of history. There would have been no sign of the remarkable regeneration of his powers which was reserved for the years to come.

The worst seemed to be over for the present, but his health was not restored. Though the fact that he had coughed up no blood in May encouraged the false belief that his lungs were really sound, it was clear that he must spare his strength. He stayed at Rudolstadt till the beginning of July, when he made with Lotte and Caroline the journey to Carlsbad to take the waters. In four weeks he re-cuperated rapidly, and then the party set out for Erfurt. On this journey Schiller took the opportunity to visit Eger, the scene of the assassination of Wallenstein in 1634. They stayed five weeks in Erfurt, where Schiller was much lionized, and returned to Jena on October 1, 1791.

Schiller longed to get back to the quiet intimacy and harmony of his domestic life. He had been very fond of Lotte before; but the prospect of death and the loving care she had expended on him had roused in him a livelier perception of her affection and devotion. It was in warmer and happier tones than before that he wrote of her to Körner:

> By making me inactive, my illness had made us so used to each other that I am reluctant to leave her by herself. Even when I am busy, it is a pleasure to think that she is near me; and her sweet ways and the childlike purity of her soul and the depth of her love give me a calm and a harmony which, with my tendency to gloom, would be impossible for me otherwise. If only we were both healthy, we should need nothing more to live like gods. [Letter of October 24, 1791.]

Back at Jena he still felt unequal to the task of continuing *The History of the Thirty Years War*. He needed some unexacting and pleasant literary activity, and found it in translating the second and fourth books of *The Aeneid* into rhymed stanzas (*ottava rima*). Done with great skill, the rendering into a form so remote from the original results in a personal *tour de force* rather than an attempt to reproduce Virgil for German readers. This pastime provided him with material for *Die neue Thalia*, into which Göschen transformed *Die Thalia* on changing its lay-out and appearance at the beginning of 1792. But translating Virgil, though a suitable recreation for Schiller's weak state, brought him no money. His health would not permit him to lecture, and he saw his income dwindle at the moment when he needed it most. He turned to the Duke of Weimar for help, but Karl August, always short of money himself, could not afford to increase his pension, though he made him a single grant of 250 talers. The situation was not yet desperate, but as the year 1791 drew to its end Schiller viewed the future with growing concern.

On December 10, 1791, Schiller received a packet from Copenhagen. He opened it without great curiosity or anticipation, for it was presumably from a Danish admirer named Jens Baggesen, who had visited him in Jena the year before. The packet contained not one letter but two. One was indeed from Baggesen; the other came from two Danish noblemen, Prince Friedrich Christian von Augustenburg and Count Schimmelmann. Schiller read it and read it again, scarcely able to believe his eyes. Suddenly the full significance dawned on him. These two noble Danes offered him a pension of a thousand talers a year for three years; it meant release from care and want, the chance to build up his health, and to create the works he felt he had still to write. His heart overflowed, and so great was the shock that he felt ill. Once Lotte was told, he felt that he must let his faithful friend Körner know too. In a transport of delight he sat down and dashed his letter off.

I must write to you at once, dear Körner, I must pour out my joy to you. What I have so ardently desired as long as I live is now fulfilled. I am free from all cares for a long time, perhaps for good; my mind can have the independence I have so longed for. To-day I have received letters from Prince Augustenburg and Count Schimmelmann, who offer me a thousand talers a year for three years; I am free to remain where I am, and the aim is to let me recover from my illness. The delicacy and tact with which the Prince makes this offer moves me almost more than the offer itself. . . .

. . . Confess, how happy is my lot.

SCHILLER'S LETTER OF DECEMBER 10, 1791, TO KÖRNER
(reduced)

Chapter Twelve

THE FIRST YEARS OF FREEDOM
1792–94

THE generous help which so surprised Schiller and his wife
in December 1791 had its origins in Jens Baggesen's visit to
Jena sixteen months before. Baggesen, a minor Danish writer, was
already an admirer of Schiller when he came. What he learned
during this visit filled him with sorrow, for he saw Schiller hard
pressed financially and working himself to a standstill over his
history, and he was deeply moved by Professor Reinhold's story of
Schiller's struggle for existence.

On his return to Denmark Baggesen did much to popularize
the name of Schiller there, and among those who listened sympatheti-
cally to his praise of the great poet struggling against adversity were
Prince Friedrich Christian and Count Schimmelmann. In the
summer of 1791 Baggesen planned a private Schiller festival in
Copenhagen, to be attended by a select circle of friends, including
Count Schimmelmann. On the eve of the party news came that
Schiller was dead, and the celebration became a memorial ceremony.
The rumour, occasioned by Schiller's desperate illness in May
1791, was soon corrected, but it had brought home to his Danish
admirers the gravity of his situation and his need of help. Urged by
Baggesen, the Prince and Count Schimmelmann decided to come to
Schiller's assistance; and towards the end of November the letters
offering Schiller a pension were sent off from Copenhagen.

The first and most obvious benefit which Schiller expected from
his improved financial situation was the re-establishment of his
health. The fearful choice between illness and want had vanished;
he was free of exhausting hack-work, which dulls the finer edge of
the mind. He could rest and recruit his strength, which was again
much tried by an attack of his asthmatic malady early in January
1792.

Schiller could hope, too, that his creative powers might return.
In four and a half years he had produced practically nothing; the
fire had burned lower and lower, till nothing but grey ash was visible.
But he knew that the glow existed and could, if fortune were kind to
him, be rekindled to a blaze. Early in 1792 he wrote to Körner,
" I am a poet, and as a poet I shall die " [February 27]; and though
he was still busy with his *History of the Thirty Years War*, which

he was determined not to leave unfinished, the idea of a tragedy about Wallenstein was beginning to stir in his mind.

Schiller had neglected poetic activity too long. Discussion with Körner, with Wieland and Herder had sharpened his critical faculties and roused his mind to exceptional alertness, and he had reason to fear that his formidable analytical powers had become an obstacle to his creative ability:

> Criticism has indeed harmed me, for I have lacked for years tne boldness and the living fire I once had, before I knew any rules. I now *see* myself *creating* and *shaping*, I observe my own enthusiasm, and since my imagination knows that it is watched it behaves with less spontaneity. [Letter to Körner, May 25, 1792.]

He knew that he could not recapture his earlier spontaneity, which had been a part of his youth, and he determined to grasp the theoretical basis of his art so thoroughly that it would become a second nature and be a substitute for the youthful freshness that was gone:

> Once I am so far that *deliberate art* has become *nature* for me, as education is for a cultured man, my imagination will regain its former liberty and only submit to those limits which it imposes itself. [Letter to Körner, May 25, 1792.]

He now had time to devote to the mastery of the principles of artistic creation. Once he had probed, verified, and absorbed the aesthetic theories which interested him his creative genius would gain new strength.

In the early months of 1792 he nursed his health carefully, and, though he was never well, the remainder of the winter passed without any more severe attacks. In April and May he and his wife paid a visit to the Körners in Dresden, when the two friends had the first opportunity, for five years, of personal contact and direct intellectual discussion. Their principal topic was the philosophy of Kant, in which Schiller, overcoming an initial reluctance, was becoming increasingly interested.

In mid-May Schiller and Lotte returned to Jena, where he took up again the *History of the Thirty Years War* and began to edit his minor prose works (*Kleine prosaische Schriften*), which Göschen was to publish in four volumes, the first appearing in the autumn of 1792. The *History* especially put a great strain on his feeble constitution; he had often to write far into the night. But in September it was finished at last, and with immense relief, he wrote to Körner: " Now I am free and intend to remain so for good. There shall be no more work thrust on me by others or imposed by anything but my own interest and inclination " (September 21, 1792).

Schiller's parents in far-off Würtemberg had watched with pride their son's mounting fame, but they were filled with anxiety at his

CHARLOTTE SCHILLER IN 1794
Ludovike Simanowiz

SCHILLER AGED THIRTY-FIVE
Ludovike Simanowiz

153

serious and obstinate illness. These misgivings about his health, coupled with the desire to make the acquaintance of their daughter-in-law, led them to discuss a visit to Jena. Captain Schiller's duties forbade such an expedition for him, but in September 1792 Frau Schiller bravely set out on the two-hundred-mile journey to Jena. She took with her her youngest daughter, Nanette, then aged fifteen. Fritz Schiller had not seen his mother since he had left Mannheim for Bauerbach in 1782. She was now sixty, but in far better health than he had expected after her serious illness in the winter of 1789-90. She seemed, indeed, stronger and healthier than her thirty-two-year-old son. Now that the *History* was finished, Schiller had leisure to devote to her, and Frau Schiller's visit of three weeks passed quickly by in quiet harmony. Early in October, before the roads became too deep, she set out for home with the hope that the young couple might next year pay a return visit.

As the cold weather came on Schiller became a hermit in his house. By close attention to his health he avoided any grave crisis that winter, but could not entirely shake off the asthmatic attacks, nor the persistent pain in his side. It was a gloomy time with the irritation of his continued ill-health and the prospect of months of virtual imprisonment in his house. The thought of a happy and prosperous future in Mainz, which had borne him up, now failed him, as the French conquest evolved into apparently permanent occupation.

Like most of his intelligent contemporaries, he had had some sympathy with the Revolution. But when in December the trial of King Louis XVI began, Schiller was shocked into writing a pamphlet in the hope of influencing the outcome. He was no ardent royalist, but the trial of a King was the climax to a long series of acts which had bred a slow mistrust. Events, however, moved too swiftly for him; on January 20, 1793, Louis XVI was convicted of treason and condemned to death. Schiller's pamphlet remained unfinished; but his disgust was expressed in his words to Körner: " I'm so revolted by these butchers that I haven't been able to read a French newspaper for the last fortnight " (February 18, 1793).

He made no further attempt to intervene in political matters, believing that his sphere of influence as a poet was wider and more important.

The spring of 1793 was uneventful for Schiller. He battled with his illness and wrestled with aesthetic problems. In February he began to expound his views to Körner in a series of letters, since known as the *Kallias-Briefe* (*Callias Letters*).[1] In April the Schillers for the first time began to keep house for themselves. The move, which coincided with a spell of raw wintry weather, precipitated

[1] See below, p. 159*f.*

L

one of Schiller's periods of illness, while Lotte, too, was far from well. Nevertheless Schiller worked at his aesthetic studies, writing the essay *Über Anmut und Würde* during May and June. In July he began a series of letters to Prince Friedrich Christian on the value of art in human affairs.

Ever since his marriage the thought of a visit to his parents had been in Schiller's mind. Now that he had the Danish pension there was no longer any financial difficulty; only his state of health and the attitude of the Duke of Würtemberg made him hesitate. The summer of 1793, however, gave him the longest period of immunity he had enjoyed since his illness had begun in January 1791. As he was still apparently the deserter of 1782 for Duke Karl Eugen, Schiller decided that he would not attempt to cross the Würtemberg border, but would establish himself with Lotte in the Imperial city of Heilbronn, some thirty miles to the north of Stuttgart. Though he would not be able to visit his parents, they at least would be able to come to him.

He looked forward to seeing a Swabian landscape and to breathing Swabian air. He longed, too, to see his father again. Captain Schiller was almost seventy, and his son felt that the opportunity of meeting must be taken soon, if it were not to be lost for ever.

It was not a fleeting visit that Schiller planned to pay. He intended to stay in Swabia through the whole autumn and winter. As the time for his departure drew near, something happened which promised not merely to raise his spirits but to change his whole outlook. Since the early months of 1793 Lotte had been ailing for no apparent reason. In July, shortly before the date fixed for the journey, it was realized that she was expecting a baby, which would probably be born in October. Heartened by this news, Schiller looked forward to his journey with even greater pleasure than before, delighted with the thought that his own native Swabia would be the native country of his first-born, too. So full were his thoughts of home, that he began to believe that its air would do more to cure his illness than all the doctors in Jena.

Schiller and his wife left Jena on August 2, 1793. Travelling by way of Nuremberg, they reached Heilbronn on the eighth. There they put up at an inn and sent news of their safe arrival to the Solitude. Living in furnished lodgings at Heilbronn, however, proved expensive, and it was too far away. Encouraged by a successful visit to his parents, he boldly moved on September 8 to Ludwigsburg, well inside Würtemberg territory. He did not regret the step, for it soon became evident that Karl Eugen would take no action against him.

In Ludwigsburg lived Schiller's old friend von Hoven, now a well-known physician, and Schiller was glad to place Lotte in the hands of a doctor who commanded his confidence. The move was scarcely completed before she felt the first pangs. Her confinement was a long and exhausting one, but late on the evening of September 14 a healthy boy was born. A new feeling of immortality assured came upon Schiller as he looked at his little son.

Mother and child were soon stronger and healthier than the father. Far from profiting by the climate, Schiller's health deteriorated. Throughout the autumn and winter he had repeatedly to battle with the severest asthmatic attacks, and their continual and disappointing recurrence threw him into a state of depression and nervous irritability. In the respites between his attacks of illness he pursued his philosophical and aesthetic studies and embodied some of the results in his letters to Prince Friedrich Christian, which he resumed in November after a pause of five months.

In October Duke Karl Eugen, who had steadfastly ignored Schiller, fell gravely ill, and on the twenty-fourth he died. Though Schiller was moved by this news and the national mourning he witnessed, his natural dislike of the man whom he felt to be the author of many of his misfortunes soon reasserted itself. He could write to Körner in December:

> The death of the old Herod has no influence on me or my family except that it is agreeable for all who are in close contact with the Duke to have a *human being* over them now. [December 10, 1793].

Under the new Duke Ludwig Eugen, Schiller's father was not only maintained in his situation as superintendent of the ducal gardens, but also promoted major in March 1794.

Since his first serious illness in 1791 Schiller had learned to dread the month of January; but in 1794 it passed without any serious crisis, and in the last ten days of the month he felt better than he had done for years. In his new-found energy he began to think of departure, and so great was his impatience to return home, that he was prepared to risk the winds and frosts of March; his haste to be gone was augmented by the report that a military hospital, probably full of patients with infectious diseases, was to be set up in Ludwigsburg.

Schiller had thought but poorly of his former friends when he had first met them in the autumn. Before leaving, however, he paid visits to them in Stuttgart and Tübingen, meeting Abel, Petersen, Scharffenstein, Zumsteeg, and Dannecker. On closer acquaintance they improved, and the atmosphere of Stuttgart pleased him so much that he decided to postpone his departure and to spend some weeks there.

Schiller particularly liked and admired the sculptor Dannecker, and Dannecker, idolizing Schiller, put all his energy, enthusiasm, and skill into a bust of his friend, which is the most impressive and, according to Schiller's contemporaries, the most faithful portrait of the poet. At the same time a portrait in oils was done by a woman, Ludowike Simanowiz, whose work, also reckoned a good likeness, shows a gentle and melancholy Schiller, contrasting sharply with the keen and energetic representation by Dannecker. Frau Simanowiz also painted Lotte's portrait.

In the previous autumn an old schoolfellow of Schiller's, Friedrich Haug, had put Schiller in touch with the Stuttgart bookseller and publisher Cotta, an energetic young man of twenty-nine. In the spring Schiller and Cotta met at Tübingen, and soon afterwards Schiller offered Cotta German translations of Greek tragedies done by himself, a Professor Nast, and Conz, a playmate of his days at Lorch. The idea did not attract Cotta, but on the eve of Schiller's departure the two men made an excursion together to Cannstadt. Cotta was determined to win Schiller's support for his firm, and he now came forward with an entirely new proposal. He intended to publish the first German newspaper with a national circulation, and invited Schiller to become its editor. The terms he offered were handsome: a basic salary of 2,000 gulden (£200), to be increased as the circulation grew, compensation if the paper failed, and, if he should die in harness, a pension for his widow. These were tempting conditions, and Schiller, though he was disinclined for such a post, promised to consider it. He had a counter-proposal to make.

Cotta was perhaps the man for a project which Schiller had very much at heart. *Die Thalia* in its various forms had been useful, but most one-man periodicals depreciate with time, and this was no exception. *Die Thalia* was inevitably associated with his earlier views, and he had therefore felt for some time that he ought to found a new journal for his new ideas. He had discussed it with Körner in the spring of 1792, and suggested it tentatively in the following October to Göschen, who failed to see the need of it. For eighteen months Schiller nursed the project without taking any practical steps. Now it seemed to him that Cotta might do what Göschen would not. On the way back to Stuttgart he put the idea to the publisher. Cotta agreed to visit Schiller in Jena, when they could discuss the two proposals at length, after each had had an opportunity to think matters over.

Schiller had spent nine months in Würtemberg, marred at first by ill-health, but ending on a note of promise for the future. It was sad to part from his father and mother, but he left them in good health and might yet be able to visit them again. Stronger, and feeling the richer for this contact with his parents, happy, too, in the little child who had extended his life into an indefinite future, Schiller left Stuttgart on May 6, 1794, on the long journey back to Jena.

Chapter Thirteen

THE STUDY OF PHILOSOPHY

1792-95

"IT is fairly certain that I shall read Kant and perhaps study him."
These words from Schiller's letter to Körner, written during his
first visit to Jena in August 1787, were to be more amply fulfilled
than Schiller could at that time foresee. His first interest remained
for some time the study of history. But his approach to history was
such as to suggest that he might find philosophical reflection a
more congenial occupation than wrestling with historical fact.

When Schiller settled at Jena in 1789 he was at the very centre of
the new faith in Kant, whose reputation stood higher only in his
native Königsberg. Professor Reinhold, when Schiller met him
on his first visit to Jena, maintained that in a hundred years the
name of Kant would be venerated like that of Jesus Christ, and men
of middle age left their estates in the hands of bailiffs and submitted
themselves to university discipline in order to hear the new gospel.
Philosophy, usually the step-child among the faculties, became the
most popular branch of study.

The enthusiasm with which Kant's philosophy was greeted is
surprising. Not only is his thought difficult to follow; but it is
expressed in language of such obscurity and specialized technicality
that it seems almost incomprehensible to all but the professional
philosopher. Indeed, so great is the difficulty that a German scholar
has ' translated ' the *Critique of Pure Reason* into normal language.[1]
Yet the popularity of Kant's ideas among his educated contemporaries
was undoubted and genuine.

Three conceptions had predominated in the philosophical thought
of the eighteenth century before Kant. The growing body of
scientists accepted the world around them as reality, and in doing
so they accepted the law of cause and effect (mechanistic causation).
The idealists and the sceptics, on the other hand, maintained that
the everyday world was appearance, not reality; the idealists believed
in final causation, in the fulfilment of an ultimate purpose, and the
sceptics (of whom Hume is the outstanding representative) rejected

---

[1] *Kants Kritik der reinen Vernunft ins Gemeindeutsche übersetzt von Wilhelm
Stapel* (Hamburg, 1919).

all causation as illusory. These three philosophies existed side by side, and none could command general assent. Kant provided the long-awaited system which countered the objections of materialists, idealists, and sceptics and gave an acceptable and apparently incontrovertible explanation of the problems which had beset the conflicting schools of thought.

Kant's most famous work, *The Critique of Pure Reason*,[1] had been published in 1781, in the same year as Schiller's *Die Räuber*. The philosopher was then fifty-seven. A period of almost complete silence ensued which was broken in 1788 by the publication of *The Critique of Practical Reason*.[2] Schiller was at that time in Weimar. Two more important works of Kant appeared during Schiller's years at Jena, *The Critique of Judgment*[3] in 1790 and *Religion within the Limits of Mere Reason*[4] in 1793.

Unlike the pure idealists, Kant did not deny the existence of the material world, but he considered that we cannot know its nature because in the act of knowing we impose on it the pattern of our own thought. The world of things, as we perceive it, is a combination of the things themselves and of our own minds, and we cannot separate from them the mental and subjective element. What we know is coloured by the conditions of knowing them. One such condition is the law of cause and effect. It is in nature because we put it there. Kant admits that things outside ourselves exist, but denies that we can know them through the senses.

This limitation of knowledge does not apply to the moral sphere. In moral experience, says Kant, we make direct contact with reality. In the moral world we are free of the illusion of cause and effect, which is part of the appearances of things (phenomena), and by exercising our will we come to know the true reality (noumena). But this moral knowledge only occurs when the will is truly free. If our actions are influenced by desires, and are not the decisions of the will alone, we are not free, but subject to cause and effect. The will should operate independently of and free from desire or inclination; such action is virtuous. It follows that an act, to be virtuous, must be performed exclusively from motives of duty and that desire or pleasure must have no part in it; Kant maintains that the participation of pleasure or inclination in an act does rob it of its virtuous character. In aesthetics Kant removes beauty from utilitarian considerations and interprets it as a symbol of the moral order—

[1] *Kritik der reinen Vernunft.*
[2] *Kritik der praktischen Vernunft.*
[3] *Kritik der Urteilskraft.*
[4] *Religion innerhalb der Grenzen der blossen Vernunft.*

that is, of the true (noumenal) reality; yet he regards the judgment of taste as subjective.

Few men were more impressed with Kant's work than was Schiller. No philosophy could appeal to him more than this system which, while admitting the existence of the phenomenal world, maintained the reality and superiority of the moral world and suggested that art could be the harmonizing mediator between the true and the apparent reality.

Schiller was temperamentally suited to Kant's outlook and interpretation of the world. But he found himself in strong disagreement with two of Kant's contentions. His whole nature revolted against the idea that the participation of inclination in an act automatically deprived it of virtuousness, and he could not accept the view that taste—that is, the judgment of beauty—is purely subjective. His philosophical work is largely an acute and lucid exposition of Kant's views on aesthetics and, to a less degree, on ethics, but with vital and far-reaching reservations about virtue and taste.

The study of Kant's philosophy was an arduous and exacting task, and Schiller could not have attempted it as long as he had to maintain himself and his wife by his writings. The Danish pension had altered that situation and he turned with eagerness and energy to this new field. He was not content merely to absorb; being a poet, he had to communicate his mental activity to others.

In the winter of 1792–93 his ideas on aesthetics began to crystallize. Just before Christmas he wrote to Körner:

> I have a much clearer idea of the nature of the Beautiful . . . I believe I have found an objective conception of the Beautiful, which would automatically give an objective principle of taste which Kant has despaired of finding. I shall arrange my thoughts on this and publish them next Easter in a dialogue: *Callias, or On Beauty.*

In thus affirming the objectivity of taste Schiller diverges from Kant at the very outset of his philosophical studies. The dialogue was never written, but the ideas which it would have embodied were largely worked out in a series of four letters (the so-called *Kallias-Briefe*) addressed to Körner in February 1793.[1]

In the first letter Schiller defines beauty. Since the world of appearances (phenomena) conforms always to the laws of cause and effect, true freedom (that is, from previous determining causes) is not possible in the phenomenal world. It is nevertheless possible for phenomena to take such a shape that they *appear* to be free. This freedom in the phenomenal world (*Freiheit in der Erscheinung*),

---

[1] February 8, 18 (with 19 as enclosure), 23 and 28.

or apparent freedom, is beauty: " The analogy of a phenomenon with the form of the pure will or of freedom is *beauty* (in its widest sense)."

The second letter contains Schiller's view of taste. An aesthetic judgment, he says, is independent of subject-matter and of morality; it is simply the assessment of the apparent freedom in the work of art: " Whenever we judge it aesthetically all we want to know is—is it what it is through itself alone? " Schiller has achieved objective definitions of beauty and aesthetic judgment, but he does not attempt to show how taste operates. As long as this gap remains, the practical application of his conception remains uncertain.

In his third letter Schiller seeks to meet this difficulty. He stresses the wholeness of a work of art and the inseparability of form and content. Beauty is nature in the sphere of art (*Natur in der Kunstmässigkeit*), a perfect harmony of essence with form. The recognition of this harmony is the task of taste. It occurs in poetry when every word and every line seems to be there necessarily and of its own accord:

> Versification is beautiful when every single line seems to determine its own length, its motion, and its pause, when every rhyme seems to come of an inner necessity and yet at just the right moment. . . .

Schiller concludes in the fourth letter that objectivity is a characteristic of great art. The elements with which the artist contends are the material in which he works and his own personality. In the greatest art both of these are unnoticed:

> The great artist . . . shows us his object (his presentation is purely objective), the mediocre one reveals himself (his presentation is subjective), the bad one shows us his material (his portrayal is determined by the nature of his medium and his limitations as an artist).

At this point the letters to Körner revert to their normal length and personal subject-matter. Though he did not finish this exposition of his views to his friend, nor write his projected *Kallias*, Schiller has said enough in these four letters to give a clear idea of his basic position. Its principal characteristic is its objectivity: beauty can be judged by an objective criterion; and art (which aims at beauty) should be objective. A thing is beautiful which appears free and independent of physical cause; a work of art is beautiful if it sheds all signs of the causes which have produced it— that is, the medium and the hand of the artist.

In May 1793 Schiller wrote in a few weeks an essay entitled *Über Anmut und Würde* (*On Grace and Dignity*), which he published in *Die neue Thalia*. It is a tentative and inconclusive work dealing with the moral implications of aesthetics, but it is important for its clear revelation of Schiller's decisive divergence from Kant's ethical position. Grace, Schiller says, is a spiritual quality added to beauty: " Die Natur gab die Schönheit des Baues, die Seele gibt die Schönheit des Spiels."[1] The state in which this " beauty of movement " takes place is one in which reason (Kant's word for the moral judgment) and sensuality are in harmony, the state in which duty and inclination coincide. Schiller goes on:

> Der Mensch nämlich ist nicht dazu bestimmt, einzelne sittliche Handlungen zu verrichten, sondern ein sittliches Wesen zu sein. Nicht Tugenden, sondern die Tugend ist seine Vorschrift, und die Tugend ist nichts anders " als eine Neigung zur Pflicht ".[2]

In the passages which follow, Schiller openly states his disagreement with Kant and gives as his own ideal " the beautiful soul " (die schöne Seele), who acts rightly by instinct and whose emotions are not at war with his duty, but always direct him along the right path. This is the character whose expression in action is grace: " In einer schönen Seele ist es also, wo Sinnlichkeit und Vernunft, Pflicht und Neigung harmonieren, und Grazie ist ihr Ausdruck in der Erscheinung."[3] This is an ideal state which, Schiller recognizes, cannot be permanently maintained in practice. Wherever the passions are concerned, there will be a conflict between desire and will, between duty and inclination. The expression of a successful struggle of the will against desire is termed dignity: " Beherrschung der Triebe durch die moralische Kraft ist Geistesfreiheit, und Würde heisst ihr Ausdruck in der Erscheinung."[4] Dignity, which appears in suffering ($\pi \acute{a} \theta o \varsigma$), and grace, which appears in conduct ($\mathring{\eta} \theta o \varsigma$), can be united in one character, and where this occurs the expression of a person's humanity is complete.

The interest of Über Anmut und Würde is primarily ethical. Schiller's next philosophical work, treating of the idea of suffering linked with dignity, is concerned with aesthetics. Über das Pathetische (On the Pathetic[5]), also published in Die neue Thalia in 1793, deals with tragedy. It was not his first effort in this field. In 1791

[1] Nature conferred beauty of structure, the soul gives beauty of movement.

[2] Man is not destined to perform single moral acts but to be a moral being. The ideal is virtue, not virtues, and virtue is nothing other than " a desire for duty."

[3] In a beautiful soul sensuality and reason, duty and inclination, are in harmony and their visible expression is grace.

[4] Control of the impulses by moral power is freedom of the spirit, whose visible expression is dignity.

[5] The word is used as Schiller uses it in conformity with its derivation from $\pi \acute{a} \theta o s$.

he had given some private lectures on tragedy, and these had formed
the basis of two essays published in *Die neue Thalia* in 1792, *Über den
Grund des Vergnügens an tragischen Gegenständen* (*On the Reason
for Pleasure derived from Tragic Subjects*) and *Über die tragische
Kunst* (*On Tragic Art*). In the former he had claimed that the
pleasure in tragedy arises from the victory of a higher moral principle
over a lower one, in the latter he emphasized the necessity of human
suffering in tragedy.

Über das Pathetische deals with this suffering, resistance to which
constitutes the tragic conflict. Tragedy shows us the free principle
in man, which expresses itself when he rises superior to adversity.
Schiller maintains that suffering is only aesthetic (that is, suitable
for art) as long as it is *sublime*. The doctrine of the sublime is based
upon Kant's views in the *Critique of Judgment* and is a cardinal
feature of Schiller's attitude. He had already touched upon it in
Über Anmut und Würde, when he proclaimed dignity to be the
expression of a sublime attitude of mind. In a short essay, originally
prefixed to *Über das Pathetische* and called *Vom Erhabenen* (*Of the
Sublime*), he summarizes Kant's views; indeed so closely does he
adhere to his model that he subsequently omitted the essay because
it added nothing original to another man's work. *Vom Erhabenen*
puts Kant's theory of the sublime in clear and arresting form. The
sublime occurs when we are at the same time conscious of our
dependence as natural beings and our independence as spiritual
ones. It can only occur in misfortune and suffering:

> Gross ist, wer das Furchtbare überwindet. Erhaben ist, wer es,
> auch selbst unterliegend, nicht fürchtet . . . Gross kann man sich im
> Glück, erhaben nur im Unglück zeigen.[1]

In *Über das Pathetische* Schiller shows how this sublimity is the basis
of all tragic art.

In another essay written during this year, but not published till
1801, Schiller puts a still higher valuation on the sublime. In
Über das Erhabene he points out that the exercise of the will only
becomes apparent when there is opposition. The stronger this
opposition, the greater is the power of the will which subdues it.
But the hostile force confronting a man may reach such a magnitude
that he must succumb to it; for instance, he may be faced with
death. How then can his will remain free? Schiller answers that
it can do so if he submits of his own free will to the inevitable, so
that he himself wills the fate which overtakes him: "Der moralisch
gebildete Mensch, und nur dieser, ist ganz frei. Entweder ist er

[1] He who conquers what is fearful is *great;* he who, while succumbing to it,
does not fear it, is *sublime.* . . . One can be great in *good fortune*, only in *misfortune*
can one be sublime.

der Natur als Macht überlegen, oder er ist einstimmig mit derselben."[1] The tragic hero, faced with overwhelming force, retains his freedom by willing what he cannot avoid. In this essay on the sublime Schiller also advances an interesting plea on behalf of the theatre. Real adversity may find us unprepared, but the artificial misfortune which tragedy provides finds us ready, and so exercises in us the independent principle of free will which is the source of the sublime. Tragedy trains us to encounter adversity. It is an instrument of moral education.

So far Schiller had been concerned with life as much as with art. He had discussed the value of conduct of various kinds, but had only been partly concerned with its representation in literature or art. His next philosophical work, published in three numbers of *Die Horen* in 1795, dealt specifically with the moral value, not of conduct, but of art.

This work, which bore the title *Über die ästhetische Erziehung des Menschen, in einer Reihe von Briefen* (*On the Aesthetic Education of Man, in a Series of Letters*), had its origin in the series of letters which Schiller had written to his Danish patron. This correspondence, rewritten and polished, forms the basis of the first instalment of nine letters. They begin with a reference to the times. Schiller realizes that many, in the age of the French Revolution and the cannonade of Valmy, will consider that men should give their efforts rather to politics than to art and poetry. But the deplorable use which they have made of their great opportunity proves that they are not yet well enough educated to be able to build the moral state: " Die moralische Möglichkeit fehlt, und der freigebige Augenblick findet ein unempfindliches Geschlecht."[2]

Modern man has specialized, to the detriment of his personality as a whole; and though the realm prospers, the individuals that compose it are one-sided and ill-developed. The totalitarian state was already a potential danger, and Schiller, with a rhetorical question to which the answer is clear, takes his stand against it: " Kann aber wohl der Mensch dazu bestimmt sein, über irgend einem Zwecke sich selbst zu versäumen? "[3]

The means by which man can regain the complete personality that he has lost in an age of specialization is art, which exerts its influence when he is most susceptible, in his hours of leisure:

Der Ernst deiner Grundsätze wird sie [deine Zeitgenossen] von dir

[1] The morally educated man alone is free. Either he is superior in power to nature, or he is in harmony with it.

[2] The moral possibility is lacking, and the moment wastes its treasure on a race of men incapable of appreciating it.

[3] Can it be man's destiny in fulfilling any one aim to lose himself?

scheuchen, aber im Spiele ertragen sie sie noch . . . Ihre Maximen wirst du umsonst bestürmen, ihre Taten umsonst verdammen, aber an ihrem Müssiggange kannst du deine bildende Hand versuchen.[1]

There were seven letters in the second batch, numbered from ten to sixteen. They sketch out a strikingly new view of art, rejecting all *direct* moral effect, and combining apparent uselessness with the very highest conception of morality. Following Kant, Schiller sees man's activity as dominated by two impulses: a material (or sensual) one (*Stofftrieb*), and a formal (or moral) one (*Formtrieb*). These impulses would appear to be opposed; nevertheless (and this is Schiller's original contribution) they can and do work together, and where this happens they arouse a third force, the play impulse (*Spieltrieb*), the object of which is beauty. To this idea of beauty Schiller gives a psychological interpretation; beauty is recognizable, not by qualities which it possesses objectively, but by what happens in us when we perceive it. A thing is beautiful, in fact, when it produces in us a state of harmony and equilibrium:

> . . . befinden wir uns zugleich in dem Zustand der höchsten Ruhe und der höchsten Bewegung, und es entsteht jene wunderbare Rührung, für welche der Verstand keinen Begriff und die Sprache keinen Namen hat.[2]

In the sixteenth letter Schiller is even more explicit, and himself uses the word ' equilibrium ' to denote the aesthetic state: " das Schöne . . . dessen höchstes Ideal also in dem möglichst vollkommensten Bunde und Gleichgewicht der Realität und der Form wird zu suchen sein."[3]

The third instalment (Letters 17–27) treats of the beautiful and the sublime under the new terms of " melting " and " energetic " beauty (*schemelzende* and *energische Schönheit*). The beautiful was most suited, Schiller declares, to man's primitive and barbaric state; the sublime is the most vital form of art in the refined and civilized condition which he has since achieved. With the aid of the sublime, man will become first aesthetic and then moral: " Es gibt keinen andern Weg, den sinnlichen Menschen vernünftig zu machen, als dass man denselben zuvor ästhetisch macht."[4]

---

[1] The weight of your principles will drive them [your contemporaries] away, but they will bear with them if they are lightened in play. . . . You will attack their maxims and condemn their acts in vain, but you can try your educative hand upon their leisure.

[2] We find ourselves at one and the same time in the state of the greatest repose and the greatest movement, and there arises in us that wonderful emotion for which the intellect has no conception and language no name.

[3] The beautiful, whose highest ideal is to be found in the most perfect union and equilibrium of reality and form.

[4] The only way to make the sensual man a moral man is to make him an aesthetic man first.

In his twenty-second letter Schiller states the signs by which the aesthetic state may be recognized:

> Haben wir uns . . . dem Genuss echter Schönheit dahingegeben, so sind wir in einem solchen Augenblick unsrer leidenden und tätigen Kräfte in gleichem Grad Meister, und mit gleicher Leichtigkeit werden wir uns zum Ernst und zum Spiele, zur Ruhe und zur Bewegung, zur Nachgiebigkeit und zum Widerstand, zum abstrakten Denken und zur Anschauung wenden.[1]

If on the other hand we feel a greater readiness for one sort of action than another, then we have not reached the aesthetic state, either because the work of art was faulty, or because we were inattentive, or, more usually, because of a combination of both. With this formulation of an aesthetic state of harmony and equilibrium Schiller has brought theory into line with experience. The argument *a priori* and the test of experiment coincide in their result. In discovering an objective touchstone in the mind for the experience of beauty, Schiller made an enormous stride forward; its full significance has only become apparent in recent years.

It is clear that the views of art which Schiller expounded in the years 1792 to 1794 fit his own talents and inclinations. He himself was a tragic dramatist, and he held tragedy to be the highest form of art. The approach to art of which he most approved was the objective one; his own natural bias had always sought to repress the personal element in his work and crystallize the objective, immutable essence of an experience. The ideal was very early his goal in art, and he strove for it all the more eagerly when he discovered that Kant rejected phenomena as our subjective perception of an unknowable reality.

Some of Schiller's qualities are hardly compatible with good philosophical writing. His enthusiasm is always liable to sweep him away from a standpoint of cool detachment; and the rhetoric, in which it naturally expresses itself, often lends an emotional colour to what should be an intellectual argument. Allied to this vigorous enthusiasm is Schiller's impatience of detail. Hardly once does he quote an author accurately, relying on his remarkable memory to give him the spirit of the original.

The faults of Schiller's method do not, however, invalidate his conclusions, which conform to the structure of his mind and can stand independently of flaws in the train of thought by which they

---

[1] If we have given ourselves up to the enjoyment of true beauty, at that moment we are completely masters of our passive and active powers and can turn with equal facility to work or play, repose or movement, can yield or resist, can retire within ourselves for abstract thought or contemplate with open mind the world around us.

have ostensibly been reached. Schiller repeatedly stated that Kant gave a theoretical basis for a number of generally accepted truths. This applies also to Schiller, whose truths still remain true, even if some features of his method are impugned.

What Schiller came to believe about art was this. The true approach is the idealistic and objective one, which ignores the incidental and transitory details and concerns itself with essentials. It was on this principle that he had always worked himself, though his view was to be broadened later by contact with Goethe. He held that the greatest kind of art was tragic art, in which man is shown succumbing physically to adversity but rising morally superior to it. Most important of all is Schiller's conception of beauty as a state of balance and harmony of our impulses. This most modern of Schiller's views combines in a remarkable way the subjective and objective elements; for the perception of beauty is a mental event, recognized by signs which are constant. The rejection of the didactic conception and the elaboration of the theory of balance are the great and generally valid achievement of Schiller's aesthetic studies.

The greatest value of Schiller's work in this field was for himself. In his three years of intensive study of aesthetics he clarified his ideas, justified his mission in his own eyes, and discovered satisfying answers to problems of form and artistic creation which had long preoccupied him. These years were not wasted. Without the reassurance, courage, and certainty which his researches gave him, it is likely that he would never have broken the silence into which his artistic genius had lapsed since 1787.

Chapter Fourteen

ALLIANCE WITH GOETHE

1794–96

SCHILLER returned to Jena with his family on May 15, 1794.
His health was not permanently improved, but his mental
vigour had benefited by the change. His intellectual powers
developed in the course of time an almost complete independence of
his physical state, so that his normal ill-health no longer impeded
his creative work.

Shortly after Schiller's return Cotta visited him in Jena. The
publisher was still anxious to have Schiller as the editor of his
projected political newspaper, and Schiller was even more eager to
persuade Cotta to publish the literary monthly which meant so
much to him. Contracts for both plans were drawn up and signed
but not exchanged, and the final decision was deferred. The more
Schiller thought about the political newspaper, the less inclined
he felt to undertake it. He had no experience of newspapers and
no interest in politics; only the tempting financial conditions and the
desire to win Cotta for his own scheme made him hesitate to refuse
the offer. In mid-June he decided against editing the newspaper
and Cotta agreed to concentrate upon the new monthly journal, which
was to be called *Die Horen* (*The Horae*).

Die Horen was to be a literary monthly enjoying the collaboration
of the best writers in Germany. Schiller himself was to be its
editor, and its policy would be controlled by a committee of eminent
contributors living within easy reach of Jena. In June he drew up a
circular announcing the scope and organization of the new periodical
and he was busy for some weeks after, distributing printed copies
of this among the most reputable German writers of the day.

The intellectual level of the monthly was to be high, its cultural
appeal wide: " Alles, was entweder bloss den gelehrten Leser
interessieren oder was bloss den nicht gelehrten befriedigen kann,
wird davon ausgeschlossen sein."[1] The difficulty was to find
contributors who could carry out the editorial policy. Schiller
realized that here lay the key to the success or failure of *Die Horen*,

[1] Everything which interests the scholar only or appeals alone to the unscholarly
will be excluded.

and he spared no pains to gather together a company of distinguished authors. By the late autumn twenty-six writers of repute had accepted his invitation to collaborate. They included Herder, Fichte, Jacobi and Schiller's own friends, Körner and Wilhelm von Humboldt. The most important acquisition of all was Goethe.

In June 1794 Schiller had sent Goethe a copy of his circular, together with a polite personal invitation to join the select committee of *Die Horen*. Ten days later he received Goethe's acceptance. This was a great triumph for *Die Horen* and a token that the antagonism which Goethe had long felt towards Schiller was at an end.

Since Schiller had left Weimar for Jena the bitterness of his resentment against Goethe had passed away. He recognized frankly the greatness of Goethe's genius, but felt that the type of mind was uncongenial to him. At Jena they had met repeatedly without friction, but also without cordiality. Neither was aware of a change in the other, but a mutual respect had sprung up. To Goethe, who had felt very much alone since his return from Italy six years before, the invitation to join the committee of *Die Horen* was a very welcome one; for he had long ago realized that Schiller was no longer the violent and undisciplined writer of *Die Räuber*.

In the middle of July both men attended, as they had often done before, a meeting of the Scientific Society of Jena. They chanced to leave the hall together and walked along the street in conversation. Goethe was agreeably surprised at a chance remark by Schiller, criticizing the fragmentary, piecemeal approach which characterized the lecture they had heard. An animated discussion followed which was interrupted by their arrival at Schiller's house. Goethe accepted an invitation to come in, and they continued their argument in Schiller's study. A wide divergence in their methods of approach became obvious. Goethe placed his trust in the evidence of the senses, Schiller in the deductions of reason. Goethe was struck by the power of Schiller's intellect and the integrity of his thought. The argument, which concerned the reality of Goethe's concept of the primary plant (*Urpflanze*), was indecisive, but it prepared the way for future contact.

The decisive step came on August 23, 1794, when Schiller wrote Goethe a letter setting forth his view of the nature of Goethe's genius. The desire to secure Goethe's maximum collaboration for *Die Horen*, and the very real admiration which Schiller had long felt for Goethe, combined to produce a tone which was both persuasive and cordial, while the content bore the stamp of Schiller's uncompromising honesty. Such praise was very welcome to Goethe, who warmed to the prospect of a union between minds so opposed in method and yet so united in their aim.

What you can hardly realize [wrote Schiller] (for to itself genius is always the greatest of all mysteries) is the splendid way in which your philosophic instinct harmonizes with the purest results of the speculative reason. It is true that it seems at first sight that there could be no greater opposites than the speculative mind, which starts from unity, and the intuitive, which starts from multiplicity. But if the former seeks experience in a loyal and disinterested spirit, and the latter searches for laws with an active and independent intellect, then the two cannot fail to meet half-way.

This acute and generous letter built a bridge between the two men. The last obstacles of prejudice were swept away, and Goethe took the first opportunity of getting to know Schiller. Several letters passed between them, and then, at the beginning of September, Goethe asked Schiller to stay with him so that they could pursue their discussions better and get to know each other thoroughly. Schiller arrived in Weimar on September 14. Goethe took great pains to make his invalid guest comfortable, and for a fortnight they lived together, seeing very little company, clarifying their ideas, and forming plans for the future.

A real personal regard began to grow up between them. It was not to be expected that mature men of forty-five and thirty-four would quickly form the same intimate kind of friendship which had sprung up so swiftly between Schiller and Körner nine years earlier. But it became something much stronger and deeper than a purely intellectual bond. Goethe grew to be a regular visitor to the Schillers' house at Jena, and constant communication became a necessity for both men. When they could not meet they exchanged letters, which, though predominantly intellectual, were written in a tone of warm understanding and firm friendship. They form a striking monument to the alliance of these two great men.

Schiller devoted the last months of 1794 to his preparations for *Die Horen*. He gave close attention to its make-up and presentation, carefully selecting types, specifying margins, and choosing design and paper for the cover. Cotta proved prompt and efficient in the dispatch of business and was more than ready to meet Schiller's wishes. The contents of the first number caused Schiller a great deal of worry. Promises were more numerous than contributions, and repeated reminders still failed in many cases to secure the hoped-for articles; in the end Schiller had to implore Körner to fill the gap at short notice. Goethe's help was negligible, for *Wilhelm Meisters Lehrjahre* (*Wilhelm Meister's Apprenticeship*) was already in the hands of a publisher when Schiller first wrote to Goethe; and though the *Elegien* (usually termed *Römische Elegien*) were to appear in *Die Horen*, Goethe insisted that they should not figure in the first number.

M

This first issue of *Die Horen* appeared in January 1795. Its most important feature came from Schiller himself and was the first instalment (Letters 1–9) of *Über die ästhetische Erziehung des Menschen*. This essay was not well received, many critics and subscribers complaining of obscurity and abstraction, but Schiller was undeterred. He had launched *Die Horen* in order to educate and train German taste, without any concession to popularity. And so the second and third instalments of his *Aesthetic Letters* were in due course published. Nevertheless works of this calibre required time and unhurried throught, and through the default of so many contributors Schiller found himself obliged to provide a far larger proportion of the copy for *Die Horen* than he had originally intended. He had therefore to turn to easier tasks than the problems of philosophy.

It was in this way that his last historical work of note came to be written. Already in November 1794 the shortage of copy was appreciable, and Schiller began a short essay on the siege of Antwerp by the Spaniards in the sixteenth century, intending to use it to give variety to the first number. He was unable to finish it before the spring, and the *Belagerung von Antwerpen durch den Prinzen von Parma in den Jahren 1584 und 1585* (*Siege of Antwerp by the Prince of Parma in the Years 1584 and 1585*) eventually appeared in the fourth and fifth numbers of *Die Horen*. It is a well-written and authoritative account of the siege, clear and vivid in style, reliable in fact, and sound in judgment.

Late in the year Schiller made a further philosophical contribution to *Die Horen*. *Über naive und sentimentalische Dichtung* (*On Naive and Sentimental Poetry*) ranks with the *Aesthetic Letters* as a mature, balanced, and original contribution to the study of aesthetics. It was begun in the autumn of 1794 in the early days of Schiller's friendship with Goethe, written for the most part in the second half of 1795 and published in *Die Horen* in three instalments in November and December 1795 and January 1796. This essay takes a wider view than any of Schiller's previous aesthetic writings, not restricting itself to Schiller's own type of poetry, but seeking to explain the working and estimate the value of other manifestations of the poetic mind.

An obvious contrast existed between the literatures of ancient Greece and modern Europe; but similar and almost equally striking disparities divided individual poets of the modern world, such as Goethe and Schiller. At the root of this diversity Schiller sees two fundamentally different methods of approach, which are determined by the character and circumstances of the poet and which he calls " naïf " and " sentimental."

Über naive und sentimentalische Dichtung falls into three sections, corresponding to the original three instalments. The first part treats of *naïf* poets and poetry. *Naïvety* is natural as opposed to artificial behaviour or thought in human beings: " Zum Naiven wird erfordert, dass die Natur über die Kunst den Sieg davon trage."[1] It is the characteristic of genius—" Naiv muss jedes wahre Genie sein "[2]—and it can also characterize whole epochs and peoples, and of these the greatest example is ancient Greece. Schiller points out that the Greeks paid no special attention to the beauties of landscape and to all that we call *nature*, because they were a part of nature themselves. Their whole world was nature, and the antithesis of nature and civilization could not arise for them. They were *naïf*. Even in the modern world, in which the contrast between natural and artificial has become very clear, it is possible for individual poets to be at one with themselves and the world around them in such a way as to be *naïf*, and Schiller points to Shakespeare as an example. But, in general, modern man is much more conscious of *nature* than his Greek predecessors; he sees it as something desirable, existing outside himself, which he has lost.

To the ancient Greek and the modern European types of mind correspond two types of poetry, that which *is* nature and that which *seeks* it—" Sie [die Dichter] werden also entweder Natur sein, oder sie werden die verlorene suchen."[3] The second type of poet yearns for and seeks his lost home. By the art of the ideal he regains the unity he has lost—" Die Natur macht ihn [den Menschen] mit sich eins, die Kunst trennt und entzweit ihn, durch das Ideal kehrt er zur Einheit zurück."[4]

It is with these poets, who are searching for a lost identity with nature, that the second section deals. Schiller terms them *sentimental*, in contrast to the *naïf* writers. The latter move us by truth to nature, the former by ideas. By the very nature of their integrity and unity with themselves, the naïf poets are not subdivisible into categories. The *sentimental* poets, however, may be divided into two main groups, the *satirical* and the *elegiac*. Schiller emphasizes that he uses these terms to denote, not formal qualities, but the nature of the emotion felt by the reader; in other words his approach is psychological, as it had been in the letters *Über die ästhetische Erziehung des Menschen.*

---

[1] For the naïf it is necessary that nature should be victorious over art.

[2] Every true genius must be naïf.

[3] They [poets] are either themselves nature, or they seek nature which they have lost.

[4] Nature makes him [man] one with herself; art separates and brings discord to him, through the ideal he returns to unity.

The *satirical* poet stresses the contrast between the ideal state of nature and the defective reality, and his satire may be either *pathetic* or *comic*, according to whether his treatment is serious or light. The *elegiac* poet emphasizes, not the contrast between ideal and reality, but the ideal alone. Either, as the elegiac poet proper, he mourns the loss of the ideal, or else he portrays the ideal as if it really existed, in which case he is an *idyllic* poet. At this point the essay descends from the realm of theory into the world of experience. Modern poets are, with very few exceptions, *sentimental* and *elegiac*, and Schiller conducts a rapid review of German literature in the eighteenth century, commenting shrewdly, justly, and forthrightly on his contemporaries and many of his predecessors.

The third instalment contained a discussion of the idyll and the sketch of a psychology based on the theory of the *naïf* and *sentimental*. The *realist* character in life corresponds to the *naïf* poet in literature. the *idealist* to the *sentimental* poet. Inferior versions of the same types are the empiricist and the dreamer.

In his survey of the literature of his age Schiller had discussed Goethe's *Werther*, which he saw as the work of a *naïf* poet treating a *sentimental* subject. This estimate of Goethe lies at the heart of *Über naive und sentimentalische Dichtung*. Schiller had previously made no attempt in a published work to assess the relationship between his type of work and Goethe's. He felt the power of Goethe's writing, its vigour, its ease, and its truth to nature. There were often moments when he felt depressed in the presence of a greater genius whom he could not aspire to equal. His own path was much harder, his aim much less certain. In *Über naive und sentimentalische Dichtung* he grappled with the problem of harmonizing Goethe's genius and his own. He and Goethe are not a lesser and a greater poet of the same type, but representatives of two different and opposed categories; Goethe the *naïf*, Schiller the *sentimental* poet. Neither category is, in his opinion, superior to the other. The *naïf* poet's work comes nearer to perfection, the *sentimental* poet's aim is higher. This conception is a fuller working out of the ideas Schiller had first expressed in his letter to Goethe of August 23, 1794. The categories of *naïf* and *sentimental*, of which Goethe and he were representative, are complementary and bound together by their ultimate aim.

Contact with Goethe had broadened Schiller's outlook and led him to a view of the artist which could include his new friend and himself without detriment to either. Goethe's influence is visible elsewhere in this essay. The abstract deduction of Schiller's earlier philosophical writings (which had been deliberate, since he wished to attain his results without the assistance of the ' real ' phenomenal world) gave place to a method which drew liberally on experience, not for proof, but for illustration. *Über naive und sentimentalische Dichtung* is, as a result, more readable than any of Schiller's earlier philosophical works. Contact with the realist Goethe enabled Schiller, the idealist, to write philosophy which was popular in the best sense.

Happy in his new friendship with Goethe and absorbed in his journalistic work, Schiller refused the offer of a professorship made to him early in 1795 by the University of Tübingen in his native Würtemberg. He felt that Saxe-Weimar was now his spiritual home and that he could not abandon the newly won contact with Goethe. Throughout the year 1795 he devoted nearly all his energies to *Die Horen*, the only relief being the writing of a number of poems, the first he had written for six years. Some of these, too, were destined to find their way into the pages of *Die Horen*, though the majority were intended for a year-book of verse (*Musenalmanach auf das Jahr* 1796), which Schiller had undertaken to edit. Schiller had worked for his periodical with energy and perseverance. It had been an ungrateful task. The initial interest of the public had waned. Many readers objected to the theoretical character of the letters *Über die ästhetische Erziehung des Menschen*, others were scandalized by Goethe's *Römische Elegien*. By August 1795 Schiller was tired of *Die Horen*; but he had called it into being, had gathered colleagues, some of whom had worked hard for it, and he had been loyally supported by Cotta. He could not drop it merely because he was losing interest. So he struggled on into the winter, feeling increasingly resentful of the lack of understanding which his and Goethe's ideas encountered. It seemed to the two friends that malice, vulgarity, and stupidity had combined against them, and that by far their worst enemies were, not the readers, but envious men of letters.

In December, when it had been decided, to Schiller's regret, to continue *Die Horen* through the year 1796, Goethe hit upon an idea which was to develop into a campaign against the mediocrity and malice which had clogged the popularity of the periodical. Goethe proposed to write a number of epigrams, one directed against each rival journal in Germany. As a model he chose the *Xenia* (or " Gifts ") of Martial, two-lined epigrams consisting of a hexameter followed by a pentameter, and he sent the first few samples to Schiller two days before Christmas 1795.

Schiller took to the idea at once. Before the New Year the two men had decided to extend their scheme to include individual authors and works as well as journals, and early in January 1796 Goethe spent a fortnight in Jena, during which they worked at their epigrams, and in March and April Schiller paid a return visit to Weimar. When they were not together they sent each other their epigrams by letter. The *Xenien*, as they were soon called by both authors, were an attack upon the German literary world, and Schiller and Goethe enjoyed themselves paying off various old scores. By the middle of 1796 they had finished their task. Four hundred and fourteen *Xenien* were published as the last part of the *Musenalmanach auf das Jahr* 1797. It was an essential part of the plan that the work of the two friends should be indistinguishable (though subsequent research has established the authorship of each epigram), and emphasis was on unanimity and close collaboration.

A few impersonal comic epigrams open the collection, which then continues with malice, sometimes stinging the quarry with a single dart, sometimes striking it down with a battery of bludgeon-like blows. The most vicious are naturally aimed at the strongest opponents of *Die Horen*. Among a number of other ' gifts ' Friedrich Nicolai received this:

> Ominös ist dein Name, er spricht dein ganzes Verdienst aus;
> Gerne verschafftest du, ging' es, dem Pöbel den Sieg.[1]

And Reichardt, a former supporter who had turned against Goethe and Schiller, was overwhelmed with a blunt personal attack:

> Setze nur immer Motto's auf deine Journale, sie zeigen
> Alle die Tugenden an, die man an dir nicht bemerkt.[2]

The brothers Stolberg (who had so bitterly attached Schiller's *Die Götter Griechenlands*) were the third main target, but a host of other figures received more or less ambiguous ' gifts.' Here and there a serious and impersonal epigram was embedded in strata of malice and irony and satire, but in the main the personal and pointed predominated. The targets were not explicitly named, but they were unmistakably indicated.

Schiller and Goethe had set out to avenge much stupid or coarse criticism and to laugh at the expense of some opponents and many mediocrities. But the weapon of mockery is a dangerous one. They had been much less vulnerable in their aloof and dignified silence; although it was exasperating to have to suffer in silence the assaults of fools, at least the enemy could not know whether his blows had struck home. Indeed their detached and superior attitude had given their opponents a feeling of angry impotence. With the publication of the *Xenien* they left their serene Olympian heights and

---

[1] Your name is an ominous one and sums up your entire merits; willingly would you help the mob to victory, if you could. (' Nike,' ' laos' for people is Greek for ' victory',)

[2] Go on putting mottoes in your journals; they indicate all the virtues which are not perceptible in you.

descended into the plain to give battle, thereby forfeiting their strongest weapon—their apparently invulnerable remoteness. Not only had they condescended to controversy; they had also stooped to personalities. There are allusions to Huber's private life and insulting comments on the intelligence of many writers and scholars. The publication of this collection of epigrams was, in fact, an act of recklessness and represents an unfortunate consequence of the new friendship between Schiller and Goethe. Alone, neither of them would have written them; together they urged each other on. The sharpest thrusts came from Schiller, the loftiest scorn was Goethe's.

The *Xenien* achieved an immediate and striking success, but it was a *succès de scandale;* the *Musenalmanach* was eagerly bought because of these personal attacks on living writers, and not on account of the serious poems which made up its principal content. It was not to be expected that all of the many authors and scholars who were so roughly handled in the *Xenien* would submit passively. Reviews, mostly unfavourable, began to appear in places as far apart as Hamburg and Salzburg. Towards the end of 1796 and in the following year books of *Anti-Xenien* were published, some of which—especially those by Manso[1] and by Fulda[2]—hurled the bitterest and coarsest personal gibes and insults at the two poets. Retorts of various kinds likewise came from Nicolai, from Claudius, and from Gleim. The savagery of these counter-attacks pleased Goethe, but they disquieted Schiller, who did not possess his friend's self-sufficiency and imperturbable contempt for the opinion of others.

The contrast in the attitude of the two men to the aftermath of the *Xenien* emerges very clearly in their correspondence. Goethe, completely unruffled, enjoys the uproar; Schiller feels uneasy and uncertain. In December 1796 he wrote to Goethe:

> What you wrote in your last letter about the higher and eventual advantages of such quarrels between contemporaries may well be true: but to enjoy them, one must be able to do without calm and the encouragement of others.

Schiller could not feel happy in an atmosphere of disapprobation, and the reception of the *Xenien* had a disturbing effect upon him. Goethe, conscious of his superiority and unneedful of the approval of any but his closest friends, could afford to antagonize two-thirds of the literary world. Schiller now realized that it had been a mistake to join Goethe in this dangerous game.

The *Xenien* claimed poetic virtues as well as controversial ones.

---

[1] *Gegengeschenke an die Sudelköche in Jena und Weimar von einigen dankbaren Gästen.* 1797.

[2] *Trogalien zur Verdauung der Xenien.* 1797.

Many of the epigrams are beautifully turned and pointed, leaving a sense of completeness and satisfaction. The best of these are by Goethe; Schiller's have more venom with less balance. Occasional variety is given by a few epigrams of a more general character, such as these lines comparing Greek and modern tragedy:

> Unsre Tragödie spricht zum Verstand, drum zerreisst sie das Herz so;
> Jene setzt in Affekt, darum beruhigt sie so ![1]

Throughout there is some variety in theme and tone, but there is no diversity of form, except for slight and subtle changes of rhythm. For four hundred and fourteen *Xenien* the sequence of hexameter and pentameter is maintained inflexibly with inevitable monotony, and this rigidity has often cramped and blunted the satire. Add to this the fleeting significance of many of the epigrams, whose understanding now requires copious notes, and it will be seen that as poetry the *Xenien* have serious shortcomings. They exhibit an unsatisfactory compromise between form and subject-matter, in which formal beauty and pungent satire prove to be mutually hostile.

The gulf between Schiller's life and his work and between his work and the political events of the day emerges very clearly in the first nine months of 1796. The *Xenien* and a number of impersonal poems were the only products of his poetic powers at a time of great anxiety. Early in the year his father fell seriously ill with gout. In March his youngest sister, Nanette, fell ill with fever, and within a few weeks the remaining sister, Louise, contracted the same disease. Frau Schiller, sixty-three and in frail health, now had three desperately sick patients on her hands and no one to help her. Schiller learned the full gravity of the situation in April. His own health was too poor to allow him to undertake the journey; neither could Lotte go, for she was now expecting a second child. The sense of his powerlessness distressed and tormented Schiller, and in a letter full of anguish and deep affection he implored his sister, Christophine Reinwald in Meiningen, to go to the assistance of the stricken family.

To his great relief he learned early in May that Christophine had set out on the long journey to the Solitude. Before she could arrive the youngest sister had died. Nanette had been born after Schiller had left home for the Duke of Würtemberg's academy, but he had become much attached to her when, as a sixteen-year-old girl, she had visited Jena with her mother in 1792. Louise gradually recovered; but it soon became clear that Kaspar Schiller was failing. In the easier intervals when his pain receded he was cheered by the

---

[1] Our tragedy speaks to the intellect, that is why its effect is heart-rending; theirs stirs the emotions, therefore it leaves us afterwards calm.

thoughts of his son's success and the good relations existing between them. In a letter written towards the end of August occur these touching words from Christophine: " I had to read your splendid letter to our dear father; he cried like a child over it and thanked God fervently that He had given him such a son."

On September 7, 1796, Kaspar Schiller died at the age of seventy-two. The news reached Schiller twelve days later, and, though he was expecting it and regarded it as a release from hopeless suffering, it shocked him deeply.

The year was darkened, too, by the war between Austria and the new French Republic. Most of the fighting was in northern Italy, where the young general Bonaparte was gaining his first victories. Desultory campaigning took place also in southern Germany, and the repercussions were felt in Thuringian towns such as Weimar and Jena. The uncertainty of communications with Cotta in Stuttgart and Tübingen obliged Schiller to turn his house into a packing and dispatch department for the *Musenalmanach auf das Jahr* 1797 (containing the *Xenien*), which was being printed in Jena because of war conditions.

But the year 1796 was not an entirely black one. In July Lotte bore Schiller a second son, who was christened Ernst. Letters reveal Schiller's delight; yet no trace of this joy, or of his sorrows, or of the unrest of 1796, is to be found in his work. This was the vehicle for his deepest convictions, but not for the physical and emotional experiences of his life.

Chapter Fifteen

POETIC RENASCENCE
1795–99

THE first indication of the revival of Schiller's creative impulse manifested itself as he was recuperating in Swabia in the winter of 1793–94. It took the form of a renewed interest in the composition of a tragedy about Wallenstein. At the time, however, he was still deeply committed to the study of philosophy. His dramatic plan therefore made no headway. He had to overcome considerable inertia, for by the time he drew closer to Goethe in the winter of 1794–95, it was fully five years since he had written anything of a poetic character. The acquaintance with Goethe released no accumulated store of themes; yet frequent contact with so fertile and creative a mind imperceptibly braced Schiller's mind for poetry. In less than a year after the establishment of the friendship Schiller had begun to write poems again, and he found that he still retained his power and skill.

Six years earlier Schiller had worked long and hard at his philosophical poem *Die Künstler*, had revised and rejected, polished and expanded. He had many lines on paper which he could not incorporate in the poem. In the interval the problems of art had continued to be his main preoccupation. It was therefore not surprising that, on his return to poetry at the age of thirty-five, in the summer of 1795, he should take up again the thoughts and fragments associated with the poem of 1789. His first effort, *Poesie des Lebens* (*Poetry of Life*), was a brief philosophical dialogue in verse between the stern philosopher who rejects appearances and the artist for whom they mean joy and happiness. It is a neat, well-executed, but not very convincing trifle.

Die Macht des Gesanges (*The Power of Song*), which followed it, makes use of the original opening lines of *Die Künstler*:

> Ein Regenstrom aus Felsenrissen,
> Er kommt mit Donners Ungestüm,
> Bergtrümmer folgen seinen Güssen,
> Und Eichen stürzen unter ihm;
> Erstaunt, mit wollustvollem Grausen,
> Hört ihn der Wanderer und lauscht,
> Er hört die Flut vom Felsen brausen,

Doch weiss er nicht, woher sie rauscht:
So strömen des Gesanges Wellen
Hervor aus nie entdeckten Quellen.[1]

These lines are a fair example of Schiller's declamatory style in poetry; they have power and vigour, but they also reveal two recurrent weaknesses of his non-dramatic verse—obscurity which conceals from the reader the application of the image, and the use of final rhyming couplets so short as to be trite. The choice of stanza, with its alternate rhyming pairs, alternate strong and weak endings, short lines, and final couplet, is an unfortunate one. Its brevity and regularity is ill-adapted to Schiller's rhetorical style, which requires flexible rhythms and a greater sweep, such as he had found in the blank verse of *Don Carlos*. Packing his sense into two short lines at a time only resulted in abrupt and elliptical thought. And in this poem it is thought which Schiller seeks to convey, and not emotion. The starting-point is purely intellectual, and the magic of poetry is something which is wrapped round it afterwards.

Pegasus im Joche (*Pegasus in Harness*) contrasts the correct use and the misuse of poetic genius, and *Die Würde der Frauen* (*The Dignity of Women*) is based on the conventional contrast of the active, dominant man and the passive, yielding woman. In *Das Ideal und das Leben* (*The Ideal and Life*) Schiller expresses his preference for the ideal to the ' real ' and his belief that the acceptance of fate offers the truest path to freedom.

As this poem embodies the ideas expressed in *Über das Erhabene*, so does *Der Genius* (*The Genius*) reflect the thought of *Über naive und sentimentalische Dichtung*. All these poems seek to give shape to an idea; their form does not grow, but is imposed upon an already existing basis of thought. In spite of all the skill Schiller has bestowed upon them, they cannot shake off the dry abstraction of their origin.

There are, however, four poems written in 1795 to which this objection does not apply. In *Der Tanz* (*The Dance*) the process is reversed; observation of the material world leads to the enunciation of general ideas. But the form is still conceived separately from the content. Schiller handles classical elegiacs with dexterity, lightness, and rhythmic grace. Nevertheless *Der Tanz* is not a natural growth, but a *tour de force* in classical form.

Der Abend (*Evening*), which uses an ancient lyrical strophe, is a still greater achievement of technical skill. It makes no pretence

---

[1] The torrent streams from rocky clefts with a roar of thunder, boulders follow it and oaks are swept away before it; astonished and seized by a pleasant shudder, the traveller listens to the flood surging down from the rocks, but whence it comes he does not know: just so do the waves of song stream down from undiscovered sources.

to be anything but a piece of deliberate verse-shaping. Consequently its starting-point is its form, which has shaped the content, producing a little gem of artificial versification:

> Senke, strahlender Gott — die Fluren dürsten
> Nach erquickendem Tau, der Mensch verschmachtet,
> Matter ziehen die Rosse —
> Senke den Wagen hinab![1]

The other two poems differ from the rest of Schiller's output in these months in having an emotional content. *Die Ideale* (*The Ideals*) laments the loss of youth and its noble and generous ideals. Personal emotion in a minor key infuses the poem and leads here and there to lines of a simple and subdued sincerity:

> Und immer stiller ward's und immer
> Verlass'ner auf dem rauhen Steg;
> Kaum warf noch einen bleichen Schimmer
> Die Hoffnung auf den finstern Weg.[2]

But *Die Ideale* still contains too much rhetoric inappropriate to its theme and mood.

Der Spaziergang (*The Walk*) was the poem of which Schiller himself was proudest. The poet on his walk surveys the rural scene, and his thoughts follow the history of man from the serene simplicity of antiquity to the cruel confusion of the present; at last there comes to him the consoling thought that in eternal nature we still have a link with the idyllic past:

> Unter demselben Blau, über dem nämlichen Grün
> Wandeln die nahen und wandeln vereint die fernen Geschlechter,
> Und die Sonne Homers, siehe! sie lächelt auch uns.[3]

The walk is a unifying factor which enables Schiller to link together separate ideas. Moreover in contrast to poems such as *Der Tanz* he re-introduces the physical world at the close. He no longer seeks to escape into a tenuous sphere of ideas, but deliberately returns to the experience from which he first set out. Not that the landscape, with which the poem begins, is a real one. Elements of reality have been fused together into a composite countryside, with a truer existence in Schiller's imagination than any actual landscape he had seen. Imaginative truth is the key to the poem. Unfettered by actual scenes and events, Schiller is able to concentrate all that is

---

[1] O radiant God, drive down your car beneath the horizon — the meadows thirst for quickening dew, man languishes, and the horses pull wearily.

[2] The rough path became ever more silent and ever more deserted; scarcely a pale gleam of hope now lit the dark way.

[3] Beneath the same blue of heaven, across the same green fields present and past generations wander together; and look, Homer's sun smiles upon us too.

essential into his countryside and to cover in the narrowest compass the whole history of mankind.

His powers are perfectly adapted to the task of summarizing in pregnant phrases a wide range of themes. He is equally at home in describing the walk itself. It is not any particular experience, but the *idea* of a walk that he wishes to communicate. He uses elements of reality to make his ideal picture, and has secured just the right combination of the concrete and the abstract. *Der Spaziergang* also derives unity from its pervading mood of nostalgic regret, occurring elsewhere only in *Die Ideale*.

The year 1796 was very largely occupied with the *Xenien*, and Schiller had little time to spend on other poetry. Apart from the overrated allegory, *Das Mädchen aus der Fremde* (*The Stranger*), the elegy *Klage der Ceres* (*Ceres' Complaint*), which fails because of disparity between its robust form and regretful mood, and the excessively antithetical poem, *Die Geschlechter* (*The Sexes*), Schiller wrote only a number of *Votivtafeln* (*Votive Tablets*) for his *Musen-almanach*. They were epigrams, similar in form to the *Xenien*, but serious in aim.

As the winter of 1796–97 approached, Schiller's energy and interest continued, despite his domestic joys and griefs, to be devoted much more to his intellectual and imaginative life. He led a life of voluntary imprisonment within his four walls, spending the long evenings in intellectual discussion with Goethe and Wilhelm von Humboldt—who with his wife Caroline was now living at Jena—or in intensive work on the tragedy which was to have Wallenstein as hero.

The friendship between Goethe and Schiller meant something different for each of them. Schiller provided Goethe in his loneliness with an appreciative critic and an ally against the philistinism of the German world of letters. For Schiller, Goethe was not only a penetrating critic, but a link with the physical world. Standing firmly on the ground and taking pleasure in the exercise of his five senses, Goethe was at home in a world which Schiller had forsaken. In scaling the philosophical heights Schiller had learned to understand his own genius. As soon as he turned again to the creation of works of art he needed to descend from the rarefied atmosphere of speculation to the sights and sounds of common things. None could help him in that descent better than Goethe, who lived always in touch with concrete reality, yet never allowed it to dominate him; Goethe, he felt, could help him to bridge the chasm between the ideal and the real.

The necessity, now that he was again a poet, to see and hear as well as to think and imagine, made this winter within doors a long and tiresome one for Schiller. He wearied of the bleak outlook on

to another house thirty feet away. He felt that he must live some-
where where he could see more than a stone wall. He needed a
garden, too, in which he could take the little exercise that his
constitution would stand. Early in the New Year he began accord-
ingly to negotiate for the purchase of a house and garden on the
outskirts of Jena. After much deliberation and some bargaining
he bought it, and moved into it in May 1797.

It was in this new environment that Schiller wrote his ballads.
As in the year 1795 his output of poems was confined to the summer
and autumn. They were poems produced under pressure, for he
was preparing for his third annual *Musenalmanach*, to which he and
Goethe were to be the chief contributors. Schiller wrote six ballads
between June and September 1797, in addition to several other
poems. They were *Der Taucher, Der Handschuh, Der Ring des
Polykrates, Ritter Toggenburg, Die Kraniche des Ibykus*, and *Der Gang
nach dem Eisenhammer*.

Der Taucher (The Diver) is among Schiller's three best-known
poems. A nameless youth, to satisfy a king's caprice, dives into a
whirlpool, is preserved almost by a miracle, but perishes on attempt-
ing to repeat the feat. The incidents are concentrated and cover
only a few minutes. The construction falls clearly into four parts:
the king's challenge to any man to retrieve the golden goblet he has
flung into the torrent; the youth's first and successful dive; the
repeated challenge for a higher reward; and the youth's second
and fatal effort. Three stanzas suffice for the first part and three
more for the third; the catastrophe is told with the utmost terseness,
and the greater part of the poem is given up to the young man's
first plunge and his astonishing reappearance.

The ballad begins with a sudden brusque onset, transporting us
without preliminary explanation into a swiftly developing crisis
as the king bluntly utters his challenge. No explanation is given
of how the party comes to be on the height overlooking the whirlpool. The poem is not concerned with the full picture or with
the whole reality, but with the concentrated essence of truth as
Schiller saw it. Everything irrelevant to his purpose is excluded.
He states the situation in *Der Taucher* in minimum space, but this
economy results in an important omission. He offers no explanation
of the king's caprice in suddenly hurling the goblet into the waters,
nor are we allowed to infer his reason from his character, of which
we are told nothing. The king's actions are autocratic and ruthless.
We know enough about him to cause us to speculate further, but
not enough to be able to arrive at conclusions. It is an unfortunate
initial miscalculation that the whole situation depends upon a
problematic and unexplained feature. The course of events is not

POETIC RENASCENCE   183

comprehensible without a more detailed knowledge of this character, and yet such detail would have been inconsistent with style and conception, and would have distracted from the central theme.

Schiller makes no attempt to portray the youth as an individual character. He has only the most general qualities: courage, determination, nobility, and readiness to risk all for a great reward. Nothing more is necessary in this poem, in which the vital element is conflict between man and the terrible powers of nature.

This central portion, occupying eighteen of the poem's twenty-seven stanzas, is narrated with great skill and verve. Schiller first makes clear the magnitude of the task facing the youth: the flood rushes surging, foaming, and grinding through the rocks below, and he must wait and watch until, for a few moments, it subsides. Schiller uses his carefully chosen, expressive words to produce a cumulative effect, corresponding perfectly to the mounting climax as the flood reaches its height:

> Die Wasser, die sie hinunterschlang,
> Die Charybde jetzt brüllend wiedergab,
> Und wie mit des fernen Donners Getose
> Entstürzen sie schäumend dem finstern Schosse.

> Und es wallet und siedet und brauset und zischt,
> Wie wenn Wasser mit Feuer sich mengt,
> Bis zum Himmel spritzet der dampfende Gischt,
> Und Flut auf Flut sich ohn' Ende drängt,
> Und will sich nimmer erschöpfen und leeren,
> Als wollte das Meer noch ein Meer gebären.[1]

As the tumult subsides the youth takes a header into the depth and is lost to sight. Schiller makes no attempt to follow his course beneath the waters, but adopts the more dramatic method of remaining on the height with the spectators, arousing by their fear and horror tense expectation and anxiety in the reader. The flood returns and with it, to the surprise of all, the young man; only now do we learn from his lips of the ghastly minutes spent beneath the surface, the horrors that surrounded him, and the lucky chance to which he owes his preservation and the retrieval of the goblet.

There follows the king's second challenge. Such good fortune as the young man enjoyed at the first attempt cannot happen twice; and yet in the world of noble thoughts and feelings in which this young man moves we cannot doubt for one moment that, for such a reward as the hand of the princess, he will face death again. Since

[1] With a roar Charybdis gives forth again the waters it had but just devoured, and with a noise as of thunder they pour foaming forth from the dark womb.

And they surge and seethe and roar and hiss, as if water were poured on fire; the steaming spray springs up to the heavens, and wave follows wave as if they would never end or the sea would give birth to another sea.

catastrophe is inevitable, Schiller ends abruptly. The second plunge is told in a single stanza. In those six lines Schiller has indicated only the breathless wait of the onlookers, while hope sinks as the minutes pass, and the flood comes and recedes and comes again:

> Wohl hört man die Brandung, wohl kehrt sie zurück,
> Sie verkündigt der donnernde Schall;
> Da bückt sich's hinunter mit liebendem Blick,
> Es kommen, es kommen die Wasser all,
> Sie rauschen herauf, sie rauschen nieder,
> Den Jüngling bringt keines wieder.[1]

Within its limits *Der Taucher* is a remarkable piece of work. True, those limits are very narrow. The anonymity of the figures and the abstention from the portrayal of character, though they assist the presentation of the elements in conflict with man, are the antithesis of drama, and Schiller's whole method was a dramatic one.

The stanzas describing the raging waters are frequently singled out as a striking instance of Schiller's capacity to imagine what he had never seen. Goethe writing from Switzerland in 1797 told Schiller how perfectly these lines applied to the Rhine Waterfall at Schaffhausen, and Schiller, in reply, admitted that he had never observed anything of this kind more considerable than a mill-race. It is a particularly obvious example of a constant and common feature of Schiller's work, his great power of imaginative reconstruction from isolated fragments of experience, which, when welded together by him, have a higher and more intense life than they possessed in their original form.

The theme of *Der Handschuh* (*The Glove*) is familiar to English readers as the subject of Browning's well-known poem. It has obvious resemblances to that of *Der Taucher*, for there is a similar challenge, and a similar daring conflict with elemental forces. But the issue, the tone, and the treatment of the characters are different. Mademoiselle Cunégonde throws her glove into the lions' arena and dares her lover Delorges to retrieve it. Having successfully brought it back, he hurls it into her face and turns from her in contempt. Not only are the characters of *Der Handschuh* named, but the event is fixed in time and place at the court of King Francis I of France. Detailed portrayal is not attempted. The interest of the poem is a dual one—narration, and a description of the great beasts, tiger, lion, and leopard; this is the best feature of the poem, which is written in lines that are too heavily accented and uncomfortably short.

---

[1] They hear the surf and the flood returns, heralded by a thunderous roar; the princess looks down with loving gaze as the waters swirl below. But no wave brings the youth again.

Schiller's third ballad is of a totally different character. *Der Ring des Polykrates* (*Polycrates' Ring*) is terse and bald, without any descriptive passage such as the whirlpool of *Der Taucher* or the great beasts of prey of *Der Handschuh*. The idea on which it is based, the envy of the gods and the fearful calamity which threatens the fortunate, lies bare and exposed. Schiller drew the story of Polycrates, Tyrant of Samos, from Herodotus. Polycrates enjoys such phenomenal good fortune that he is persuaded by his guest, the King of Egypt, to sacrifice what he prizes most highly, as an insurance against disaster. He throws into the sea a treasured ring, which is restored to him the following day, having been found in the belly of a newly caught fish. His good fortune survives even this test. Appalled at this proof that the gods have vowed Polycrates' doom, the Egyptian guest hastily takes his leave. Schiller's ballad goes no further, but Herodotus tells how Polycrates was captured by the Persians and crucified.

Schiller's poem is the skeleton of a drama. The two main figures, Polycrates and the Egyptian king, are not individualized. Their purpose is graphically to portray Schiller's fundamental idea, and for that they need no further details than their royal office. The limitless good fortune of Polycrates is mirrored by a rapid series of events: the internal enemies of his state die, his foreign foes are dispersed, and his merchant fleet escapes the dangers of rock and tempest. In order to achieve a maximum concentration in time and a minimum outlay of words, Schiller presents these episodes with the aid of messengers, as in Greek tragedy. This part of the ballad bears also a striking resemblance to the first chapter of the Book of Job, with good tidings substituted for evil. The breathless haste with which messenger follows messenger is in itself impressive; but the poignancy of the situation derives from the fear, nourished by the Egyptian king, that this apparent good fortune is in reality part of an impending hideous and dreadful catastrophe.

Schiller does not pursue the career of Polycrates to its end, but halts it immediately it is clear that the attempt to appease the gods has failed:

> Hier wendet sich der Gast mit Grausen:
> So kann ich hier nicht ferner hausen,
> "Mein Freund kannst du nicht weiter sein.
> Die Götter wollen dein Verderben,
> Fort eil' ich, nicht mit dir zu sterben."
> Und sprach's und schiffte schnell sich ein.[1]

---

[1] His horrified guest turns and speaks: " I can no longer stay here, nor can you be my friend. The gods seek your destruction, I hasten away that I may not die with you." Thus he spoke and straightway took ship.

N

Schiller's stringent economy leaves the catastrophe to the imagination, and this conclusion, far from presupposing a knowledge of Herodotus, is the more impressive for the scope it offers for fearful speculation. No ballad of Schiller's is more dramatic than *Der Ring des Polykrates*, and none is reduced more closely to its basic elements. It more than atones for its lack of colour by its spare vigour, its expressiveness of gesture, and its pregnant omissions.

Die Kraniche des Ibykus (*The Cranes of Ibycus*) began as a gift from Goethe, who was also engaged on the writing of ballads for the *Almanach*. Schiller, having taken over the theme from his friend, wrote his ballad in the early autumn of 1797. *Die Kraniche des Ibykus* illustrates the slow but certain course of divine justice. The singer Ibycus is waylaid and murdered on his way to the Isthmian Games at Corinth. As he dies he cries to the migrating cranes passing overhead to bear witness against his murderers. His body is discovered, but there is no trace of the criminals. A few days later, during the performance of a tragedy portraying the certain course of divine justice, a flock of cranes passes over the theatre, and a voice cries in fear, " Look, Timotheus, Ibycus's cranes! " The murderer has revealed himself, driven to this involuntary exclamation by sudden association of the cranes with Ibycus's dying appeal.

Die Kraniche des Ibykus is a drama divisible into two scenes, the murder and its detection. It would have been possible to omit the first, conveying its essence in the narration of the second, but Schiller no longer aimed in this ballad at the stark bleakness of *Der Ring des Polykrates*. He had discovered in his new theme possibilities of poetic effects which more than compensated for the loss of intensity. The murder story is a little tragedy in itself, beginning in hope and optimism, ending in disaster and gloom, in which there is no glimmer but the apparently vain appeal to the cranes.

The discovery of the crime and the thought that the murderer may well be among the crowd, unrecognized and unsuspected, leads to the final scene at the performance of a tragedy (apparently the *Eumenides* of Aeschylus, though its identity is immaterial). Schiller seizes eagerly the opportunity of describing theatre, audience, and play. He does not allow the pleasure of portraying a scene, every detail of which was full of interest for him, to distract him from his aim. But the passage is long enough to withdraw the attention from the murder of Ibycus. Suddenly the cry is heard, and the mind is forcibly brought back to the fate of the singer. This effect of surprise, in which reader as well as murderer is caught off his guard, makes the episode doubly impressive. It is the deep absorption in the theatrical presentation of divine justice which makes the murderers (and the reader) at once link the cranes with Ibycus. At any other calmer moment they would have known that these were not and could not be Ibycus's birds. It is a particularly satisfying passage, which is equally convincing from whatever standpoint it is regarded —psychological, poetic, or realistic.

The actual moment of discovery is remarkably well done; the voice gives the first warning of the cranes, and only when attention has been drawn to them by the cry do other members of the audience notice the birds:

> Da hört man auf den höchsten Stufen
> Auf einmal eine Stimme rufen:
> "Sieh da, sieh da, Timotheus,
> Die Kraniche des Ibykus!"
> Und finster plötzlich wird der Himmel
> Und über dem Theater hin
> Sieht man in schwärzlichtem Gewimmel
> Ein Kranichheer vorüberziehn.[1]

This story of the exposure of crime also gave Schiller the chance to develop an impressive picture of the potent effect of tragic art. For the discovery is primarily due to the state of mind induced by the tragic events and moving speeches on the stage. The arrival of the cranes is immediately preceded by this stanza:

> Und zwischen Trug und Wahrheit schwebet
> Noch zweifelnd jede Brust und bebet
> Und huldiget der furchtbar'n Macht,
> Die richtend im Verborg'nen wacht,
> Die unerforschlich, unergründet
> Des Schicksals dunkeln Knäuel flicht,
> Dem tiefen Herzen sich verkündet,
> Doch fliehet vor dem Sonnenlicht.[2]

It was, too, an opportunity to praise the power, not merely of tragedy, but of Greek tragedy—a welcome chance at a moment when his eye was fixed keenly on the achievements, the dramatic practice, and theory of the Ancients.

Die Kraniche des Ibykus is—with *Der Taucher*—Schiller's most popular ballad. This it owes partly to its convincing completeness partly to the skilful preparation of its climax, partly to the

---

[1] And suddenly from the highest row is heard a voice: " Look, Timotheus, look, Ibycus' cranes! " And at once the sky is dark and over the theatre a great, dark flock of cranes wings its way.

[2] And every breast hovers doubtfully and fearfully between illusion and truth, filled with reverence for the terrible power which watches and judges unseen, which inscrutably weaves the dark web of fate, which flees the light of the sun and makes itself known only to the recesses of the heart.

conspicuous role allotted to the cranes (so clearly belonging to the sensual world), but most of all to a feeling of mystery—to a sense of unsuspected hidden connexions binding together the gods and men and brute creation into one indivisible world. It is a poem in which more seems implied than stated, a rare event with Schiller, who was no poet of the half-light and the veiled horizon, and who usually said clearly and openly what he had to say.

Ritter Toggenburg (*The Knight of Toggenburg*) and *Der Gang nach dem Eisenhammer* (*The Errand to the Foundry*) have medieval settings. The former is the story of a returning Crusader, who finds that the woman he loves has entered a convent. He abandons wealth and castle, horse and hounds and, becoming a hermit, spends the remainder of his life gazing at his love's window. It is perfunctorily treated, the mere amusement of an idle hour, and is chiefly noteworthy as the source of the legend about Rolandseck and the Convent of Nonnenwerth on the Rhine. In *Der Gang nach dem Eisenhammer* divine justice rectifies the erring ways of men. The Count of Saverne, unjustly suspecting his servant Fridolin of adultery with the Countess, orders his foundrymen to throw into the furnace the first man sent to inquire whether orders have been carried out. He dispatches Fridolin with this message, and after a decent interval sends Fridolin's false accuser to find out if the fiery execution has been successfully performed. Fridolin stops to attend mass, and the accuser arrives first, suffering the fate intended for his victim. The Count realizes that God has protected his own. Schiller has treated this gruesome story in a light and humorous fashion, but though the element of horror can be attenuated, it cannot be removed. In spite of many neat touches of humour, the terrible end of Fridolin's accuser remains cruel and repellent. Schiller was at fault in his choice of theme, which has a blemish which he could lessen but could not erase.

Soon after the work on the *Almanach* for 1798 was completed Schiller moved back to his town flat, in accordance with his plan of spending the winter inside and the summer outside the town. His life was uneventful, and he was glad enough that this was so, for he wanted freedom from interruption, so that he could live his intense intellectual and imaginative life. What little contact he needed with the outside world he obtained through his friendship with Goethe, who became his eyes and ears. Now and then some event from his past life or from the political current of the time would touch him. In March 1798 he received a diploma, drawn up in 1792, conferring on him honorary citizenship of the French Republic for his services to the cause of liberty. It was a curious historical document, signed by Danton, Roland, and Clavière, all long before

1798 victims of the revolution they had once led. It seemed a silent confirmation of the wisdom of Schiller's own unpolitical life.

Early in 1799 he was reminded of his own early struggles by a pathetic appeal for help from Frau Hölzel, who with her husband had so generously helped Schiler in his desperate situation fifteen years before. Schiller came very willingly to the assistance of the old couple, asking Cotta, who acted as his banker, to send them immediately a sum of five " Carolins " (equal to about £4), to be followed by the same amount again in the autumn.

Each summer Schiller had to tear himself away from work on his tragedy in order to write a few poems for the current *Almanach*. Their number diminished year by year. Among those written in 1798 were two ballads, *Der Kampf mit dem Drachen* (*The Fight with the Dragon*), which emphasizes the necessity of self-discipline and obedience to law, and *Die Bürgschaft* (*The Pledge*), a poem in praise of friendship and integrity. *Der Kampf mit dem Drachen* is a concentrated drama, for its action is complete and the dragon already slain, and the poem concerns itself only with the moral consequences of the action. The dragon is slain against orders, and the slayer can only be pardoned when he admits that he is wrong. *Die Bürgschaft*, however, is narrative in form, swift in movement, yet arousing breathless suspense. Its conclusion, the triumph of a noble humanity over barbaric cruelty, recalls Goethe's *Iphigenie auf Tauris*. But Schiller, with a single word, hints at some undisclosed reason for the king's cruelty in past experience; amazed at Möros's high sense of honour and loyalty, the tyrant exclaims, " Und die Treue, sie ist doch kein leerer Wahn,"[1] and with the one word " doch " (after all) opens up a region for speculation and wonder which enormously enhances the magic of the poem.

In *Das Eleusische Fest* (*The Eleusinian Festival*), a hymn-like poem written for the *Almanach* in this summer, Schiller surveys the history of human activity without achieving the poetic vision which he had shown in *Der Spaziergang*. *Das Glück* (*Fortuna*) his last appreciable contribution for that year, expresses in a mature style Schiller's mature character. Without ever suffering extremities of want, Schiller had through the first thirty years of his life encountered adversity in many forms and had waged a perpetual struggle to keep his genius alive. Even after the stroke of good fortune, which in 1791 made him for a time independent of his pen for his livelihood, he had to contend constantly with ill-health which would have worn down the resistance of a less determined and more materially minded man. He had been no child of fortune, but his fairness and integrity of mind gradually overcame the resentment and envy with which he

[1] Then loyalty after all is no idle dream.

had once regarded Goethe's easier career. *Das Glück* is a generous recognition that good fortune is a gift of the gods to those they love:

> Vor Unwürdigem kann dich der Wille, der ernste, bewahren,
> Alles Höchste, es kommt frei von den Göttern herab,"[1]

and there must be no thought of envy:

> Zürne dem Glücklichen nicht, dass den leichten Sieg ihm die Götter
> Schenken, dass aus der Schlacht Venus den Liebling entrückt.[2]

Preoccupation with a play about Mary Queen of Scots left Schiller with little interest in shorter poems in the summer of 1799, and he hoped to be able to fill up the *Almanach* for 1800 with contributions from others, especially from Matthisson[3] and from Amalie von Imhoff[4]; but at the last moment he found energy to add a poem of his own. It was *Das Lied von der Glocke (The Song of the Bell)*, which he had first begun in 1797. Its theme is the whole range and scope of human life. Its vehicle is not the erudite elegiac metre of *Der Spaziergang*, but flexible rhyming verse, such as Goethe had often used in his pre-classical days. The bell is the witness and the symbol of all the joys and sorrows of human life:

> Was unten tief dem Erdensohne
> Das wechselnde Verhängnis bringt,
> Das schlägt an die metall'ne Krone,
> Die es erbaulich weiter klingt.[5]

The poem is dramatic in form, for it is put into the mouth of the master bell-founder as he supervises the casting of the bell, maintaining all the while a commentary on the vicissitudes of life. *Das Lied von der Glocke* never forgets the molten metal and the form, the blazing furnace, and the sweating foundryman; the care and attention of the master-founder are constantly diverted back to his delicate task, and the poem is punctuated with orders, hopes, and fears, which make his framework a reality. When time and duty allow, the master makes his survey of human life, of childhood and early love, of happiness and prosperity, of catastrophe and early bereavement; he turns from the individual lot to that of

---

[1] Earnest will can preserve you from indignity, but the highest gifts come freely from the gods.

[2] Do not envy the happy man, to whom the gods grant victory or whom Venus rescues from the battle.

[3] Friedrich von Matthisson (1761–1831). Schiller had met him in Würtemberg in 1794.

[4] Amalie von Imhoff (1776–1831) a poetess and novelist living in Weimar.

[5] Whatever wavering fortune brings here below to the sons of earth, strikes the metal crown of the bell, which echoes it abroad for the edification of all.

nations, contrasting the security of settled, civilized life with the fury and savagery of revolution:

> Gefährlich ist's den Leu zu wecken,
> Verderblich ist des Tigers Zahn,
> Jedoch der schrecklichste der Schrecken,
> Das ist der Mensch in seinem Wahn.[1]

till he looks at last with confidence and hope to the future, dedicating the bell to peace and happiness:

> Freude dieser Stadt bedeute,
> Friede sei ihr erst Geläute.[2]

By conceiving the poem as a monologue Schiller was able to adopt a homelier and more popular style of reflection, whose weight and memorable quality have made *Das Lied von der Glocke* one of the richest quarries for quotation in Schiller's works. It ranks among his better poems, because the robust character of the master bell-founder gives it a firm link with common experience and counter-balances the tendency towards abstraction, which is a feature of so many of Schiller's poems. This tendency is not surprising when it is realized that his normal procedure was to write a summary of ideas in prose for subsequent conversion into verse, a process visible as it were in petrified form in the poetic fragment which later received the title *Deutsche Grösse* (*German Greatness*).

For five years Schiller had given up some part of each summer to the writing of poems, but since the " ballad year " of 1797 he had done it with increasing reluctance. The poetic summers had provided an easy method of reviving his interest and his skill, demanding only limited inspiration and application. But he was neither a lyrical nor a narrative poet, and none of the themes of his poems had seized and dominated him as the subject of his tragedies had done. They were conscious, deliberate exercises which he could have left undone if he had chosen. But the story of Wallenstein was a different matter; and this tragic theme gripped his imagination and gave him a goal and an urge to reach it which a lifetime of poems would never have given him. He had taken it up again in 1796, but it was not till the winter of 1797–98 that it became a powerful and absorbing interest; from that time the writing of poems receded into the background.

Schiller spent the summer of 1798 chiefly in preparing *Wallensteins Lager* (*Wallenstein's Camp*) for the stage, and in September he went to Weimar to assist Goethe in supervising the production.

---

[1] It is dangerous to waken the lion, destructive is the tiger's fang, but the most terrible of all terrors is fanatical man.

[2] May its first peal bring happiness and, above all, *peace* to this town.

The first performance took place on October 12th, 1798, in the newly decorated Weimar Court Theatre. Schiller returned to Jena immediately afterwards and worked furiously at the next play of his vast trilogy, *Die Piccolomini*. It was ready at the end of 1798, and again Schiller moved to Weimar for the rehearsals. As soon as the first performance, on January 30, 1799, was over, Schiller hastened to complete the last part, *Wallensteins Tod* (*Wallenstein's Death*), returning to Weimar with his manuscript in April. As the effect of the first two parts had naturally faded, it was decided to produce all three plays in quick succession. *Wallensteins Lager* was acted on Monday, April 15, *Die Piccolomini* on the Wednesday, and the first performance of *Wallensteins Tod* followed on Saturday, April 20, 1799. The week was, in fact, though not in name, a Schiller Festival, and the poet, now in his fortieth year, could be more than satisfied with its success. The interest and enthusiasm were immense, and he could write to Körner:

> Wallenstein had an extraordinary success in the Weimar theatre, and even the least sensitive were carried away. Every one spoke with the same voice about it, and it was the only subject of conversation for the whole of the next week. [May 8, 1799.]

It was a notable and splendid climax, but Schiller gave himself no leisure to enjoy his triumph. Once *Wallenstein* was performed his interest in it rapidly lapsed, and though he returned to Weimar to see it performed in July in the presence of King Frederick William III of Prussia and Queen Louise, whose gracious presence charmed Schiller as it did every one else, all his vital attention in the spring and summer of 1799 was given to a new play, whose subject was Mary Queen of Scots.

The autumn, however, brought an interruption. Lotte was again expecting a child, and on October 11 she was delivered of a healthy daughter, who was christened Caroline. Ten days later Lotte began to exhibit alarming symptons. She became feverish and delirious and would tolerate no one near her but Schiller and her mother. In spite of his own poor health he watched at her bedside every other night, listening to her incoherent ramblings and tormented by the thought that her mind might have given way. At the end of a nerve-racking week signs of recovery began to appear, but though Lotte's life seemed safe, her mind remained dark for some weeks and Schiller began to fear that her reason was permanently lost. But Starke, the family doctor, remained confident, and by mid-November his confidence was justified by an appreciable improvement in Frau Schiller's condition. It seemed very desirable that she should have a complete change of surroundings, and fortunately Schiller had already made preparations during the summer to move from Jena to Weimar.

Jena had been a very suitable environment between 1789 and 1794 when Schiller had been absorbed in philosophy, but now that his dramatic urge had returned it had little to commend it but its cheapness. Frequent visits to Weimar for the rehearsals of the *Wallenstein* trilogy had convinced Schiller that living in Weimar would be more agreeable. Constant contact with the theatre also would provide him with a valuable stimulus. The move would mean that he would be able to meet Goethe much more regularly. The greatest drawback was the increased expense of living in Weimar, but in September 1799 Karl August agreed to double Schiller's pension, and no obstacle remained to the change of quarters once Lotte's confinement was over. Now, after Lotte's illness, both were more than ever glad of the prospect of completely new surroundings. Schiller had negotiated in September for the tenancy of the house which Frau von Kalb had occupied in Weimar, and on December 3, 1799, he and his family arrived safely in Weimar.

Chapter Sixteen

" *WALLENSTEIN* "

1799

N O completed work of Schiller's, not even *Don Carlos*, occupied him for so many years as did *Wallenstein*. From January 1791, when he first conceived the idea, to March 1799, when he put the finishing touch to *Wallensteins Tod*, he had spent more than eight years at it. His first acquaintance with the subject reached even farther back, for it was in April 1786 that his imagination was first stirred by Gustavus Adolphus and Wallenstein, the great figures of the Thirty Years War, which had devastated Germany in the seventeenth century. Born in 1583, Wallenstein fought on the Imperial and Catholic side, raised a considerable army, and conquered large tracts of North Germany, He was created Duke of Mecklenburg by the Emperor Ferdinand II, but was in 1630 deprived of his command at the instance of the Catholic party which feared his power. In 1632 the successes of the Protestants under Gustavus Adolphus forced the Emperor to recall Wallenstein, who after the battle of Lützen, negotiated with the Protestants, was again dismissed by the Emperor, and assassinated at Eger in 1634.

It was during the visit to Erfurt, which witnessed his first serious illness, that Schiller began to consider taking these events as the subject of a tragedy. But he got no further then than thinking about it, for alternate bouts of sickness and of frenzied work at his *History of the Thirty Years War* absorbed all his energy. The idea, however, continued to ferment, even in the years 1792 to 1794 when he was mainly preoccupied with aesthetic theory. From 1794 to 1796 he wavered between Wallenstein and an earlier idea dealing with the Knights of Malta. Then in March 1796 he decided to concentrate on the theme from the Thirty Years War.

He found it hard going, for he had to wrestle with facts and to create characters with whom he did not sympathize, but by the end of the year the work had taken shape and his imagination was fired. From January 1797 he worked steadily at it, only laying it aside when forced to do so by illness or the approach of publishing day for the year's *Almanach*. By February 1797 he had decided to write a prelude, at first called *Die Wallensteiner*, and later *Wallensteins Lager* (*Wallenstein's Camp*). It was written in short rhyming verse, considered suitable to the period represented, and was finished in the summer of 1797. In October Schiller began to rewrite his original prose *Wallenstein* in blank verse. At this time it was still one large play with a short prelude. By Christmas 1797 the first two acts were finished, two more were roughly completed in March 1798, and the fifth and last in the summer.

But neither Schiller nor Goethe, with whom he constantly discussed the play, was satisfied. The work was much too long, and the sacrifices, which would be involved by drastic shortening, were too serious. In September 1798, while Schiller was at Weimar assisting with the preparations for the first performance of *Wallensteins Lager*, Goethe suggested to him that the play could be divided into two. It was the only course which could both preserve what Schiller had written and enable the play to be performed on the stage. In this way *Wallenstein* became two distinct but connected five-act plays, *Die Piccolomini* (*The Piccolominis*) and *Wallensteins Tod* (*Wallenstein's Death*). The former was completed in the last days of 1798, the latter at the end of March 1799.

Wallensteins Lager contrasts remarkably with the second and third plays of the cycle. Its fundamental conception is different, for it has no real plot. It is a continuous series of pictures of camp life during the Thirty Years' War. Soldiers of all arms in Wallenstein's army come and go—cuirassiers and carabineers, lancers and dragoons, musketeers and Jägers—and the *cantinières* joke and flirt with them all. Each soldier is a representative of his regiment and reflects in some manner the character of his colonel; and so anticipations are formed in the spectator's mind, which the important officers of *Die Piccolomini* and *Wallensteins Tod* justify when they appear; it is a valuable form of preparation, which makes the principal characters familiar before they are seen. The soldiers are also representative of their various nationalities, for the army, ostensibly Imperial and Catholic, has been recruited from most of the races and both the religions in Europe. Men from Holstein and Würtemberg, Ireland and Italy, make the camp a world in miniature. Actually, Schiller's men are more than representative, for each has his own personal and individual character. In the pomposity of the Wachtmeister, the raffishness of the Jäger, the touchy jealousy of the dragoon, and the blunt honesty and rough humanity of the Pappenheim cuirassier, the army shows itself as disparate in temperament as in origin.

This vast assemblage of diverse elements is not a mob but an army, and the secret of its unity lies in its commander, whose shadow lies across the whole of the *Lager*. Wallenstein is every soldier's constant thought, whether the soldier is speculating about his invulnerability, defending him against the invective of the Capuchin monk, or, like the wiseacre of a Wachtmeister, openly recognizing that the General and none other holds the army together:

> Wer hat uns so zusammengeschmiedet,
> Dass ihr uns nimmer unterschiedet?
> Kein andrer sonst als der Wallenstein.[1]

Not all the characters of *Wallensteins Lager* are soldiers. The Capuchin friar represents the Church, and the peasant symbolizes the misery of all his fellows. They are in the midst of an army which has little time for religion and regards the peasant as a scarcely human provider of food and loot.

The voluble and vituperative Capuchin is a last-minute addition and his whirlwind sermon, with its racy abuse and monstrous puns, is a versified adaptation of passages from the sermon *Auf, auf, Ihr Christen* of Abraham a Santa Clara which Schiller found in a volume lent him by Goethe in October 1798. The Capuchin sums up the reproaches of supineness and indifference and of vice and violence directed against the troops; and he typifies the narrow Catholic party which had deposed the General in 1632 and was now agitating against him again.

Wallensteins Lager, however, has a significance beyond the period it represents. Its soldiers are characteristic of the profession of arms throughout the centuries—restless, active men, united in their contempt of the civilian's restricted life, in their flight from responsibility, and their desire for freedom, summed up in the refrain of the closing song:

> Der Soldat allein ist der freie Mann.[2]

One motive which can animate the soldier is lacking. Patriotism has no place in this cosmopolitan horde, which fights for pay and plunder.

Though *Wallensteins Lager* is diverse in incident and character, its style is consistent. Vocabulary, syntax, and the octosyllabic rhyming verse, already used by Goethe in several early works are deliberately archaic. By this use of a poetic style appropriate to the period Schiller attained his end by non-realistic means, for the impression of the age is more satisfactorily communicated by its own verse-form than it could have been by naturalistic detail. The uneven metre and homely speech are also admirably suited to the comic incidents and characters which abound in

---

[1] Who has welded us together so that there is no distinction between us? None other than Wallenstein.

[2] None but the soldier is a free man.

this prelude. The distinctive verse serves, too, as a frame, clearly separating *Wallensteins Lager* from the tragedy which is to follow.

Though this prelude has no plot of its own, it reflects the events of the play proper. It is in *Wallensteins Lager* that we first learn that Questenberg is in the camp, that Wallenstein is hated at Court, that a part of the army is to be detached, and that many suspect that there is a plot to weaken and depose the General. All this appears as rumour, distorted and vulgarized by the multitude of mouths through which it has passed. Its impact on the soldiery reveals three factors vital to the career and fate of Wallenstein: the army's devotion to its general, its respect for the oath of allegiance, and its regard for discipline.

The restless, ever-changing human scene of *Wallensteins Lager* provides an explanatory background and enables Schiller to concentrate in the two following plays solely upon events and motives. Having no plot, it might easily have disintegrated, but it is held firmly together by the comradeship of the soldiers, the shadow of Wallenstein, and its unity of style. It is in short a perfect overture to the tragedy.

Die Piccolomini and *Wallensteins Tod* constitute one giant ten-act play conveniently divided into two halves for theatrical representation. Their present bulk proves how impossible was the original five-act form. The division has been well contrived, so that although neither is fully satisfying by itself, each can stand as an evening's entertainment. Their titles indicate a real difference, for the first is concerned primarily with the Piccolominis' relation to each other and to Wallenstein, and the second with Wallenstein's fate. Each play has a distinct focus.

The theme of this vast tragedy is the failure of Wallenstein's attempted revolt against the Emperor Ferdinand. When the play begins, his plans are already far advanced. He has called his generals together at Pilsen and fetched his wife and daughter from Austria. The defection of one or two commanders is the first warning of possible failure. At this critical moment the Emperor's envoy, Questenberg, comes to the camp to upbraid Wallenstein and to demand the detachment of eight thousand of the best troops to the Low Countries. Octavio Piccolomini, a general whom Wallenstein blindly trusts, is hand in glove with Questenberg. Before his assembled officers Wallenstein repudiates the envoy's accusations and rejects his demands. Yet he does not feel secure in his plans as long as his subordinates are bound by their oath of allegiance to the Emperor. Two of his closest confederates, Illo and Terzky, undertake to substitute a new loyalty for the old. At a riotous banquet they circulate a form of oath of fidelity to Wallenstein, containing a clause reserving allegiance to the Emperor. When the floor is littered with bottles, the party about to break up, and few of the guests capable of suspicion or even of thought, they ask for signatures. All append their names except Max Piccolomini, the son of Octavio. The document which the officers sign, however, is not the one they have read; it is a copy which omits all reference to the Emperor.

Though he refuses to sign the declaration, Max Piccolomini has no suspicions of Wallenstein, who before the play begins had charged him as a sign of favour with the duty of escorting his wife and Thekla, his daughter, from Carinthia. On this journey Max Piccolomini has fallen deeply in love with Thekla to the alarm of Octavio, who now endeavours to open his son's eyes to Wallenstein's treasonable plans. Max is impatient with his father's crooked course and disingenuous silence, and determines to discover the truth about Wallenstein's aims. He knows that he must lose either his father or his friend. This crisis in the Piccolomini household ends the play.

Throughout *Die Piccolomini* Wallenstein has kept a route open for retreat. *Wallensteins Tod* begins with a Swedish ultimatum, which must force him at last to commit himself. Reluctantly he takes the final step. At this moment, when his power seems most terrible, the ground begins to slip beneath his feet, as Octavio Piccolomini wins first one general then another back to allegiance to the Emperor. Blow after blow falls upon Wallenstein; regiments silently ride away; others refuse to obey orders; yet others demand an explanation of the General and judge it unsatisfactory. In a few hours Wallenstein's might has dissolved, and of his fifty regiments but five remain. A last attempt to win Max Piccolomini by the tempting bait of Thekla's hand fails in face of her noble and unflinching integrity, and Max Piccolomini goes out to seek death. Abandoned by all but a handful of intimates and the sinister figure of Buttler, whom he blindly trusts, Wallenstein rides with his family to Eger to await the Swedes. Here Buttler, fearing their approach, has Wallenstein and his confederates murdered. Octavio Piccolomini arrives too late to prevent the assassination, but in time to learn that his part in these tortuous and bloody proceedings has earned his elevation from the dignity of count to prince.

As *Wallensteins Lager* serves as prelude to the vast ten-act tragedy, so is *Die Piccolomini*, within that tragedy, a prelude to the sudden decision, swift climax, and headlong collapse of *Wallensteins Tod*, It introduces all the principal protagonists and portrays the character of each; it reveals the complex and tormented history of Wallenstein's command, his intrigues in camp, and the machinations of the Viennese Court against him. It knits together the hearts of Max and Thekla, brings dissension into the house of Piccolomini, and threatens Octavio's laborious and secret scheming with exposure and destruction. Step by step it leads the action to the point when Wallenstein can no longer dally, but must move in one direction or another.

Die Piccolomini absorbs into itself all that might have clogged the movement of the tense and keen tragedy that is to follow. Though subordinated to the last part of the trilogy, it is also a play in its own right. Its first act reveals the characters of secondary figures, the clash between forthright and quick-tempered soldiers and the suave Viennese envoy, softened by the diplomatic tact of Octavio Piccolomini.

The second act is Wallenstein's; it is his only appearance in this play. It has a dual function, first exhibiting Wallenstein without the mask among his intimate friends, then showing him in public, his superb manner commanding and receiving respect and devotion. From this scene of stern words, unyielding looks, and grim threats, the third act gives complete relief in a tender love-scene between Max Piccolomini and Thekla.

The fourth act returns to the soldiers and shows them unbelted and unbuttoned, drinking and carousing far into the night. This drunken banquet is one of the masterpieces of dramatic literature, worthy to stand beside the scene in Pompey's galley in the second act of *Antony and Cleopatra*. All the types are here: Isolani garrulous and full of good-nights; the steady, powerful, silent drinker Tiefenbach:

> Vergebt, ihr Herrn. Das Stehen wird mir sauer.
>
> .   .   .   .   .   .
>
> Das Haupt ist frisch, der Magen ist gesund,
> Die Beine aber wollen nicht mehr tragen;[1]

abstemious Buttler with his stiff, unsociable bearing; Octavio, his insinuating manner mellowed and softened by the wine. Finally there is the figure of Illo, riotously drunk, seized by a foolish liking for Octavio, pouring out confidence after confidence which should never have reached his hearer's ears, flaming up into impotent anger when Max Piccolomini refuses to sign the oath, drawing a sword which he is too drunk to hold and disclosing in a strident voice, which his confederates try in vain to silence, the secrets of the dishonest trick by which the signatures have been gained. This is living drama, convincing in every word, every figure a man of flesh

---

[1] Forgive me, gentlemen. Standing is too much for me. . . . My head is fresh and my belly sound, but my legs won't bear me any longer.

and blood, with passions and inhibitions, with opinions and prejudices, each interlocking with the others, all alive throughout,
whether speaking or silent.

The sound of crunching broken glass, of voices raised in ribald
laughter or raucous reproach, gives way in the fifth act to an interview between the two Piccolominis in the small hours following
the banquet. It takes place in an atmosphere of fatigue and weariness
which contrast and are yet related to the forced gaiety and over-
heated quarrelsomeness of an hour before. Such a quiet, sober,
and yet tense, ending was necessary to keep *Die Piccolomini* subordinate to the play which is to follow.

When *Wallensteins Tod* begins the General is consulting the
stars, whose oracles seem to shine propitiously upon his enterprises:

Denn Jupiter, der glänzende, regiert — —[1]

The time has come for action, and no sooner has this thought formed
in his mind than grim necessity comes hammering at the door,
requiring him to strike or fall. It is a fine dramatic stroke to follow
Wallenstein's words:

Jetzt muss
Gehandelt werden, schleunig, eh' die Glücks-
Gestalt mir wieder wegflieht überm Haupt,
Denn stets in Wandlung ist der Himmelsbogen —[2]

with Terzky's urgent knocking and the news that the commander-
in-chief's secret envoy has been taken and that, unless he acts
quickly, his ruin is certain. The entire first act is devoted to Wallenstein's struggles with himself. A succession of resolute characters
come and go, each endeavouring to thrust the hesitant and reluctant
General to the point of decision, which he at last reaches at the end
of the act.

The second act comprises two scenes. In the first the waters
eddy and swirl for a time, till at last they begin slowly to set against
Wallenstein's course; in the second the current flows decisively
against the rebel. The first is an interview with Max Piccolomini,
in which Wallenstein exerts his utmost powers of persuasion
to keep Max, whom he values and loves, on his side. But the
straight and honest Max can see only one upright course—loyalty
to his oath of allegiance; and once he learns that Wallenstein has
already acted against the Emperor and that all argument is too late,
he turns on his heel and goes without a further word. The climax

---

[1] For Jupiter, the shining planet, rules.

[2] Now I must act, and quickly, before the constellation of fortune flees from
above my head, for the vault of heaven is constantly changing.

of the scene is achieved by a wonderful stroke of visual imagination as Wallenstein brings home to Max the futility of protests and the irrevocability of what is already done:

> Es ist zu spät. Indem du deine Worte
> Verlierst, ist schon ein Meilenzeiger nach dem andern
> Zurückgelegt von meinen Eilenden,
> Die mein Gebot nach Prag und Eger tragen.[1]

The excellence of Schiller's technique of contrast and juxtaposition appears in the episode which follows this scene.

Between the forthright integrity of Max Piccolomini in the preceding scene and the tortuous and double-faced honesty of Octavio which is to come, Schiller introduces a dialogue in which Wallenstein's confederates try, but fail, to inspire him with distrust of the two Italians. Both Wallenstein and his friends make the mistake of classing both Piccolominis together; the Italians (" die Welschen "), by their mere presence, are a perpetual source of annoyance to Illo. Schiller has shown how wrong are Illo and his friends and how right is Wallenstein about Max. The scene that is to follow reveals their rightness and Wallenstein's more fatal error with regard to Octavio. Behind locked doors Octavio interviews subordinate commanders and recalls them to their allegiance to the Emperor. Two of them, Isolani and Buttler, suffice for Schiller's dramatic purpose. Isolani exemplifies the average unpolitical and unprincipled soldier; Buttler is the stern, resentful, vengeful man, who becomes the chief agent in Wallenstein's destruction. With such coarse natures Octavio succeeds, and the situation of Wallenstein is gravely threatened. But Octavio fails just as badly as Wallenstein in the attempt to win over Max, who cannot follow a crooked path to please either friend or father.

The first two acts of grim but secret preparation are followed by a third act in which rebellion becomes overt and is immediately met by paralysing counter-strokes. When Wallenstein joins the women, who, with the exception of the Countess Terzky, are as ignorant as the army and the outside world of his designs, all is still apparently well. The messenger bringing news of the capture of Prague is awaited every moment. But while Wallenstein discloses his ambitions, riding rough-shod over Thekla's love for Max and his wife's hopes, events are taking place in the camp. First Terzky, then Illo, comes with astonishing and alarming reports. Regiment after regiment has paraded without orders, mounted, and ridden away into the night. Wallenstein feels that he is assailed and shot

---

[1] It is too late. While you stand wasting words the swift messengers carrying my order to Prague and to Eger pass milestone after milestone.

at by lurking, unseen enemies; he does not know where and from whence the next blow may come. It falls when he realizes that Octavio Piccolomini, whom he had obstinately trusted against all advice, has worked all the time against him and now encompasses his destruction.

Meanwhile something very like mutiny has spread through the camp, the cause of which Wallenstein cannot at first discover. Presently he learns of his greatest misfortune yet—the stroke against Prague has failed and the news of his treason has become public throughout the army. The total helplessness and weakness of Wallenstein at this crucial time is underlined by his long anxiety about the cause of the mutinous behaviour of his troops. He has eagerly awaited the news from Prague, only to learn that his messenger has arrived hours before and has been stopped by Wallenstein's soldiers in Wallenstein's own camp; only long after the meanest soldier has heard it does the message reach the commander-in-chief to whom it is addressed. Wallenstein's fall is catastrophic; in the short space of this scene the formidable and feared commander has become a mere fugitive. For the spectator the effect of this descent is heightened by dramatic irony; the spectator knows, while Wallenstein does not, that the ground on which the General stands is hollow. The surprises are surprises for the General alone.

In the second scene of this act the violence of the first landslide is over. It remains for Wallenstein to gather what he can from the ruins. Terzky's five regiments are assured; for the rest his hopes are fixed on Max's corps, the Pappenheim Cuirassiers, and on Max himself, who is not to be found. In a long interview, in which he exerts all his authority, persuasiveness and prestige, Wallenstein fails to win over a deputation of cuirassiers because Buttler at the critical moment brings proof of the General's treasonable intentions. When Max Piccolomini appears, a long and heart-breaking scene takes place in which love conflicts with duty in Max, and Wallenstein wavers between affection and hatred. Max decides against Wallenstein and goes away in despair, with the harsh call of duty symbolized by the short, shrill and ever-louder trumpet-blasts and the heavy, grinding tread of the determined troopers who gradually fill the hall ready to rescue their colonel from the hands of Wallenstein. These impressive accompaniments preserve the elevated sentiments of this scene from the risk of cold and unsympathetic analysis; they distract the attention of the emotional tight-rope walker Max, and of those who watch him, from the dangers of the ridiculous into which he might so easily fall.

With the third act the last glimpse of martial splendour is past, and it is clear that Wallenstein is lost. But the nature of his disaster is not yet apparent. The fourth act is devoted to the preparation of the murder. It is set at Eger, whither Wallenstein has withdrawn to await a junction with the Swedes. Schiller has introduced Gordon, the governor of the fortress, as a contrast to Buttler. Against the latter's ruthless and implacable hatred the weak but well-meant protests of Gordon can make no headway, and it is evident that Wallenstein's murder is resolved. Schiller, however, still has on his hands the fate of the unhappy lovers. The second half of the fourth act is given up to the receipt by Thekla of the news of Max Piccolomini's end and to her determination to join her dead lover. With the quiet resolution of Thekla and the laconic but practical sympathy of the head-groom who offers to accompany her, the fourth act closes. With it fades the last glimpse of a purer, nobler world.

The fifth act begins in sordid horror as Buttler issues his orders for the murder of Wallenstein to his two selected desperadoes. The horror is augmented by the reluctance of these merciless and callous products of sixteen years of ruthless and inhuman war. Both of them shrink from the almost sacrilegious thought of turning their weapons against their general.

The scene shifts to Wallenstein's chamber, and Schiller exerts every device to arouse sympathy at this fateful moment for the often un-attractive character of his hero. Generosity to his servants, a soft and reminiscent mood, auguries of approaching disaster, enlist our thoughts for Wallenstein, and all the more easily because we expect at any moment to see the shadow of the murderers in the lantern light, turning the corner of the stairs. The efforts of the astrologer and Gordon to make Wallenstein conscious of his danger fail. Buttler meanwhile is determined to make an end, and his excuse is the proximity of the Swedes and the impossibility of holding Wallenstein a prisoner once they arrive. There follows a simple but masterly moment. As Buttler stands with the assassins upon the stairs a distant trumpet-call is heard. For Buttler it is the signal of the Swedes' arrival, and in a few moments Wallenstein is dead. But it is not the Swedes. Marching through the city gates come the Imperial troops, headed by Octavio Piccolomini. The intensity of horror is past, and the figure of Octavio, honest in intention, limited in mind and unlimited as to means, remains. It is mediocrity that survives, while perverted greatness such as Wallenstein's and pure integrity such as Max Piccolomini's have fallen in one common disaster.

The hero of this vast tragedy is not of superhuman stature. Schiller's problem was to maintain respect for a character for whom he himself could feel little sympathy. He had somehow to balance the requirements of art and truth. Wallenstein was hesitant and vacillating, ambitious and timid, more inclined to threaten than to act. Schiller has shown him gradually and reluctantly thrust by events to the point where he must make a decision. In the second act of *Die Piccolomini* he disguises his reluctance as deliberate incalculability:

> Es macht mir Freude, meine Macht zu kennen;
> Ob ich sie wirklich brauchen werde, davon, denk' ich,
> Weisst d u nicht mehr zu sagen als ein andrer.[1]

Behind an inscrutable mask Wallenstein conceals his own irresolution. He has not advanced a step farther in the first act of *Wallensteins Tod*, where he is determined both to play with an alliance with the Swedes and to avoid any definite commitment.

When Wallenstein at last makes his decision, it is a step which is thrust upon him. Illo and Terzky seek to persuade him to revolt, and are joined by the Countess Terzky with her stinging reminder:

> Wie? Da noch alles lag in weiter Ferne,
> Der Weg sich noch unendlich vor dir dehnte,
> Da hattest du Entschluss und Mut — und jetzt,
> Da aus dem Traume Wahrheit werden will,
>
> . . . . . .
>
> . . . da fängst du an zu zagen?[2]

Wallenstein still tries hard to avoid committing himself, to keep all roads open:

> Wenn eine Wahl noch wäre — noch ein milderer
> Ausweg sich fände.[3]

Influenced by the Countess's repeated inflammatory speeches, he does at last make his decision. He has played with fire until it has escaped his control, invoked the spirit till it has appeared. As Schiller has so far portrayed Wallenstein there is nothing of greatness in him; mean and vulgar souls like Terzky and Illo, an ambitious woman like the Countess, can dominate him and determine his course. If there were nothing more in the hero, the play would lack its centre and the parts seem greater than the whole.

But Wallenstein *has* greatness, and Schiller wisely shows it already in the second act of *Die Piccolomini*. Whatever doubts Wallenstein

---

[1] It gives me pleasure to feel my power; whether I shall really use it, *you*, I think, know as little as any other.

[2] What? when all still lay far off, when the road still stretched endlessly before you, then you had resolution and courage—and now that the dream is about to become true . . . you begin to be faint-hearted?

[3] If there were but still a choice—if there were some less drastic way out.

may have in private, he can conceal them in public. To Questenberg he betrays no hint of the doubts which disquiet him. Long
though he hesitates and wavers, he is resolute and swift in action
once his mind is made up. He has the great commander's gift of
winning the soldier's loyalty by the personal recollection of individuals, as in the conversation with the cuirassiers in Act III of
Wallensteins Tod; and his popularity with the rank and file is clearly
demonstrated in *Wallensteins Lager*. He can be kind too, and at the
last reminiscent and regretful. Yet coarseness and brutality lurk
beneath the surface—suddenly emerging, as in the scene in Act III
in which Max takes his final leave. He is, too, an unprincipled
opportunist, ready to profit by every chance that comes his way.
He flirts with the enemy, makes up again to his allies, is apparently
open-hearted and bluff, yet secretly treacherous, as in his political
contacts with the Swedes and his personal conduct towards Buttler.
Such a character can with difficulty command sympathy, and it is a
remarkable feat that Wallenstein's end stirs us as much as it does.
Schiller achieves this not only by the softer mood of his hero, but
also by the grim horror and brutality with which the murder is
prepared and executed.

The absence of Wallenstein from *Wallensteins Lager* and from all
but one act of *Die Piccolomini* is significant proof that the *Wallenstein*
trilogy does not depend solely or even primarily upon its central
figure. The play is more than the personal fortunes of a single man;
it is a picture of a world. In this world the sharpest light is focused
on Wallenstein, but every other character is equally essential to the
whole scene.

Wallenstein's closest associates are his brother-in-law Terzky,
and Illo. Both are men of even coarser fibre. Terzky acts as
Wallenstein's secretary, signing documents so that the general can
remain uncommitted. He tries to persuade his commander to
rebellion, but is himself incapable of any heroism. Illo is conceived
on a grander scale. Jealous and brutal, he is quick to action, rash
and swift to anger; and when Buttler's men set upon him in the
Castle of Eger, he fights like a wounded tiger till he is overwhelmed
and killed. Illo has courage and strength, but no likable human
feature. There is no gentleness in this harsh, vengeful and bloodthirsty man:

> Nicht ruhn soll dieser Degen, bis er sich
> In österreich'schem Blute satt gebadet.[1]

By emphasizing the nobler side of Wallenstein and the baser passions
of Illo, Schiller succeeds in enlisting our sympathy for the General,

---

[1] This sword shall not rest till it has drunk its fill of Austrian blood.

while withholding it from his lieutenant, though both meet a like fate almost at the same moment.

There is no grandeur or nobility of character in Octavio Piccolomini, whose appearance at the end as Wallenstein's successor emphasizes the gap which assassination has left and Octavio cannot adequately fill. He is honest in his aims, but careless in his means, and he would rather punish crime than prevent it. He is a limited and narrow character, the ordinary man elevated to high station.

Buttler, the successful adventurer who remains sensitive about his humble origin, is a much more sinister figure. He is at first an ally of Wallenstein and hostile to the Emperor, because he believes that the latter has rebuffed his pretensions to the rank of count. In the second act of *Wallensteins Tod* Octavio reveals to him that it was Wallenstein who engineered the snub. So deeply does this strike at Buttler that he has to hold on to a chair to save himself from falling. The change in him is immediate and complete; from Wallenstein's most loyal friend he becomes his bitterest and most treacherous enemy. Buttler has none of Octavio's inhibitions, and flinches from no action, however ruthless and cruel, in his pursuit of Wallenstein's destruction. He executes his plan without qualm or misgiving, experiencing, unlike Octavio, no remorse.

Two very different figures negotiate with Wallenstein in the two plays. Questenberg presents in Act II of *Die Piccolomini* the accomplished diplomat. Adroit and confident in debate, dignified and firm in bearing, he conceals entirely in public the misgivings he has admitted in private conversation with Octavio. To this skilful courtier, so obviously out of place in an armed camp, the Swedish colonel stands in sharp contrast. Colonel Wrangel, whose brief but memorable appearance falls in Act I of *Wallensteins Tod*, is a blunt, direct soldier, a balanced, mature and fixed character. In his negotiations with Wallenstein, though he does not fail to pay proper formal respect to the officer of higher rank, he takes the lead, and does not shrink from frank words. His whole bearing is fearless and yet unprovocative. Wallenstein wavers and swerves, tries first this line of approach then that; Wrangel remains unmoved, firm and constant in his aim. In his integrity, courage, and self-control he is a convincing portrait of a fine type of soldier, and a typical figure of the Swedish Protestant forces. These forces are conscious defenders both of their faith and of their nation , in strong contrast to the vast and fluctuating army of godless mercenaries under Wallenstein's command.

There are many lesser but equally impressive portraits. The generals Isolani and Tiefenbach, Captain Neumann, Terzky's butler, Gordon and the two assassins—these live in the few lines allotted to them. Rosenberg, Wallenstein's head-groom, speaks with Thekla for a mere two minutes at the end of the fourth act of *Wallensteins Tod*. The longest of his six speeches consists of only eight words. Yet in this short space are conveyed not only the man's sympathy and fidelity, but his independent existence as a living person.

Two women share Wallenstein's fortunes and misfortunes, his wife and his sister-in-law, Countess Terzky. Wallenstein's wife is no more than his shadow, a woman made for an obscure, happy, untroubled life, who suffers much from the insecurity, the dangers, and the excitement which she has reluctantly to share. Her sister, Countess Terzky, is a woman of a more heroic temper. It is she who in the first act of *Wallensteins Tod* stings and goads the General to his fateful decision. She plays a decisive part in the tragedy, but her courage, adequate to one sharp crisis, falters under prolonged strain, as does that of Lady Macbeth, whom she clearly resembles.

In contrast to this world of egoists great and small (among whom only Rosenberg and Wrangel stand out as exceptions) Schiller has portrayed two characters of striking nobility and purity. Max Piccolomini and Thekla Wallenstein differ conspicuously from their fathers. The vision, which for their elders has become clouded and dimmed, is still fresh and luminous for them. Pure in thought, attached to noble ideals, they and their happiness are destroyed by the hideous forces which Wallenstein and Octavio handle but cannot control. Both react instinctively, and their reactions are unerringly correct. Thekla senses the falseness of those round her, and Max alone declines to sign the document with which Illo intends to incriminate the generals and commanding officers. That he has no conscious reason for his refusal only serves to emphasize how much his just reaction is instinctive.

The stress of life threatens this youthful wholeheartedness, and Max finds himself wrenched from the state of the " beautiful soul " (the *schöne Seele* of *Über Anmut und Würde*) and thrust into a situation where duty and inclination are irreconcilably opposed. True to her more intuitive nature, Thekla quickly senses the right and upright course, and Max appeals to her to help him in the maze of conflicting self-interests in which he is entangled. In the second act of *Wallensteins Tod* he confidently asserts:

Dem Herzen folg' ich, denn ich darf ihm trauen.[1]

Yet in the crisis his instinct fails him:

[1] I follow my heart, for I can trust it.

Wo ist eine Stimme
Der Wahrheit, der ich folgen darf? Uns alle
Bewegt der Wunsch, die Leidenschaft.[1]

Though he no longer knows the right course, yet Max knows at
least where he will be advised with integrity and unselfish truth.
When he turns to her Thekla confirms his original impulse.

Max and Thekla speak a different language from that of the rest
of the characters. But they themselves speak at different times in
divergent keys. In monologue or in the presence of indifferent
persons they express themselves in a rhetoric which often sounds
artificial and stilted, particularly from the lips of the sensitive,
womanly Thekla, as at the end of the speech on Max's death:

— Da kommt das Schicksal — Roh und kalt
Fasst es des Freundes zärtliche Gestalt
Und wirft ihn unter den Hufschlag seiner Pferde —
— Das ist das Los des Schönen auf der Erde.[2]

—four lines so much out of character and situation and so trite in
form that they need all the skill and tact of a great actress to save
them from ridicule. Yet when Max and Thekla are together Schiller
has written tender love scenes, rendered more moving by an occasional stab of premonition. These scenes are on a different plane
from the rest of the work. The failure to link their beauty with the
harsh realism of the baser world around them is a significant flaw in
a remarkable play.

Max and Thekla were for Schiller a relief from the atmosphere
of sordid baseness which pervaded the rest. With them he escaped
from the vast conflict of self-interest into a pure and ideal world.
There was no other prominent character in the play whom he liked.
He loved idealists and disliked realists, and in *Wallenstein* he found
himself obliged to portray a succession of realists and opportunists.
This distaste for his subject enabled him for the first time to achieve
his goal of objectivity of treatment. He formulated the situation
clearly in a letter to Goethe:

So far I am treating the principal character and most of the minor
ones with the pure love of the artist; only for the second character,
young Piccolomini, do I feel a personal attraction. [November 28,
1796].

There are two worlds; an ideal one infused with Schiller's own
enthusiasm, and a real one which could engross but not fire his

[1] Where is there a voice of truth that I can follow? We are all moved by wishes
and passions.
[2] Then comes fate. Brutally and coldly it seizes my friend's delicate form and
hurls it beneath the hooves of his horses. That is the lot of the beautiful on earth.

imagination, and which forced him into contact with detail. The result, for most of the play, is a perfect balance; the subject will not let Schiller leave the earth for a more ethereal air.

Schiller felt some misgivings about the causes of Wallenstein's fall. It seemed the consequence of crime and not the work of a fate beyond man's control. He studied the Greeks and saw Oedipus, the victim of fate, as his ideal; but he read Shakespeare, too, and found in Macbeth a precedent for the criminal as hero. Although reassured, he still felt that some form of fate was needed. Otherwise Wallenstein could be viewed simply as meeting his deserts, thus forfeiting all sympathy. From this desire came the astrological element in the play. Misleading interpretations of star and planet induce Wallenstein to trust the very man who is in fact his most dangerous enemy, just as the deceptive prophecies of the witches lure Macbeth to destruction. The stars seem often in harmony with the events in *Wallenstein*, especially in the final act when Seni, the astrologer, appalled at what he has observed in the sky, hastens to warn Wallenstein of impending catastrophe. Schiller makes the General misinterpret the warning and fail to heed the stars at the very moment when they foretell the truth. But he does not say whether there is a real connexion between the planets and human destiny, whether this is mere coincidence, or whether Seni's warning is just a projection of his own anxiety. His abstention both from belief and disbelief gives to his astrological device an atmosphere of mystery without which it would have seemed trivial.

In *Wallenstein* Schiller achieved a perfect style, so perfect as to be imperceptible, for, except in certain scenes involving Max or Thekla, there are no mannerisms, no pose, and no conscious gesture. A flexible, subtle, and memorable blank verse has become as natural to him as the play of his muscles, and fits itself unostentatiously to each character, giving variety by its adaptability and unity by its constant basic rhythm.

The indebtedness of *Wallenstein* to *Macbeth* is obvious in the misinterpreted prophecies of the stars and in the resemblance of Countess Terzky to Lady Macbeth. Schiller's work is not in any way an imitation; it is influenced by an intelligent study of the principles on which *Macbeth* and other plays of Shakespeare are built. *Wallenstein* is Schiller's first truly Shakespearean work. It is also his vastest work. From the outset he was aware of its colossal proportions and manifold ramifications. Over and over again he refers to the recalcitrant and intractable material which refused to be simplified and distilled to an essence. Not till he had extended its plan on a huge scale could he begin to see some sort of order emerging from chaos. But it was the chaos of a living world.

Schiller himself put *Wallenstein's* true significance to Körner, calling
it " a little world " (*ein kleines Universum*[1]).

There are plays which interest us by their profound or subtle
analysis of the hero's or heroine's heart, such as Racine's *Phèdre* or
Kleist's *Penthesilea*. Schiller himself had at first pursued this path
in *Don Carlos*. There are others which present not one person in
detail, but a whole world in broad yet convincing outline; of this
kind are the histories of Shakespeare, which Schiller studied with
interest and approval in November 1797 while he was at work on
Wallenstein. Very rarely the two are united, and there emerges a full-
length portrait of the hero combined with a living and varied picture
of the world about him, as in *King Lear*, and *Hamlet* and *Antony
and Cleopatra*. In *Wallenstein* Schiller has come very close to this
highest pitch of dramatic art. His Wallenstein is a life-size portrait
and yet the play will stand the test of the hero's removal. Take
Karl Moor from *Die Räuber* and what is left collapses; but take
away the figure of Wallenstein, and the world around him still
lives. Schiller's Isolani and Wrangel, his Tiefenbach and Rosenberg,
are as independently alive as Gloucester and Kent, Enobarbus and
Ventidius. Only in the central figure does Schiller fall short.
Wallenstein has not the stature of Lear or Hamlet. He fails to
dominate his world as Shakespeare's greatest tragic heroes dominate
theirs.

Wallenstein's chief title to glory remains its wonderfully live,
kaleidoscopic pageant of human character and action, in which
economy and breadth combined have resulted in one of the most
satisfying of Schiller's plays.

[1] January 8, 1798.

Chapter Seventeen

"*MARIA STUART*" AND
"*DIE JUNGFRAU VON ORLEANS*"
1799–1801

BY mid-December the Schiller family was established in the
new home and Friedrich Schiller had begun the even and
uneventful course of his life in Weimar. He saw much of Goethe,
visited the few other people he wanted to see regularly, and frequently attended the theatre. These visits were an invaluable stimulus to his work, which had become the all-embracing interest of his
life. After *Wallenstein* Schiller's productivity surpassed even the
intensity of his early twenties, and major plays followed at the rate
of about one a year, while the intervals between them were filled
out with dramatic plans, adaptations, and translations. In the
three and a half years that Schiller spent in this first house in Weimar
he composed *Maria Stuart* and *Die Jungfrau von Orleans*, worked
at plays on the Knights Templar of Malta and Perkin Warbeck, and
adapted for the German stage *Macbeth* and Gozzi's *Turandot*.
Writing for the theatre had become the focal-point of his life.

The idea of writing a play about Mary Queen of Scots, had
occurred to Schiller at Bauerbach in 1783, after he had finished
Kabale und Liebe. He wavered for a time between Mary Stuart
and Don Carlos. Having decided on the latter, he laid the Scottish
subject on one side and forgot it.

After finishing *Wallenstein* in March 1799 he experienced a feeling
of unrest, aimlessness, and sterility, instead of the relief and satisfaction he had expected. The creative urge had revived in him to
such purpose that even the completion of such a monumental task
as *Wallenstein* could not leave him satiated. He himself knew
clearly the meaning of his restlessness, as his words to Goethe show:
" I shall not be settled until I see my thoughts fixed with hope and
pleasure on a definite subject " (March 19, 1799). He felt a desire
to turn h's back on princes and soldiers and all the figures of historical
tragedy. Yet when in April 1799 his imagination took fire over a
new subject, it was again an historical one. The story of Mary
Queen of Scots, however, at least offered an escape from the generals

and soldiers who had peopled the recent world of his work and of whom he had grown utterly weary.

Schiller began to write the first act of *Maria Stuart* in June 1799 and he finished the play in June 1800. He had worked at it through the summer of 1799, had then been interrupted by Lotte's illness, by the move to Weimar, and finally by an attack of his own bronchial complaint. He had resumed work early in 1800, and, for the last act, had withdrawn in mid-May from Weimar to the rural seclusion of Ettersburg, about seven miles distant. Immediately after its completion, *Maria Stuart* was performed on June 14, 1800, at the Weimar Court Theatre.

The play concerns itself only with the last phase of Mary's career, from the announcement of sentence to its execution. Schiller's sources which included Brantôme, Camden and a history of Queen Elizabeth by a German historian, Archenholz, were mostly favourable to Mary Stuart.

The whole of the first act takes place in Fotheringay Castle, where Mary is imprisoned. She is informed of the sentence of death passed upon her, and at this dark moment receives new hope from Mortimer, a leading member of the latest conspiracy to free her. The second act shows Queen Elizabeth wishing her rival dead, but fearing to confirm the death sentence. She is persuaded by the Earl of Leicester, a secret supporter of Mary, to meet her royal prisoner at Fotheringay. This interview takes place in the third act with terrible and unforeseen consequences. All Mary's good resolutions disappear and she heaps bitter denunciations and scorching home-truths upon Elizabeth, exacting a short-lived satisfaction for all the wrongs she has suffered. As Elizabeth returns from this meeting an unsuccessful attempt is made upon her life. Its failure means the miscarriage of Mortimer's conspiracy. The fourth act is divided into two scenes: the first portrays the death of Mortimer; the second shows Leicester's attempt to exculpate himself, followed by Elizabeth's signature of the death warrant, which she deliberately hands without proper instructions to the frightened Secretary of State, Davison. The execution takes place in the fifth act, and a final scene depicts its reaction upon Elizabeth's reputation, summed up by the Earl of Shrewsbury with:

> Du hast von nun an
> Nichts mehr zu fürchten, brauchst nichts mehr zu achten.[1]

It is an extremely concentrated play. Mary's sensational early career is made known only by allusion, and the action occupies only

---

[1] Now you have nothing more to fear, now you need have respect for nothing more.

the last two days of her life. To achieve this Schiller has compressed his geography, making it possible for Elizabeth to spend the morning in London, hunt in Northamptonshire in the afternoon, visit Fotheringay Castle, and return before dark to London. Not that this foreshortening of distance is any worse than Shakespeare's gift of a sea-coast to Bohemia. It is justifiable because the play is not concerned with any sort of realism.

The contrast of *Maria Stuart* with the plays which Schiller had so far written is immense. Instead of the vast scene and wide panorama of *Die Räuber*, *Fiesco*, or *Wallenstein*, the vigorous action of *Kabale und Liebe*, or the long-drawn-out lyrical eloquence of *Don Carlos*, Schiller has given us in *Maria Stuart* a play almost as compact and intense as Ibsen's *Ghosts* or Racine's *Phèdre*. Not only in subject-matter, but even in structure Schiller felt the need of a complete contrast with *Wallenstein*.

It is not only the external action that has been concentrated. The psychological interest of *Maria Stuart* is confined to a very few figures —to the two queens, and, in a much slighter degree, to Lord Leicester. There are many more characters in the play beside these three, but each is seen only in his or her relationship to one or other queen. Some who scarcely touch the main persons, such as the French envoys, are the merest lay figures. Others display only one quality such as Davison's timidity in the face of enormous responsibility. Hannah Kennedy is Mary's devoted and affectionate servant, and nothing else. Melvil is her masculine counterpart, whose deep devotion to his queen goes the length of taking holy orders so that she may receive the absolution of her own Church in her hour of need.

What is true of the minor characters applies also to the more important ones, Burleigh, Mortimer, and Shrewsbury. Burleigh is the opportunist in politics, the 'realist' in the bad sense, who subordinates justice to the national interest. But he is carefully subordinated to Elizabeth who listens to his advice only when it suits her purpose and never allows him to dominate her; and in his one encounter with Queen Mary he is completely worsted. Burleigh, who had all the material for a strong and dominant character in the tragedy, is carefully kept in the background, and shown only in relation to the central figures. Elizabeth is the principal; he is never more than her agent.

Mortimer is a swifter, more violent character, a fanatic, whose religious zeal develops into a furious physical passion for Mary, bordering on lunacy. But Schiller is not interested in Mortimer's unbalanced psychology, he uses his passion only to show the catastrophic influence which Mary exerts, and always has exerted, on so many of the men she meets. Similarly Burleigh serves to show us how Elizabeth both exploits her advisers and shelters behind them.

Between Elizabeth's minister and Mary's conspirator-lover stands Shrewsbury, honourable, selfless, and forthright, equally fearless in defence of Mary's rights and Elizabeth's life or reputation. His impartial position in the play might have given him independence, but he, too, is only portrayed in relation to the two queens.

Leicester, like Shrewsbury, occupies a central position. But while Shrewsbury is detached and objective, Leicester is emotionally entangled with both the queens. He is in love with Mary, yet deeply attached to the honours and privileges which his peculiar relationship to the Queen of England gives him. Since he embodies the conflict of ambition and love, he is a potential hero of the tragedy; and Schiller, in order to guard against his becoming too prominent, has given him a weak and mean character. Leicester is selfish, ruthless where his interests are involved (witness his treacherous treatment of Mortimer), faithless to the woman he loves, as soon as his fidelity is exposed to the slightest strain, and eternally anxious about his position and prestige at Court. As Mortimer contemptuously remarks:

Wie kleine Schritte
Geht ein so grosser Lord an diesem Hof![1]

He is no more than a fifth-rate personality, gifted with pleasant form and features, and born to wealth and rank. Schiller has conceived his character thus because he was determined to focus the light on Mary and Elizabeth and to subordinate to them all other characters. Thus every figure looks towards the two queens and in so doing directs the spectator's and reader's gaze to the focal-point of the play.

Schiller's Mary Queen of Scots is guilty of complicity in the murder of Darnley, her second husband. Since that dark episode there has been nothing in her life of which she need feel ashamed. She makes no secret of her longing to escape from Elizabeth's hands, but she has not supported with word or thought any of the attempts which have been made on the life or power of Elizabeth. Schiller succeeds in making this contrast between Mary's immaculate present and her sombre past fully comprehensible. Hers is a passionate nature, ruled by impulse; now calmed and chastened by years of imprisonment (though not the nineteen years of history, for Schiller's Mary as he wrote to Iffland on June 22, 1800, is only twenty-five). Schiller needed, not merely to talk about the passion which caused Mary's misfortunes, but to bring it before our eyes, and he used the third

---

[1] What anxious little steps so great a lord must take at this Court!

act for this purpose. Without any explanation Mary suddenly finds herself released from captivity within the castle and free to wander about its grounds. The unexpected change is too much for her balance. An extravagant uprush of excited joy expresses itself in lyrical passages, admirably conveying the irrepressible surge of long-pent-up emotion. The change goes deeper. The sudden association of liberty with her earlier life awakens desires and passions which she had forgotten. A just instinct opposes the meeting with Elizabeth which her friends have arranged with such excellent intentions, and when the meeting takes place the worst occurs: humility turns to reproach, submission to anger, and self-accusation to vehement and triumphant reproof of a rival. The emotional character and the necessity of this outburst is reflected in words betraying satiation and exhaustion as she gasps:

> O, wie mir wohl ist, Hanna! Endlich, endlich,
> Nach Jahren der Erniedrigung, der Leiden,
> Ein Augenblick der Rache, des Triumphs!
> Wie Bergeslasten fällt's von meinem Herzen,
> Das Messer stiess ich in der Feindin Brust.[1]

This scene of earthly passion, in which Mary returns to her former nature, is followed by another in which she finds herself the object of Mortimer's almost insane physical passion. A violent shock brings her once more to the humility which she had acquired with so much suffering during her imprisonment.

The consequence of Mary's scarifying attack upon Elizabeth is death. Under its inescapable approach her character changes. With all hope gone, she finds courage, and her deluding passions die. She draws strength from the thought that, innocent of the offence for which she is condemned, by her death she can expiate the dreadful crime committed in her youth:

> Gott würdigt mich, durch diesen unverdienten Tod
> Die frühe schwere Blutschuld abzubüssen.[2]

With the shadow of death already upon her, she can face even the final test of meeting on her way to the scaffold Leicester, whom she had loved. Mary Stuart is the first of Schiller's tragic heroes and heroines who accept the inevitable and face their end in greatness of soul. They maintain their freedom of will by voluntarily submitting to what they cannot evade, in accordance with Schiller's view in *Über das Erhabene*.

---

[1] Oh, how much good that has done me, Hannah! At last, at last, after years of humiliation and suffering, one moment of revenge—of triumph! A weight falls from my heart now that I have thrust the dagger into my enemy's heart.

[2] God permits me by this unmerited death to expiate my early bloody guilt.

Unlike Mary, Queen Elizabeth is capable of malice. Vain and arrogant, she detests her Scottish kinswoman because she is a pretender to Elizabeth's own throne. Those pretensions are a perpetual reminder of the stigma of bastardy, once fastened on Elizabeth by her own father. She detests Mary, too, for quite personal and feminine reasons—for her looks and her success with men. Elizabeth is a jealous, envious woman, capable of any meanness, though eager for the good opinion of the world. She therefore feigns sentiments which her secret actions belie, seeking to have Mary quietly poisoned because she fears the repercussions of an execution. Not only is she a hypocrite, she is also a moral coward, endeavouring always to thrust the responsibility for her own actions on to others, blaming, for instance, Davison for the execution. Except for one genuine movement of compassion, when in the second act she reads her rival's humble letter, her course is one of intrigue, subterfuge, and dissimulation. But her continual efforts to do evil by the hand of others are only partly successful. She sweeps her rival from her path:

> Jetzt endlich hab' ich Raum auf dieser Erde ——[1]

In doing so she loses the supporters whose good opinion she values most. Shrewsbury withdraws when he has failed to save her from herself, and Leicester, after his own fashion, takes French leave:

> Der Lord lässt sich
> Entschuldigen, er ist zu Schiff nach Frankreich.[2]

Schiller's portrait of Queen Elizabeth raises the question of the tragic dramatist's treatment of history in a form which is particularly acute for the English reader. Accustomed to the picture of a genial, popular, and wise ruler, he is roused to sharp antagonism by Schiller's portrayal of a rancorous and hypocritical tyrant. Schiller had, of course, no intention of offending national susceptibilities. He agreed with Lessing that the stage is no proper medium for interpreting historical periods or analysing great men. He had been a historian himself and saw clearly that the aims of history and tragedy were divergent.

This division between history proper and history in drama, though true in principle, cannot always be maintained in practice. Schiller himself had found his great knowledge of the Thirty Years War something of a hindrance in writing *Wallenstein*. He could not shake off what he knew. And what is true for the author is also true for the spectator. He, too, cannot lay aside his knowledge; hence

---

[1] At last there is room for me on this earth!

[2] His lordship begs to be excused, he has taken ship for France.

the unsatisfactory response of the English reader to *Maria Stuart*. Nationalism, with which Schiller did not reckon at all, has seriously impaired the value of the play as an article for export. Yet on the basis of his restricted facts (for Schiller confines his view of Elizabeth solely to her relationship with Mary) Schiller's view is a plausible one, and, indeed, he felt that he was if anything too faithful to historical fact, complaining to Goethe of the difficulty of freeing his imagination from the ties of history (July 19, 1799). If the play is to be appreciated, a constant effort must be made to see Elizabeth as a figure belonging to this tragedy alone and not to the ' real ' world of history.

Schiller's verse is of the same high quality as that of *Wallenstein;* but it has less need to adapt itself to individual character, because the concentration of *Maria Stuart* upon two figures demanded unity rather than diversity. In the third act he makes a considerable variation of style to express, not character, but emotion. When, in the third act, Mary is permitted to go into the garden, a torrent of long-repressed joy pours forth in successive waves, and the short spontaneous outbursts of ecstasy are conveyed by the impulsive hurrying beat of a lyrical measure:

> Lass mich in vollen, in durstigen Zügen
> Trinken die freie, die himmlische Luft![1]

Shortsighted contemporaries reproached Schiller with Catholic sympathies. Certainly his heroine is a Roman Catholic and is shown in favourable contrast to the Protestant Elizabeth, and Roman rites are presented on the stage in the last act with dignity and reverence. But this is no sign of partiality; it is the outcome of Schiller's objectivity. His earlier opposition to the Catholic Church was personal; his detachment in *Maria Stuart* proves how much he had done towards eliminating personal and private partiality from his plays.

With *Maria Stuart* Schiller ventured for the first time into the portrayal of a heroine. But there was nothing in the private life of this most masculine writer which could cause this change. Just as the concentration of this play afforded the completest relief from the breadth of *Wallenstein*, so, too, did a play about two women offer the opposite pole to the world of coarse and robust soldiers which he had just quitted.

However different in character *Maria Stuart* was from its predecessor, it had in common with it Schiller's wonderful command of the stage and a dramatic sense—especially in the third and fifth acts—which we should now call superb " theatre." He was profiting

---

[1] Let me in long, deep draughts drink in this free and heavenly air.

rapidly by the renewed practical experience which the rehearsals of *Wallenstein* had given him.

Even when the disturbance of moving house and his own illness had interrupted work on *Maria Stuart* in the early months of 1800, Schiller could not leave the theatre alone. In January he began an adaptation of *Macbeth*, intended to be the work of a mere fortnight. It actually occupied him until April, because he found that the existing translations were useless and that he must translate as well as adapt.

Macbeth was in part the outcome of Schiller's contact with the Weimar Theatre, for it was intended as an extension of the repertoire. It was also a pot-boiler, for he could sell the manuscript to other theatres. Above all he was interested in the task because *Macbeth* had been much in his mind during the writing of *Wallenstein*, and his translation was a tribute to a work he admired.

Schiller's *Macbeth* is a refined version; it uses blank verse throughout, and substitutes for the coarse jesting of the Porter a " morning song." But the witches remain unaltered, and the standard of translation in all the serious passages is remarkably high. Schiller himself was under no illusions about the inferiority of his adaptation to the original. He was no 'improver' of Shakespeare; he was only concerned to prepare an acting version for the German stage. His translation is certainly superior to anything which had appeared before.

No sooner was *Maria Stuart* finished than Schiller turned his attention to his next tragedy, which was to deal with Joan of Arc. This was to occupy him from June 1800 to April 1801. As Duke Karl August objected to its performance because he did not wish his favourite actress, Caroline Jagemann, to appear in public in a semi-masculine part, *Die Jungfrau von Orleans (The Maid of Orleans)* was first acted in Leipzig on September 18, 1801. In Weimar it was eventually performed on April 23, 1803.

Here, in *Die Jungfrau von Orleans*, the pendulum of Schiller's structural style swings back again from concentration to breadth. In striking contrast to the retrospective technique of *Maria Stuart*, this play brings before our eyes, incident by incident, the whole career of Joan of Arc. The normal five acts proved insufficient, and Schiller added a sixth in the guise of a prelude.

This prelude reveals Joan as a much deeper nature than her sisters, and shows her suspected of witchcraft by her sombre father. Before it ends she prophesies the liberation of France and recognizes that it is her destiny to achieve it. In the first act we see the pitiable state of the uncrowned King Charles VII, his armies defeated, his kingdom rent by dissension, his treasury empty, his last great city threatened. The Maid arrives, already famous for her victory at Vaucouleurs, and a sudden confidence in victory sweeps the weary and depressed French Court. Orleans having been relieved, the defeated English and Burgundians are in the second act again routed by Joan, who proves a ruthless and merciless enemy in battle. She crowns her success in arms by persuading the Duke of Burgundy to abandon the invader and rejoin Charles's cause.

In the third act the reconciliation between Charles VII and the Duke takes place, after which Dunois and La Hire sue for Joan's hand. She rejects both offers, for her destiny is not an earthly one. Once again battle is joined, and Talbot, the mightiest of the English, is defeated, but the Maid, when the English knight Lionel is at her mercy, is seized with love for him and spares him. The coronation of Charles VII follows in the fourth act, and Schiller sets his scene outside the west doors of Reims Cathedral. Joan, now at the height of her fame, is heartsick at the thought of her treasonable love for an enemy of her country. At this moment her half-crazed father publicly denounces her as a witch. She makes no attempt to defend herself and is expelled from the Court. In the fifth act she falls into the hands of the English, is delivered by a miracle (she breaks treble chains asunder), joins the battle, and perishes heroically and beautifully in the field, while (in the words of the stage direction), a rosy hue suffuses the sky.

From this story to the facts of history is a far cry. The divergence from fact was deliberate, since Schiller had studied the history of the period with great care. He believed the dramatist should be free to adapt and alter the events of history for his purpose. But if the use he made of history in *Maria Stuart* is still defensible, his practice in *Die Jungfrau von Orleans* reveals the limits beyond which his theory fails. Any historical play must involve distortions. Considerable divergences can be made, provided the outlines of history are maintained. But if such a salient point as the burning of Joan of Arc is altered into a glorious death on the battlefield, the play will encounter resistance and disbelief from the normally educated spectator or reader. Schiller chose in *Die Jungfrau von Orleans* to ignore this principle.

His large-scale distortion of history in this play would still be accounted a fault even if his changes were in the nature of improvements. They are very far from being so. The death of Joan seems a violent and arbitrary device to avoid the truly tragic ending of the original story. Its treatment, turning the closing scene into a glowing apotheosis (thereby recalling the final scene of *Egmont*, which Schiller had condemned in 1788), takes us even farther from the tragic. Nor is this all. Schiller has added a number of episodes of his own invention. Of these the sentimental scene in which Joan recalls Burgundy to his duty, the slaying of Montgomery, Joan's love for Lionel, the ghost of Talbot, the denunciation of the Maid by her father, and her expulsion by order of Charles VII are the most striking. So numerous are these fantasies, so romantic and sentimental is their character, that *Die Jungfrau von Orleans* can scarcely claim to be anything more than a dramatized fairy-tale. The lavish use of pageantry and music, most conspicuous in the fourth act, is symptomatic of Schiller's abandonment of a tragic purpose; the play needs their help because it does not possess the intensity of tragedy.

Though *Die Jungfrau von Orleans* forms a complete contrast to *Maria Stuart* in all but the sex of its chief character, it is no reversion to the manner of *Wallenstein*. It has breadth but no variety. *Wallenstein* offered to our view a world full of real characters of the most diverse types. *Die Jungfrau von Orleans* exhibits only a tedious succession of conventionally noble figures, who neither by speech nor act at any moment come to life as credible individuals. It is astonishing to find this great student of the human heart abandoning his psychological penetration and contenting himself with an array of lay figures. He did not term his work a " romantic tragedy " for nothing; his fifteenth century is an age which has never been, an age in which thought, conduct, and speech are on a stylized level which eliminates individuality and hides all that is harsh and unpleasant in a rosy haze of romanticism.

The human problem embodied in *Die Jungfrau von Orleans* is complex. Joan is torn between patriotism and love, but also between her personal interest and her divine mission. The voice of God tells her:

> Nicht Männerliebe darf dein Herz berühren
> Mit sünd'gen Flammen eitler Erdenlust ——[1]

The sense of a single-minded mission develops in her to the point of arrogance:

> Ihr blinden Herzen! Ihr Kleingläubigen!
> Des Himmels Herrlichkeit umleuchtet euch,
> Vor eurem Aug' enthüllt er seine Wunder,
> Und ihr erblickt in mir nichts als ein Weib.[2]

[1] The love of men may not touch thy heart with the sinful flames of vain earthly joy.

[2] You blind hearts! You men of little faith! The radiance of Heaven surrounds you, before your eyes it unfolds its wonders, and yet you see in me nothing but a woman.

This is the *hubris* of the Greeks, and Joan's overweening self-confidence promptly meets disaster when to Lionel she really does become a woman and no more. This sense of failure in her mission is crossed with another failure, since, as France's liberator, she falls in love with one of France's enemies.

Schiller's Joan is undoubtedly a nationalist who believes in France for the French just as ardently as Bernard Shaw's Joan does. In the fury of her patriotism she becomes herself a Fury, ruthlessly killing with her own hands the Welsh youth Montgomery, who tries vainly to surrender, and seeking to kill Lionel in the same fashion. Indeed, it is this extreme nationalism that brings disaster upon Joan, for it leads to her abortive attempt to kill Lionel, and thence to her love for him. To see in the play, as many German commentators have done, a panegyric of nationalism, or even a patriotic German play in French disguise, is a gross perversion. With all its many faults, it must be acquitted of any flattery to German nationalism.

Schiller's values were not political but spiritual. The one work which betrays any national feeling, the fragment of a poem written in 1801 and since called *Deutsche Grösse* (*German Greatness*) by the scholar Suphan, who unearthed it, praised the Germans for turning their backs on politics, war, and wealth, and for devoting themselves instead to the things of the spirit.

Alone among Schiller's mature plays *Die Jungfrau von Orleans* has a uniform style which fails to adapt itself to the characters. Whether King Charles looks hopefully towards a better future:

> Frankreich steigt,
> Ein neu verjüngter Phönix, aus der Asche,
> Uns lächelt eine schöne Zukunft an.
> Des Landes tiefe Wunden werden heilen,
> Die Dörfer, die verwüsteten, die Städte
> Aus ihrem Schutt sich prangender erheben,
> Die Felder decken sich mit neuem Grün ——[1]

or whether the charcoal-burner deplores the war-making of man:

> Wie eine losgelassne Hölle tobt
> Der Sturm, die Erde bebt, und krachend beugen
> Die altverjährten Eschen ihre Krone.
> Und dieser fürchterliche Krieg dort oben,

---

[1] France will rise up, a newly risen Phœnix, from these ashes and meet a splendid smiling future. The land's deep wounds will heal, the devastated villages and cities rise more prosperous from their rubble, the fields be covered with fresh verdure.

> Der auch die wilden Tiere Sanftmut lehrt,
> Dass sie sich zahm in ihre Gruben bergen,
> Kann unter Menschen keinen Frieden stiften ——[1]

the style is the same.

The deadening monotony is varied only by a few changes of metre —by lyrical measures in the Prologue and the fourth act, and by iambic trimeters, the metre of Greek tragedy, in the Montgomery scenes of the second act. But these are changes of form; the style itself does not change. And Schiller disregards the method (adopted so successfully in *Wallenstein*) of varying the manner of speech to conform with the character of the speaker. Only in the speeches of Talbot, the realist, whom he dislikes, does Schiller sound any but a purely rhetorical note:

> Bald ist's vorüber, und der Erde geb' ich,
> Der ew'gen Sonne die Atome wieder,
> Die sich zu Schmerz und Lust in mir gefügt.
> Und von dem mächt'gen Talbot, der die Welt
> Mit seinem Kriegsruhm füllte, bleibt nichts übrig
> Als eine Handvoll leichten Staubs. — So geht
> Der Mensch zu Ende — und die einzige
> Ausbeute, die wir aus dem Kampf des Lebens
> Wegtragen, ist die Einsicht in das Nichts
> Und herzliche Verachtung alles dessen,
> Was uns erhaben schien und wünschenswert.[2]

a speech simple in movement and convincing in tone with an undoubted echo of *Macbeth*, which Schiller had recently translated.

The influence of Shakespeare, however, was not always so beneficial. It is to Schiller's admiration for the ghosts in *Hamlet* and *Macbeth* that we owe the appearance in the third act of this play of a spectre, which is apparently that of the newly slain Talbot. This ghost conceals his ghostliness not only from Joan, but also from the audience, till he unexpectedly sinks through the floor amid thunder and lightning. It is a puerile and pointless episode, introduced for no other reason than to heighten the romantic atmosphere.

Though *Die Jungfrau von Orleans* now seems by far the weakest of Schiller's plays, Schiller and his friends were particularly pleased

---

[1] The storm rages like hell let loose, the earth quakes and venerable ash-trees bend. And yet this fearful war in the heavens, which teaches even animals gentleness, so that they quietly hide in their lairs, can not persuade men to make peace.

[2] Soon it will be over, and I shall give back to the earth and to the everlasting sun the atoms which were joined in me for joy and sorrow, and nothing will remain of mighty Talbot, who filled the world with his martial glory, but a light handful of dust.—So man ends—and the only profit which we gain from the struggle of life is an insight into nothingness and a hearty contempt for everything which seemed sublime and desirable.

with it. Goethe praised it highly, Körner considered it his best work, and Schiller himself not only valued it highly, but was especially satisfied with the last act. He thoroughly enjoyed writing the work. On January 5, 1801, he had written to Körner:

> The very subject makes me enthusiastic; I am in it with all my heart, and it flows more from my heart than previous plays, in which my intellect had to grapple with the subject-matter.

Here is the clue to the quality of *Wallenstein*, the defects of *Die Jungfrau von Orleans*, and the middle position of *Maria Stuart*.

Schiller had been repelled by the figure of Wallenstein, and could not wholeheartedly approve of Mary Queen of Scots; but Joan of Arc was a heroine after his own heart, a Max Piccolomini thrust into the very centre of a play and dominating it. Joan of Arc had nothing in her that was earthly, except for the brief period of her love for Lionel. Schiller's enthusiastic fantasy could range freely regardless of reality. It was his enthusiasm for his heroine which drove him so grossly to disfigure history, for the Joan of his imagination could have nothing to do with so sordid an end as burning at the stake. With less congenial subjects (including in this play the figure of Talbot), he had to grapple more vigorously with his material. Conflict is the essence of drama, and it was also the essence of Schiller's writing of drama. Only when he had to wrestle with a recalcitrant subject, which held him in contact with reality, did he write great drama. Where the subject was too much to his taste, he would fly off into exalted moods, divorced altogether from reality. Such was his enjoyment that he valued highly what he produced under their spell. These works, of which *Die Jungfrau von Orleans*, several poems and parts of plays are examples, were the product of emotional self-indulgence. Schiller had rightly concluded that he was an objective writer. But when he identified himself with his subject, as he did in *Die Jungfrau von Orleans*, he turned his back for the time being on objectivity. He had strayed from the right path. Soon, however, he was to find it again.

After *Die Jungfrau von Orleans* more than a year elapsed before Schiller began seriously to work at the next of his completed plays. Meanwhile he was not idle. He spent some time on *Wilhelm Tell*, which he then laid aside. He also worked at a project, which he was never to carry out—a play on the story of Perkin Warbeck.

This was only one of many projects. From 1798 onwards playwriting was the essence of Schiller's life, and he was constantly occupied with numerous schemes. Some of these developed into the plays of the Schiller canon, some were fully planned and even exist as fragments, others progressed no farther than general ideas and rudimentary scenarios. Of all these projects the most important were *Die Malteser* (*The Knights of Malta*) and *Perkin Warbeck*.

Die Malteser, which was the older subject, occupied Schiller for many years. It is first mentioned in a letter to Körner written during Schiller's summer in Rudolstadt (May 28, 1788), though the story occurs even earlier, being briefly told in the third act of *Don Carlos*. His dramatic urge was then at its weakest, and several years passed without further reference to it. During his visit to Würtemberg in the winter of 1793-94 he toyed with the idea again, and he expounded the plan to Goethe during the fortnight he spent as the latter's guest in Weimar in September 1794. All through 1795 the plan was in his mind. Eventually it was shelved in favour of *Wallenstein*. But Schiller did not abandon it completely, and he was still pondering on it in 1797 when work on his trilogy was at its height. He found both then and later that the thought of another play in a less advanced and more flexible state was at once a relaxation and a help to the task he already had in hand. He worked at it occasionally until March 1803. Whether he would have finished it, had he lived longer, is doubtful, for his interest had clearly waned after the completion of *Die Braut von Messina*.

Die Malteser was based on the story of the heroic defence of the island of Malta by John of Valetta in 1565, in the face of overwhelming force without, and despair and mutiny within. All the characters were to be men, and Schiller contemplated treating it after the manner of a Greek tragedy, with chorus and no division into acts. His long preoccupation with the theme is a certain indication that he had not solved the problem of presenting it in dramatic form. He achieved his aim of writing a neo-Greek play more successfully with *Die Braut von Messina*.

Perkin Warbeck also had a fairly long history, being first mentioned during the writing of *Maria Stuart* in the summer of 1799. Two years later he took it up again, laying it aside in the autumn of 1801. He continued to brood on it until the year before his death, but the moral difficulty caused by the fact that the hero is a conscious impostor proved insuperable. His decision to treat the similar, though morally less questionable, story of Demetrius meant the final abandonment of Warbeck.

Schiller left plans for several other plays. *Die Polizei* was to have been an analytical tragedy on the plan of *Œdipus Rex*, in which the Paris police were to assume the role of fate. He also considered, with some reason, treating this theme as a comedy. *Die Kinder des Hauses* was another attempt at a tragedy after the manner of *Œdipus:* the story of a successful criminal setting in motion inquiries which lead eventually to his own exposure. *Die Prinzessin von Celle* dealt with a *cause célèbre;* the story of the consort of the Elector George of Hanover (later King George I of Great Britain) and of the assassination of Count Königsmark in 1694. The princess in Schiller's play would have been an innocent victim of the coarseness, brutality, and malice of others. All these were projects of the last years of Schiller's life, and are evidence of the constant, restless activity of his mind, which had now reached a high pitch of dramatic creativeness. Some were still-born, mere waste products of his tireless energy, but others might have developed, had he lived, into finished plays.

In the summer of 1801, when he was still undecided whether his next play would be *Die Malteser, Perkin Warbeck,* or *Die Braut von Messina,* Schiller planned to take a holiday by the Baltic, at Doberan near Rostock. He and his family had not left the little state of Saxe-Weimar since the visit to Würtemberg, during which Karl was born. That was more than seven years before. The family now numbered three children and Schiller and Lotte felt that they all needed a change. They hoped to spend six weeks away altogether visiting Berlin and Dresden on the return journey. At the last moment, however, Lotte was unwell, the whole plan was abandoned, and a prolonged visit to the Körners at Dresden substituted. From early August till mid-September Schiller and Lotte were the guests of their old friends. In spite of the long interval since they had last met, Schiller and Körner re-established at once the sincere, open-hearted, and cordial relationship which had characterized their friendship ever since it had emerged from the first effusiveness of 1785.

Schiller was now without question one of the great names of contemporary German literature. An outward sign of this was his demand in October 1801 for higher payment, which Cotta most readily granted. The unhurried care he gave to his later work prevented him from ever becoming a really prosperous author, but at least the consciousness of his worth gave him deep satisfaction: " At last [he wrote to Cotta] I believe that as far as writing is concerned I have reached the position for which I have striven for years."

In the late autumn, while still uncertain about his next play, he spent his time adapting Gozzi's *Turandot* for the German stage. It was a pleasant recreation and, in view of the slight expenditure of time and energy, a remunerative one. When *Turandot* was finished Schiller began to prepare Goethe's *Iphigenie* for the Weimar stage. All this time his creative powers were working at low pressure, storing energy for the task ahead. Nevertheless these adaptations and continuous contact with the Weimar stage were giving him an increasingly sure sense of the theatre.

In this same winter of 1801–2 Schiller and his wife derived much pleasure from Goethe's Wednesday circle (Mittwochskränzchen). Founded in October 1801, it formed a little private and select artistic society, devoted to conversation, readings, and music. Unfortunately the Wednesday circle came to an end in March 1802, when Kotzebue, the popular dramatist, annoyed at Goethe's refusal to admit him, alienated some of the members and so broke up the gathering. Kotzebue even attempted to drive a wedge between Schiller and Goethe by ostentatiously arranging a Schiller festival from which Goethe was to be excluded. The attempt failed, and the festival never took place, but the Wednesday circle did not recover from the dissension sown by a clever intriguer.

Early in 1802 Schiller saw the chance of buying a house in the Esplanade from Joseph Mellish, an Englishman who had spent some time in Weimar and had translated *Maria Stuart*. Schiller was now forty-two, with three children, the eldest of whom was already eight, and he felt that he needed the security of a house of his own. He bought the house in February and planned to move into it in May.

The intervening period was one of strain and worry, not so much because he had to cope with carpenter and mason, glazier and paper-hanger, but because depressing news was reaching him from Würtemberg. His mother was failing in health. Schiller, tied down by sickness, could do no more than ask his doctor-friend von Hoven to attend her and write encouraging letters to his sister Luise, who was nursing her. Frau Schiller died on April 29, 1802, on the day on which Schiller moved into his new home. The news made him more deeply aware of his family responsibilities and of the precariousness of his own life.

Chapter Eighteen

"*DIE BRAUT VON MESSINA*"
1802–3

THE summer months of 1802 were barren ones for Schiller. No sooner had the workmen gone from his new house than sickness came; for weeks he was incapacitated by a feverish catarrh. In September his work again began to gather momentum, and once he was busy with *Die Braut von Messina* (*The Bride of Messina*) he felt happy again.

In the late autumn he received a new token of public recognition. He was raised to the nobility, acquiring the simple prefix 'von.' It was a grant of arms, made at Vienna by the Emperor Francis at the request of Karl August and valid throughout the whole of Germany. Schiller was glad of it chiefly for Lotte's sake, for she had suffered a little at seeing her sister Caroline, now the wife of Wilhelm von Wolzogen, enjoy access to Court, which she herself as the wife of a commoner had been denied. The story behind this grant of nobility diminished its value for Schiller, for it was done as much for Herder's discomfiture as for Schiller's gratification. It was, in fact, an act of retaliation by the Duke, for Herder had presumed that his recently acquired Bavarian nobility gave him a prescriptive right of entry to the court of Weimar; Karl August sought rather pettily to annoy Herder by obtaining for Schiller a rank that would unquestionably be valid at any German Court.

Expectations which Schiller had centred on another noble patron revived a little in 1802, only to fade soon afterwards. In July Karl Theodor von Dalberg succeeded at last to the Electoral throne of Mainz. Conditions were now so much altered and prospects so uncertain that there was no longer much likelihood that he would become the Maecenas that Schiller had once hoped. Though he could not invite Schiller to settle in Mainz, Dalberg gave him appreciable help, including a substantial present of money at New Year 1803.

The earliest really vital event in Schiller's life after the move to his new house was the first performance of *Die Braut von Messina* in the Court Theatre of Weimar on March 19, 1803. The play made a deep impression, and Schiller had a gratifying feeling of having tapped a new vein in the German theatre—possibly the purest that had yet been struck.

The seed of *Die Braut von Messina* can perhaps be detected as far back as Schiller's studies and translations of the Greek tragic writers in the autumn of 1788. His interest in the theatre of the Ancients later waned, and did not revive until 1797, during the writing of *Wallenstein*, when it is very clearly reflected in the ballad *Die Kraniche des Ibykus* (August 1797). The first clear evidence of work on *Die Braut von Messina* occurs in March 1799, immediately after the completion of *Wallenstein*, when Goethe, in a letter to their mutual friend Meyer, wrote of Schiller turning to a new subject of his own invention. Schiller himself first referred to the theme in a letter to Körner (May 13, 1801), but said that it did not yet interest him vitally.

It seemed likely that either *Die Malteser* or *Perkin Warbeck* would be written first. After an interval of groping with these subjects and of adaptation (with *Turandot*), Schiller dropped everything else and began seriously to work at *Die Braut von Messina* in the late summer of 1802. On September 9 he wrote to Körner: " I . . . am now working fairly seriously at a tragedy, the subject of which I mentioned to you. It is the hostile brothers, or, as I am now going to christen it, *Die Braut von Messina*." He hoped to have the play finished in time for performance on the birthday of the dowager Duchess, January 30. He was well advanced by the end of the year, but still failed to adhere to his self-imposed time schedule. He put the last touches to the play on February 1, 1803, and read it to the Duke of Meiningen and a large circle of listeners three days later.

Die Braut von Messina occupies a very special place in Schiller's work, for without trying to recreate Greek tragedy, he has sought to adapt some of its methods and to achieve its intense effect on the modern stage. The model which guided Schiller was the *Œdipus Rex* of Sophocles, as the story itself, which is Schiller's own invention, proves. Isabella, widow of the Prince of Messina, has two sons who live in perpetual hostility towards each other. She also has a daughter, of whom an oracle has foretold that she would cause the death of her two brothers and the ruin of her house. The husband has ordered the infant daughter's death, but Isabella saves her and has her brought up secretly in a convent, where she is ignorant of her own identity. Years pass, the daughter grows up, and her father is dead. Isabella plans to reconcile her sons and to produce her daughter at the same time. But the two brothers have both fallen in love with Beatrice, not knowing that she is their sister; and neither knows of the other's love. The brothers are indeed reconciled and happiness seems about to crown Isabella's life, when Don Cesar, the younger, finds his chosen bride in the arms of Don Manuel and immediately stabs him. Now the whole story unfolds, and Cesar learns that he has loved his sister and murdered his brother out of jealousy of her; and Isabella finds that all her efforts to ward off prophesied evils have been instrumental in bringing them to pass. Don Cesar then determines to expiate his crime by killing himself and resists all persuasion to stay his hand.

If the plot owes a debt mainly to Sophocles, the presentation of it reflects in its austere grandeur the influence of Aeschylus, four of whose plays Schiller read in Stolberg's translation in the autumn of 1802. Their powerful effect on him was transferred to the play he was writing, as he wrote to Wilhelm von Humboldt (February 17, 1803):

> I will not deny that without the closer acquaintance which I had meanwhile made with Aeschylus, this transference into former times would have presented greater difficulty.

Schiller aimed in *Die Braut von Messina* at creating a new type of tragedy which was to have more in common with the practice of the Ancients than either the realistic or the neo-classical tragedy of the moderns. He was engaged only on a private experiment, and did not imagine that his success would have any effect in diverting the German theatre from its course. He wrote *Die Braut von Messina*, in fact, primarily for his own edification:

> I will confess [he wrote to Iffland on April 22, 1803] that in *Die Braut von Messina* I essayed a little contest with the ancient tragic writers in which I thought more of myself than of the public.

Although Schiller entered into deliberate rivalry with the Greek dramatists, he made no attempt to write a pastiche; he attempted rather to adapt the principles of the ancient drama to the modern stage.

He began by adopting a plot which deals with fundamental human relationships, interwoven and crossed with such intensity that the extremes of horror, incestuous love, and fratricide result. He modelled this subject on the lines of the most famous of all Greek tragedies by making its catastrophe turn upon the fulfilment of oracles and by presenting only the final catastrophe to the spectators. It is the analytical construction of Sophocles in less pure form; for in Schiller's play one important action, the murder of Manuel, occurs during the play, which is thus not exclusively the unfolding of past history. The difference is a decisive one. The figures of Sophocles are passive, Schiller's characters are active. This change relegates fate in Schiller's play to a secondary place.

Schiller did not divide his play into acts and so appears to have given it a further superficial resemblance to Greek tragedy. This appearance is deceptive, and there are, in fact, five sub-divisions, each of which involves a change of scene. They are symmetrically arranged and occur in this order: colonnaded hall, garden, room in the interior of the palace, garden, colonnaded hall. The sequence of events is such that it is necessary on the stage to give at any rate some indication of a change of scene—if only by the lowering of a curtain—for the corpse of Don Manuel, murdered in the second garden-scene, has to be borne on to the stage in the last scene in the colonnaded hall. In this respect Schiller's play is not 'Greek'; his aim was not pastiche, but a play for the contemporary stage with front curtain and artificial lighting.

The most striking and obvious similarity to the drama of the Ancients is Schiller's introduction of a chorus. He makes both an ancient and a modern use of it; an ancient one when it follows the action and comments upon it in lyrical tones; a modern one when it divides into two, splits into individuals, and takes a part in the action of the play. Schiller has been abundantly criticized, both for the introduction of the chorus and for its dual role. He foresaw the criticisms and wrote his own defence, which he prefaced to *Die Braut von Messina* when it was published in 1803.

Über den Gebrauch des Chors in der Tragödie (*On the Use of the Chorus in Tragedy*) devotes itself first to a general repetition of Schiller's view of art as the means by which reality is to be made accessible to man:

> Die Natur selbst ist nur eine Idee des Geistes, die nie in die Sinne fällt. Unter der Decke der Erscheinungen liegt sie, aber sie selbst kommt niemals zur Erscheinung. Bloss der Kunst des Ideals ist es verliehen, oder vielmehr, es ist ihr aufgegeben, diesen Geist des Alls zu ergreifen und in einer körperlichen Form zu binden.[1]

Schiller's chorus is an emphatic declaration that the play is not realistic, but is " art of the ideal." By its mere presence it serves as a wall dividing the ideal from the real world.

> . . . eine lebendige Mauer . . . die die Tragödie um sich herumzieht, um sich von der wirklichen Welt rein abzuschliessen und sich ihren idealen Boden, ihre poetische Freiheit zu bewahren.[2]

The chorus also purifies the tragedy by separating action and reflection, for the latter is its own special sphere. Since it must express itself in poetic terms, the chorus imposes on the rest of the play a

[1] Nature itself is only an idea of the mind, which the senses cannot perceive. Nature lies behind appearances, but is never herself visible. It is in the power, or rather it is the task of the art of the ideal to seize this fundamental spirit of the whole and give it a corporeal form.

[2] . . . A living wall, with which tragedy surrounds itself, in order to shut itself off from the real world and to preserve its ideal territory, its poetic freedom.

higher and nobler tone, if harmony is to be preserved; and it brings to the action periods of repose which are equally valuable for the spectator and for the *dramatis personae*.

All these aspects of the chorus are true of the Greek conception, and there is nothing in them to justify or explain Schiller's modifications. But at the end of the essay he points out that he has given his chorus two distinct functions; when it comments upon the action and reflects upon human life it is one united body, but when it takes part in the action it divides. Schiller does not try to demonstrate in his essay that these two roles can be combined, for the proof is in the performance. There is no *a priori* reason why a crowd of men should not be unanimous at one moment and disunited at another, and Schiller's treatment of his chorus rests upon mass psychology.

In the final paragraph of *Über den Gebrauch des Chors in der Tragödie* Schiller mentions another possible objection to the play, the mingling of Christian and ancient Greek religions in one play. He defends it on the ground that the scene was Messina, where Christianity and the monuments of ancient Greece existed side by side. He had no need of any such excuse. The scene is no more a real, concrete Messina than Sophocles' tragedy plays in historical Thebes. *Die Braut von Messina* is placeless and timeless. It plays in a poetic world and a poetic age, where geographical and historical touchstones do not apply.

Schiller has deliberately gone farther from realism in *Die Braut von Messina* than in any of his preceding plays. He has simplified the situation and eliminated all irrelevant detail. Isabella, her sons Manuel and Cesar, her daughter Beatrice, her servant Diego, the Chorus, two anonymous messengers, and a silent group of elders of Messina make up the entire *dramatis personae*. All features of their lives which do not relate to this central crisis are rigidly excluded. The characters are purged of incidentals, although not romanticized like those of *Die Jungfrau von Orleans*. They are credible human beings set in a situation of uncommon intensity, removed from all distracting influences, fundamentally true in their thoughts, emotions, and reactions. The action, too, is simplified to its barest requirements; nothing is allowed to distract from the swelling surge of tragic emotion, nothing is retained which has not its clear and obvious relationship to the essential dramatic conflict.

The play begins in repose. Isabella unfolds to the elders of Messina the story of her house. It is exposition in its simplest form of monologue. Accompanied by her sons, she initiates the action by her attempt at reconciliation. With the three members of the family together, each individual and divergent, the spectator can yet see that they share a generic likeness. For all of this family are quick to anger, brutal and tyrannical in action. The strong will and harsh energy of the dead husband of Isabella had successfully curbed the rebellious tempers of his sons. Isabella is of a similar temper, regarding suspicion and force as the means by which her sons can maintain their authority:

> Von eurer Macht allein und ihrer Furcht
> Erhaltet ihr den gern versagten Dienst.[1]

The source of the brothers' imperious and haughty nature is plain.

Isabella pleads in mounting anguish, but all her passionate persuasion seems to produce no effect upon her silent sons. Wounded and exhausted she pauses:

> Jetzt weiss ich nichts mehr. Ausgeleert hab' ich
> Der Worte Köcher und erschöpft der Bitten Kraft.
> Im Grabe ruht, der euch gewaltsam bändigte,
> Und machtlos steht die Mutter zwischen euch.[2]

Schiller successfully turns the long monologue, a feature of his new technique, to psychological account; for Isabella in this speech lives through a tormenting experience, strains every nerve in love for her sons, and then reveals the decisive resolution of her character when, having pleaded to no purpose, she suddenly stops and angrily and defiantly faces disaster:

> — Vollendet! Ihr habt freie Macht! Gehorcht
> Dem Dämon, der euch sinnlos wütend treibt,
> Ehrt nicht des Hausgotts heiligen Altar,
> Lasst diese Halle selbst, die euch geboren,
> Den Schauplatz werden eures Wechselmords. . . .[3]

The two brothers remain alone, irresolute and not unmoved. Suddenly the reconciliation is there; but the brothers' love is as quick as their anger, and its swiftness gives little hope of permanence. As the friendship ripens we learn that both brothers are in love, and our first suspicion rises that Manuel unknowingly loves his sister. Even at the moment of apparent unanimity the jealous and passionate nature of Don Cesar flickers up:

---

[1] Only your power and their fear will retain for you the service they would fain refuse.

[2] I can go on no longer. I have used every weapon and the power of my pleadings is all in vain. He who once tamed you lies in his grave, and your mother stands powerless between you.

[3] Go on! You have full power! obey the spirit that drives you on in senseless rage, dishonour the holy altar of the house and let this hall become the scene of brother killing brother.

Denk' nicht ich fühle weniger als du,
Weil ich die festlich schöne Stunde rasch zerschneide.[1]

and the Chorus underlines the precariousness of this sudden peace:

Sorge gibt mir dieser neue Frieden,
Und nicht fröhlich mag ich ihm vertrauen,
Auf der Lava, die der Berg geschieden,
Möcht' ich nimmer meine Hütte bauen.[2]

and goes on to point out the inescapable consequences of past actions:

Denn zu tief hat schon der Hass gefressen,
Und zu schwere Taten sind geschehn.
Die sich nie vergeben und vergessen.

The garden scene which follows is the weakest feature of the play. So that Don Cesar, claiming Beatrice at their second meeting as his bride, may be left ignorant of her attachment to Don Manuel, Beatrice remains silent as long as Cesar is present. She is shocked and terrified by Cesar's appearance when she had so confidently expected Manuel whom she loves. Even if Beatrice's behaviour is not impossible, it still seems unbelievable that Cesar could leave without hearing even *one* word from his beloved. This garden scene makes one further stage in the tragedy pitilessly clear. Both brothers love the same woman, and each is ignorant of the other's claims. In view of Cesar's rash temper and Manuel's determination, alarming dangers already threaten the new alliance.

The dark foreboding of this scene is soon past, and we see the joy and happiness of Isabella in the reconciliation of her sons and the prospect of reunion with her long-hidden daughter. She reveals the existence of this sister to her two sons and explains why she had concealed the child. Her happiness seems about to reach its height when news is brought that the daughter has disappeared. For the spectator the chain is now complete. The woman whom both brothers love is Beatrice, their own sister. Every person on the stage possesses some links of the chain; none possesses all. Don Manuel alone is beset by a fearful suspicion.

The scene changes to the garden where Beatrice anxiously waits.

[1] Do not think that I feel less than you because I cut short this solemn and splendid hour.

[2] This new peace disquiets me, and I cannot greet it with joy and confidence. I would never dare build my house on the lava which the mountain has poured forth.

[3] Already this hatred has eaten too deep and deeds have been done which can never be forgiven or forgotten.

Q

The atmosphere is sultry with the quarrelling of the two groups of the Chorus sent by the rival lovers. The anxious Manuel arrives and questions Beatrice. Just as it becomes clear that she is his sister Cesar appears and promptly strikes his brother down. Schiller carefully minimizes the physical side of the murder. His aim is to get it done, and quickly, so that he can turn to the consequences. There is therefore no prolonged quarrel; black venom surges through Cesar's veins and he strikes. Manuel can hardly utter a word before he dies. All the emphasis is on the psychological and moral aspects; brutal satisfaction in one half of the chorus, vengeful indignation in the other, while Cesar proudly asserts the justice of his act in spite of a latent horror lurking beneath his arrogance:

> Ein furchtbar grässlich Ansehn hat die Tat,
> Doch der gerechte Himmel hat gerichtet.[1]

With the murder of Manuel the first stage in the catastrophe is reached. The anxious spectator knows there is more to come. Isabella has still to know that son has slain son, Cesar to learn that he has killed his brother out of jealousy of his own sister. In a scene arousing pity and horror in the last degree, Isabella, Cesar, and Beatrice learn slowly and remorselessly of the web of incestuous love and fratricidal strife in which they are enmeshed. Isabella finds her daughter unconscious. This causes her distress enough, but it is nothing to the next blow, when the body of Don Manuel is solemnly borne on to the stage. She still does not know how he has met his end, and all the oracles and prophecies seem to have missed the mark. Isabella, from whose proud and imperious nature suffering strikes fire, turns upon the gods with angry derision:

> Warum besuchen wir die heil'gen Häuser
> Und heben zu dem Himmel fromme Hände?
> Gutmüt'ge Toren, was gewinnen wir
> Mit unserm Glauben? So unmöglich ist's
> Die Götter, die hochwohnenden, zu treffen,
> Als in den Mond mit einem Pfeil zu schiessen.
> Vermauert ist den Sterblichen die Zukunft,
> Und kein Gebet durchbohrt den eh'rnen Himmel.[2]

With the approach of Don Cesar the last dreadful discoveries await the mother and the son. *She* learns that Manuel has fallen by his brother's hand, *he* that his bride and his sister are one. Again catastrophe wrings no tears from Isabella; angrily and bitterly she admits

---

[1] This act looks terrible and grim, but just Heaven decreed it.

[2] Why do we visit the temples and lift pious hands to Heaven? Well-meaning fools, what do we gain by our faith? For it is as impossible to reach the gods as to touch the moon with an arrow. The future is an impenetrable wall, and no prayer can pierce the iron rampart of Heaven.

the truth of what the gods foretold, angrily and bitterly she renounces her surviving son. In words that have the power and surge of Lear's speech she rises to her fullest stature in her deepest despair:

> ... den Rachegeistern überlass' ich
> Dies Haus. Ein Frevel führte mich herein,
> Ein Frevel treibt mich aus. Mit Widerwillen
> Hab' ich's betreten und mit Furcht bewohnt,
> Und in Verzweiflung räum' ich's. Alles dies
> Erleid' ich schuldlos; doch bei Ehren bleiben
> Die Orakel, und gerettet sind die Götter.[1]

As Isabella sweeps out, Cesar remains with Beatrice and the body of their brother. Determined to kill himself, he is still tormented by his love for Beatrice and by jealousy of the silent eloquence of Manuel, who still survives in the remembrance of his sister-lover:

> Weine um den Bruder, ich will mit dir weinen,
> Und mehr noch — rächen will ich ihn! Doch nicht
> Um den Geliebten weine![2]

Isabella returns, having humanly repented of her rash denunciation of her son. Anxiety and fear for him have revived, now that the crisis of passion is over. There follows one of the most moving scenes in the whole of drama as first Isabella, then Beatrice, pleads and persuades with so much love—though with hearts of lead and gnawing foreboding of the end—while Cesar resists them and his own struggling wishes. His death is inevitable, and the onlooker is made to feel it, for in this play Schiller's heart-penetrating gaze and sublime conception are in perfect harmony. Cesar does not die in order to fulfil Schiller's theory that acceptance of fate makes the free man, although he certainly does fulfil it. His resolution begins impurely—he is envious of dead Manuel's superiority in his mother's heart:

> Denkst du, dass ich den Vorzug werde tragen
> Den ihm dein Schmerz gegeben über mich?[3]

and he is jealous, too, of the love which Beatrice still feels for her lost lover:

[1] I leave this house to the gods of vengeance. A crime brought me into it, a crime drives me out. I entered it with repulsion, lived in it with fear, and in despair I leave it. All this I suffer without guilt; but the oracles are justified and the gods saved.

[2] Weep for our brother and I will weep with you—nay, more, I will avenge him. But do not weep for your beloved!

[3] Do you think that I can bear the advantage which your grief gives him over me?

Wir mögen leben, Mutter, oder sterben,
Wenn sie nur dem Geliebten sich vereinigt.[1]

Eventually the pleas of the two women are successful, and all three
are united in harmony. But Cesar knows that this happiness can be
for one moment of exaltation only. If he were to live, silent reproach
and bitter thoughts must slowly wear down his proud spirit. Now
he makes his free resolve, and follows Don Manuel to death.

Schiller has nobly vindicated his experiment. No play of his is
barer of the elements of ' reality ', no play is truer in its portrayal of
the suffering human heart and tormented human relationships.

The peculiar quality of the play is determined by its choral passages. In the theatre manuscript he sent to Vienna Schiller broke
them up, allotting strophes to individuals, and this sub-division,
published by Körner in 1814, is now normally retained. But
Schiller himself published the play without them, and it seems that,
at any rate in the theatre of the mind, he wished the Chorus to be
true to its name and speak in unison in lyrical passages of general
reflection, such as the praise of the peasant's obscure life:

Wohl dem! Selig muss ich ihn preisen,
Der in der Stille der ländlichen Flur,
Fern von des Lebens verworrenen Kreisen,
Kindlich liegt an der Brust der Natur.[2]

The most impressive of Schiller's choral poetry is not the moral
comment, but the passages in which the chorus abandons cold
detachment, when, for instance, Don Manuel's body lies on the
stage and Don Cesar approaches. Then the Chorus, with its

Brechet auf, ihr Wunden!
Fliesset, fliesset!
In schwarzen Güssen
Stürzet hervor, ihr Bäche des Bluts![3]

achieves a quasi-musical effect which transcends the meaning of
the words. This is true also of the repeated cries of " Woe! "
which could sound so foolish, and yet in the early part of the final
scene do so much to heighten the fearfulness of the situation as
Isabella pours forth her imprecations, regardless of the effect on the
appalled Chorus.

There is an obvious musical element in *Die Braut von Messina*

---

[1] We may live or die, mother, if only *she* is united with her lover.

[2] Happy is the man, I deem, who, in the quiet of the countryside and far from
the confused tangles of life, lies childlike at the breast of nature.

[3] Burst open, wounds! Flow, flow! Pour forth in black torrents, you streams
of blood!

in the use of the funeral march which heralds the arrival of the procession bearing the body of Don Manuel. Musical feeling also pervades the entire play, most conspicuously in the last scene, which marches as a perfect ensemble to its inevitable and inspiring end.

The basic metre of *Die Braut von Messina* is blank verse. Beatrice uses *ottava rima* to express her anxiety in the first garden scene, and the grave and solemn dialogue in which Don Cesar bids the Chorus prepare for his obsequies is conducted in the iambic trimeters which Schiller had already used for the heroic Montgomery scene in *Die Jungfrau von Orleans*. His verse in this play matches and often transcends the superb music of *Don Carlos*. It is language which is in perfect harmony with the thought and emotion it expresses. And it has profited in speed and intensity by the possibility of relegating all reflection to the speeches of the Chorus. For this reason the blank verse of *Die Braut von Messina* has not yielded many popular tags. It is something better than a quarry of quotations, it is a perfectly forged and subtly tempered instrument for the working out of the drama.

The scope given to the Chorus for reflection has sometimes suggested that its speeches are an embodiment of Schiller's own philosophy. An instance is a famous passage expressing the fear of sudden disaster, which had already formed the burden of the ballad, *Der Ring des Polykrates*:

> Wenn die Wolken getürmt den Himmel schwärzen,
> Wenn dumpftosend der Donner hallt,
> Da, da fühlen sich alle Herzen
> In des furchtbaren Schicksals Gewalt.
> Aber auch aus entwölkter Höhe
> Kann der zündende Donner schlagen.
> Darum in deinen fröhlichen Tagen
> Fürchte des Unglücks tückische Nähe!
> Nicht an die Güter hänge dein Herz,
> Die das Leben vergänglich zieren!
> Wer besitzt, der lerne verlieren,
> Wer im Glück ist, der lerne den Schmerz.[1]

To interpret this, or the final moral words of the Chorus at the end of the play as the personal view of Schiller is to overlook the important fact that Schiller is first, last, and all the time a dramatist. His chorus is a body of men involved in the tragic scene and profoundly

---

[1] When the towering clouds darken heaven and the thunder booms, then all hearts feel themselves in the power of terrible fate. But the thunderbolt can strike, too, from a cloudless sky. Therefore fear the treacherous approach of misfortune in your days of happiness. Cling not to the goods which adorn life for a brief space. He who possesses should learn to lose, and the happy man should learn grief.

moved by its outcome; touched by but not entangled in the tragic events it witnesses, it reacts very humanly in making such general comment. Schiller, like Shakespeare, was too great a dramatist to use his tragedy as a direct expression of personal opinion. *Die Braut von Messina* is not at any point a moral tract, it is a sublime embodiment of human grandeur.

Chapter Nineteen

"WILHELM TELL"
1803-4

AFTER the completion of *Die Braut von Messina* there was a short pause in Schiller's creative activity. Yet so absorbed was he in the theatre that even these two months of recuperation were spent in translating for the Weimar Theatre two comedies of Picard (1767–1828), *Le Médiocre rampant* and *Encore des Menechmes*, which he entitled *Der Parasit* and *Der Neffe als Onkel*. These were nothing more than serviceable contributions to the theatre and to his own exchequer.

In April 1803 came signs of new creative work. He busied himself again with his *Perkin Warbeck* and thought of following it with a play about William Tell. By July, however, the priority was changed and Tell had displaced Warbeck. In August he began to work intensively on the new play. The story of Tell was not a new one for Schiller. His attention had been drawn to it in 1797 and 1798 by Goethe, who at that time thought of making Tell the subject of an epic poem. But Goethe's idea lapsed, and Schiller did not at that time think of adopting the theme for himself. In 1801 a rumour became current that he was writing a new play with Tell as hero. This quite groundless report roused Schiller's interest and led him to study the sixteenth-century Swiss chronicle of Tschudi. By March 1802 he was writing to Cotta for a map of the region round the Lake of Lucerne.

Tell, however, took second place to *Die Braut von Messina*, and though Schiller had made some progress in the summer of 1802 (letter to Körner, September 9, 1802), it was almost a year later that Tell's story gripped him with an intensity that drove him irresistibly to forge this new drama. His diary records that he began to write the play on August 25, 1803. On February 18, 1804, it was complete. It was performed in Weimar on March 17, and achieved a success surpassing that of any previous work by Schiller. In Berlin on July 4 the play encountered a similar enthusiastic reception. It appeared in book-form in October 1804. Seven thousand copies were sold in the first three months, and a new edition was called for before the end of the year.

The story suited Schiller well after his work on *Die Braut von*

Messina. Just as he had turned to *Die Jungfrau von Orleans* after *Maria Stuart*, so now he found relaxation in the breadth and movement of *Wilhelm Tell*. It is the story of a revolt of the three Swiss cantons, Uri, Schwyz, and Unterwalden against Habsburg oppression in the years 1307 and 1308. There are two parallel actions; the conspiracy and revolt of the Swiss, and the private and individual revolt of Tell against his oppressor, whose tyranny is the link which binds the two plots together.

Wilhelm Tell, unlike any other of Schiller's plays, opens with a full description of the scene:

> The lake makes a bight into the land, not far from the shore is a small wooden cottage, the *Fisher Boy* is in his boat. Across the lake one sees the green meadows, villages, and farms of Schwyz bathed in bright sunshine. To the left of the spectator is the peak of Haken, half hidden by clouds; to the right, far off, are ice-capped mountains.

It is a striking change from the meagre indications of setting in Schiller's earlier plays, which rarely go further than " In the house of the Mayor of Eger " or " In the country; in the right foreground is a chapel with a saint's effigy, on the left a tall oak-tree." The new policy is a result of the effect on Schiller's imagination of reading about Swiss landscape; the mental picture which ensued moved him deeply. From the study of books and maps he obtained the materials for a Switzerland of the imagination. This is not the replica of any actual scene, but a reconstruction of the essential features of Swiss landscape. In this wider significance it is truer than an individual reproduction of any one scene could be.

Schiller's landscape painting is not limited to stage direction, it pervades the speech of the play. His farmers and shepherds, fishermen and hunters are not living in a vacuum, but are constantly aware of the scenes around them, so that a *Wilhelm Tell* without background or machinery would still possess in its verse a setting of towering mountains, alpine pastures, still lakes, and sudden storms.

Against this rugged landscape the opening scenes portray the contented life of the Swiss peasants. But the calm symbolized by the harmony of fisherman, cowherd, and hunter is soon interrupted. The farmer Baumgarten, who has defended his wife and honour against the assault of a vicious sheriff in Unterwalden, flees from the mounted police of the Austrians and hopes to cross the Lake of Lucerne to safety on the farther bank. These short scenes contain the basic elements of the play; the peaceable countryman, asking nothing better than to be left in quiet, is oppressed by the wanton tyranny of the intruding feudal Austrians.

The appearance of Tell brings to the conflict a new force. While

Baumgarten stands forlorn and helpless by the shore, because the fisherman will not risk his life in the storm, Tell takes the oars, commends himself and his passenger to God, and successfully traverses the lake. He is the embodiment of individual willingness to help.

The second scene deals with tyranny and the reaction it arouses in the many who are weak alone but strong in concert. Stauffacher of Schwyz sows the first seed of communal effort when he decides to seek a remedy in consultation with the men of Uri. So far there have been individual acts of violence, but the third scene reveals the tyranny of Gessler, the governor of Uri, who tramples underfoot the rights of a whole people when he builds the castle of Zwing Uri and orders the populace to uncover themselves before his hat. The total disregard of local tradition, the lawless abuse of power, and cruel violence of the Austrian governors are focused in the fourth scene in the house of Walther Fürst of Uri. Here Fürst, Stauffacher, and Melchthal of Unterwalden, whose father has been blinded by the wicked and vengeful whim of the governor of the Canton, resolve to right their wrongs themselves and to summon a council from the three cantons on the Rütli meadow.

The second act opens with a scene between two contrasting types of the Swiss nobility. The aged Attinghausen typifies the older generation, men who lived with the peasants, wore the same dress, and kept the same customs. The young noble, Rudenz, despises the peasant, copies the foreigner, and sides with him against his own countrymen.

The most important part of the second act is the secret assembly on the Rütli. Together on the moonlit meadow the armed men of three cantons meet on a still October night to deliberate means of freeing themselves from Austrian tyranny. Schiller's revolutionists, however, are no firebrands; they are sober, responsible men, ready to wait in patience for the attainment of their end, yet absolutely determined to achieve it. Conspiracy by such level-headed and deliberate men is a slow and blunt weapon against ruthless and well-armed power.

The third act is the critical one. After a scene in which Tell's domestic virtues are displayed, and another in which Rudenz returns to the path of patriotism, Tell's ordeal at Altdorf in Uri approaches. The hat stands upon its pole, guarded by armed sentries, and the inhabitants of Altdorf avoid its neighbourhood. William Tell, passing by with his son, ignores the symbol of tyranny and is promptly seized by the guards. A hue and cry is raised and the angry peasants seem about to rescue Tell, when Gessler and his escort arrive. At once the unorganized and improvised revolt collapses, and Tell remains at the mercy of the tyrant, who bids him at eighty paces distance shoot at an apple placed on his son's head.

At this point Schiller had to decide between three possibilities. He could have the shooting incident off-stage and allow one of the characters to tell the story; he could let it happen unseen by the audience, but visible to the actors on the stage; or he could present it boldly on the stage, with all the technical difficulties and possible absurdities, which the performance of such a feat must risk. He chose the last and most daring expedient, because his broad and episodic treatment of Tell's story brought so much incident on to the stage that the central and most popular feature of the legend could not be omitted. He overcame his difficulties by letting Tell loose his arrow at a moment when the spectators' attention is elsewhere. It is concentrated at that moment on Gessler and on Rudenz, who is roused to vehement protest against Gessler's inhumanity. This threat from a member of his own suite, expressed in impassioned eloquence, turns Gessler's mind from Tell and his ordeal, when suddenly Stauffacher's cry rings out—

Der Apfel ist gefallen![1]

It is an obvious and simple device, but an effective one, for this silent resolve and swift action entirely fits Tell's character. With this successful shot the crisis seems past. Immediately another and more threatening one looms up, as Gessler tricks Tell into the admission that the second arrow was destined for the tyrant if the first had killed the boy. Tell is bound and carried away and the peasants stand impotently by, unable to prevent it.

The fourth act contains another, almost superhuman, episode of the legend—Tell's escape from Gessler's ship. To have shown this to the spectators would have imposed on the stage manager an impossible task; to have narrated it as a past event would have been too cold. Schiller compromises. From a hill a fisher boy watches the ship, which neither the fisherman nor the spectators can see, and describes its hazardous course. Although he follows the general direction of the ship he fails, by reason of darkness and distance, to observe Tell's leap. The details are supplied by Tell himself, who appears a moment later and gives his own story. Schiller has done this in order to make Tell's sudden appearance a complete surprise. It is narration of a past event, but it is red-hot narration, for we know that the incident happened a moment before while the fisher boy was watching and giving us a commentary on the ship's progress.

[1] The apple has fallen!

"JÄGERLIEDCHEN FÜR WALTHER TELL" IN SCHILLER'S HANDWRITING
(reduced)

Jägerliedchen für Walther Tell womit Actus III. anzufangen

Mit dem Pfeil, dem Bogen
Durch Gebirg' und Thal
Kommt der Schütz gezogen,
Früh im Morgenstrahl.

Wie im Reich der Lüfte
König ist der Weih,
Durch Gebirg' und Klüfte
Herrscht der Schütze frei.

Ihm gehört das Weite,
Was sein Pfeil erreicht,
Das ist seine Beute,
Was da fleugt und kreucht.

It accords with Tell's resolute and active nature that he should immediately set out to avenge himself upon Gessler. For stage purposes an intervening scene had to be devised which, by distracting our attention for a while, would make Tell's reappearance at a distance plausible, which would, in fact, " give him time to get there." This scene contains the death of Attinghausen and culminates in the united resolve of the cantons to make an immediate end of tyranny. It serves therefore not only to speed Tell on his way to the narrow gorge where Gessler cannot evade him, but also to show that Tell's single-handed action, coinciding with a general rebellion, will not be in vain.

In the third scene of the fourth act Tell's arrow, deadly this time, kills the tyrant before the eyes of the spectators. With this action the most dangerous enemy of the people is eliminated and the path of the revolt, which occupies the first scene of the fifth act, is made smooth. The finale is a scene of general rejoicing. Before it is reached there is an episode of the utmost importance, an interview between Tell and Duke John of Swabia, known as Johannes Parricida.

The success of the Swiss revolt was made complete by Duke John's assassination of his uncle, the Emperor. Tell had killed the man who had done him injury, so too had Duke John. It was Schiller's aim in this scene to emphasize the differing motives and the widely separated moral planes of the two acts, and in so doing to justify Tell, who energetically rebuts Parricida's claim to kingship:

> Darfst du der Ehrsucht blut'ge Schuld vermengen
> Mit der gerechten Notwehr eines Vaters?[1]

Schiller's plays were plays of the theatre, and the scene with Parricida is designed to make the moral quality of Tell's deed unmistakably clear to the spectator. The reader, however, hardly requires such assistance, for Tell had already declared his public-spirited motive as he had waited for Gessler in the sunken road:

> Die armen Kindlein, die unschuld'gen,
> Das treue Weib muss ich vor deiner Wut
> Beschützen, Landvogt![2]

But there are potential depths in Tell which Schiller did not probe. Gessler's tyranny has in a very short space transformed Tell's whole character:

---

[1] Dare you mingle ambition's bloody guilt with the justified self-defence of a father?

[2] I must protect poor innocent children and faithful wives against your fury, vice-roy.

> Ich lebte still und harmlos, das Geschoss
> War auf des Waldes Tiere nur gerichtet,
> Meine Gedanken waren rein von Mord.
> Du hast aus meinem Frieden mich heraus
> Geschreckt, in gärend Drachengift hast du
> Die Milch der frommen Denkart mir verwandelt;
> Zum Ungeheuren hast du mich gewöhnt.[1]

Tell himself gives the obvious explanation of this change in terms of reflection and conscious resolve. Schiller hints at another and deeper emotional change:

> Da, als ich den Bogenstrang
> Anzog, als mir die Hand erzitterte,
> Als du mit grausam teufelischer Lust
> Mich zwangst, aufs Haupt des Kindes anzulegen,
> Als ich ohnmächtig flehend rang vor dir —
> Damals gelobt' ich mir in meinem Innern
> Mit furchtbarm Eidschwur, den nur Gott gehört,
> Dass meines nächsten Schusses erstes Ziel
> Dein Herz sein sollte.[2]

The suggestion here of a vital emotional reshaping of Tell, whose too cruelly tormented nature has cracked and taken on new shape, was one which Schiller could not pursue without turning his play of swift and abundant incident into a personal and individual tragedy. He therefore renounced the deeper probings, leaving us with Tell's resolution to prevent further tyranny as the chief motive of his action. It was in any case a very important motive.

In the scene with Parricida Tell might leave an impression of priggishness and self-righteousness, were it not for his final reassertion of his natural readiness to help:

> Was ihr auch Grässliches
> Verübt — Ihr seid ein Mensch — ich bin es auch;
> Vom Tell soll keiner ungetröstet scheiden —
> Was ich vermag, das will ich tun.[3]

With that we are again won over to his character. As Tell helps Parricida because he cannot leave a fellow-creature in despair, so

[1] I lived quietly and harmlessly, my arrows were aimed only at the beasts of the forest, murder had no part in my thoughts. *You* have shocked me out of that peace, have turned the milk of my pious thought to fermenting dragon's venom; have accustomed me to what is monstrous.

[2] When I drew the bow string and my hand trembled, when you with cruel devilish glee compelled me to aim at my boy's head, when I pleaded impotently to you—then I swore a fearful oath, heard only by God, that the target of my next shot should be your heart.

[3] Whatever your crime, you are a man—and so am I. It shall not be said of any man that he parted from Tell without help. I will do what I can.

he had helped Baumgarten because he could not stand by and witness another's destruction:

> Landsmann, tröstet Ihr
> Mein Weib, wenn mir was Menschliches begegnet.
> Ich hab' getan, was ich nicht lassen konnte.[1]

He begins and ends the play with a readiness to help which is compounded of human kindness and healthy love of action. But though he acts promptly and vigorously, he has little to say. Because he is unwilling to waste words he will not join the conspiracy, and is absent from the Rütli though he will clearly not fail when action is needed:

> Doch was ihr tut, lasst mich aus eurem Rat!
> Ich kann nicht lange prüfen oder wählen;
> Bedürft ihr meiner zu bestimmter Tat,
> Dann ruft den Tell, es soll an mir nicht fehlen.[2]

In the same spirit, he wastes no words when he sets out with steady hand and firm step to kill Gessler:

> *Fischer*
> Was habt ihr im Gemüt? Entdeckt mir's frei!
> *Tell*
> Ist es getan, wird's auch zur Rede kommen.[3]

Of all the Swiss peasant and farmer characters Tell is the only one who stands out clearly. Stauffacher and Fürst and Melchthal and a host of others are adequately delineated, but not highly individualized. This treatment was required by Schiller's plan, which contrasted the group to which they belong with the solitary independent figure of Tell. Two figures of the Swiss scene, apart from Tell, are differentiated from all the rest. The noble Lord of Attinghausen, eighty years of age, feeble of hand but indomitable of spirit, the last repository of the ancient sound traditions of a changing and decadent nobility, recalls in character, speech, and significance the John of Gaunt of *Richard II*.

The portrait of his nephew, Ulrich von Rudenz, who represents a newer generation with new ideas of honour, taste, and fashion, is less successful. Rudenz undergoes a change and turns from the

---

[1] Friend, console my wife if I am unlucky. I have done what I could not help doing.

[2] Whatever you do, leave me out of your counsels. I cannot long deliberate and choose. If you need me for definite action, then call for Tell and I shall not be absent.

[3] *Fisher*. Tell me openly what you have in mind to do.
Tell. When it's *done* it will be known soon enough.

oppressor to side again with his countrymen. But his patriotism is determined only by his love for Bertha von Bruneck and the scorn with which she treats his pro-Austrian conduct. Personal interests determine his public attitude, but being a great self-deceiver, he views himself as a disinterested patriot. Even in the crisis of the war, it is the rescue of Bertha and not the recovery of Swiss liberties that is the motive of his actions. Schiller, who gives him the last lines of the play, obviously regards him with an approval which we cannot share. He is one more example of the young men who roused Schiller's enthusiasm and chloroformed his critical sense. It is a pity that he has not been omitted from the play altogether, where both he and Bertha von Bruneck are incongruous figures.

Opposed to all the Swiss characters stands Gessler, the Austrian tyrant, as solitary a figure as Tell himself. Modern as well as medieval, his type is eternal and as characteristic of Gestapo cell or gangsters' hide-out as of the predatory baron's castle. Brutal, cold, and cynical, Gessler can sneer at his victim in his extremity or treacherously lure him to a fancied and illusory security. His strength is not in himself, but in his position and his armed guards. Alone he is no match for such a strong personality as Tell. Once on a narrow mountain path he had met Tell and had been afraid; white-faced and speechless he had flattened himself against the rocky wall. It is an incident which Schiller uses to reveal not only the real weakness of his character, but also the source of his sadistic persecution of Tell.

Wilhelm Tell could not help in some measure being a political play. Its course confirms in the successful struggle against tyranny and the destruction of the tyrant the unshakable confidence of Stauffacher:

> Nein, eine Grenze hat Tyrannenmacht.
> Wenn der Gedrückte nirgends Recht kann finden,
> Wenn unerträglich wird die Last — greift er
> Hinauf getrosten Mutes in den Himmel
> Und holt herunter seine ew'gen Rechte,
> Die droben hangen unveräusserlich
> Und unzerbrechlich wie die Sterne selbst.[1]

Seventeen years after *Don Carlos* Schiller returned to the theme of resistance to oppression and recaptured in such a speech as this the fluent persuasive rhetoric with which Posa had pleaded his cause. There the resemblance ends. There is no place in *Wilhelm*

---

[1] No, there is a limit to the tyrant's power. When the victim of oppression can find no legal remedy and the burden becomes intolerable, then he raises his hand with firm spirit to Heaven and grasps his eternal rights which dwell above, inalienable and indestructible as the stars themselves.

Tell for the intellectualized love of all mankind, for the generous and all-embracing impulse which make Posa so just to the human race and so unjust to the one individual he loves. The farmers and peasants of *Wilhelm Tell* are limited in education and outlook and see no farther than the oppression under which they themselves suffer. Yet what they lose in breadth and distance of vision they gain in balance and solidity. That is why *Wilhelm Tell* is no tragedy like *Don Carlos*, but a chronicle with a happy ending.

The tyrannies in both plays are foreign oppressions. The liberators of the Swiss cantons are not internationalists like Posa, but patriots. Posa was a foreigner ardently engaged in a quarrel not his own, or his only since he saw himself as " a representative of all humanity." Such high-flying sentiments are unknown luxuries to Schiller's Swiss peasants, who wish to be left alone and only become conscious of their nationality when foreign intervention threatens their laws, traditions, and freedoms. Even then it is no abstract concept that animates them, but a sense of community, the necessity of standing together:

> Wir wollen sein ein einzig Volk von Brüdern,
> In keiner Not uns trennen und Gefahr!
> Wir wollen frei sein, wie die Väter waren,
> Eher den Tod, als in der Knechtschaft leben![1]

The Lord of Attinghausen speaks, to be sure, in more conventionally patriotic tones when he admonishes Rudenz to hold fast to his native land:

> Ans Vaterland, ans teure, schliess' dich an,
> Das halte fest mit deinem ganzen Herzen.[2]

Yet the moving thought with him, as with all the Swiss of humbler origin, is not the magic of nationality or the intrinsic superiority of his own race; it is the necessity of unity if the free peoples are to remain free. For one moment Attinghausen rises above the narrow local view and—a mature, balanced, experienced Posa—urges not only the Swiss, but all free peoples to stand together:

> Drum haltet fest zusammen — fest und ewig —
> Kein Ort der Freiheit sei dem andern fremd ——[3]

Attinghausen's appeal to the *free* is the clue to the patriotism of *Wilhelm Tell*. It is a purely defensive and resistant patriotism,

---

[1] We will be a single people of brothers and separate neither in hardship nor danger! We will be free as our fathers were. Rather death than servitude.

[2] Cleave to your dear fatherland and hold it fast with all your heart.

[3] Hold firmly and eternally together—let no free place be foreign to another.

created by oppression and aiming only at safeguarding and maintaining ancient liberty. The full accent of the closing words falls
on freedom, not on nationality:

Bertha
So reich' ich diesem Jüngling meine Rechte,
Die freie Schweizerin dem freien Mann!

Rudenz
Und frei erklär' ich alle meine Knechte.[1]

Wilhelm Tell finishes as a humanitarian and not as a patriotic play.
Schiller was no more a nationalist at forty-five than at twenty-five.
Attempts to turn this play into a disguised patriotic tract or to interpret it as foreshadowing the national movement of 1813 are frankly
distortions of a work which is an objective, dramatic re-creation of
the historical legend.

The style of *Wilhelm Tell* is uneven. It is at its worst in the
conventionally conceived and perfunctorily executed scenes between
Rudenz and Bertha von Bruneck, who declaim in a steady, undiffer-
entiated stream of stilted formal rhetoric. In the scenes of conspiracy
Schiller uses a less artificial language, which is nevertheless elevated
above the individual level and serves, by spreading its mantle over
all characters alike, to bind them together into one community.

Two characters, Tell and Gessler, speak another language altogether. Gessler in his two appearances in the third and fourth acts
might easily have been presented as a ranting, storming stage tyrant,
a treatment which would have accorded with Schiller's talent and
predilection for rhetoric. But Gessler had seized Schiller's imagination, and when that happened the character spoke no longer in
Schiller's dramatic manner, but in his own fashion, as his nature and
circumstances required. Gessler's manner is simple, at moments
misleadingly friendly, at others bitterly ironical; and this simplicity
fits exactly the cold unimpassioned cruelty of the man:

Wer sagt Euch, dass ich scherze? Hier ist der Apfel.
Man mache Raum — er nehme seine Weite,
Wie's Brauch ist — achtzig Schritte geb' ich ihm —
Nicht weniger, noch mehr. Er rühmte sich,
Auf ihrer hundert seinen Mann zu treffen.
Jetzt, Schütze, triff und fehle nicht das Ziel![2]

[1] *Bertha.* So I, the free Swiss woman, give to this free man my hand.
Rudenz. And I declare all my serfs free.

[2] Who told you I was joking? Here is the apple. Make room. Let him pace
his distance in proper fashion—I give him eighty paces, not one less or more. He
boasted that he could hit his man at a hundred. Now, bowman, shoot, and see that
you don't miss your target!

R

In the last line all the hard, stony ferocity of the man is exposed, and we see him bend forward slightly in the saddle and fix his victim with eyes full of hatred and vengeful joy.

With Tell Schiller needed simplicity of another kind. Tell is a direct and simple character of sterling sincerity. In conversation with others his homely and short phrases reflect that character. Even when he speaks at greater length, as when he tells the story of his escape, his language is still direct and only slightly elevated above his normal tone. At the beginning of the scene in which he intends to kill Gessler in the sunken road near Küssnacht, Schiller has allotted to Tell his only monologue, one of considerable length. Here, too, he keeps for the most part to his natural style:

> Sonst, wenn der Vater auszog, liebe Kinder,
> Da war ein Freuen, wenn er wiederkam;
> Denn niemals kehrt' er heim, er bracht' euch etwas,
> War's eine schöne Alpenblume, war's
> Ein seltner Vogel oder Ammonshorn,
> Wie es der Wanderer findet auf den Bergen,[1]

where, except for the unnecessary final line, we hear the simple, homely Tell we know. But Schiller has not been quite able to resist the temptation of his rhetoric, and in the following lines he departs altogether from character and gives himself up to handsome verse:

> Hier geht
> Der sorgenvolle Kaufmann und der leicht
> Geschürzte Pilger, der andächt'ge Mönch,
> Der düstre Räuber und der heitre Spielmann,
> Der Säumer mit dem schwer beladnen Ross,
> Der ferne herkommt von der Menschen Ländern,
> Denn jede Strasse führt ans End' der Welt.[2]

Here we hear Schiller; we no longer hear Tell. And so the inconsistency of style, which is one of the work's chief defects, penetrates even to the principal figure of the play. It is a sign that *Wilhelm Tell* was produced at relatively low pressure, which enabled Schiller to write here and there as he wished and not as the characters made him.

One of the most remarkable features of this rather uneven play is its scenic completeness and vivid local atmosphere—products of

[1] Formerly when your father left, dear children, there was great joy when he returned; for he never came back without bringing you something, a lovely alpine flower, a rare bird or an ammonite, such as the traveller in the mountains finds.

[2] Here pass the worried merchant and the unburdened pilgrim, the sombre robber and the happy minstrel, the packman with his heavily laden horse, coming from far-off lands, for every road leads to the end of the world.

Schiller's power of imaginative creation out of second-hand literary and artistic impressions. The capacity to do this enabled him to ignore the world around him and to write powerfully with no other source of experience but the living and active world of his own mind.

Wilhelm Tell proved to be one of Schiller's most popular plays and has remained so ever since. It owes this favoured position to many factors: to the simple and easily grasped opposition of tyrant and plain countryman; to the vigour with which the character of Tell is presented; and to the eloquence with which widely felt popular sentiments are expressed. Most of all it is popular because of the phenomenal skill of its hero with oar and crossbow, the range of adventure vividly presented on the stage, and the unmistakable satisfaction of poetic justice by Gessler's death. Virtue is threatened by the direst perils, and triumphs completely. To its fine character-drawing and noble sentiments it adds the appeal to the juvenile element present in most of us.

Chapter Twenty

CLOSING SCENE
1804-5

WILHELM TELL was not a climax or an end. Its author had turned to a new theme even before he had prepared the manuscript of *Tell* for the press. He now explored territory far away from the settings of his recent plays, for the action of his next one took place in Russia and Poland.

In the summer of 1803 the Crown Prince of Weimar was in St Petersburg wooing the Czar's daughter, the Grand Duchess Maria Paulovna. With him went Wilhelm von Wolzogen, Schiller's brother-in-law. This fortuitous circumstance focused Schiller's interest on the borderland of eighteenth-century Europe. It would hardly otherwise have caught his attention. The story which seized his imagination was the expedition of the Pretender Demetrius (Dmitri), his invasion of Russia, involving the death of Boris Godounoff, and his final overthrow in 1606.

The first reference to Schiller's *Demetrius* occurs in his diary on March 10, 1804. The first allusion in a letter was made to Wilhelm von Wolzogen on June 16, 1804. Work on it suffered from manifold distractions through illness, court festivities, and the passage of *Wilhelm Tell* through the press, and the play remained unfinished at Schiller's death. He left in manuscript the whole of the first act and the greater part of the second in almost completed form; in addition there is a great quantity of notes, drafts, and sketches among his papers. The fragment was published in 1815 by Körner, who added a synopsis of the three unwritten acts.

Schiller was attracted to the theme by the figure of Demetrius himself, who while being a false pretender to the Russian throne, nevertheless believes his claims to be true. It was a psychological problem analogous to that of Perkin Warbeck, which had already occupied Schiller for several years. Demetrius had the advantage of being initially a more upright character, since Warbeck is from the outset aware of his own deceit. Schiller's Demetrius was eventually to learn that his claims were unfounded and then to find that what he had acquired, believing it to be his right, he must hold because it had become a necessity for him which he could not and would not renounce. Hence he is driven to maintain one deceit by another, by violence and cruelty, until he finally brings about his own destruction.

On a lower level *Demetrius* gave Schiller the opportunity of paying tribute to the Russian royal house, to which Prince Karl Friedrich's bride belonged, for the death of Demetrius coincides with the rise of the Romanoffs to Imperial power.

Schiller's first act shows Demetrius pleading his case before the Polish House of Lords, fully believing that he is the son of Czar Ivan. Simultaneously it is made clear that he is the unwitting tool of an ambitious and intriguing Polish noble house. In the second act, Marfa, mother of the true Prince Dmitri, learns of the Pretender's invasion. Uncertain whether he is really her son or not, she resolves to support him for motives of revenge against Boris Godounoff. Demetrius is then seen crossing the Russo-Polish frontier, only too well aware of his equivocal position, a Russian ruler at the head of an invading foreign army, bringing war and devastation to his own land. A glimpse of the illiterate inhabitants of a Russian village confused by the claims of the rival rulers, Boris and Demetrius, closes the fragment.

In the scene in the Polish parliament Schiller handles a crowd in masterly fashion and paints a bitter but recognizable picture of democratic institutions in decay. He shows a penetrating poetic imagination in the wonderful short scene in which Demetrius surveys the Russian plain from a frontier height:

Demetrius

Ist das der Dnieper, der den stillen Strom
Durch diese Auen giesst?

Odowalsky

                    Das ist die Desna.
Dort fliesst der Dnieper hinter Tschernigow,
Und was du siehst ist deines Reiches Boden.

Razin

Was dort am fernen Himmel glänzt, das sind
Die Kuppeln von Sewerisch Novgorod.

Demetrius

Welch heitrer Anblick! Welche schöne Auen!

Odowalsky

Der Lenz hat sie mit seinem Schmuck bedeckt,
Denn Fülle Korns erzeugt der üpp'ge Boden.

Demetrius
Der Blick schweift hin im Unermesslichen.[1]

Schiller had already exhibited this power to evoke in a few short sentences a poetic mood at the contemplation of landscape when William Tell describes to his son the German plain, so that a wide sunlit countryside is spread out before his mind's eye and ours. It is a striking revival in drama of a power he had revealed more than twenty years before in the scene by the Danube in *Die Räuber*. But there is a profound difference between the later scenes and the earlier one. Tell and Demetrius look with steady objective gaze, Karl Moor's eyes were turned inward, and the sunset glow lit up his own soul.

Demetrius did not, however, progress far enough to offer great intrinsic interest. Its chief claim to our attention is the light it throws upon Schiller's method of writing, for here alone are papers extant showing all stages of his work. The first phase consisted of historical, geographical, and other studies, whose results were preserved in careful notes. Then Schiller made an outline plan and wrote sketches of the principal characters. The plan was expanded into a detailed scenario, and the scenes were then written in prose. He next converted the prose into verse, leaving blank any phrases or lines which proved particularly obstinate, with the intention of filling them in later. Finally he meticulously revised the work to eliminate all minor blemishes in characterization, motivation, or verse. Fragments of *Demetrius* exist at every stage but the last.

Throughout these years in Weimar Schiller's life had pursued its even outward tenor, interrupted only by periods of illness, occasional journeys, and visitors. In December 1803 Madame de Staël paid a visit to Weimar and made a most favourable impression on Schiller. She seemed at first a remarkable woman—alert, clear in thought, and intellectually inquisitive; and he wrote of her in approving terms to Goethe and Körner and other friends, while the lady on her side was equally impressed: " I was much struck (she wrote) by this simplicity of character." But in so small a town a prominent visitor could not be avoided, and as her stay lengthened from the

---

[1] *Demetrius:* Is that the Dnieper, whose quiet stream flows through these meadows?
Odowalsky: That is the Desna. The Dnieper flows beyond Tchernigoff, and what you see is territory of your empire.
Razin: The turrets of Severich Novgorod glitter on the far horizon.
Demetrius: What a peaceful sight, what lovely fields!
Odowalsky: The spring has decked them, for this rich countryside brings forth abundant corn.
Demetrius: The eye can find no pause in this immeasurable space.

projected three weeks into nearly three months Schiller found her loquacity and insatiable curiosity a source of irritation. His work suffered from social engagements which he could not evade and from the poor health which the winter usually brought him.

His low state was made worse that year by a series of deaths which depressed and saddened him. In the late summer of 1803 Wilhelm von Humboldt had lost his eldest son, and Schiller, himself a devoted father, felt deeply for his friend and keenly realized how hard such a blow must be. In December Herder died at the age of fifty-nine, and in the first days of January 1804 Schiller learned of the death of the Duke of Meiningen, an occasional patron, who had granted him the title *Hofrat* on the eve of his marriage. Only with Humboldt was there any close link, but these deaths filled Schiller with the thought of mortality and of the meagre provision which he, a sick man with poor expectation of life, had so far been able to make for his three children.

Restlessness and dissatisfaction took possession of him. He turned again to the thought of a post in Mainz and weighed up the alternative of Berlin. In April he went to Leipzig with his wife and two sons and quite suddenly decided to go on to Berlin. The journey was undertaken with an impulsive abruptness reminiscent of Schiller's earlier years. On May 1, 1804, after a wearisome journey across the sandy plain of Brandenburg, they arrived unannounced in Berlin. It did not take Schiller long to establish contacts, nor the Berliners to discover the famous figure that their city was unexpectedly harbouring. No sooner had Iffland, who directed the Berlin Theatre, learned of Schiller's arrival than he arranged performances of *Die Jungfrau von Orleans*, *Die Braut von Messina*, *Wallensteins Tod*, and *Die Räuber* in his honour. Each time Schiller attended the theatre he was the centre of an ovation, and applause and demonstrations greeted him in the streets whenever he was recognized. On May 5 he was the guest of Prince Louis Ferdinand at a banquet, and on the thirteenth he and Lotte with the two children were received in audience by Queen Louise, to whom they had first been presented in Weimar five years before.

Schiller was much encouraged by the reception he encountered and delighted with the artistic and intellectual activity of Berlin, but he realized that life there would be more expensive for him, and a carriage and horses a necessity. In the last few days of his stay negotiations were opened with the object of securing him for Berlin. It was Iffland who took the first steps, and his efforts met with a willing response from the King and Queen. When Schiller left in mid-May it seemed almost certain that he would shortly return to Berlin with an annual pension of 3,000 talers (say £450), membership of the Berlin Academy, and possibly an appointment as tutor in history to the Prussian princes. His object in coming to Berlin seemed more than amply fulfilled.

On the way home he had leisure to weigh the pros and cons of the new situation. The money seemed less tempting when it was measured by the expensive style of life in Berlin. It seemed to him that he would be as well off with his present income in Weimar as he would be with 600 Friedrichs d'or (about £500) in Berlin. It was true, he felt, that the stir of the city's life and the keen edge of its intellectual intercourse might stimulate his mind to a quicker and more incisive production. On the other hand he would have much less time to himself, and he needed solitude for his writing. That was a familiar lesson which the recent visit of Madame de Staël had taught him again. It seemed that he wished to be able to divide himself into two, one half living in Berlin, the other in Weimar. He could not forget, either, that in going to Berlin he would lose Goethe. Besides, the whole family would have to rebuild friendships and acquaintanceships. It was a less enthusiastic Schiller who arrived back in Weimar on May 21, 1804.

Though he had put nothing in writing, he had gone far enough to feel uneasy as to how he could extricate himself with a good grace. The best course, he thought, would be to ask Karl August for a higher pension and to offer his part-time services to Berlin. He still hankered to live in both places at once. Since this was not possible, he compromised with the idea of living six months in one, then six months in the other. In this way he hoped to secure for himself the stimulus of the great city and the reflective quiet of Weimar. It is difficult to imagine that Schiller, with his poor health and dislike of disturbance, could ever have adhered to such an arrangement, but it was never put to the test. Karl August agreed to all that Schiller asked, and raised his pension from 400 to 800 talers, with a promise of a further increment to bring it up to 1,000. But the letter Schiller wrote on June 18, 1804, to Hofrat Beyme, the functionary in Berlin who had charge of the negotiations, remained unanswered. It seemed that Schiller's change of ground had aroused the royal disapprobation. The whole project lapsed. Subsequently it transpired that no offence had been taken and that the delay was solely due to the King's dilatoriness in the transaction of business.

If Schiller's Berlin visit had served no other useful purpose, it had at least occupied him at a time when he had felt restless, discontented, and in need of change. It had given him hope and tided him over into the better weather of the spring and the awakening interest in a new play. The visit had afforded him a gratifying realization, too, of the esteem in which he was held as the outstanding German dramatist of the age.

Frau Schiller was expecting a fourth child in the summer of 1804; indeed, some of the haste over the Berlin journey was due to the knowledge that, if they did not go at once, Lotte's condition would prevent her from travelling later. In July Schiller and his wife moved to Jena for the confinement, for they had confidence only in Dr Starke of that town, who had been their family physician since their marriage. Lotte gave birth to a second daughter, Emilie, on July 25, 1804, and this time made a very speedy recovery. At the moment of the birth it was Schiller, and not Lotte, who was seriously ill. He was attacked by a colic of such violence that Starke himself doubted whether he would survive it. The savage pains, lasting intermittently for three or four days and accompanied by a weakening dysentery, took a serious toll of Schiller's strength, and all through August he lay on his bed or sat about his room, listless and despondent and with no real belief in eventual recovery. It was not till October that he began to feel his strength gathering and energy and purpose returning. By then the winter he always feared so much was but a few short weeks away.

Schiller was not able for long to concentrate his mind on *Demetrius*. The arrival of Prince Karl Friedrich and his Russian bride was awaited in November. At the end of October Goethe, who had made no special preparations for this occasion, panicked and asked Schiller, who was less dependent on momentary mood, to help him out with a festive dramatic piece. Early in November Schiller wrote in four days *Die Huldigung der Künste* (*The Homage of the Arts*), a " lyric drama " of some two hundred and fifty lines, which was performed in the presence of the court on November 12, 1804. It is an elegant and pleasing trifle, symbolizing the welcome which Weimar accorded its new princess and the one advantage it could offer, communion with the arts:

> So wollen wir mit schön vereintem Streben,
> Der hohen Schönheit sieben heil'ge Zahlen,
> Dir, Herrliche, den Lebensteppich weben!
>
> .   .   .   .   .   .
>
> Denn aus der Kräfte schön vereintem Streben
> Erhebt sich, wirkend, erst das wahre Leben.[1]

This unimportant but graceful essay in allegory and compliment was Schiller's last completed work.

---

[1] May we, the seven sacred numbers of noble beauty, weave with united endeavour the carpet of your life . . . for from the united endeavour of our powers arises the true and active life.

The festivities for the Princess's arrival meant constant functions and much standing about in draughty and rarely used state rooms for all members of the Court. Before the celebrations were over Schiller had caught a cold which left him with the obstinate catarrh from which he so often suffered, but which now seemed much harder to shake off than formerly. All through December and well into January this malady plagued him, depriving him of all energy and concentration for creative work. Dramatic writing was none the less a necessity, and since the effort needed for *Demetrius* was too much for him, he turned once again to translation. In mid-December he began to translate Racine's *Phèdre*, completing it a month later. It was produced in the Court Theatre at Weimar on January 30, 1805. Schiller expended on this translation the same skill and care that he had formerly devoted to *Iphigeneia in Aulis* and to *Macbeth*, but with less success. The comparative failure of *Phädra* is no reflection on Schiller's ability. It is a demonstration that the precision and austere discipline of thought in the best French Alexandrines are not reproducible in German blank verse.

The New Year of 1805 began gloomily enough for Schiller with news of the death of his old friend Huber at the early age of forty. Since Huber had jilted Dora Stock twelve years before, their lives had hardly touched, and Schiller had thought many hard things about Huber. His regret was all the keener now that the news of his former friend's death evoked vivid memories of the happiness and enthusiasm of those Leipzig and Dresden years. Death also softened the sense of the wrong done to Dora Stock and Körner which Schiller had felt deeply. Huber's early end prompted again in Schiller thoughts of his own precarious health and of the insecurity of his family if he should die.

Towards the end of January he began to feel better, and he imagined that for him the winter was past. February brought a sharp return of his illness, with an exceptionally high temperature which left him in a state of unusual lassitude and discouragement, It was Schiller's worst winter, and it imposed an even heavier strain on him because he had had no chance to recuperate during the preceding summer.

The approach of spring, however, quickened his faculties, and he began to work again at *Demetrius*, yet with all his enthusiasm he found that he could not shake off the after-effects of his miserable winter. But he was not discouraged. At the beginning of April he wrote to Wilhelm von Humboldt a long letter in which he spoke confidently of his hope of providing effectively for his family in spite of the failure of the Berlin project. Cotta treated him generously and was readier to offer higher terms than Schiller was to ask for them. Iffland in Berlin paid handsomely for his plays. All over Germany directors of theatres were eager to secure the performing rights of Schiller's plays.

A new play by Schiller had become an event of importance and Schiller himself a national figure. He had really achieved the fame which had been such a spur to him in his early years in Stuttgart, Mannheim, and Bauerbach. Yet for the last fifteen years he had had other standards than applause, and though he did not despise popularity, it no longer roused in him an answering enthusiasm. He valued it most for the financial help it gave in building up the future of his family of four children, to whom he was deeply attached. The birth of his first son had been one of the decisive crises in his life, and ever since the love for his children had deepened and become a greater and greater part of his life. William Tell is no mirror of the poet, but Schiller could not have created the bond between Tell and his son Walter with such moving truth and simplicity, if he himself had not experienced a similar love. The thought of his children and their future was a chief preoccupation of his mind, and when he remembered the deaths of Herder and Huber and his own sickly state, it was a saddening one. Writing to Humboldt on April 2, 1805, he felt that five more years would see his family in a very much improved and even secure financial situation. If he could reach fifty all would be well. This confidence was not only a reflection of the higher market price of his works, but an affirmation of his own dramatic fertility, an act of faith in his yet unwritten plays.

April passed uneventfully, and Schiller's work advanced, though slowly. The damage done to his health by the winter still troubled him, but he felt that fifty was an age that he could set before him as a realizable goal, for he mentioned it again in a letter written to Körner on April 25, 1805.

On April 28, Schiller was at court. On the following evening he went to the theatre and met Goethe for a few moments just as he was setting out. It was their last meeting. Two evenings later he remarked to his sister-in-law, Caroline von Wolzogen, on their way to the theatre, that the pain he had felt for years in the left side, and presumably in the left lung, was no longer there. It seemed a hopeful sign. It fortunately did not occur to him that it might mark the total destruction of the lung. In the course of the evening he became feverish, and when a young friend, Voss, brought him home his teeth were chattering.

The following day he suffered one of his worst feverish attacks, and passed soon into a state between sleeping and waking. By May 5 his condition was grave. Many thought it hopeless, though Lotte steadfastly believed in his recovery. He continued to grow worse and presently was too feeble to sustain a conversation. On the morning of Sunday, May 8, his youngest daughter, the nine-months-old Emilie, was brought to him. The watching Voss saw from Schiller's inexpressibly sad and yearning eyes that he knew that he was looking at her for the last time. Schiller turned on his side and buried his face in the pillow. The next day he lay unconscious and uttered from time to time detached phrases. He raised himself up in bed and repeated the word " judex " several times. In the afternoon his strength failed rapidly. About four o'clock his whole body suddenly twitched, then he lay still. Lotte still sought to warm his hand as the slow minutes passed. It was Monday, May 9, 1805.

Fifty had been too difficult a goal. The tragedies, alas, remained unwritten. But he had fought a good fight.

APPENDIX

ORIGINAL TEXT OF PASSAGES QUOTED FROM
LETTERS OR CONVERSATIONS

P. 1.   ... einen blonden, blauäugigen, schüchternen jungen Mann ...,
dem die Tränen in die Augen standen und der kaum wagte uns
anzureden. (MARIE KÖRNER.)

P. 1.   Ich meinte, er müsse so im Laufe eines Gesprächs etwa wie
sein Posa in der berühmten Szene mit König Philipp sprechen.
Zu meinem Erstaunen nun stellte er sich in seiner Unterhaltung
als ein sehr lebenskluger Mann dar, der namentlich höchst
vorsichtig in seinen Äusserungen über Personen war. (HENRIETTE
HERZ.)

P. 2.   Dies Jahr folgte uns Schiller nach dem ersten Ort [Lauchstädt],
und seine Ankunft daselbst erweckte ein grosses Interesse bei den
versammelten Badegästen, denn alt und jung schwärmte doch
weit mehr für ihn als für Goethe. Aber wie anders bewegte
sich Schiller in der Gesellschaft Goethe gegenüber! Die bunte
Menge beängstigte ihn förmlich, und Ehrenbezeigungen, die
Goethe als etwas Selbstverständliches aufnahm, wurden ihm
unheimlich und machten ihn schüchtern; darum suchte er
zunächst die einsamen Wege auf, um den ewigen Begrüssungen
zu entgehen; aber wenn es hiess: "Schiller ist dahin ausge-
gangen," wählte man gewiss den Weg wo man ihm begegnen
musste. Er ging gewöhnlich gebeugten Hauptes durch die
Massen, jedem, der ihn grüsste, freundlich dankend. Wie ganz
anders war Goethe unter diesem Publikum, das alljährlich fast
dasselbe war, einhergeschritten, stolz wie ein König, mit hoch-
erhobenem Haupte, dasselbe bei einem Gruss nur gnädig neigend.
(GENAST.)

P. 2.   ... je le trouvai si modeste et insouciant dans ce qui ne con-
cernait que ses propres succès, si fier et si animé dans la défense
de ce qu'il croyait la vérité, que je lui vouai, dès cet instant, une
amitié pleine d'admiration. (MME DE STAËL, *De l'Allemagne.*)

P. 18.   Gott weiss, ich vergass alles, alle andere neben Dir! ich
schwoll neben Dir, denn ich war stolz auf deine Freundschaft,
nicht um mich im Aug der Menschen dadurch erhoben, sondern
im Aug einer höhern Welt, nach der mein Herz mir so glühte,

261

welche mir zuzurufen schien: das ist der einzige, den Du lieben
kannst, . . . und doch war ich nie so gedemüthigt, als wenn ich
Dich ansah, . . . da that ich auch Wünsch an Gott, mich Dir
gleich zu machen! . . . D u   h a s t   n i c h t s   a u f   m i c h   g e-
h a l t e n ! — wie oft (aber immer nur, wenn Du in Zorn geriethst,
sonst heucheltest Du Achtung und Bewunderung,) wie oft
hab ichs hören müssen von Dir und dem Boigeol, bitter,
bitter, wie mein ganzes Wesen eben ein Gedicht sey, wie meine
Empfindung vorgegebne Empfindung.

P. 18.   Der Sangir, den ich so liebe, war nur in meinem Herzen . . .
und ich betete ihn an in Dir, seinem ungleichen Abbilde!

P. 19.   Ich bin noch nicht ein und zwanzig Jahr alt aber ich darf es
Ihnen frei sagen, die Welt hat keinen Reiz für mich mehr, ich
freue mich nicht auf die Welt, und jener Tag meines Abschieds
aus der Akademie, der mir vor wenig Jahren ein freudenvoller
Festtag würde gewesen seyn, wird mir einmal kein frohes
Lächeln abgewinnen können.

P. 22.   Ich fange an in Activitaet zu kommen, und das kleine hunds-
vöttische Ding hat mich in der Gegend herum berüchtigter
gemacht, als 20 Jahre Praxis.

P. 46.   Und doch bereue ich beinahe die glüklichste Reise meines
Lebens, die mich, durch einen höchst widrigen Kontrast meines
Vaterlands mit Mannheim, schon so weit verleitet hat, dass mir
Stuttgardt und alle schwäbische Szenen unerträglich und
ekelhaft werden.   Unglüklicher kann bald niemand seyn, als ich.
Ich habe Gefühl genug für meine traurige Situation, vielleicht auch
Selbstgefühl genug für das Verdienst eines besseren Schiksals,
und für beides nur — eine Aussicht.
Darf ich mich Ihnen in die Arme werfen, vortreflichster Mann?

P. 46.   Noch bin ich wenig oder nichts.   In diesem Norden des
Geschmaks werde ich ewig niemals gedeyhen, wenn mich sonst
glüklichere Sterne und ein g r i e c h i s c h e s   K l i m a zum wahren
Dichter erwärmen würden.

P. 53.   Sobald ich Ihnen sage, i c h   b i n   a u f   d e r   F l u c h t, sobald
habe ich mein ganzes Schiksal geschildert.

P. 63.   Was Sie thun, lieber Freund, behalten Sie diese praktische
Wahrheit vor Augen, die Ihren unerfahrnen Freund nur zu viel
gekostet hat: Wenn man die Menschen braucht, so muss man
ein H . . . t werden, oder sich ihnen unentbehrlich machen,
Eines von beiden, oder man sinkt unter.

P. 63.   Es ist ein Unglük meine Beste, dass gutherzige Menschen so gern in das entgegengesetzte Ende geworfen werden, den Menschenhass, wenn einige unwürdige Karaktere ihre warmen Urtheile betrügen. Gerade so gieng es mir. Ich hatte die halbe Welt mit der glühendsten Empfindung umfasst, und am Ende fand ich dass ich einen kalten Eisklumpen in den Armen hatte.

P. 63.   Sie glauben nicht, wie nöthig es ist, dass ich edle Menschen finde. Diese müssen mich mit dem ganzen Geschlechte wieder versönen, mit welchem ich mich beinahe abgeworfen hätte.

P. 63.   Ein Freund soll mich mit dem ganzen Menschengeschlecht, das sich mir auf einigen hässlichen Blössen gezeigt hat, wiederum aussönen, und meine Muse halb weegs nach dem Kozytus wieder einholen.

P. 64.   Es wohnt ein ausserordentlicher Geist in ihm, und ich glaube, Deutschland wird einst seinen Namen mit Stolz nennen. Ich habe die Funken gesehen, die diese vom Schicksal umdüsterten Augen sprühen, und den reichen Geist erkannt, den sie ahnen lassen.

P. 65.   Itzt bester Freund fangen die herrliche Zeiten bald an, worinn die Schwalben auf unsern Himmel, und Empfindungen in unsere Brust zurükkommen. Wie sehnlich erwarte ich sie!

P. 65.   Einsamkeit, Misvergnügen über mein Schiksal, fehlgeschlagene Hoffnungen, und vielleicht auch die veränderte Lebensart haben den Klang meines Gemüths, wenn ich so reden darf, verfälscht, und das sonst reine Instrument meiner Empfindung verstimmt. Die Freundschaft und der Mai sollen es, hoff ich, aufs neue in Gang bringen.

P. 66.   Ihr Herr Bruder muss menschliche Charaktere viel kennen, weil er sie auf der Bühne schildern soll, item, er muss sich durch Gespräche über Natur und Kunst, durch freundschaftliche, innige Unterhaltung aufheitern . . . Die Gegend, wo er sich jetzt aufhält, . . . und ein zweiter Winter da zugebracht, wird Herrn Dr S. völlig hypochondrisch machen.

P. 80.   Der Mann ist ganz Feuer, aber leider nur Pulverfeuer, das plötzlich losgeht und eben so schnell wieder verpuft.

P. 80.   . . . die ich schon lange nicht mehr genossen habe, weil die Unbestimmtheit meiner Aussichten, und der nagende Gedanke meiner Schulden mich unaufhörlich verfolgten.

P. 81.   Um zugleich die Ungeduld des Theaters, und die Erwartungen des hiesigen Publikums zu befriedigen habe ich unter meiner Krankheit mit dem Kopf arbeiten müssen, und durch starke Porzionen China meine wenigen Kräfte so hinhalten müssen, dass mir dieser Winter vielleicht auf Zeitlebens einen Stoss versezt.

P. 84.   Sehen Sie meine Beste — so kommen zuweilen ganz unverhofte Freuden für Ihren Freund, die desto schäzbarer sind, weil freier Wille, und eine reine, von jeder Nebenabsicht reine Empfindung und Simpathie der Seelen die Erfinderin ist. So ein Geschenk von ganz unbekannten Händen — durch nichts als die blosse reinste Achtung hervorgebracht — aus keinem andern Grund, als mir für einige vergnügte Stunden, die man bei Lesung meiner Produkte genoss, erkenntlich zu seyn — ein solches Geschenk ist mir grössre Belohnung, als der laute Zusammenruf der Welt, die einzige süsse Entschädigung für tausend trübe Minuten.

P. 84.   Und wenn ich das nun weiter verfolge, und mir denke, dass in der Welt vielleicht mehr solche Zirkel sind, die mich unbekannt lieben, und sich freuten mich zu kennen, dass vielleicht in 100 und mehr Jahren — wenn auch mein Staub schon lange verweht ist, man mein Andenken seegnet, und mir noch im Grabe Tränen und Bewunderung zollt — dann meine Theuerste freue ich mich meines Dichterberufes, und versöne mich mit Gott und meinem harten Verhängnis.

P. 92.   (Hier bin ich neulich durch einen unvermuteten Besuch unterbrochen worden, und diese 12 Tage ist eine Revolution mit mir und in mir vorgegangen, die dem gegenwärtigen Briefe mehr Wichtigkeit gibt, als ich mir habe träumen lassen — die Epoche in meinem Leben macht.) Ich kann nicht mehr in Mannheim bleiben. In einer unnennbaren Bedrängniss meines Herzens schreibe ich Ihnen, meine Besten. Ich kann nicht mehr hier bleiben . . . Ich habe keine Seele hier, keine einzige, die die Leere meines Herzens füllte, keine Freundin, keinen Freund; und was mir vielleicht noch theuer seyn könnte, davon scheiden mich Konvenienz und Situationen.

P. 93.   Etwas grosses, etwas unaussprechlich angenehmes muss mir da aufgehoben seyn, denn der Gedanke an meine Abreise macht mir Mannheim zu einem Kerker, und der hiesige Himmel ligt schwer und drükend auf mir, wie das Bewusstseyn eines Mordes — Leipzig erscheint meinen Träumen und Ahndungen wie der rosigte Morgen jenseits den waldigten Hügeln.

P. 94.   Bis hieher haben Schiksale meine Entwürfe gehemmt. Mein Herz und meine Musen mussten zu gleicher Zeit der Nothwendigkeit unterliegen.

P. 96.   O, wie schön und wie göttlich ist die Berührung zweier Seelen, die sich auf dem Weege zur Gottheit begegnen.

P. 96.   Das sollen göttliche Tage sein.

P. 99.   Aber ein Jahr wenigstens lass mir die Freude, Dich aus der Nothwendigkeit des Brodverdienens zu setzen.

P. 102.   Der Dichter mus weniger der Mahler seines Helden — er mus mehr dessen Mädchen, dessen Busenfreund seyn.

P. 102.   O lieben Kinder wie sehne ich mich nach euch. Wie sehr verstimmt mich diese freundelose Einsamkeit.

P. 103.   Täglich wird mir die Geschichte theurer. . . .

P. 106.   Wird mein Bild nicht früher bei euch erlöschen, als das eurige bei mir? . . . Ihr wart mir so viel und ich euch so wenig.

P. 106.   Hätte ich nicht die Degradation meines Geistes so tief gefühlt, ehe ich von Euch ging, ich hätte Euch nie verlassen.

P. 107.   Ich finde, dass diese Geschichte mehr Einheit und Interesse zum Grunde hat als ich bisher geglaubt, und mir Gelegenheit zu starken Zeichnungen und erschütternden oder rührenden Situazionen gibt. Der Karakter eines feurigen, grosen und empfindenden Jünglings, der zugleich der Erbe einiger Kronen ist, — einer Königin, die durch den Zwang ihrer Empfindung bei allen Vortheilen ihres Schiksals verunglükt, — eines eifersüchtigen Vaters und Gemals — eines grausamen heuchlerischen Inquisitors, und barbarischen Herzogs von Alba u.s.f. solten mir, dächte ich, nicht wol mislingen.

P. 108.   Karlos würde nichts weniger seyn, als ein politisches Stük — sondern eigentlich ein Familiengemälde in einem königlichen Hausse.

P. 108.   Vier grosse Karaktere, beinahe von gleichem Umfang Karlos, Philipp, die Königin und Alba.

P. 108.   Karlos hat, wenn ich mich des Maases bedienen darf, von Shakespears Hamlet die Seele — Blut und Nerven von Leisewiz Julius, Und den Puls von mir.

s

P. 109.   Ich muss gestehen, dass ich ihn gewissermassen statt meines Mädchens habe. Ich trage ihn auf meinem Busen — ich schwärme mit ihm durch die Gegend — um Bauerbach herum.

P. 120.   Ich kann mir es jezt nicht vergeben, dass ich so eigensinnig, vielleicht auch so eitel war, um in einer entgegengesezten Sphäre zu glänzen, meine Phantasie in die Schranken des bürgerlichen Kothurns einzäunen zu wollen, da die hohe Tragödie ein so fruchtbares Feld, und für mich, möcht ich sagen, d a ist; da ich in diesem Fache grösser und glänzender erscheinen, und mehr Dank und Erstaunen wirken kann, als in keinem andern, da hier vielleicht nicht e r r e i c h t, im andern ü b e r t r o f f e n werden könnte.

P. 125.   Mit der Hälfte des Werths den ich meiner historischen Arbeit zu geben weiss, erreiche ich mehr Anerkennung in der sogenannten gelehrten und bürgerlichen Welt als mit dem grössten Aufwand meines Geistes für die Frivolität einer Tragödie. . . . Für meinen Carlos — das Werk dreijähriger Anstrengung bin ich mit Unlust belohnt worden. Meine Niederl. Geschichte, das Werk von 5 höchstens 6 Monaten wird mich vielleicht zum angesehenen Manne machen.

P. 126.   Ist es wahr oder falsch, dass ich darauf denken muss, wovon ich l e b e n soll, wenn mein dichterischer Frühling verblüht?

P. 126.   Ich bin in Gefahr mich auf diesem Wege auszuschreiben.

P. 127.   Die Geschichte wird unter meiner Feder, hier und dort, manches, was sie nicht war.

P. 129.   Die Vorstellung unserer Wiedervereinigung steht hell und heiter vor mir. Alles soll und wird mich darauf zurückführen. Alles wird mich an Sie erinnern und mir theurer seyn durch diese Erinnerung.

P. 129   Die Zeiten sind nicht mehr, wo ich auf ein einziges Object alle meine Kräfte zusammenhäufte.

P. 130.   In den nächsten 2 Jahren, habe ich mir vorgenommen, lese ich keine moderne Schriftsteller mehr. Vieles, was D u mir ehemals geschrieben, hat mich ziemlich überzeugt. Keiner thut mir wohl; jeder führt mich von mir selbst ab, und die Alten geben mir jetzt wahre Genüsse. Zugleich bedarf ich ihrer im höchsten Grade, um meinen eigenen Geschmack zu reinigen, der sich durch Spitzfündigkeit, Künstlichkeit und Witzeley

sehr von der wahren Simplizität zu entfernen anfieng. Du wirst
finden, dass mir ein vertrauter Umgang mit den Alten äusserst
wohlthun, — vielleicht Classizität geben wird.

P. 134. Oefters um Goethe zu seyn, würde mich unglücklich machen:
er hat auch gegen seine nächsten Freunde kein Moment der
Ergiessung, er ist an nichts zu fassen; ich glaube in der That,
er ist ein Egoist in ungewöhnlichem Grade. Er besitzt das Talent,
die Menschen zu fesseln, und durch kleine sowohl als grosse
Attentionen sich verbindlich zu machen; aber sich selbst weiss
er immer frei zu behalten. Er macht seine Existenz
wohlthätig kund, aber nur wie ein Gott, ohne sich selbst zu
geben — dies scheint mir eine consequente und planmässige
Handlungsart, die ganz auf den höchsten Genuss der Eigenliebe
calculirt ist. Ein solches Wesen sollten die Menschen nicht um
sich herum aufkommen lassen. Mir ist er dadurch verhasst, ob
ich gleich seinen Geist von ganzem Herzen liebe und gross von
ihm denke.

P. 135. Aber mit Goethe messe ich mich nicht, wenn er seine ganze
Kraft anwenden will. Er hat weit mehr Genie als ich, und
dabei weit mehr Reichtum an Kenntnissen, eine sichrere Sinnlichkeit, und zu allem diesem einen durch Kunstbekenntnis aller
Art geläuterten und verfeinerten Kunstsinn.

P. 135. Dieser Mensch, dieser Göthe ist mir einmal im Wege, und er
erinnert mich so oft, dass das Schicksal mich hart behandelt hat.
Wie leicht ward sein Genie von seinem Schicksal getragen,
und wie muss ich biss auf diese Minute noch kämpfen!

P. 135. . . . ich habe mir eigentlich ein eigenes Drama nach meinem
Talente gebildet, welches mir eine gewisse Excellence darin
giebt, eben weil es mein eigen ist. Will ich in das natürliche
Drama einlenken, so fühl ich die Superiorität, die er und viele
andere Dichter aus der vorigen Zeit über mich haben, sehr
lebhaft.

P. 141. Wir führen miteinander das seligste Leben, und ich kenne
mich in meiner vorigen Lage nicht mehr.

P. 141. Ich zittre vor dem Kriege, denn wir werden ihn an allen Enden
Deutschlands fühlen.

P. 143. Ich sehe nicht ein, warum ich nicht, wenn ich ernstlich will,
der erste Geschichtschreiber in Deutschland werden kann.

P. 144. Dein Ideal von Universalgeschichte ist vortrefflich, aber um es zu Deiner Befriedigung zu erreichen, müsstest Du aller anderen Thätigkeit absterben. Es fordert den ganzen Mann durch ein ganzes Menschenleben.

P. 145. Ich wollte dass ich zehen Jahre hintereinander nichts als Geschichte studiert hätte. Ich glaube ich würde ein ganz anderer Kerl sein. Meinst Du, dass ich es noch werde nachhohlen können?

P. 147. Es wäre doch schön, wenn wir noch länger zusammenblieben.

P. 147. So gerne, wünschte ich das noch zu erreichen, wozu eine dunkle Ahndung von Kräften mich zuweilen ermuntert.

P. 148. Meine Krankheit hat dadurch, dass sie mich ganz ausser Thätigkeit setzte, uns so aneinander gewöhnt, dass ich sie nicht gern allein lasse. Auch mir macht es, wenn ich auch Geschäfte habe, schon Freude, mir nur zu denken, dass sie um mich ist; und ihr liebes Leben und Weben um mich herum, die kindliche Reinheit ihrer Seele und die Innigkeit ihrer Liebe, gibt mir selbst eine Ruhe und Harmonie, die bey meinem hypochondrischen Übel ohne diesen Umstand unmöglich wäre. Wären wir beide nur gesund, wir brauchten nichts weiter, um zu leben wie die Götter.

P. 149. Ich muss Dir unverzüglich schreiben, ich muss Dir meine Freude mittheilen lieber Körner. Das, wonach ich mich schon so lange ich lebe, aufs feurigste gesehnt habe wird jetzt erfüllt. Ich bin auf lange, vielleicht auf immer aller Sorgen los, ich habe die längst gewünschte Unabhängigkeit des Geistes. Heute erhalt ich Briefe aus Koppenhagen vom Prinzen von Augustenburg und vom Grafen von Schimmelmann, die mir auf drey Jahre jährlich 1000 Thlr. zum Geschenk anbieten, mit völliger Freiheit zu bleiben, wo ich bin, bloss um mich von meiner Krankheit völlig zu erhohlen. Aber die Delikatesse und Feinheit mit der der Prinz mir dieses Anerbieten macht könnte mich noch mehr rühren, als das Anerbieten selbst. . . .
. . . Sage Dir selbst, wie glücklich mein Schicksal ist.

P. 151. Ich bin und bleibe bloss Poet, und als Poet werde ich auch sterben.

P. 152. Geschadet hat sie mir in der That, denn die Kühnheit, die lebendige Glut, die ich hatte, eh mir noch eine Regel bekannt war, vermisse ich schon seit mehreren Jahren. Ich sehe mich jetzt erschaffen und bilden, ich beobachte das Spiel der Begeisterung, und meine Einbildungskraft beträgt sich mit minder Freiheit, seitdem sie sich nicht mehr ohne Zeugen weiss.

P. 152. Bin ich aber erst soweit, dass mir Kunstmässigkeit zur Natur wird, wie einem wohlgesitteten Menschen die Erziehung, so erhält auch die Phantasie ihre vorige Freiheit zurück, und setzt sich keine andern als freiwillige Schranken.

P. 152. Jetzt bin ich frei, und ich will es für immer bleiben. Keine Arbeit mehr, die mir ein anderer auflegt, oder die einen andern Ursprung hat als Liebhaberei und Neigung.

P. 153. Ich kann seit 14 Tagen keine franz. Zeitung mehr lesen, so ekeln diese elenden Schindersknechte mich an.

P. 155. Der Tod des alten Herodes hat weder auf mich noch auf meine Familie Einfluss, ausser dass es allen Menschen, die unmittelbar mit dem Herrn zu thun hatten, wie mein Vater, sehr wohl ist, jetzt einen Menschen vor sich zu haben.

P. 157. Dass ich Kant noch lesen und vielleicht studieren werde scheint mir ziemlich ausgemacht.

P. 159. Uber die Natur des Schönen ist mir viel Licht aufgegangen . . . Den objectiven Begriff des Schönen, der sich eo ipso auch zu einem objectiven Grundsatz des Geschmacks qualifiziert, und an welchem Kant verzweifelt, glaube ich gefunden zu haben. Ich werde meine Gedanken darüber ordnen, und in einem Gespräch: Kallias, oder über die Schönheit, auf die kommenden Ostern herausgeben.

P. 160. Analogie einer Erscheinung mit der Form des reinen Willens oder der Freiheit ist Schönheit (in weitester Bedeutung.)

P. 160. Sobald wir es ästhetisch beurtheilen, so wollen wir bloss wissen, ob es das, was es ist, durch sich selbst sei.

P. 160. Eine Versifikation ist schön, wenn jeder einzelne Vers sich selbst seine Länge und Kürze, seine Bewegung und seinen Ruhepunkt gibt.

P. 160. Der grosse Künstler . . . zeigt uns den Gegenstand (seine Darstellung hat Objectivität), der mittelmässige zeigt sich selbst (seine Darstellung hat Subjectivität), der schlechte seinen Stoff (die Darstellung wird durch die Natur des Mediums und die Schranken des Künstlers bestimmt).

P. 169.   Was Sie aber schwerlich wissen können (weil das Genie sich immer selbst das grösste Geheimnis ist), ist die schöne Übereinstimmung Ihres philosophischen Instinktes mit den reinsten Resultaten der speculirenden Vernunft. Beym ersten Anblicke zwar scheint es, als könnte es keine grössern Opposita geben, als den spekulativen Geist, der von der Einheit, und den intuitiven, der von der Mannichfaltigkeit ausgeht. Sucht aber der erste mit keuschem und treuem Sinn die Erfahrung, und sucht der letzte mit selbsttätiger freier Denkkraft das Gesetz, so kann es gar nicht fehlen, dass nicht beide einander auf halbem Wege begegnen werden.

P. 175.   Was Sie in ihrem letzten Brief über höhern und entfernteren Vortheile solcher Zankereyen mit den Zeitgenossen sagen, mag wohl wahr seyn: aber die Ruhe muss man freilich und die Aufmunterung von aussen dabey missen können.

P. 177.   Deinen herrlichen Brief musste ich dem lieben Vater vorlesen; er weinte wie ein Kind darüber und dankte Gott mit Inbrunst, dass er ihm einen solchen Sohn gegeben.

P. 192.   Der Wallenstein hat auf dem Theater in Weimar eine ausserordentliche Wirkung gemacht, und auch die Unempfindlichsten mit sich fortgerissen. Es war darüber nur Eine Stimme, und in den nächsten acht Tagen ward von nichts Anderem gesprochen.

P. 208.   Der Hauptcharakter so wie die meisten Nebencharaktere traktiere ich wirklich bis jetzt mit der reinen Liebe des Künstlers; bloss für den nächsten nach dem Hauptcharakter, den jungen Piccolomini, bin ich durch meine eigene Zuneigung interessiert.

P. 211.   . . . ich werde nicht eher ruhig seyn, bis ich meine Gedanken wieder auf einen bestimmten Stoff mit Hofnung und Neigung gerichtet sehe.

P. 223.   Schon der Stoff erhält mich warm; ich bin mit dem ganzen Herzen dabei, und es fliesst auch mehr aus dem Herzen, als die vorigen Stücke, wo der Verstand mit dem Stoffe kämpfen musste.

P. 225.   Endlich glaube ich mich, was die Schriftstellerei betrift, auf dem Standpunkte zu befinden, wohin ich seit Jahren gestrebt habe.

P. 228.   Ich . . . arbeite jetzt mit ziemlichem Ernst an einer Tragödie, deren Sujet Du aus meiner Erzählung kennst. Es sind die feindlichen Brüder, oder, wie ich es taufen werde, die Braut von Messina.

P. 229. Ich will indess nicht läugnen, dass mir ohne eine grössere Bekanntschaft die ich indess mit dem Aeschylus gemacht, diese Versetzung in die alte Zeit schwerer würde angekommen sein.

P. 229. Bei der Braut von Messina habe ich, ich will es Ihnen aufrichtig gestehen, einen kleinen Wettstreit mit den alten Tragikern versucht, wobei ich mehr an mich selbst als an ein Publicum ausser mir dachte.

P. 240. Der See macht eine Bucht ins Land, eine Hütte ist unweit dem Ufer, Fischerknabe fährt sich in einem Kahn. Über den See hinweg sieht man die grünen Matten, Dörfer und Höfe von Schwyz im hellen Sonnenschein liegen. Zur Linken des Zuschauers zeigen sich die Spitzen des Haken, mit Wolken umgeben; zur Rechten im fernen Hintergrund sieht man die Eisgebirge.

P. 254. Je fus si frappée de cette simplicité de caractère.

SELECT BIBLIOGRAPHY

I. EDITIONS OF SCHILLER'S WORKS

The first collected edition of Schiller's works was:

Sämtliche Werke (edited by C. G. Körner), 12 volumes (Stuttgart, 1812–15).

The principal critical editions of Schiller's *Sämtliche Werke* are:

Säkularausgabe (edited by E. v. der Hellen), 16 volumes (Stuttgart, 1904–5).

Bongs Goldene Klassiker (edited by A. Kutscher), 15 volumes (Berlin, 1908).

Deutsche Klassiker-Bibliothek (edited by O. Güntter and G. Witkowski), 20 volumes (Leipzig, 1909–11).

Horenausgabe (edited by C. Schüddekopf and C. Höfer), 22 volumes (Munich-Berlin, 1910–26). (Works arranged in chronological order.)

Meyers Klassiker (edited by L. Bellermann, R. Petsch, A. Leitzmann, W. Stammler), 15 volumes (Leipzig, 1919–22).

II. LETTERS, ETC.

Briefwechsel zwischen Goethe und Schiller (Stuttgart, 1828–29).

Schiller und Lotte (edited by W. Fielitz) (Stuttgart, 1879).

Schillers Briefe (edited by Fr. Jonas), 7 volumes (Stuttgart, 1892–96).

Schillers Briefwechsel mit Körner (edited by K. Goedeke and L. Geiger) (Stuttgart, 1893).

Briefwechsel zwischen Schiller und Wilhelm von Humboldt (edited by A. Leitzmann) (Stuttgart, 1900).

Schillers Persönlichkeit (edited by M. Hecker and J. Petersen), 3 volumes (Weimar, 1904–9).

Schillers Gespräche (edited by J. Petersen) (Leipzig, 1911).

Briefwechsel zwischen Schiller und Goethe (edited by H. G. Gräf and A. Leitzmann), 3 volumes (Leipzig, 1912).

III. BIOGRAPHICAL AND CRITICAL WORKS

The following are noteworthy as early biographies:

C. G. Körner: *Schillers Leben* (Stuttgart, 1812).

T. Carlyle: *The Life of Fr. Schiller* (London, 1825).

Caroline v. Wolzogen: *Schillers Leben* (Stuttgart, 1830).

A. Streicher: *Schillers Flucht von Stuttgart* (Stuttgart, 1836).

The following are the principal modern biographical and critical works:

J. Minor: *Schiller: sein Leben und seine Werke*, 2 volumes (Berlin, 1890).

J. Wychgram: *Schiller* (Bielefeld, 1895).

C. Weitbrecht: *Schiller in seinen Dramen* (Stuttgart, 1897).

O. Harnack: *Schiller* (Leipzig, 1898).

L. Bellermann: *Schiller* (Leipzig, 1901).

K. Berger: *Schiller: sein Leben und seine Werke*, 2 volumes (Munich, 1905–9).

J. G. Robertson: *Schiller after a Century* (Edinburgh, 1906).

L. Bellermann: *Schillers Dramen* (Leipzig, 1911).

E. Kühnemann: *Schiller* (Munich, 1927).

F. Strich: *Schiller: sein Leben und sein Werk* (Berlin, 1928).

H. Cysarz: *Schiller* (Halle, 1934).

INDEX

[The page numbers in heavy type relate to the principal discussions of Schiller's works.]